WINE
and the
WHITE HOUSE

A HISTORY

WINE
and the
WHITE HOUSE

A HISTORY

Frederick J. Ryan, Jr.

THE WHITE HOUSE *HISTORICAL ASSOCIATION*

First edition
10 9 8 7 6 5 4 3 2 1
Library of Congress Control Number: 2020933568
ISBN 978-1-950273-07-2

Designed by Luke Hayman, Jenny Hung, Shannon Jager, and Janny Ji
Pentagram, New York

Printed in Italy

*To Genny, Genevieve, Madeline, and Caroline—
who encouraged me to write this book and who
have patiently tolerated many years of quizzes
on White House history and "guess the wine"
games around the family dinner table.*

HERBLOCK
©1953 THE WASHINGTON POST CO.

CONTENTS

INTRODUCTION

In vino veritas—in wine there is truth.

—*Pliny the Elder*

This personally signed bottle of Château Mouton Rothschild 1955 was a birthday gift to the author from President Ronald Reagan.

IT'S A RARE PLEASURE to be able to write a book about a longtime personal passion. It's even rarer to be able to write about two such passions in the same book.

Since my days as a political science major in college, I've been fascinated by the unique role of the American president and the history of the White House. As for my decades-long interest in wine, I wish I had an original, thrilling story to tell. But I got into it for a remarkably typical reason: I wanted to impress a date.

When I was an undergraduate at the University of Southern California, I had planned what I thought was a surefire success of a first date. I reserved a table at the Brown Derby, a Hollywood hot spot that had once been the preferred dining establishment of A-list actors and movie moguls. I went all-out on our meal, ordering the prime rib. But when the sommelier came by, I was in trouble. Almost all the items on the extensive list of Bordeaux treasures were unpronounceable to me at the time. I latched onto Château d'Arche, confident I could at least manage to say that much without stumbling. The sommelier politely urged me to reconsider, offering several other recommendations, but I was firm, explaining to him that I thought it would be an excellent pairing with our entrée. The extent of my faux pas was revealed when he returned and opened the bottle—a chilled sweet white wine from Sauternes, ideal for dessert but a tragic mismatch with roast beef. My date was not impressed, and the relationship went no further.

It was clear that I needed to begin taking wine seriously. Up to that point, I'd actually had more experience with wine than many Americans my age: When my father's career in the U.S. Air Force brought our family to Italy during my preteen years, I took full advantage of the country's lack of a drinking age and freehanded approach to wine service. I finished high school in California, a world-renowned wine region, but my tastes at the time inclined toward Boone's Farm and, on special occasions, Mateus Rosé. My palate obviously needed work, so in addition to enrolling in wine appreciation and tasting courses in college, I made a point of exploring the wineries in Napa Valley whenever traveling north for USC football games against Stanford and UC-Berkeley.

This was useful preparation, as it happens, for my early career, which was rooted in my other passion: the American presidency. In 1982, I found myself working in the White House of President Ronald Reagan, one of the most sophisticated and engaged presidents when it came to the subject of wine. He had been governor of California at a time when the state's wine industry was gaining prominence on the global stage, and he played an important role in the rise of many California winemakers. In appreciation of his support, when he left office, those winemakers sent him many cases of their finest wines—a gift he thoroughly enjoyed.

President Reagan brought that knowledge of and enthusiasm for wine with him to the White House, where he took pride in showcasing America's finest wines. Though certainly very different from California, Washington had a wine culture of its own, especially as the many embassies in the city put great effort into presenting the best wines from their countries. It was also the place where, on many Saturday mornings, wine enthusiasts could find a young, emerging wine critic named Robert Parker at Addy Bassin's MacArthur Beverages in Northwest D.C.

Reagan's presidency coincided with a moment when wine was achieving a new level of popularity across America. His decision to serve only American wines at official events sent an important message to an attentive public. But it also created a challenge within the White House. After all, his predecessors had spent decades stocking the White House cellar with an impressive collection of the best wines from France. Under an American-only wine regime, what was to be done with them?

As a young White House aide, I thought I had come up with a clever solution. I offered to exchange the First Growth French Bordeaux and top Burgundies in the cellar with current vintage California wines. The White House would no longer have to figure out what to do with its collection of well-aged French treasures, and I would gain a first-class wine collection—a true win-win. But it didn't take long for word to come back from the office of John F. W. Rogers, who managed White House operations, that my generous offer had been declined. Despite that rejection, John and I have been the best of friends for decades, and I have enjoyed many of my favorite wine experiences in his company.

While I did not succeed in acquiring an entire cellar's worth of wine, my time with President Reagan did provide me with some excellent bottles. Knowing of my interest in wine, he would thoughtfully gift a bottle from his own cellar on special occasions. I was especially touched to receive a personally signed bottle of Château Mouton Rothschild 1955—my birth year—as a birthday gift.

Another perk of serving on the Reagan White House staff was the chance to sit in the president's box at the John F. Kennedy Center for the Performing Arts. The box had a refrigerator well-stocked with small bottles of champagne engraved with the Presidential Seal. Each visit presented a dilemma: whether to enjoy the bottle in the course of the evening or save it as a unique souvenir.

I remained interested in wine well after the White House, and in 2008, my enthusiasm and curiosity led me to enter the world of winemaking myself. Peggy Ryan—a very talented (and unrelated) Napa Valley winemaker—and I formed a joint venture called, appropriately, Ryan Cellars. Our roles were clear: Peggy used her brilliant skills to produce what went into the bottle, and I did my best to try to help with the business on the outside. We also had a well-defined production strategy: we'd limit annual output to a few hundred cases so that if the wine didn't sell, we could at least consume it all within the scope of a few wild parties. My time with Ryan Cellars was a firsthand education in

This special half-size bottle of Great Western Natural Champagne from New York is one of those produced during the Reagan administration exclusively for the president's box at the Kennedy Center. It features the Presidential Seal.

the winemaking business, but also the source of tremendous gratification, especially when we saw our wine served by the Prince of Wales at Buckingham Palace and enjoyed at a formal dinner at Decatur House honoring First Lady Michelle Obama.

Over the years, I've been fortunate to have opportunities to explore both wine and White House history in great depth. I've had the honor of meeting most of the men who served as president in my lifetime, as well as the chance to visit many of the world's top wineries and engage with some of the world's great winemakers. In pursuing both of these avocations, I came to observe that oenophiles and people fascinated by the White House actually have a lot in common.

At their core, both groups are people who love learning about the past and connecting that history to the present. The White House has borne witness to America's darkest moments and its greatest triumphs; the men and women who lived there are part of an unbroken chain across more than two centuries, connecting the ideals of our country's founding to the daily lives of nearly 330 million Americans today. Enthusiasts have an insatiable appetite for inside knowledge about the presidents who have lived this history.

Wine aficionados, meanwhile, love history in their own way. A bottle of wine is in many ways a historical artifact. Millions of years of geology have gone into making just the right soil. Generations of careful viticulture have produced today's grape varietals. Winemaking philosophies have developed over decades, often passed down as part of the rich histories of winemaking families. Depending on the value of the bottle, the wine itself is the product of grapes grown years—sometimes even centuries—ago. It's no coincidence that many of the people I know who really love wine are also huge history buffs.

And just as people interested in the presidency will often argue zealously as to why their favorite leader is the best president in history and will often claim intense attachment to a political party, wine enthusiasts have rivalries and loyalties of their own. They have favorite vineyards, vintages, and regions; pitched battles will emerge over whether Bordeaux or Burgundy is truly superior. Wine lovers will collect mementos, such as bottles, corks, or labels, to express their interest in history and their attachment to specific wines, much as political junkies collect campaign memorabilia. A proudly displayed empty bottle of Bordeaux from the 1950s is the wine equivalent of an original "I Like Ike" button. In short, both camps are known for their strength of feeling; neither wine enthusiasts nor followers of White House history are passive consumers.

The author's long interest in wine led to the establishment of Ryan Cellars. Ryan wine was served by the Prince of Wales at Buckingham Palace on June 20, 2013, and enjoyed at a farewell dinner honoring First Lady Michelle Obama, which was hosted by the White House Historical Association, November 15, 2016.

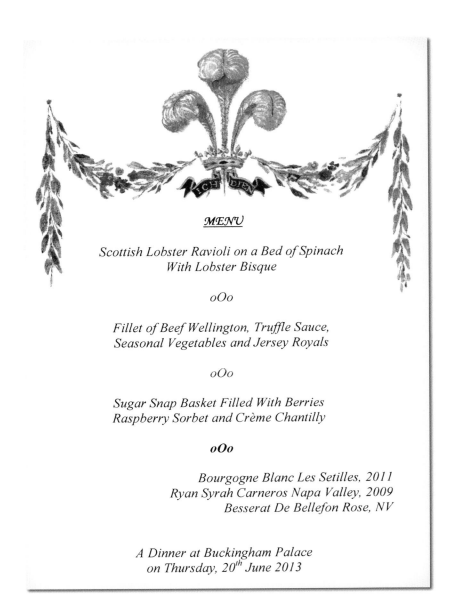

MENU

Scottish Lobster Ravioli on a Bed of Spinach
With Lobster Bisque

oOo

Fillet of Beef Wellington, Truffle Sauce,
Seasonal Vegetables and Jersey Royals

oOo

Sugar Snap Basket Filled With Berries
Raspberry Sorbet and Crème Chantilly

oOo

Bourgogne Blanc Les Setilles, 2011
Ryan Syrah Carneros Napa Valley, 2009
Besserat De Bellefon Rose, NV

A Dinner at Buckingham Palace
on Thursday, 20ᵗʰ June 2013

This overlap suggested that there might be interest in a comprehensive history of wine in the White House. Books have been published on several aspects of life in the White House, including music, art, food, and entertaining, but never a volume completely devoted to wine. This book is an attempt to fill that void and, I hope, satisfy the thirst of an eager audience.

In chapter 1, I've tried to include material about every president's experience of wine in the White House. While some genuinely appreciated and enjoyed wine, others considered it merely a ceremonial necessity. Still others campaigned to outlaw it and banned it from the White House; their successors celebrated its return.

More recently, all presidents, regardless of whether they enjoyed wine themselves, have used the White House as a venue to showcase the finest wines made in America. Chapter 2 explores how presidents have selected the wines they've chosen to serve their guests and explains the detailed process through which wine is acquired, stored, and served in the White House.

White House Historical Association
Dinner honoring
First Lady Michelle Obama
Tuesday, November 15, 2016

M·E·N·U

AUTUMN VEGETABLE HARVEST SALAD
Carrot Oil and Arugula Chimichurri
Dahig Vineyard · Ryan Chardonnay 2009

PAN ROASTED HALIBUT *and* SEA BEAN SALAD
Grape Verjus and Lemongrass Sauce
RISOTTO-STYLE POTATO *and* SUNCHOKE PURÉE
HARICOTS VERTS *with* TOMATO CONCASSE

Van der Kamp Vineyard · Ryan Pinot Noir 2010

PECAN, CHOCOLATE *and*
SWEET POTATO CHARLOTTE
Brown Butter Pecan Ice Cream
and White House Honey
Scharffenberger Brut

Before the recent "America only" policy for wine service in the Executive Mansion, presidents chose their wines from some of the top regions across Europe; many of those winemaking traditions, along with several vines, were transplanted in the United States, yielding American vineyards and labels that are now household names. Chapter 3 reviews the grape varietals and growing regions around the world that have furnished wine throughout the history of the White House and includes reflections from some of the most prominent winemakers operating in these regions today.

Wine lovers know that much more goes into the experience of a fine wine than simply the drink itself. The glasses, decor, food, ambience, and company all contribute, especially in a setting as stunning and memorable as a formal White House dinner. While no book can fully re-create that atmosphere, I've tried, to the extent possible, to provide some flavor of it. Chapter 4 tells the fascinating history of White House glassware, as presidents and first ladies have acquired glasses, decanters, and other wine-related accessories to serve as objects of beauty and instruments of enjoyment for their guests. Chapter 5 attempts to capture a sense of the social atmosphere of White House wine drinking and the central role wine has played in American diplomacy, through photographs of and quotations from memorable presidential toasts.

Over the years, the White House developed the custom of creating beautifully calligraphed menu cards to place at each guest's seat for formal presidential events. Each documents the food and wine served with each course. Chapter 6 contains an assortment of these menu cards from historic White House gatherings—and provides an opportunity for intrepid chefs and wine collectors to try to re-create some of the meals themselves.

For readers interested in the specific wines and vintages that have been served at presidential events since World War II, chapter 7 contains a detailed list. It is the first time a comprehensive catalog spanning multiple presidencies and detailing the specific wines and vintages served at major social occasions has ever been assembled.

For as long as humans have kept records of our civilization, wine has inspired profundity and wit among writers, thinkers, and historical figures. Quotations from these men and women are placed throughout the book for your enjoyment, along with essays devoted to major events in the history of winemaking.

Whether you're a devotee of presidential history, a lover of wine, or, like me, a longtime fan of both, I hope you enjoy the book and find it informative and entertaining. And if it inspires you to raise a glass to those who have led our nation over the years and to the talented winemakers who have supplied them, I hope these pages will also provide some useful ideas for what to drink.

CHAPTER ONE

THE PRESIDENTS AND THEIR WINES

**Wine to gladden
their hearts.**

—Psalm 104:15

Noah is seen tasting wine in
his vineyard in this mosaic
in Saint Mark's Basilica in
Venice, Italy.

BY THE TIME the first glass of wine was served at a presidential table, wine had already been at the center of human civilization for several millennia. The Bible tells us that after surviving the Great Flood, Noah, a man of the soil, was the first to plant a vineyard. His ark is thought to have come to rest on Mount Ararat, about 60 miles from the Armenian village of Areni, which, archaeological evidence suggests, may have been the first place in the world to make wine with grapes.

In ancient Egypt, wine was considered the drink of the gods, royalty, and the wealthy. When King Tut was buried in the fourteenth century BCE, he was sent off to the afterlife with twenty-six vessels of wine enclosed in his tomb.

The Phoenicians enjoyed wine as they colonized the Mediterranean in 1100 BCE; 350 years later, the early Greeks celebrated wine as a gift from the god Dionysus. The Romans believed that the god Bacchus had taught humankind winemaking—a skill that was apparently flourishing by the time Mount Vesuvius erupted, when the disaster wiped out the many wine merchants operating in Pompeii. It was a Roman philosopher, Pliny the Elder, who in 77 CE first coined the enduring Latin phrase *in vino veritas*—"in wine there is truth."

And it was in the Roman Empire that perhaps the most famous consumption of wine in human history—the Last Supper—occurred. The influence of that single meal kept European winemaking alive throughout the following centuries, as Catholic monks—for whom wine played a central role in the sacrifice of the Mass—helped save viniculture during the Dark Ages and from the destructive rampages of barbarian invasions. A group of Franciscan brothers eventually brought this European winemaking tradition to the New World, developing viticulture alongside their missions in modern-day California.

GEORGE WASHINGTON
First President of the United States, 1789–1797

A glass decanter shaped like President George Washington was one of thousands of commemorative items produced in celebration of America's Bicentennial in 1976.

Published by Nathaniel Currier in 1848, this lithograph (opposite) portrays General Washington making a farewell toast to his officers at Fraunces Tavern in New York in 1783. Influenced by the temperance movement, later printings of the image included a hat in place of the carafe and wineglasses on the table.

AMERICA'S WINE STORY BEGINS with the earliest colonists, who enjoyed fortified European wines such as Port, sherry, and Madeira. These varieties could withstand a range of weather conditions enclosed in a ship's hold, enabling them to survive long transatlantic journeys. By the time the colonies were declaring their independence from England in 1776, Madeira had become the most popular wine in America.

It was also popular with America's first president. As a "Madeira Man," George Washington often drank three or four glasses of Madeira—which has an alcohol content of around 20 percent—in an evening, according to biographer Ronald Chernow.

But Washington's interests reached beyond Madeira, and when it came to discovering new grape varietals and the wines they produced, he relied heavily on his minister to France—Thomas Jefferson. Jefferson's predecessor in that role, Benjamin Franklin, had immersed himself in all the delights France had to offer, including its wines. He reportedly loved to drink champagne and established an impressive wine cellar of his own containing more than one thousand bottles. Perhaps inspired by this example, Jefferson, too, used his time abroad to discover for himself all that Europe's winemakers had to offer. While roaming the countryside or enjoying the elegant salons of Paris, young Jefferson explored the Continent's wines with great enthusiasm. He traveled extensively through Europe's major wine regions and vinicultural areas, not only in France, but in Germany and Italy as well.

Though Washington could not match Jefferson's knowledge of wine, he appreciated the libation enough to ensure that it was served properly. Records show the president placing an order for "4 Neat and fashionable Cut glass Decanters with broad Bottoms, that they may stand firm on the Table," and "2½ Dozen Wine Glasses, to be rather low and strong as well as Neat."

Further evidence of Washington's esteem for wine can be found in a July 1781 letter to a French army general, the Marquis de Chastellux. The president had a policy of refusing all gifts, but he was making an exception for a cask of wine from the marquis:

You have taken a most effectual method of obliging me to accept your Cask of Claret, as I find, by your ingenious manner of stating the case that I shall, by a refusal, bring my patriotism into question, and incur a suspicion of want of attachment to the French Nation, and of regard to you. . . . In short, my dear sir, my only scruple arises from a fear of depriving you of an Article that you cannot conveniently replace in this Country. You can only relieve me by promising to partake very often of that hilarity which a glass of good Claret seldom fails to produce.

JOHN ADAMS
Second President of the United States, 1797–1801

Wine stimulates the mind and makes it quick with heat; care flees and is dissolved in much drink.

—*Ovid*

WASHINGTON WAS AMERICA'S FIRST PRESIDENT, but not the first to live in the White House. That distinction belongs to President John Adams. Little is known about Adams's wine service in the President's House, but there are records of his experiences with wine prior to becoming president. In 1774, Adams served as a Massachusetts delegate to the First Continental Congress in Philadelphia, and he wrote to his wife Abigail:

I shall be killed with kindness in this place. We go to Congress at nine, and there we stay, most earnestly engaged in debate upon the most abstruse mysteries of state, until three in the afternoon; then we adjourn, and go dine with some of the nobles of Pennsylvania at four o'clock, and feast upon ten thousand delicacies, and sit drinking Madeira, Claret, and Burgundy, till six or seven and then go home fatigued to death with business, company, and care. Yet I hold out surprisingly.

President John Adams welcomed Federal City society by invitation to his 1801 New Year's Day reception, the first large-scale social event ever held at the White House.

John Adams (center) shares wine with his wife Abigail and his friend Thomas Jefferson in a scene from the miniseries *John Adams* (2008).

Adams had a better experience during a 1779 diplomatic trip to Europe, where he enjoyed a sumptuous meal with the French consul and others in Spain. He wrote in his diary: "We had every Luxury . . . the Wines were Bordeaux, Champagne, Burgundy, Sherry, Alicante, Navarre, and Vine de Cap. The most delicious in the World."

During his diplomatic posts at The Hague and in Paris, Adams developed a strong appreciation for European wines. He accumulated a large cellar and enhanced it with an order of five hundred bottles of French wine to be sent to England, where he intended to use his purchases as America's first minister in London. Upon learning that the significant importation tariffs the English imposed on French wine would not be waived even with his diplomatic immunity, he scrambled to reverse the shipment. Writing to his friend Thomas Jefferson, Adams said, "I beg you to take the wine, at any price you please. . . . Or accept it as a present or sell it."

THOMAS JEFFERSON
Third President of the United States, 1801–1809

Wine from long habit has become an indispensable for my health.

—Thomas Jefferson

President Thomas Jefferson employed dumbwaiters at the White House to allow guests to serve themselves at dinner, reducing the need for servants.

IT WAS THOMAS JEFFERSON who, during his presidency, became the "Founding Father" of American wine appreciation. While every American president contributed to the development of wine as an instrument of diplomacy and entertaining, Thomas Jefferson truly distinguished himself as America's first wine aficionado. His role in the discovery of wines and his contributions to wine education and enjoyment have earned him a position far above any of his fellow presidents.

Jefferson can be credited with establishing many of the White House traditions that endure to this day, including cherished social customs, which he recognized as an important part of presidential leadership. In March 1801, soon after his Inauguration, Jefferson began hosting dinner parties for friends, politicians, and diplomats. The dinners were lavish affairs with many courses of food and wine. Jefferson's guests, usually twelve to fourteen people, were seated at a round table where each seat was of equal importance. This arrangement allowed for group conversation, unlike the period etiquette of alternating conversation right and left. Jefferson employed dumbwaiters, small tiered tables placed near the main table, which allowed guests to serve themselves, reducing the need for servants and keeping discussions private.

French cuisine and the stately setting impressed the president's guests as intended, while flowing wine—Jefferson spent an average of $3,200 annually ($70,124 in 2020 dollars) on wine alone—helped the attendees relax. In this atmosphere of intimate entertaining, President Jefferson steered conversation to politics and the issues of the day. The president was careful to refer to these dinners as "unofficial," asserting that he did not, in fact, host official dinners but kept the business of the presidency separate from his private entertaining. As one senator described the new White House social scene, "You drink as you please . . . and converse at your ease."

The wine Jefferson served was extraordinarily diverse for the time and place. While most Americans drank only Madeira and Port, Jefferson served whites and reds, drys and sweets, from Germany, France, Italy, Spain, Portugal, and Hungary. As Jefferson's letters and household memorandums demonstrate, the wines selected for presidential dinners were dictated by his tastes, the seasons, and cost. He compiled a document titled "Wine provided at Washington," a comprehensive list of the varieties he served while president, recording country of origin and price. When his favorite Burgundies and Bordeaux became too expensive, he switched to cheaper varieties from Italy and Portugal. The list includes Madeira, Sauterne, Pedro Ximénes Mountain, Montepulciano, and White Hermitage, to name a few. Many of Jefferson's favorite wines, such as Château Margaux and Château d'Yquem, are still prized by connoisseurs today.

Most of Jefferson's wine orders were in quantities of a "pipe," a large barrel that contained 110 gallons on average, according to Jefferson's notes. He also ordered his wine

Thomas Jefferson's wine cellar at Monticello is seen here in the twenty-first century.

by the bottle. In November 1804, for example, he ordered 240 bottles of "Hungary wine, Tokay." At the end of the list he recorded forty wines from five countries—France (12), Italy (11), Spain (10), Portugal (5), and Hungary (2)—clearly indicating the wide range of his tastes. During his eight years as president, records show, Jefferson purchased more than 20,000 bottles of wine from the top European wine regions, including the premier wines of Bordeaux, Burgundy, and Rhone.

Thomas Jefferson viewed wine as a preferred beverage for Americans and sought to make it more available at reasonable prices, including by working to reduce importation tariffs on European wines. Writing to the French minister to the United States, he expressed his opinion that the legislature would act, saying, "I rejoice, as a Moralist, at the prospect of a reduction of the duties on wine, by our national legislature. It is an error to view a tax on that liquor as merely a tax on the rich. It is a prohibition of its use to the middling class of our citizens, and a condemnation of them to the poison of whiskey, which is desolating their houses."

Jefferson also believed that America was capable of furnishing its own supply. Near the end of his presidency, he wrote, "We could in the United States, make as great a variety of wines as are made in Europe: not exactly of the same kinds, but doubtless as good." Jefferson may have been anticipating his postpresidential endeavors; in 1807 he began cultivating grapes to make his own wine at Monticello.

WINE PROVIDED AT WASHINGTON

An Inventory

TO THE JOY of historians and scholars, Thomas Jefferson kept extraordinarily detailed notes of his activities and interests. This is especially true of his wine collecting, as he maintained meticulous records of his various acquisitions and the sources and prices of each. One particularly noteworthy example is Jefferson's documentation of his White House wine collection, prepared during his retirement years. "Wine provided at Washington," as Jefferson called the memorandum, is the most complete account of any president's wine cellar. His list, in its entirety, appears here, in his original hand.

1801. Wine provided at Washington — D

May 3. a pipe of Brazil Madeira from Col^o. Newton . . . . 350.

20. a pipe of Pedro Ximenes mountain from Yznardi. 126. gall^s @ 2 D. — 252.

424. bottles of it sent to Monticello. Feb. 1803.

a Quart^r. cask of Tent from d^o. 30. gall^s. @ 1.50 — 45.

a keg of Pacharetti doux. from d^o.

doz. of claret from d^o

15. doz. Sauterne from H. Sheaff. @ 8. D . . . . 120.

~~148. bottles claret @ 10 D. p^r doz.~~ . . . .

~~6 doz. d^o @ 12 D.~~ . . . .

June. 12. 2. pipes of Brazil madeira. from Taylor & Newton . . . 700.

148. bott. claret @ 10. D. p^r doz. 123.33

72. d^o. @ 12. D. 72. . . . . 195.33

220

Sep. 28. 2. pipes of Brazil Madeira from Taylor & Newton . . . 700.

Nov. 28. 30. doz. = 360. bottles of Sauterne from Sheaff . . . 240.

1802 Jan. 7. a tierce (60. gall^s.) Malaga from mr. Yznardi. Lacryma Christi — 106.

the above is 56. years old. viz. vintage of 1755

2. doz. bottles of claret from mr Barnes. @ 8. D. . . . . 16.

Feb. 24. 1. pipe dry Pacharetti. from mr Yznardi . . . . 202.

1. pipe Sherry of London quality 10. y. old 188

1/2 pipe of Sherry of a different quality . . . . 94.

278. bottles of it sent to Monticello. Feb. 1803.

1/2 pipe of white Sherry . . . . 84.

insurance on the wines of Feb. 24. D 22.72

May. 6. duties pd Yznardi on d^o. . . 156. . . . . 178.72

claret from J. Barnes.

Nov. a half barrel of Syracuse from Capt. M^c. Niel

Dec. 1. 100. bottles Champagne from the Chevalr. Yrujo. } 172.50

1803 Jan. 10. 100. d^o. @ .86 1/2 viz. .75 first cost + 11 1/4 duty

2. halfpipes of wine of Oeyras from mr Jarvis at Lisbon. — 98.17

sent to Monticello

Mar. 3. 2 pipes of Brazil Madeira from James Taylor Norfolk. — 700.

21. 12. doz. Sauterne from Sheaff. @ 8 2/3 D. 104.33

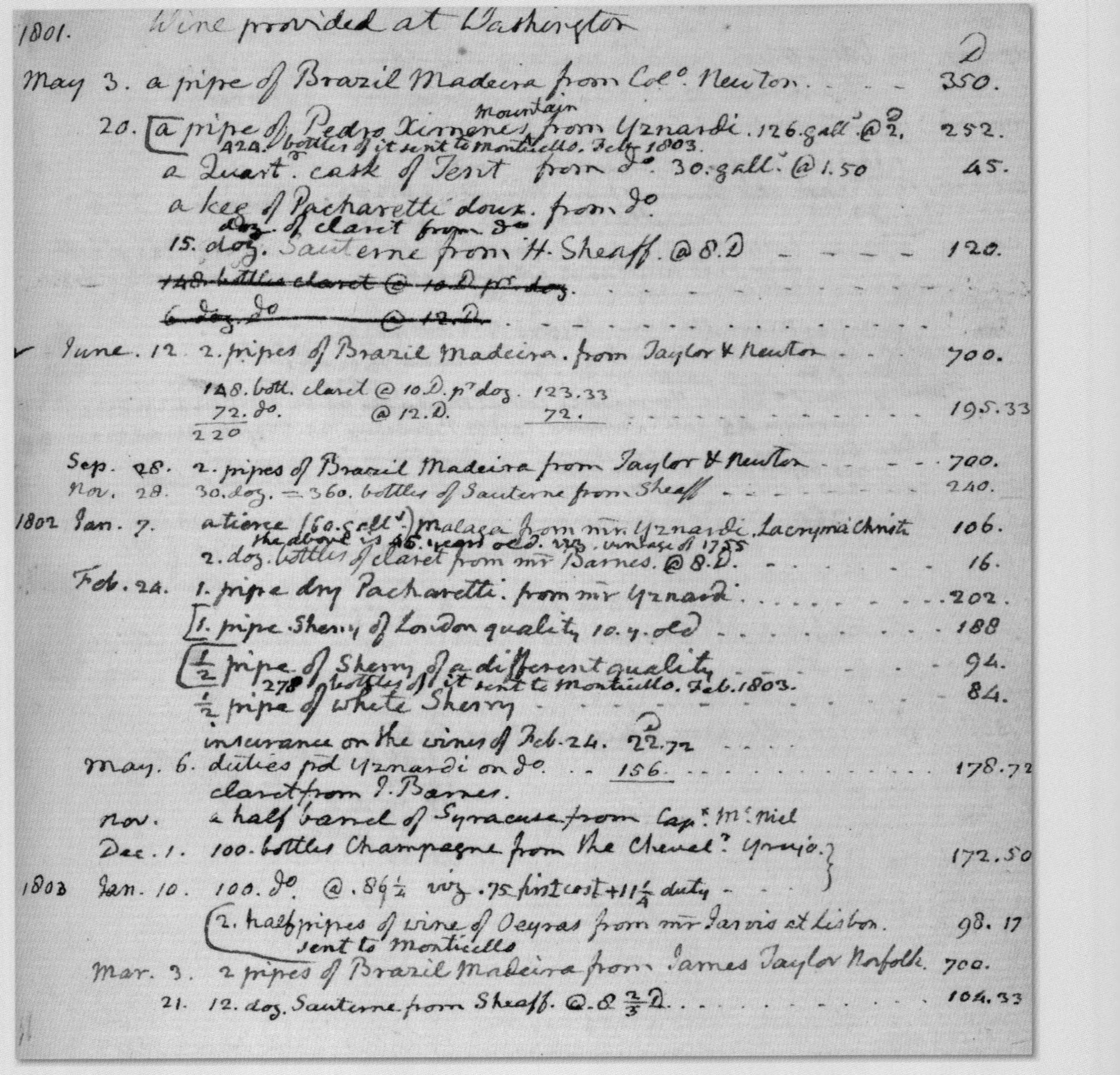

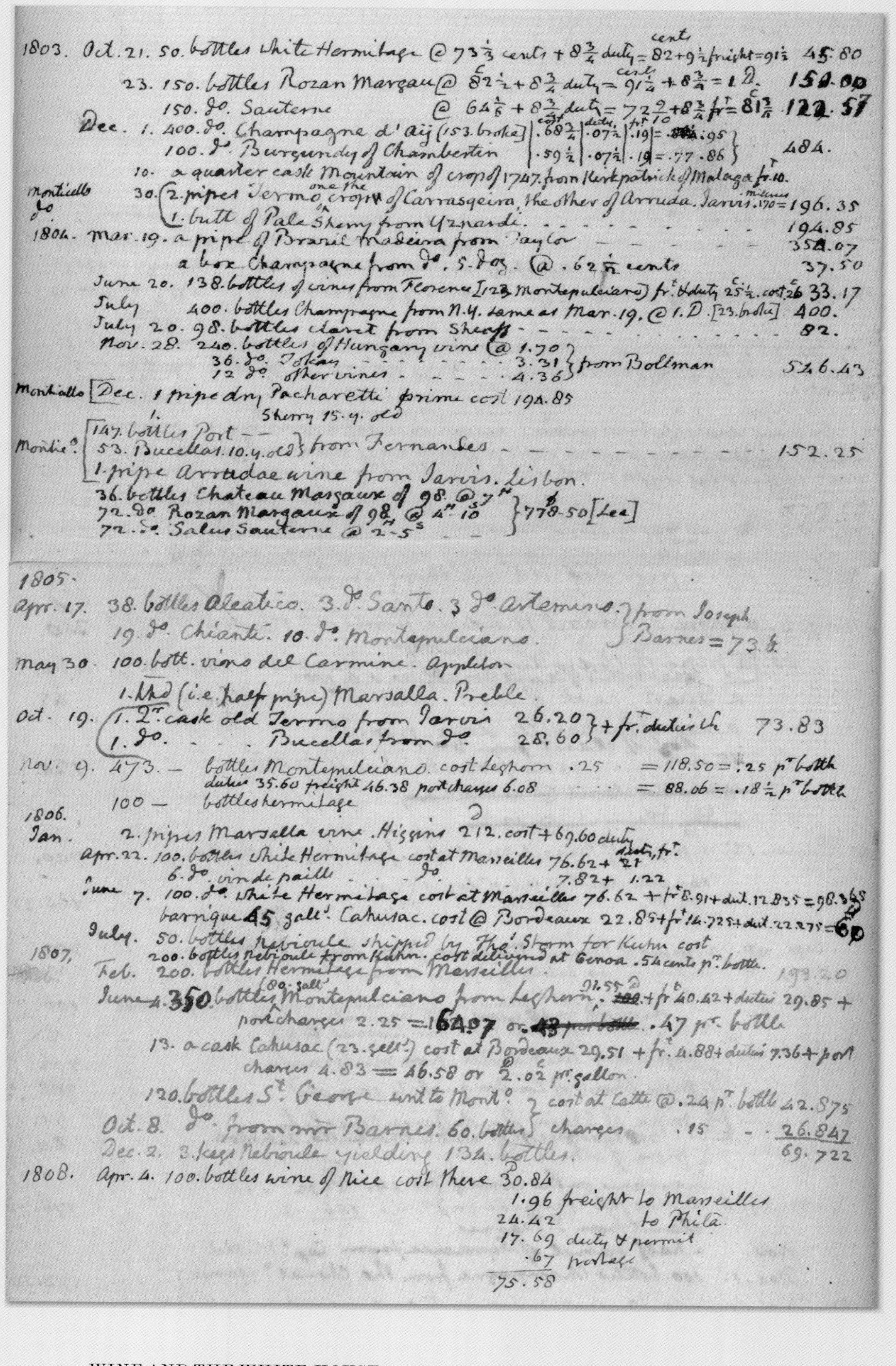
1803. Oct. 21. 50. bottles White Hermitage @ 73 1/3 cents + 8 3/4 duty = 82 + 9 1/2 freight = 91 1/2 cents 45.80
23. 150. bottles Rozan Margau @ 82 1/2 c + 8 3/4 duty = 91 1/4 cents + 8 3/4 = 1 D. 150.00
150. do. Sauterne @ 64 1/6 + 8 3/4 duty = 72 9/10 + 8 3/4 fr^t = 81 5/8 c 122.57
Dec. 1. 400. do. Champagne d'Aij [153. broke] | cost .68 3/4 | duty .07 1/2 | fr^t .19 | = .95 } 484.
100. do. Burgundy of Chambertin | .59 1/2 | .07 1/2 | .19 | = .77 .86 }
10. a quarter cask Mountain of crop of 1747. from Kirkpatrick of Malaga fr^t 10.
Monticello 30. 2. pipes Termo one the crop of Carrasqueira, the other of Arruda. Jarvis. 170 milreis = 196.35
do. 1. butt of Pale Sherry from Yznardi. 194.85
1804. Mar. 19. a pipe of Brazil Madeira from Taylor 350.07
a box Champagne from do. 5. doz. @ .62 1/2 cents 37.50
June 20. 138. bottles of wines from Florence [123 Montepulciano] fr^t & duty 25 1/2 c cost 26 c 33.17
July 400. bottles Champagne from N.Y. same as Mar. 19. @ 1. D. [23. broke] 400.
July 20. 98. bottles claret from Sheaff 82.
Nov. 28. 240. bottles of Hungary wine @ 1.70 }
36. do. Tokay 3.31 } from Bollman 526.43
12 do. other wines 4.36 }
Monticello [Dec. 1 pipe dry Pacharetti prime cost 194.85
1. Sherry 15. y. old
Montic^o. [147. bottles Port
53. Bucellas. 10. y. old } from Fernandes 152.25
1. pipe Arruda wine from Jarvis. Lisbon.
36. bottles Chateau Margaux of 98. @ 7^{tt} }
72. do. Rozan Margaux of 98. @ 4^{tt} 10^s } 778.50 [Lee]
72. do. Salus Sauterne @ 2^{tt} 5^s }
1805.
Apr. 17. 38. bottles Aleatico. 3. do. Santo. 3 do. Artemino. } from Joseph
19. do. Chianti. 10. do. Montepulciano. } Barnes = 73.6
May 30. 100. bott. vino del Carmine. Appleton
1. hhd (i.e. half pipe) Marsalla. Preble.
Oct. 19. 1. Q^r. cask old Termo from Jarvis 26.20 } + fr^t. duties &c 73.83
1. do. Bucellas from do. 28.60 }
Nov. 9. 473. bottles Montepulciano. cost Leghorn .25 = 118.50 = .25 p^r bottle
duties 35.60 freight 46.38 port charges 6.08 = 88.06 = .18 1/2 p^r bottle
100 bottles hermitage
1806.
Jan. 2. pipes Marsalla wine. Higgins 212. D cost + 69.60 duty
Apr. 22. 100. bottles White Hermitage cost at Marseilles 76.62 + 21 duty, fr^t.
6. do. vin de paille do. 7.82 + 1.22
June 7. 100. do. White Hermitage cost at Marseilles 76.62 + fr^t 8.91 + dut. 12.835 = 98.365
barrique 45 gall^s. Cahusac. cost @ Bordeaux 22.85 + fr^t 14.725 + dut. 22.275 = 60
July. 50. bottles Nebioule shipped by Thos. Storm for Kuhn cost
1807. 200. bottles Nebioule from Kuhn. cost delivered at Genoa .54 cents p^r. bottle.
Feb. 200. bottles Hermitage from Marseilles. 193.20
June 4. 350. bottles (80. gall^s) Montepulciano from Leghorn. 91.55 D + fr^t 40.42 + duties 29.85 +
port charges 2.25 = 164.07 or .47 p^r. bottle
13. a cask Cahusac (23. gall^s.) cost at Bordeaux 29.51 + fr^t. 4.88 + duties 7.36 + port
charges 4.83 = 46.58 or 2.02 D/c p^r. gallon.
120. bottles S^t. George sent to Mont^o. } cost at Cette @ .24 p^r. bottle 42.875
Oct. 8. do. from mr Barnes. 60. bottles } charges .15 26.847
Dec. 2. 3. kegs Nebioule yielding 134. bottles. 69.722
1808. Apr. 4. 100. bottles wine of Nice cost there 30.84 D
1.96 freight to Marseilles
24.42 to Phila.
17.69 duty & permit
.67 postage
75.58

THOMAS JEFFERSON'S 1787 CHÂTEAU LAFITE
One of the World's Greatest Rarities?

HISTORICAL RECORDS DEMONSTRATE that Thomas Jefferson purchased thousands of bottles of wine. Some, we know, were even enjoyed by his successors James Madison and Grover Cleveland. But only one of them would become a record-setting subject of global fascination two centuries later.

In 1985, a German manager of rock bands and devotee of old Bordeaux vintages, Hardy Rodenstock, reported the discovery of a cache of very old wines hidden behind a brick cellar wall at an undisclosed location in Paris. Rodenstock was well known within the world of rare wine collectors, and his announcement was welcomed with great fanfare.

Among the wines discovered was a bottle of 1787 Château Lafite Bordeaux that, according to Rodenstock, had belonged to Thomas Jefferson. His claim was credible, as the bottle was of the shape and color used in 1787, the cap was of the type used during that period, and, most convincing of all, the bottle was engraved with the letters "Th. J."

After renowned wine expert Michael Broadbent examined the bottle and confirmed it as "one of the world's greatest rarities," the historic item was put up for auction by Christie's in London on December 5, 1985. The catalog listed the value of the bottle as "inestimable," inciting worldwide interest in the auction.

Bidding began at £10,000 ($15,000). Two minutes later, after aggressive competition between *Wine Spectator* publisher Marvin Shanken and Christopher Forbes, son of the publishing magnate Malcolm Forbes, the gavel fell at a bid of £105,000 (approximately $155,000)— enough to earn Forbes a spot in the *Guinness Book of World Records* for the most expensive wine purchase ever. The triumphant Forbes flew the treasure back to New York on his private jet, with the intention of displaying it in an exhibition of presidential memorabilia in the Forbes Galleries.

The "Th. J." bottle of 1787 Lafite was placed in a position of prominence in the galleries, viewable by the many visitors who came to see Malcolm Forbes's unique collections housed within the lobby of his magazine's New York headquarters. But the curators failed to appreciate the fragility of their prized object, and the heat of the lights in the display case caused the bottle's ancient cork to shrink and slip into the bottle, rendering the wine undrinkable. Christopher Forbes, however, remained unflappable, telling the *New York Daily News*, "We still have the original bottle with the original wine with the original wax and cork. Perhaps, not in the order we'd like."

At the same time, evidence began to emerge suggesting that the wines Hardy Rodenstock served at his exclusive wine tastings—and the vintages he sold for enormous sums in the rare-wine market, like the Jefferson bottle—were fakes. Connoisseurs tasted oddly modern notes in wines that were supposed to be centuries old. Corks seemed too short for their alleged ages. Rodenstock himself was evasive about the provenance of his wines and then, when challenged, grew angry and defensive. But allies like Broadbent and friends in the wine press—many of

Eventually proved to be a fake, this bottle was sold to Christopher Forbes under the pretense that it was a 1787 Château Lafite Bordeaux that once belonged to Thomas Jefferson.

whom had built their careers in no small part through access to Rodenstock's rare treasures—defended the German. Even chemical and radiological testing of Rodenstock's purported Jefferson bottles proved inconclusive. One test conducted at the behest of a concerned customer said the wine was too new to be real; another commissioned by Rodenstock seemed to suggest the wine was as old as he claimed it to be.

Eventually, it was the efforts of billionaire William Koch, who purchased some of the other purported Thomas Jefferson bottles, that settled the matter. A forensic expert hired by Koch determined that the initials "Th. J." were inscribed with an electric drill—meaning the bottles could not possibly date from the eighteenth century. The curator of the Thomas Jefferson Foundation also challenged the bottles' authenticity, saying, "We don't believe those bottles ever belonged to Thomas Jefferson." Then a former landlord in Germany discovered refuse and discarded equipment indicating that Rodenstock had carried out high-end wine forgery in his basement. And Rodenstock, it turned out, was not even Rodenstock at all. His real name was Meinhard Görke, and the elite credentials and prestigious family lineage he had presented to his fellow wine connoisseurs were as fabricated as the wines he sold.

Koch ultimately spent $35 million in a campaign to prove that Rodenstock's Jefferson stash was fake and to help expose fraud within the world of wine collecting. Yet he retained a sense of humor about the episode, telling the *New Yorker* in 2007: "I used to brag that I got the Thomas Jefferson wines. Now I get to brag that I have the fake Thomas Jefferson wines." Malcolm Forbes, however, seemed to suffer from more acute buyer's remorse, telling a reporter: "I wish Jefferson had drunk the damn bottle."

JAMES MADISON
Fourth President of the United States, 1809–1817

If you drink too much [champagne], it will make you hop like the cork.

—*James Madison*

The Madisons' entertainments ended in 1814 when the British torched the White House during the War of 1812 (as depicted by Leslie Salburg).

FOR JEFFERSON'S SUCCESSOR, James Madison, wine continued to play an important role in White House entertaining. The Madisons held Wednesday drawing rooms—weekly evening gatherings open to anyone who had either been formally introduced to the Madisons or came with a letter of introduction. At these receptions, members of opposing political factions were served wine as they conversed with one another and the president and first lady in a congenial atmosphere. The Madisons also held dinner parties where the wine was a central feature, as William Winston Seaton, proprietor of the *National Intelligencer*, recorded in his diary:

> There were many French dishes, and exquisite wines, I presume, by the praises bestowed on them; but I have been so little accustomed to drink, that I could not discern the difference between Sherry and rare old Burgundy Madeira. Comment on the quality of the wine seems to form the chief topic after the removal of the cloth, and during the dessert.

These pleasant evenings in the Madisons' White House ultimately came to a dramatic end. On August 24, 1814, during the War of 1812, the British burned the White House. History tells of how Dolley Madison famously saved Gilbert Stuart's portrait of George Washington from the flames; less clear, however, is exactly what happened to the White House wine. Under Madison and his predecessors, the White House wine cellar had been well stocked. Although the White House and most of its furnishings were destroyed by the fire, the brick wine cellar survived. But its contents may not have fared quite so well. Margaret Bayard Smith, writer and wife of the founder of the *National Intelligencer*, wrote that "the wine, of which there was a great quantity, was consumed by our own soldiers."

President and Mrs. James Madison were famous for their weekly drawing rooms where wine was a central part of the hospitality, as imagined by a twentieth-century illustrator.

Deniere et Matelin

JAMES MONROE
Fifth President of the United States, 1817–1825

The discovery of a wine is of greater moment than the discovery of a constellation. The universe is too full of stars.

—Benjamin Franklin

ON NEW YEAR'S DAY 1818, Madison's successor, James Monroe, officially reopened the White House with a festive reception. He and First Lady Elizabeth Kortright Monroe reinstated dinner parties and drawing room receptions. President Monroe brought to these occasions the wine education he had received while serving as President Jefferson's emissary to France, Spain, and Great Britain. He had returned to the United States in 1807 with a collection of French vines he intended to plant "with a view to making wine" himself.

As president, Monroe was given a substantial budget by Congress to refurnish the rebuilt White House. Through agents, he acquired many important pieces from France and, for himself, 1,200 bottles of champagne and Burgundy wine.

For guests at Monroe's presidential dinners, wine played a prominent role. Future First Lady Louisa Catherine Johnson Adams wrote to her father-in-law, former President John Adams, that a dinner at the Monroe White House in 1819 was "uncommonly social and pleasant. The President," she added, "gave us some Mendoza wine which was sent him as a present."

Among the most dramatic pieces acquired by President James Monroe for the reconstructed White House is a gilded bronze plateau. Over 14 feet in length, the piece was made by Denière et Matelin, in Paris, c. 1817. Charles Percier, Napoleon's architect, may have designed the plateau with its gallery of fruit and vines and figures of Bacchus and Bacchantes (opposite).

The centerpiece remains in use, as seen in this photograph of the State Dining Room taken just ahead of a State Dinner in 1970 (right).

JOHN QUINCY ADAMS
Sixth President of the United States, 1825–1829

ANDREW JACKSON
Seventh President of the United States, 1829–1837

JOHN QUINCY ADAMS, America's sixth president and son of the second, prided himself on his refined taste in wine. He frowned upon the choices of his political rival, Henry Clay; in a diary entry prior to becoming president, Adams wrote critically of a meal he shared with Clay on a trip to Belgium to settle the War of 1812. "They sit after dinner and drink bad wines and smoke cigars," Adams observed of Clay and his colleagues, "which suits neither my habits nor my health, and absorbs time which I cannot spare."

At a large White House dinner, President Adams demonstrated his superior wine knowledge at the expense of Virginia Senator Littleton Waller Tazewell. The senator had stated that Germany's Rhenish wine and Hungary's rare Tokay wine tasted the same. Adams retorted: "I do not believe you ever drank a drop of Tokay in your life."

Refinement in alcohol consumption was not exactly the hallmark of Adams's successor, Andrew Jackson. At the frontiersman's inaugural reception at the White House, whiskey was consumed in enormous proportions. The widespread inebriation led to fistfights; crystal and china flew off the shelves; and a hungry crowd stormed the kitchen. As the evening went on, guests fled the mob scene and riot by crawling through the White House windows. The muddy brawl moved outside, where the kitchen staff had smartly relocated the spiked orange punch and wine.

For all his posturing as a man of the people, Jackson's interest in wine showed another side of Old Hickory. He ordered large quantities of Madeira and claret for the new White House wine cellar, and his affection for wine was made clear in 1834, when his own personal residence in Tennessee, The Hermitage, was burned. His first question upon learning of the fire was: "I suppose all the wines in the cellar have been destroyed?"

When it came to White House entertaining, Jackson's rough frontier personality was balanced by the style and grace of his niece, Emily Donelson, who devoted substantial attention to the food and wine service at the Executive Mansion. Jackson's informal but lavish dinners began in the midafternoon and lasted four hours, with several choices of wine offered during each course. Robert C. Caldwell, who dined with the president in

It is better that wine should be spilled than blood.
—*John Quincy Adams*

The rowdy crowd that descended on the White House during President Andrew Jackson's first inaugural reception in 1829 was finally lured outside when the alcohol was moved to the lawn. The scene is depicted in this 1841 illustration by Robert Cruikshank.

December 1834, recalled that the wines served were "sherry, madeira, and champagne," and the president ended the meal with "a significant nod of the head [to] drink [to] one another's health." Another guest described a Jackson dinner:

The wines on the table were Sherry and Port to drink with soups and the first course of meats. When the wild turkey and fish were served, Madeira was handed out and while the wild fowl was eaten, Champagne was constantly poured out by the servants; after these were gone through with, Claret was substituted to be taken with the dessert and old [S]herry was put on to drink with the fruits.

A BEAUTIFUL GOBLET OF
WHITE·HOUSE CHAMPAGNE

MARTIN VAN BUREN

Eighth President of the United States, 1837–1841

Say it's the wine that leads me on, the wild wine that sets the wisest man to sing at the top of his lungs, laugh like a fool.

—*Homer*

A political cartoon depicts a smiling President Martin Van Buren holding a glass of champagne. He was heavily criticized by his opponents for what were perceived as expensive tastes and a lavish lifestyle.

IN STARK CONTRAST with Jackson's common touch, Martin Van Buren was roundly criticized for his snooty style and lavish spending. He was an aficionado of fine champagne and Madeira, though his palate spanned the full range from light table wines to begin the meal to Madeira, sherry, and brandy to cap the evening. In one order placed through his lawyer in 1819, Van Buren wrote that he wanted "about fifteen or twenty gallons of table wine—say prime Sicily, Madeira, or some other pleasant but light and low wine to drink with dinner." He also shared Thomas Jefferson's fondness for Italy's powerful red wine from Montepulciano. In the early 1830s, he reached out to the minister to France, William Cabell Rives, for help in securing his favorite French vintages.

As president, Van Buren offered stylish entertainments, overseen by his 22-year-old daughter-in-law, Angelica Van Buren, who was enamored of the practices of European courts. To some they smacked of royalty. In 1840, when Van Buren was running for reelection, his lush lifestyle was harshly attacked by U.S. Congressman Charles Ogle of Pennsylvania in a speech on the floor of the House of Representatives entitled "The Regal Splendor of the Presidential Palace." Ogle quoted receipt after receipt of public expenditures for luxuries, including gold spoons. He depicted the president as lavishing finery on himself while being stingy at public events. A White House "banquet" for distinguished guests, reported Ogle, concluded with "Saturne, Hock, Champagne, Claret, Port, Burgundy, Sherry, and Madeira, 'choisest brands,'" but for the annual New Year's Day reception, at which previous presidents had offered "good cheer" to "all the citizens of the Republic," Van Buren served "no fruits, cake, wine, coffee, hard cider, or other refreshments of any kind."

Building on Ogle's "Gold Spoon Oration," Van Buren's political opponents featured a caricature of him holding a champagne glass in their campaign attacks. Van Buren lost his bid for reelection to William Henry Harrison, who claimed to be a "teetotaler." Although the reasons for the loss are complex, the damage done by Ogle's speech may have been a factor.

The People's Line--Take care of the Lo

A cartoon made during the 1840 presidential election campaign depicts incumbent Martin Van Buren about to be unseated by challenger William Henry Harrison, who drives a "Hard Cider" locomotive. While Van Buren endured criticism for his love of champagne and other luxuries, Harrison, a one-time whiskey producer, was associated with "log cabin" simplicity.

WILLIAM HENRY HARRISON

Ninth President of the United States, 1841

JOHN TYLER

Tenth President of the United States, 1841–1845

HIS TEETOTALER CLAIMS notwithstanding, William Henry Harrison was no stranger to alcohol. Prior to becoming president, on his farm in North Bend, Ohio, Harrison had planted corn and launched a distillery to produce whiskey. But he later had a change of heart and, out of concern for the unhealthy effects of alcohol, closed the distillery and apologized for his mistake.

As for how Harrison approached wine and alcohol in the White House, there are no reports. After delivering a nearly two-hour-long Inaugural Address in miserable weather, he fell ill and died thirty-two days into his administration.

Harrison's vice president and successor, John Tyler, once invited an old Virginia friend, William Peachy, to join him for dinner at the White House. When Mr. Peachy arrived, he discovered that all that was available for dinner was an unappealing assortment of leftovers. Embarrassed by his poor hospitality, President Tyler had a brilliant idea to save the evening. As John Sergeant Wise observed:

> During the meal of ham and turnip greens a happy thought occurred to the President. "I tell you what I'll do, Peachy, to atone for this wretched entertainment," said he. "We will send for the keys of the White House cellars, and you shall go there yourself and take your choice." It was no sooner said than done. Peachy knew good wine and loved it dearly. Accompanied by the butler the two were soon rummaging the dust-covered bottles in the Presidential cellars, and, according to Mr. Peachy's account, he never had such a frolic in his life. Smacking his lips, with the memory of that afternoon's entertainment fresh in his mind, he declared that it was the only time his life when he had more good liquor than he could drink and not as many people as he wanted to divide with him.

JAMES K. POLK

Eleventh President of the United States,
1845–1849

**Champagne is
the only wine
that leaves a
woman beautiful
after drinking it.**
—*Madame de Pompadour*

Twenty-first-century artist
David Ramsey used computer
technology and period
documents to illustrate
the State Dining Room
(opposite) ready for a holiday
dinner during the Polk
administration. As described
by one of the president's
guests, Elizabeth Dixon, the
colorful glasses of wine are
set around the top of each
plate, forming "a rainbow."

PRESIDENT JAMES K. POLK kept up with evolving social customs, serving several types of wines—with a different glass for each—during dinner. These glasses would be arrayed around each guest's place at the table. Elizabeth L. C. Dixon, wife of a Connecticut congressman, described the arrangement at a dinner in December 1845:

> The table & dinner was as handsome as any I ever saw, in proportion to its size not even excepting the supper table at the Tuilleries at the Queen's ball. . . . There were 200 lights, chandeliers, candelabras & figures round the grand centre ornament, which all were of gilt burnished & very brilliant, with vases of flowers. . . . I judge 150 courses for every thing was in the french style & each dish a separate course. . . . The glassware was very handsome blue & white, finely cut, & pink champagne, gold sherry, green hock, Madeira, the ruby port & sauterne formed a rainbow round each plate with the finger glasses and water decanters.

The Polks in fact became known for relying heavily on wine for their dinners and receptions. First Lady Sarah Polk refused to serve hard liquor in the White House, doing away with the traditional whiskey or rum punches served at larger events. To compensate, she stocked the cellar with more wines and champagnes than previous administrations. This costly decision meant the Polks' wine bills would be among their biggest expenses in the White House.

It was also around this time when the fashion for the strong, fortified wines of Madeira and Port began to fade. As ships became faster, there was less time for wine to spoil or bottles to break in transit from Europe, which made the diverse varieties of red and white wines that Jefferson had imported more accessible in the United States.

ZACHARY TAYLOR
Twelfth President of the United States, 1849–1850

MILLARD FILLMORE
Thirteenth President of the United States, 1850–1853

FRANKLIN PIERCE
Fourteenth President of the United States, 1853–1857

An 1852 political cartoon (opposite) mocks presidential candidate Franklin Pierce, who was rumored to be a heavy drinker. Pierce leans against a large tree while holding a bottle out toward a passerby on horseback, who advises Pierce that the "tree looks as if it was old enough to stand alone." Pierce replies, "I'll stand as long as this tree will stand by me!" and he toasts confusion to Maine's new liquor law, the first state law to prohibit the manufacture and sale of alcoholic beverages. Despite protests, a dozen states soon passed similar laws.

AS THE TEMPERANCE MOVEMENT in America grew during the 1840s and 1850s, the White House saw presidents who personally abstained from alcohol but, recognizing its important role in diplomacy, continued to serve wine to their guests. The twelfth president, General "Rough and Ready" Zachary Taylor, maintained the discipline he had established in the army and was only an occasional drinker. When Taylor died in office in 1850, he was succeeded by Millard Fillmore, who had taken a temperance pledge in his 20s.

When Fillmore took office, Senator Salmon P. Chase of Ohio—later to serve as treasury secretary and chief justice of the Supreme Court—sent him a gift of wine. The president thanked Chase, explaining:

I am chiefly a water drinker, and consequently not a competent judge of its quality, but it will nevertheless be received by me with great pleasure and as soon as the removal of the habiliments of mourning from the White House will permit the entertainment of my friends, it shall be as you request submitted to their criticism.

Little is known about the wine served by the fourteenth president, Franklin Pierce. What is known is that, unlike his predecessor, he was certainly no teetotaler. Pierce

I have seldom tasted wine and seldom offered it to a guest.

—*Millard Fillmore*

had a reputation as a heavy drinker. He had been a "dark horse" candidate for the Democratic Party nomination, chosen on the forty-ninth ballot at the convention in 1852. He won the presidency that November, but in January his only surviving son was killed in a train accident, and he and his wife, Jane Appleton Pierce, entered the White House in mourning. Neither Pierce nor any of the presidents of the 1850s seemed able to halt the increasing sectional divisions that would soon lead to war. After failing to receive his party's nomination to serve a second term, he is purported to have said: "There's nothing left to do but get drunk." Franklin Pierce died of cirrhosis of the liver at age 64.

JAMES BUCHANAN

Fifteenth President of the United States, 1857–1861

Wine in moderation ... has a thousand pleasant influences. It brightens the eye, improves the voice, imparts a new vivacity to one's thoughts and conversation.

—*Charles Dickens*

IN THE LATE 1850s, the White House became home to James Buchanan. Buchanan had demonstrated his interest in the fruit of the vine before ascending to the presidency. In January 1846, while secretary of state, he had hosted a high-proof party at Washington's popular Carusi's Saloon. The massive feast featured lobster, beef, turkey, ham, pheasant, and wild venison. Beverages for the evening included three hundred bottles of wine and one hundred fifty bottles of champagne, as well as hard liquor.

Buchanan was America's only bachelor president, and so his hostess was his niece, Harriet Lane. The two were highly regarded by Washington society for their White House entertainments, which featured fine wines and champagnes. For his Inaugural Ball, the incoming president reportedly spent $3,000 ($88,410 in 2020 dollars) on wine alone.

Buchanan apparently preferred to consume his wine in large format bottles. As for the contents, although America had by that point embraced a range of wines from France and Italy, Buchanan preferred Madeira, the favorite of his earliest predecessors. According to John W. Forney, Buchanan's political manager, "The Madeira and sherry that he had consumed would fill more than one old cellar." Present-day visitors to Buchanan's estate, Wheatland, near Lancaster, Pennsylvania, will see an unopened bottle of 1827 Madeira from the president's cellar sitting on his desk.

Buchanan was renowned for his ability to consume high volumes of alcohol without appearing intoxicated. He is reported to have justified his drinking by saying: "I was never in better health in all of my life; I can take my glass of Old Monongahela [rye whiskey], dine heartily, indulge in Madeira, and sleep soundly."

But later in life, Buchanan's excesses caught up with him, saddling him with a case of gout. His failing health ultimately caused him to curtail his wine consumption, albeit with great reluctance. Writing to his niece in his postpresidential years, Buchanan lamented that he had attended a lavish dinner on the New Jersey Shore where he was put in an "awkward" situation by "not being able to drink a drop of wine."

An unopened bottle of 1827
Madeira belonging to James
Buchanan remains displayed
on his desk at Wheatland,
his home near Lancaster,
Pennsylvania.

ABRAHAM LINCOLN
Sixteenth President of the United States, 1861–1865

AT THE TIME OF ABRAHAM LINCOLN'S 1860 campaign for president, the temperance movement was gaining steam. Americans opposed to the consumption of alcohol were becoming a powerful voting bloc, and Lincoln preferred to be seen as a teetotaler. The strategy was not without its challenges. Bourbon was a major product in the rural Kentucky of Lincoln's upbringing, and many residents—including his father and his schoolteacher—performed seasonal or part-time work in the distilleries.

Alcohol was in fact the pretext used by Lincoln's political nemesis, Stephen A. Douglas, to try to fan the flames of scandal. In one of their famous debates during the 1858 campaign in Illinois for the U.S. Senate, Douglas accused Lincoln of selling alcohol at Berry and Lincoln, a grocery store Lincoln had owned in the 1830s. In fact all general stores sold whiskey, but it seems that Lincoln's partner acted alone in applying for a license to permit drinking on the premises and the partnership soon dissolved.

While Lincoln lost the Senate seat to Douglas, the political profile he built for himself during that campaign eventually propelled him to the White House. Once there, he tended to personally abstain from alcohol. This abstention reportedly made some of his contemporaries in Washington uneasy, so occasionally at these events he would pointedly take a sip of champagne for their benefit. According to Lincoln's assistant secretary, William Osborn Stoddard, when Lincoln's attention was called to a rare wine, he would "barely touch his lips to the glass, just to see what it was," but without any "perceptible diminution of its contents." It is therefore impossible to know whether Lincoln enjoyed what, in 1864, would have been a distinct novelty: a gift of 1859 vintage California wines from the collector of the port of San Francisco.

State Dinners were discontinued at the White House during the Civil War, but the Lincolns continued to have afternoon and evening receptions for the

President Abraham Lincoln's avoidance of alcohol did not prevent a political cartoonist of the period from depicting him as a bartender in action. Published in an 1862 issue of *Punch*, the satirical illustration meant to criticize the president's handling of the press shows Lincoln with bottles labeled "Bunkum," "Bosh," and "Brag," pouring the "New York Press" from a glass of "Victory" to a glass of "Defeat."

Dated December 16, 1864, this letter (opposite) was sent from Perkins, Stern & Co., dealers in California wines, to President Abraham Lincoln, informing him that two cases of California wines—Port and hock, both vintage 1859—were being shipped to him with the compliments of Charles James, collector of the port of San Francisco. James had received his commission from Lincoln earlier in the year.

THE LATEST FROM AMERICA;

Or, the New York "Eye-Duster," to be taken Every Day.

public at which wine was served. Records show that the president and Mary Todd Lincoln often served six different wines with dinner, followed by liqueurs in the Red Room.

On February 5, 1862, Mrs. Lincoln held what the press labeled a "Presidential Party"; one newspaper described the supper room as "a coup d'oeil of dazzling splendor, fruits and flowers, and blazing lights, and sparkling crystal, and inviting confections were everywhere." Young Willie Lincoln was ill upstairs during the ball, and following his death two weeks later, official entertaining was suspended for a year.

ANDREW JOHNSON
Seventeenth President of the United States, 1865–1869

ULYSSES S. GRANT
Eighteenth President of the United States, 1869–1877

**Then a smile,
and a glass, and
a toast and a cheer
/ For all the good
wine, and we've
some of it here.**

—Oliver Wendell Holmes

FOLLOWING LINCOLN'S ASSASSINATION, his vice president, Andrew Johnson, became the seventeenth president of the United States. When Vice President–elect Johnson came to Washington for the Inauguration in 1865, he had made quite a splash. It was reported he got drunk from the moment he arrived and remained in that condition for the day and a half of inaugural activities. In the audience for the Lincoln-Johnson Inauguration ceremony was future President Rutherford B. Hayes. He wrote to his wife, Lucy—a temperance advocate herself—saying, "It was lucky you didn't come to the inauguration. The bad weather and Andy Johnson's disgraceful drunkenness spoiled it."

The Inauguration spectacle was not the first indication that Johnson enjoyed strong drink. During Lincoln's first term, Johnson had served the president as the military governor of Tennessee. In this role, he attended a dinner party at the home of a prominent supporter. Expecting Johnson to be accustomed to the finest wines, the hosts set an elegant table that featured their most prized wineglasses. As the servant attempted to fill Johnson's glass, the governor politely refused, saying, "I never drink wine." Following the dinner, Johnson explained himself: "I refused wine at your dinner today because I don't like the stuff. Too thin." Apparently Johnson preferred whiskey.

Andrew Johnson was the first president to be impeached. Wine played a role even in that serious constitutional process. After the Senate came just one vote short of convicting Johnson and removing him from office, it was reported that William Seward, secretary of state, had bet a case of champagne that Johnson would be acquitted.

Social dining reached a new high point in the years following the Civil War. The dinners hosted by President Ulysses S. Grant were particularly lavish; each place was set with six wineglasses in anticipation of at least that many different wines being served with the sequence of courses. William H. Crook, bodyguard and clerk to twelve presidents, wrote in his memoir that President Grant "chose the wines himself, and gave directions that they should be of the proper temperature. General Grant was an open-handed, lavish host. I remember one wine bill which impressed me very much at the time—$1800 for champagne alone." The wine bill would be $35,230 in 2020 dollars.

Entitled "Let Us Have Pease," a song written during the presidential campaign of 1868 poked fun at Ulysses S. Grant's "Let Us Have Peace" campaign slogan. The sheet music bears an illustration of Grant seated at a table laden with fruit and wine ordering peas[e] from a waiter.

At a State Dinner for Prince Arthur of Britain in January 1870, Grant's wine bill reportedly totaled nearly $1,500 ($28,279 in 2020 dollars), almost the cost of the rest of the twenty-nine-course meal. The dinner began at 7:00 p.m. and lasted so long that there was no time for after-dinner conversation. Wines were served about every third course, according to one report, and six wineglasses of different sizes were arrayed with a small bouquet of flowers at every place setting. That may explain why, later in his administration, President Grant began economizing by replacing the wine service with fruit punches.

WINE AND THE WHITE HOUSE

RUTHERFORD B. HAYES
Nineteenth President of the United States, 1877–1881

God only made water, but man made wine.

—Victor Hugo

PRESIDENT RUTHERFORD B. HAYES and his wife, Lucy Webb Hayes, were both known to be aligned with the nation's growing temperance movement when they entered the White House in 1877. Yet even in this time of temperance, the diplomatic community considered the service of wine to be an essential ingredient of state hospitality. On the occasion of the Hayes administration's first official social event, the April 1877 visit of Grand Duke Alexis, son of the Russian czar, the president's advisers implored him to serve wine at the dinner to avoid a diplomatic disaster. President and Mrs. Hayes acquiesced and, for the sake of international comity, allowed the customary six wines to be served at the dinner. Never again during their tenure was alcohol served in the White House.

Although the first lady set luxurious standards for other aspects of her entertaining, organizing beautiful White House dinners with elegant place settings and stunning floral arrangements, she directed that no alcohol be served. Instead she offered her guests fruit juice, earning her the nickname "Lemonade Lucy." After attending one such dinner, Secretary of State William Evarts remarked that, at the Hayes White House, "The water flowed like champagne."

Though not included in the Republican platform published during the 1876 election (opposite), temperance became one of the most memorable aspects of Rutherford B. Hayes's administration.

During these years, Henry D. Cogswell, a temperance advocate, was installing "temperance fountains" at busy intersections in at least a dozen U.S. cities. He hoped that easy access to pure water would deter people from drinking alcohol. The fountain for Washington, D.C., adorned with a crane and a dolphin (right), was installed c. 1880 on Pennsylvania Avenue about halfway between the White House and the Capitol. It is one of the few that have survived, though it has not served up ice water for at least a century. Inscribed around the top are the words Faith, Hope, Charity, and Temperance.

JAMES A. GARFIELD
Twentieth President of the United States, 1881

**The immortal grape
. . . cheers the sad,
revives the old,
inspires the young,
makes Weariness
forget his toil.**

—Lord Byron

HAYES DECIDED NOT TO RUN FOR A SECOND TERM, but he hoped that after his exit the White House would continue to be a model of temperance. In a memorandum to his successor, President-elect James A. Garfield, Hayes argued that "to reject the reform which has been established in the White House will grievously disappoint thousands of the best people who supported you." He then went on to appeal to Garfield's political and religious sensibilities: "You . . . will be regarded as lacking the courage of your convictions if you abandon it. It will be said quite as much by men of the world as by others that you lack the grit to face fashionable ridicule." The Garfields were also hounded on the subject of temperance by religious and women's groups, and whether the new president would choose to make temperance a tradition in the White House was hotly debated in the newspapers.

In February 1881, the *Washington Post* asked:

> *Shall wine be banished from or allowed in the White House under the next Administration? Do not laugh, for the question is more serious, or rather more troublesome, than you would suspect. Ridiculous as it may appear to you, there has been got up through the country a lively agitation of this question. Temperance people, as they call themselves, are making the most intemperate appeals to General and Mrs. Garfield on the subject. . . . Make it a tradition, they urge, that the White House shall be the sanctuary of total abstinence.*

And a story in the February 1881 *Boston Independent* explained:

> *It is expected that the President will perform certain public social duties. For that reason, the public has a right to be interested in the question whether the new President will offer wine to his guests, or will continue the custom set by Mrs. Hayes. . . . If this is a public matter, then we may properly express the opinion that our best public sentiment, which rejects wine, ought to rule. It is our country and our society that are to be represented in our court, and not the society and customs of France or Austria. Our national habits are not wine drinking. If Mr. and Mrs. Garfield drink intoxicating liquors privately, we hope they will not offer them officially, at the expense of the nation, which pays, whether directly or indirectly, for these official entertainments.*

But Garfield never got a chance to settle the question definitively. Though he intended to use wines stocked in the White House cellar by Ulysses Grant for upcoming State

The administration of President James A. Garfield was cut short by an assassin's bullet before a decision was made on whether he would serve wine at the White House. A portrait published during the presidential campaign of 1880 shows the Garfield family engaged in a variety of wholesome pastimes such as sewing, music, and reading.

Dinners, he neither drank nor served wine during his first six months in office. On June 30, 1881, his wife, First Lady Lucretia ("Crete") Garfield, wrote to her husband with a wine-related request for his upcoming visit to their vacation spot on the New Jersey Shore. "My Darling," she implored, "For two nights I have taken a glass of port wine, and conclude that it is one reason I have slept better, but I have only a little more wine and if you can bring me a little more that you can trust as pure port I think it may be of advantage to me." Two days later, President Garfield was shot in Washington while preparing to board the train to New Jersey to see her. It is not known whether he had packed her request in his baggage. Severely wounded, he was brought back to the White House. He died in September.

WINE AND THE WHITE HOUSE

CHESTER A. ARTHUR
Twenty-First President of the United States, 1881–1885

TEMPERANCE ADVOCATES WERE ESPECIALLY chagrined by the elevation of Garfield's vice president, Chester A. Arthur, to the presidency. The new president was not inclined toward restraint or abstention in matters of lifestyle, including his alcohol consumption. President Arthur retained Louis Comfort Tiffany to carry out an elaborate redecoration of the White House, including heavy gold wallpaper and an immense red, white, and blue glass screen running the length of the Cross Hall. In this highly adorned entertaining space, President Arthur's meals of fourteen or more courses were accompanied by eight different wines and champagne.

As James R. Bumgarner documents in *The Health of the Presidents*, "Arthur would drink wine and after dinner liqueurs pretty much nightly." In July 1884, the *New York Times* praised President Arthur as having "far surpassed all his predecessors in the matter of entertaining at the White House, and [he] has set an example of excellence and elegance in table appointments which will be difficult for his successors to follow." The same article lists the menu for a Diplomatic Corps dinner given by the president on February 6, 1884. Accompanying the numerous courses were Chablis, sherry, "Hockheimer," "Grau Larse" (probably Château Gruaud–Larose), "Perier Jouet & Co.," and Chambertin.

President Arthur's habits set him on a course toward a testy confrontation with the women leading the temperance movement, who pressed him to ban alcohol from the White House. They also demanded that, in homage to former First Lady Lucy Hayes's tough stand, he hang a large portrait of their heroine in the East Room. Refusing both requests, President Arthur replied to one of their leaders: "Madam, I may be President of the United States, but my private life is nobody's damned business."

Included in "Bottle Alley," a display of pre–World War I liquors at the Broadmoor Resort in Colorado Springs, are two bottles that once belonged to President Chester A. Arthur: a "Fine Champagne Brandy from 1840" and an 1810 cognac. Chester A. Arthur II, the president's son, lived in Colorado and was a friend of Spencer Penrose, who founded the Broadmoor Resort.

GROVER CLEVELAND
Twenty-Second and Twenty-Fourth President of the United States, 1885–1889, 1893–1897

BENJAMIN HARRISON
Twenty-Third President of the United States, 1889–1893

Well, my dear fellow, what did you expect, champagne?

—*Grover Cleveland*

WHITE HOUSE ENTERTAINING at the end of the nineteenth century was lavish, and the presidents took an interest in wine and champagne and their service. In his memoir, Ike Hoover, who was sent to the White House in 1891 to install electricity and stayed on to manage the system, referred to this period as the time "when wine flowed freely," and he described a typical dinner in detail:

> *At the large dinners in those days from four to six glasses would surround each plate. There was a different wine for each course and champagne all through the meal. We figured on a quart of champagne for every four people, and after being once iced up for the party, it was never returned to the wine-vault. . . . There was an old steward in particular who used to do a lot of worrying when the champagne he had iced up was not being used fast enough. He would pass around the table peering over the shoulders of the guests and, seeing glasses empty, would whisper in the ears of the so-called "wine men," "let the chammy fly!"*

According to Hoover, who eventually became chief usher, President Grover Cleveland was "an epicure and connoisseur of wines." At a dinner for his cabinet on January 20, 1887, he offered seven wines. Cleveland was the only president to serve two nonconsecutive terms, but his enthusiasm for wine seems not to have diminished much during the intervening years. At a dinner for his cabinet on January 4, 1894, six wineglasses stood around every plate, except at the setting for First Lady Frances Folsom Cleveland, his young ward whom he had married in 1886, where there was, as usual, only a glass for water.

Cleveland's terms bookended the presidency of Benjamin Harrison, who, along with his wife, Caroline, also emphasized fine dining and entertaining. Pressure from the temperance movement was ongoing, and in Harrison temperance advocates seemed to have an ally. He had once written to his wife criticizing the effects of alcohol and expressing his preference for "a pleasant, cheerful dinner of the kind where only wine enough is taken to give vivacity to the mind." Despite this profession, Harrison celebrated the

This hand-colored engraving depicts guests enjoying their wine during the State Dinner hosted by President Grover Cleveland in honor of the Diplomatic Corps on January 24, 1889.

centennial of George Washington's Inauguration on April 30, 1889, with a dinner for eight hundred at New York's Metropolitan Opera House. Glasses were raised for thirteen toasts, in honor of the thirteen colonies.

The Harrisons also opened a new chapter in the story of wine at the White House. They served sweet California wine supplied by their friend Leland Stanford—railroad magnate, former governor of California, and founder of Stanford University—who owned two wineries in Northern California: the Leland Stanford Winery, established in 1869, and Great Vina Ranch, established in 1881. By the late 1890s, California's commercial vineyards had been producing for only about forty years, making their product quite a novelty, especially on the East Coast. But the Harrisons had visited the state in 1891 and tasted for themselves the distinctive flavors of California wines, even sampling a Riesling from the Schramsberg Vineyard—a winery that would become very important to presidents in the next century—during a visit to San Francisco.

WILLIAM McKINLEY
Twenty-Fifth President of the United States, 1897–1901

Wine . . . brings to light the hidden secrets of the soul, gives being to our hopes, bids the coward fight, drives dull care away, teaches new means for the accomplishment of our wishes.

—*Horace*

President and Mrs. William McKinley enjoyed wine and served it to their guests, as seen in this illustration (right) of a State Dinner for the Diplomatic Corps in 1900. The table is set in the Cross Hall, separated from the Entrance Hall by Louis Comfort Tiffany's stained-glass screen.

The McKinleys were photographed at a less formal White House dinner table set in c.1898 with wineglasses and decanters (opposite).

WILLIAM McKINLEY, the last in a series of Civil War officers from Ohio to be elected president, was known to drink only in moderation. When he first ran for Congress, in 1876, he was attacked as being a shameless drunk, but in this he had been confused with another officer is his regiment, the 23rd Ohio, a man named John McKinley. The confusion was cleared up, and McKinley was elected, and then reelected six times, to the House of Representatives. Once in the White House, he is reported to have enjoyed wine and served it to his guests.

THEODORE ROOSEVELT
Twenty-Sixth President of the United States, 1901–1909

High and fine literature is wine, and mine is only water, but everybody likes water.

—Mark Twain

THEODORE ROOSEVELT began the new century by scaling back the size and extravagance of White House dinners. The early twentieth-century presidents rarely drank, but they still recognized the importance wine played in politics and diplomacy and would partake in a diplomatic glass of champagne at official dinners during toasting.

Despite his rough-and-tumble reputation, Theodore Roosevelt avoided hard liquor, according to his aide Archibald Butt. He did enjoy occasional mint juleps and drank wine in small amounts at lunch and dinner. Butt said the president insisted on buying his own wine because he wanted only the best for the White House.

Menus from Roosevelt's administration still reflect the typical multicourse Victorian dinner, with a different beverage served for each course, but the number of wines was reduced to only four at the most, instead of the earlier standard of six or more. The Roosevelts typically served a Sauterne, a Spanish sherry or a Bordeaux, and a champagne—usually Ruinart Brut. Except for the sherry, all the wines they served were French. For a cabinet dinner on December 17, 1903, the menu listed Haut Sauterne, sherry amontillado, Claret Château Langoiran, and Champagne Ruinart Brut. Early Roosevelt menus identify wines by name, but a 1907 letter from Roosevelt aide George Bromwell to the caterer, Charles Rauscher, reveals that First Lady Edith Roosevelt eventually decided to list only generic names instead: "You are further informed that it is Mrs. Roosevelt's desire that the names of the various wines used be not placed on the menus provided for the dinner table, but that simply the words 'Ht. Sauternes,' 'Sherry,' 'Claret,' 'Apollinaris,' and 'Liqueurs' be used in their proper places."

In 1902, when Prince Henry of Prussia visited the United States to launch his brother the kaiser's new imperial yacht, the U.S. importer of Moët & Chandon champagne used the occasion to promote his products. He seems to have supplied free champagne for the State Dinner honoring the prince, to have printed the menus for the dinner and for the luncheon the next day, and even to have made sure it was a bottle of Moët & Chandon that Alice Roosevelt used to christen the ship. Evidently the kaiser, who had supplied a bottle of German champagne for the purpose, was not pleased.

Another special occasion for the Roosevelts was held on December 28, 1908, when they hosted a debut dinner at the White House for their youngest daughter, Ethel. At the midnight supper, the Roosevelts served a white wine left over from the wedding of their eldest daughter, Alice, two years earlier and served champagne with dessert. The official records indicate that the young guests were served eight cases of wine; the aide Butt, however, insisted it was ten, adding: "I did not see a single youth show any effect from it."

Roosevelt's alcohol consumption during his White House years became the subject of high drama in his postpresidency. As the temperance movement continued to gain strength, a small Michigan newspaper ran an editorial after Roosevelt left office

Wineglasses await the arrival of President Theodore Roosevelt's guests at a dinner honoring Prince Henry of Prussia on February 24, 1902. Decorations included smilax festoons, white and pink azaleas, ferns and palms, and red, white, and blue lights.

claiming that Roosevelt "gets drunk, . . . and that not infrequently, and all his intimates know about it." Roosevelt filed suit against the editor of the newspaper and personally testified against him at trial. He offered as a witness his personal physician, who said that if Theodore Roosevelt ever drank anything, it would be milk. Roosevelt himself explained:

> *I do not drink either whiskey or brandy. . . ; I do not drink beer; I sometimes drink light wine. . . . At home, at dinner, I may partake of a glass or two glasses of white wine. At a public dinner, or a big dinner, if they have champagne I will take a glass or two glasses of champagne.*

Journalists who had covered the president during his years in office also testified as character witnesses. In the end, the Hero of San Juan Hill prevailed, and the editor of the newspaper admitted he was wrong.

WILLIAM HOWARD TAFT
Twenty-Seventh President of the United States,
1909–1913

WOODROW WILSON
Twenty-Eighth President of the United States,
1913–1921

[Once] we lost our corkscrew and were compelled to live on food and water for several days.
—W. C. Fields as Cuthbert J. Twillie

PRESIDENT WILLIAM HOWARD TAFT CONTINUED the custom of serving the diverse wines expected by distinguished guests. While he seemed to prefer food over drink, he ensured the White House cellar was well stocked. Yet even though his staff were instructed to purchase the best champagne, it is not clear that these fine wines reached all of Taft's guests. The White House aide Archibald Butt recalled:

We had in the wine closet fifteen bottles of a very good champagne but the President thought it was not good enough to serve at his Harmony Dinner and told me to get some extra fine wine. I thought it perfect nonsense to serve vintage wine to most of those people so I bought four bottles of the very finest vintage wine I could get at the Metropolitan and gave direction to serve this wine to Senator Root, Senator Hale, the Speaker, the Attorney General, and several others who are bon vivants *in their way and great connoisseurs of champagne.*

Taft's successor, Woodrow Wilson, had long been known to raise a glass on special occasions. As president of Princeton University, he celebrated New Year's Eve in Scottish fashion. Toward midnight, guests gathered in the dining room, each standing with one foot on a chair and one on the table. They sang "Auld Lang Syne" and drank a toast of wine, and when the bell of Nassau Hall began to strike twelve, they rushed to open the front door, to welcome 1910. But despite his own enjoyment of wine, Wilson's administration ushered in the era of Prohibition and, with it, the "Dark Ages" for wine at the White House.

Although Wilson vetoed the Volstead Act, which detailed how the Eighteenth Amendment would be enforced, he was overridden by Congress. As Prohibition was about to take effect, Wilson was abroad attending the Paris Peace Conference with his personal physician, Dr. Cary Grayson, in his entourage. According to Grayson's diary, at

Despite the dust, the bottles of Moët champagne can be identified in this collection preserved in President Woodrow Wilson's wine cellar. These fine wines acquired during his presidency survive at his home on S Street in Northwest Washington, D.C., where they have been stored for nearly a century.

the signing ceremony for the Treaty of Versailles the French prime minister "had wine brought in and proposed a toast to the peace and good health of the party. After the toast had been drunk he turned to me [Grayson] and said, 'You had better have another one because you will not be able to get any more of this wine when you get back home.'"

When the Eighteenth Amendment took effect on January 17, 1920, it prohibited the manufacture, sale, and transportation of alcoholic beverages throughout the United States, including at the White House. But Wilson had accumulated a substantial wine collection while in the White House and wanted to enjoy it when he left. He was able to bring the bottles to his postpresidential residence in Northwest Washington, D.C., only after getting special approval from the Prohibition commissioner since, under the Volstead Act, transporting alcohol was a crime.

Fermentation and civilization are inseparable.
—*John Ciardi*

When attempting to throw out the first pitch at the 1931 World Series, President Herbert Hoover was met with the "We Want Beer" signs of angry protesters, weary of more than a decade of Prohibition.

WARREN G. HARDING
Twenty-Ninth President of the United States, 1921–1923

CALVIN COOLIDGE
Thirtieth President of the United States, 1923–1929

HERBERT HOOVER
Thirty-First President of the United States, 1929–1933

ALTHOUGH ALL OF AMERICA was officially "dry," President Warren G. Harding's White House was anything but. Drinking was a feature of Harding's twice-weekly poker games, where, according to frequent guest Alice Roosevelt Longworth, "trays with bottles containing every imaginable brand of whiskey stood about." Harding enjoyed drinking with friends as they played poker in the private quarters, and he finished off rounds of golf at the Chevy Chase Club with drinks in the clubhouse. The president's sources for his liquor supplies are not known. One historian, however, claims that some came through a Harding associate whose connections at the Justice Department gave him access to confiscated alcohol. He also tells of a party of Harding associates at which a prostitute was accidentally killed, hit by flying bottles as a table-top was cleared for dancing. The president was quickly whisked away.

With President Harding's untimely demise in 1923, his vice president, Calvin ("Silent Cal") Coolidge, assumed the presidency. The Coolidge White House was distinguished by its austere frugality, and no records suggest that wine was served at any White House event. After his presidency, however, Coolidge is said to have been introduced to the pleasure of sweet Tokay wine by publishing magnate William Randolph Hearst during a visit to Hearst's California estate. Coolidge reminded his host that he did not drink but was persuaded to accept a small glass of Tokay. After enjoying Hearst's offering, he quickly had a second glass and made a point of saying that he was noting the wine for future reference.

Herbert Hoover made campaign commitments to advocates of Prohibition and seems to have honored them at the White House, although he enjoyed wine. Prior to his government service, he collected fine wines on his travels around the world. But during the years of his presidency, the rise of organized crime—driven by bootlegging in a "dry" nation—was a challenge, and then the onset of the Great Depression caused Hoover's popularity to plummet. As he attempted to throw out the ceremonial first pitch at the 1931 World Series in Philadelphia, the angry crowd booed him and began loudly chanting, "We want beer!"

FRANKLIN D. ROOSEVELT

Thirty-Second President of the United States, 1933–1945

> **To encounter Roosevelt with all his buoyant sparkle, his iridescent personality, and his sublime confidence, was like opening your finest bottle of champagne.**
>
> —*Winston Churchill*

BY 1932, TWELVE YEARS without alcohol and the economic disaster of the Great Depression had left their mark on the voting public. Franklin D. Roosevelt saw the political opening and as a candidate for president pledged his support for repealing the Eighteenth Amendment. In one campaign speech he referred to Prohibition as a "stupendous blunder." Then, in March 1933, just a week after he was inaugurated president, Roosevelt pushed for a change to the Volstead Act that would permit beverages with 3.2 percent alcohol or less. "I believe this would be a good time for a beer," he said. By the end of his first year in office Prohibition had been banished altogether by the Twenty-First Amendment.

President Roosevelt (above) enjoys a glass of wine at a Democratic Party fund-raiser in 1938.

Vineyard workers in France (opposite), hopeful that the end of Prohibition in America would improve sales of French wine, raise a toast to Franklin D. Roosevelt's image upon his election to the presidency in 1932.

After such a long dry spell, the American public was curious to see how the new president would handle alcohol in the White House. In November 1934, the *New York Times* reported the policy announced by First Lady Eleanor Roosevelt. "Wines will be served at state dinners at the White House this season for the first time since pre-prohibition days. . . . Although about 1,800 White House wine glasses are available from storage, the pre-war customs of setting three or four for each guest, for a vintage 'with every course,' will not be revived." Mrs. Roosevelt indicated only one or two wines would be served for White House dinners, and that they would be "light wines" (wines with less than 12.5 percent alcohol). "With us it will be a very simple thing always," she remarked, "serving American wines to those who care for them."

That high-profile endorsement of domestic wines thrilled California's wine industry, which responded with an official expression of thanks to the first lady from the

directors of the California Wine Institute. But not everyone was so delighted. After a dinner at the White House, Harold L. Ickes, FDR's secretary of the interior, wrote in his secret diary:

> *Wine was served for the first time since prohibition went into effect. Mrs. Roosevelt had announced she would serve one glass each of two domestic wines and she kept her word. The sherry was passable, but the champagne was undrinkable. . . . I am bound to say that probably on only one other occasion have I ever tasted worse champagne, and it does seem to me that if decent champagne can't be made in the United States, it ought to be permissible, even for the White House, to serve imported champagne.*

The Prohibition years had left the White House wine cellar depleted, but industry leaders stepped in to improve the quality of the collection, presenting the White House with rare treasures. The noted French wine merchant André L. Simon, for example, presented President Roosevelt with ten bottles of wine that he described as "so rare as to be almost curios." Six of the bottles were Moët & Chandon champagne reportedly bottled for Queen Victoria in 1874; two were the last remaining bottles of Château Mouton Rothschild 1858; and the other two were survivors of the 1811 bottling of Chambertin.

Despite Mrs. Roosevelt's edict about serving domestic wines, occasional exceptions might have been made. One may well have been the 1939 visit of King George VI and Queen Elizabeth of England. Their trip was not only the first time a British monarch would set foot on American soil but also a crucial strategic maneuver at a moment when war with Germany loomed on the horizon. Both sides had every interest in a flawless visit, and the planned entertainments—including food and drink selections— were highly scrutinized. On June 7, 1939, the *Washington Post* reported that "President Roosevelt refused point blank yesterday to say whether imported or domestic wines would be served by the White House during the stay of King George and Queen Elizabeth. He said . . . that he was not advertising any brands or valleys noted for their grape choices."

The king and queen were not the only English visitors to get around Mrs. Roosevelt's rules. Her limits on consumption were apparently lifted when Britain's wartime prime minister and Roosevelt's close ally, Winston Churchill, visited the White House. "On his breakfast tray I was instructed to have something hot, something cold, two kinds of fresh fruit, a tumbler of orange juice and a pot of frightfully weak tea. . . . Plus a tumbler of sherry. This was breakfast," recalled White House butler Alonzo Fields. "At lunch he had Scotch and soda. For dinner always champagne, and after dinner, brandy. Then during the evening more Scotch and soda."

Winston Churchill (opposite) enjoys a glass of champagne, his signature drink.

The total cost of the wine for President Roosevelt's dinner for twenty-six in honor of Crown Princess Juliana of the Netherlands was just $4.55 or 17¢ per person (right).

```
           April 23, 1942


CROWN PRINCESS JULIANNA & PRINCE
    CONSORT BERTRAM DINNER FOR 26


Clams                       2.16
Man to open clams           1.00
Oxtailsoup                  2.50
Filet Fish                  6.13
Sauce                        .50
Rib Roast                  30.15
Spinach                     1.75
Onions                      1.25
Idahoes                      .35
Avacadoes                   1.50
Ice Cream                   6.00
Coffee, etc.                3.90
Wine                        4.55
Band                        7.75
Rolls                        .88
Crescents                   1.40
Lettuce                      .60
Grapes                      2.00
Grapefruit                   .60
Dressing                     .25
Cakes                       2.00
                          ───────
                          $77.22


    $77.22 ÷ 26 = $2.91
```

HARRY S. TRUMAN
Thirty-Third President of the United States, 1945–1953

The best audience is one that is intelligent, well educated—and a little drunk.

—*Alben Barkley*

WITH SOME EXCEPTIONS, the light wine service remained a constant for the Roosevelts as well as for President Harry Truman and First Lady Bess Truman after them. Wine was not a focal point of entertaining during the war; a single glass of champagne was served before formal dinners and, although wines were sometimes served with the meal, the process of refilling the empty wineglasses was deliberately slow.

This restrained approach to wine reflected the lasting effects of Prohibition on Americans' interest in wine and the absence of a market for the product. Prohibition had forced many American vineyards—some in operation since the mid-nineteenth century—to close, and World War II prevented the importation of European wine. The dearth of high-quality wines created a void that cocktails rushed to fill, for presidents and their guests as well as the broader public. In private, especially when he was playing poker, President Truman's favorite drink was bourbon and branch water.

Champagne flowed freely on November 3, 1948, after President Harry S. Truman surprised his critics by winning a full term as president.

Although served frugally at the White House, champagne was regularly sacrificed by the Trumans to christen military ships and planes. Here First Lady Bess Truman is seen as she breaks a bottle on an army aircraft at Washington's National Airport during the annual War Bond Show, May 1, 1945.

DWIGHT D. EISENHOWER
Thirty-Fourth President of the United States, 1953–1961

A single glass of champagne imparts a feeling of exhilaration. The nerves are braced, the imagination is agreeably stirred; the wits become more nimble.

—Winston Churchill

IN THE 1950s, with the "Greatest Generation" home from war, wine service at the White House took on added significance as the importance of State Dinners increased, especially during President Dwight D. Eisenhower's second term. One of the diplomatic highlights of that term was the October 17, 1957, visit to the White House of Queen Elizabeth II—her first as reigning queen. She and Prince Philip were feted at a glamorous State Dinner featuring Dry Sack, Château Climens 1943, Beaune Grèves 1952, and Charles Heidsieck 1949. At her luncheon with Vice President Richard M. Nixon during the same visit, the queen was reportedly served American sherry and red wine.

During the Eisenhower years, wine even functioned as a gift of state. In August 1959, in the midst of the Cold War, when ties between the United States and Western Europe were of increasing importance, West German Chancellor Konrad Adenauer presented the president with a special gift: fifty bottles of the highly acclaimed German wine Bernkasteler Doktor.

Earlier in the Eisenhower administration, White House menus listed only the variety of wine served—sherry, Sauterne, red Burgundy, and champagne. By 1958, however, all the wines were fully identified. A typical Eisenhower menu after 1958 included

President and Mrs. Dwight D. Eisenhower pose on the Grand Staircase at the White House with their guests, Queen Elizabeth II and Prince Philip of Great Britain, ahead of the State Dinner in the queen's honor, 1957.

President Eisenhower lifts a glass to toast Generalissimo Francisco Franco during a banquet at the royal palace in Madrid, Spain, December 1959.

Dry Sack, a Spanish sherry routinely served for the first course; Château Climens, a French Sauterne, for the second; and Beaune Grèves, a French Pinot Noir, for the main course—the same wines served to Queen Elizabeth II. For dessert there was often Pol Roger, the French champagne favored by Winston Churchill. The Eisenhowers also served a few other French and Spanish wines.

For luncheons and less formal dinners, the Eisenhowers chose American wines, which were still considered a novelty and frowned upon by many wine critics. But at a dinner in February 1958, President Eisenhower revealed that, throughout that social season, American wines had been secretly served to guests who believed they were tasting Europe's finest offerings. The experiment's success spoke to a promising development: the beginning of an era when American wines would come to be accepted as the equals of their European cousins. To accommodate growing interest in wine during this exciting period, the White House wine cellar was upgraded with new bins and shelves that enlarged its capacity and improved storage conditions.

JOHN F. KENNEDY
Thirty-Fifth President of the United States, 1961–1963

> I'm like old wine. They don't bring me out too often, but I'm well preserved.
>
> —*Rose Kennedy on her 100th birthday*

KNOWN FOR THEIR STYLISH entertaining, President John F. Kennedy and First Lady Jacqueline Kennedy served the best European wines at their State Dinners. Some of their offerings were German and Italian, but in keeping with Jacqueline Kennedy's love for all things French, they chose mostly French wines, including Pouilly-Fuissé, Château Haut-Brion, and Dom Pérignon champagne.

Champagne was dear to both the president and first lady. The worldly and sophisticated Jacqueline enjoyed the fine French champagne Veuve Cliquot served in an elegant

flute champagne glass. Jack, meanwhile, seems to have taken a freer approach. The legendary *Washington Post* editor Ben Bradlee described JFK as a most attentive host: "The champagne was flowing like the Potomac in flood, and the President himself was opening bottle after bottle in a manner that sent the foam flying over the furniture."

Despite their affection for European wines, the Kennedys did serve California wines at occasional luncheons and small dinners. On September 19, 1961, Almaden Pinot Noir became the first American wine to be served at a State Dinner when the Kennedys chose it for the event honoring

Soviet Premier Nikita Khrushchev is seen during his famous tour of the Moët & Chandon wine cellars in France with Jean-Rémy Moët (above).

Peruvian President Manuel Prado Ugarteche. Almaden was again served at a May 22, 1962, State Dinner for President Félix Houphouët-Boigny of the Ivory Coast, where guests enjoyed the vineyard's Pinot Blanc. It was in good company with a Puligny-Montrachet Pucelles 1958 and Dom Pérignon 1952. And at the famous White House dinner on November 13, 1961, where the cellist Pablo Casals performed for Governor Luis Muñoz Marín of Puerto Rico, the Kennedys served a California Chardonnay from Inglenook and a Cabernet Sauvignon from Almaden while finishing the evening with the French champagne Piper-Heidsieck 1953.

Although California wines were increasingly gaining prominence, President Kennedy would take no chances when appearing on the international stage, especially not when facing off against Soviet Premier Nikita Khrushchev. In addition to being Kennedy's Cold War adversary, Khrushchev had high expectations when it came to wine. During an official visit to France in 1960, the only side trip from Paris that the Soviet leader requested was a tour of the champagne cellars of Épernay. He was driven in a little electric train around the 17 miles of cellars of Moët & Chandon. To top off the visit, the head of the firm, Count Robert-Jean de Vogüé, toasted Khrushchev with an 1893 Moët & Chandon champagne that was bottled in 1894—the year of Khrushchev's birth.

Known for their elegant entertaining, John and Jacqueline Kennedy, seen enjoying champagne at the Stork Club in 1955 (opposite), were said to have kept the champagne flowing at their White House parties. Especially well considered were the wines Kennedy served on his travels, including the 1953 Château Mouton Rothschild selected for his summit with Khrushchev.

So when Kennedy and Khrushchev entertained each other with luncheons at their respective embassies during the 1961 Vienna Summit, the wine-selection stakes were high. While Khrushchev came fully loaded with vodka and Soviet wines, JFK would not risk reciprocating with California wines. Instead he served a 1953 Château Mouton Rothschild—a wine described by noted wine critic Michael Broadbent as "a most lovely wine." Not to be outdone, in September 1962, Khrushchev responded with his own grand gesture: sending a gift of five crates of Georgian wine to the White House.

The Kennedys established many of the cherished traditions associated with the White House today, one of which was the service of three wines at State Dinners. Kennedy menus list a light white wine for the first course, a red with the entrée, and

Champagne awaits President and Mrs. Kennedy as they arrive at a dinner party with French President Charles de Gaulle during their visit to Paris, 1961.

Champagne goblets and tulip champagne glasses were included on the Kennedys' glassware order for *Air Force One* from Tiffany and Co. in April 1961.

Request for Crystal for the Presidential Aircraft

P&C   PRES   27 April 1961
   Attn: Mrs. Stern

Request that the following items as listed be purchased from Tiffany & Co,
5th Avenue & 57th Street, New York for the Presidential aircraft for use
by the President and his guests:

850	10)			
50004		Old Fashion glasses	12	$15.00
	14)	High Ball glasses	12	$18.00
	29)	Cocktail glasses	12	$24.00
850	32)			
50011		Champagne Goblets	12	$27.00
	33)	Tulip Champagnes	12	$24.00

$108.00 - Total

Forwarded as per telephone conversation with Mrs. Stern and Sgt Dabney.

JAMES B. SWINDAL
Lt Colonel, USAF
Presidential Aircraft Commander

Dinner

Saarburger 1959 — Salmon à la Norvégienne en Bellevue

Châteaubriand Beauharnais
Potatoes Parisienne

Almaden Pinot Noir

Salad Mimosa
Assorted Cheeses

Dom Pérignon 1955 — Soufflé glacé Gran Marnier aux fraises
Petits fours sec

Demi-tasse and Liqueurs

Monday, June 24, 1963

My dear girl, there are some things that are just not done, such as drinking Dom Pérignon '55 above the temperature of 38 degrees Fahrenheit.

—*Sean Connery as James Bond*

President Kennedy shared an appreciation of such fine champagnes as Dom Pérignon with James Bond, the fictional British MI6 agent 007. The champagne was on the Kennedys' menu for a dinner in honor of West German Chancellor Konrad Adenaur on June 24, 1963, and enjoyed by Bond in many films, including *Thunderball* (1965).

then champagne with dessert. This three-wine service of white, red, and champagne became the norm for all succeeding administrations.

Popular culture of the early 1960s was also embracing fine wines and associating them with a glamorous lifestyle, as in the James Bond stories, which Kennedy enjoyed. He saw *Dr. No* soon after it was released and watched the second Bond film, *From Russia with Love*, in the White House shortly before his assassination in November 1963. The chronicles of 007 prominently referred to premier wines in even the most sinister scenes. As James Bond grabbed a bottle of champagne from the dining table to attack a guard, Dr. No reminded Bond, "That's a Dom Pérignon '55. It would be a pity to break it." In the Ian Fleming novel *Goldfinger*, Bond drinks Château Mouton Rothschild 1947 over dinner at the villain's house in England. Dining with his boss "M" in *Moonraker*, Bond enjoys a 1934 Château Mouton Rothschild at the exclusive Blades Club in London. As America was coming of age as a wine-appreciating country, these iconic cultural moments helped elevate fine wine to dining tables across the nation, including at the White House.

LYNDON B. JOHNSON

Twenty-Sixth President of the United States, 1963–1969

Come, come, good wine is a good familiar creature if well used; exclaim no more against it.

—William Shakespeare

PRESIDENT LYNDON B. JOHNSON was the first president to prominently feature American wines in the White House. Johnson wanted to promote the growing American wine market and give it a sense of legitimacy. If a domestic wine was good enough for the president and the White House, it could be served at any American table. Even for a dinner hosted by the President's Club of New York, at the Waldorf Astoria Hotel, President Johnson requested that only American wines be served—a departure from the hotel's usual French offerings. In 1969, Don W. McColly, president of the Wine Institute, stated, "No President has done more to further the interest of the American wine industry than President Johnson," crediting him for the growing popularity of American wines.

The Johnsons hosted fifty-three State Dinners, more than any of the previous occupants of the White House. The wines served during Johnson's tenure were mostly from California vineyards, with a few from New York—the two states at the time with the most vineyards. From New York, the Johnsons served Gold Seal Fournier Nature and Great Western Vin Rouge; the California wines served most often were Wente Pinot Chardonnay, Paul Masson Emerald Dry, Beaulieu Vineyard Cabernet Sauvignon, and Almaden Blanc de Blancs. The Almaden was the Johnson administration's sparkling wine of choice, as it was served with dessert at the majority of events. These four favorite vineyards were founded in the late nineteenth and early twentieth centuries; Almaden was established in 1852. Serving wines with historic pedigrees aided in Johnson's campaign to enhance the reputation of the American wine industry.

The Johnsons even helped make wine history. At the January 14, 1964, State Dinner for Italian President Antonio Segni—the first since the Kennedy assassination—LBJ invited a young Italian American winemaker from California and his wife to attend. Honored by the prestigious request, Robert Mondavi contacted a friend in Washington to prepare for the evening. He was told to get his wife Marjorie a full-length fur coat, to rent a tuxedo for himself, and to hire a limousine instead of a taxi to take him to the White House.

During the course of the evening, photographs of Robert and Marjorie Mondavi were taken. When Robert's sister-in-law Blanche saw the photographs, she became jealous and convinced her husband, Robert's brother and business partner Peter, that Robert must be embezzling to afford such extravagance. A fistfight broke out between the two brothers. Robert was kicked out of the family wine business, and his young son, Michael, was told to give up any hope of a job in the family enterprise. The spurned brother went on to establish his own venture, the Robert Mondavi Winery, which became one of the greatest winemaking operations in the world. Robert Mondavi's wines would be appreciated at White House dinners in the decades to follow.

Guests enjoy their wine (opposite) as President Lyndon B. Johnson speaks at a State Dinner for Chancellor Ludwig Erhard of West Germany, June 12, 1964.

RICHARD M. NIXON
Thirty-Seventh President of the United States, 1969–1974

President Richard M. Nixon often selected the wines to be served at special events himself. Although he reinstated European wines on White House menus, he also chose to highlight American wines at such special events as the formal dinner he hosted at the Century Plaza Hotel in Los Angeles honoring the *Apollo 11* astronauts for their historic lunar landing mission, 1969 (opposite).

DESPITE BEING THE ONLY U.S. president born and raised in California, Richard M. Nixon reinstated the service of European wines at the White House. His personal preference was for French wines, demonstrated by their frequent appearance on menus from his administration's dinners. Many of the top wines in the world—including Château Margaux, Château Haut-Brion, Château Latour, Pol Roger, and Dom Pérignon—were often served. Nixon also served a variety of German wines, including Bernkasteler Doktor and Schloss Johannisberg. When the Nixons entertained the Duke and Duchess of Windsor, they served European jewels from the White House wine cellar—in the form of a 1967 Bernkasteler Doktor and a 1959 Château Margaux—and toasted the royal couple with a 1961 Taittinger Blanc de Blancs.

Although Nixon preferred European varieties, he did make some effort to showcase the American wine industry. At the White House, he served select wines from larger, historic California vineyards such as Louis Martini, Inglenook, and Charles Krug. He also chose American wines for special events outside the Executive Mansion. On August 13, 1969, President and Mrs. Nixon hosted a dinner at the Century Plaza Hotel in Los Angeles to honor the successful *Apollo 11* astronauts; among the guests were popular actors and entertainers as well as another American boundary-breaker, aviator Charles Lindbergh. For this patriotic tribute, the Nixons served only California labels, featuring Wente Brothers Pinot Chardonnay, Inglenook Cabernet Sauvignon, and Korbel sparkling wine.

When the time came to celebrate the beginning of U.S.-China relations, Nixon went with American wines again. For his toast with Premier Zhou Enlai during the 1972 breakthrough visit to China, the president chose a 1969 Schramsberg Blanc de Blancs. For dinners at the American embassies in Moscow and Tehran in that same year, Nixon also served American wines only, as was the case for events honoring former Vietnam prisoners of war in 1973.

In highlighting American wines, Nixon benefited from some encouragement and help. In April 1970, the Wine Institute had delivered a large number of bottles of more than sixty varieties of wine and champagne from California to the White House for the president's use. The institute had begun this practice with the receptive Eisenhowers, but the gift was refused by the Kennedys; it was then resumed with the Johnsons. The

Men are like wine—some turn to vinegar, but the best improve with age.

—*Pope John XXIII*

gift to the Nixon White House was followed by a notable increase in the presence of California wines on the menus for dinners.

The wines served at important events were often selected by Nixon himself. According to presidential historian William Seale, "Nixon was particular about wine." Eventually Nixon wine service settled into a distinct pattern: a German Riesling with the first course, a California Cabernet Sauvignon for the main course, and a French champagne with dessert. Even though Nixon continued to serve more European wines, his placing the California varieties in the middle of the menu showed his confidence that they could hold up in quality next to European selections.

An oft-repeated story about the Nixon White House tells of a two-tier wine service. As a devotee of First Growth French Bordeaux wines, Nixon had a designated wine waiter who poured this fine selection into the president's glass while other guests at dinner were served more ordinary wines. Over the years the practice became known as "Pulling a Nixon."

The story has been denied by former Nixon White House employees but is reinforced by *Washington Post* investigative reporters Bob Woodward and Carl Bernstein. In addition to exposing Nixon's misdeeds related to the Watergate break-in, they also revealed in their book *The Final Days* that, on the presidential yacht, Nixon served inexpensive French Bordeaux wines to the congressmen he was entertaining while instructing the stewards to secretly fill his own glass from a pricey bottle of his favorite 1966 Château Margaux. The bottle was wrapped in a towel to obscure the label.

GERALD R. FORD
Thirty-Eighth President of the United States, 1974–1977

When there is plenty of wine, sorrow and worry take wing.

—Ovid

WHEN PRESIDENT GERALD R. FORD hosted his first two State Dinners, the menus followed the same three-wine pattern of Nixon dinners—probably because they had been planned prior to his resignation. But beginning with the State Dinner for Italy on September 25, 1974, all the wines served by the Fords were American, a change that would become permanent. The Fords' social secretary stated that the new commitment to serving only domestic wines was in keeping with the president's policy of "representing everything American at the White House." Nixon was thus the last president to serve European wines at official dinners.

President Ford selected wines from many of the California vineyards favored by the Johnsons, such as Paul Masson and Wente, and found favorites of his own, including Robert Mondavi, Freemark Abbey, and Mirassou. Ste. Michelle Chenin Blanc from Washington also quickly became a staple. In November 1974, at the State Dinner for Austria, Tabor Hill Vidal Blanc from the president's home state of Michigan was featured for the first course. This was the first time a wine from that state, and in fact from the Midwest, was served at the White House. Another Michigan wine would not be served for more than forty years, until President Barack Obama served Chateau Chantal 2013 Ice Wine at his State Dinner for Canadian Prime Minister Justin Trudeau on March 10, 2016.

At the risk of rubbing salt in a two-century-old wound, when the queen of England came to the White House to celebrate America's Bicentennial on July 7, 1976, President Ford made sure the wine list was all American. The Fords served the visiting monarch a 1972 Sterling Chenin Blanc, a 1968 Beaulieu Vineyard Cabernet Sauvignon, and a 1973 Schramsberg Blanc de Blancs sparkling wine. Old rivalries notwithstanding, the Anglo-American friendship was flourishing, and the wine choices—along with the entertainments that evening—were apparently a hit. First Lady Betty Ford later recalled in her memoirs, "I'd give myself four stars for the way that visit went off."

As it turns out, the Fords did not have many opportunities to plan wine lists for formal White House dinners. After serving out the remaining two years of Nixon's second term, Ford lost his bid for reelection. The administration's final hours were spent in alcohol-fueled self-consolation. As Ford's press secretary, Ron Nessen, recorded: "On Ford's last night in the White House, I and my Press Office staff, all feeling sad, gave ourselves a farewell party. First we downed several bottles of champagne purchased for the occasion. When that was gone, we drank all the liquor we could find in our cabinets and closets. And when that was gone, we even consumed an old bottle of fizzy white wine brought home from a Ford visit to Romania."

President Gerald Ford shares a toast with Queen Elizabeth II in celebration of the Bicentennial of America's independence from Great Britain, 1976.

JIMMY CARTER
Thirty-Ninth President of the United States, 1977–1981

Winemaker and former president Jimmy Carter holds two bottles of his signature wine ahead of a silent auction to benefit the Carter Center, 2006.

FORD'S SUCCESSOR, JIMMY CARTER, brought an unusual depth of firsthand vinicultural knowledge to the White House. Before his 1976 election, Carter had cultivated grapes and made his own wine on his peanut farm in Georgia. With this background, as president, he served some of America's finest wines from California, New York, and Washington. These included varieties that were also favorites of past presidents, such as wines from the California vineyards of Louis Martini and Charles Krug, previously selected by Nixon; from the New York vineyards Gold Seal and Great Western, previously selected by Johnson; and from the Washington vineyard Ste. Michelle, which had been favored by Ford.

The selection of excellent wines was also a priority for First Lady Rosalynn Carter, who preferred these refined offerings over hard liquor for White House guests. Speaking to *Vanity Fair* magazine, she said:

We served wine, punch, and cordials. That was what was served at the White House before John Kennedy. I had been to one dinner at the Nixon White House, when Jimmy was governor. It was so beautiful and so elegant and I was so impressed. Then here comes a waiter carrying a tray with bottles of liquor on it. I just did not like that. Everybody thought it was because we were Baptists, but it was not. I just thought it distracted from the elegance of the evening. And Jimmy agreed.

After leaving office, Jimmy Carter resumed his modest winemaking venture on his Georgia farm. Using a 250-year-old wine press, the former president began producing one hundred bottles of wine at a time—about seventy-five red and twenty-five white. Many were given to family and friends; the remainder were donated to the Carter Center to support President and Mrs. Carter's philanthropic causes.

There is more wit in those 100 litres [of wine] than in all the books on philosophy in the world.

—*Louis Pasteur*

First Lady Rosalynn Carter, seen with Polish First Secretary Edward Gierek in 1977 during a State Dinner in Warsaw (right), was involved in the selection of wines for White House events.

British Prime Minister Margaret Thatcher shares a toast with President and Mrs. Jimmy Carter (below) during a State Dinner, 1979.

RONALD REAGAN
Fortieth President of the United States, 1981–1989

THE ADMINISTRATION OF President Ronald Reagan saw wine service in the White House reach a level of interest unmatched since the time of Thomas Jefferson. Reagan understood the importance of wine in entertaining and diplomacy, especially during the 1980s, when wine was rapidly growing in popularity in the United States. Moreover, during his years as governor of California, he had established close relationships with California winemakers and stayed in touch with them. When in Washington, D.C., the legendary winemaker André Tchelistcheff, who led Reagan's favorite Beaulieu Vineyard, would drop by the Oval Office to see the president. And California reaped the commercial benefit from Reagan's promotion. After Canadian Prime Minister Pierre Trudeau first tasted a 1976 Jordan Cabernet Sauvignon at the White House, he ordered an entire case.

The Reagans were keen to promote a variety of winemakers from their home state. With the exceptions of Schramsberg sparkling wine as the standard for dessert and Jordan and Robert Mondavi as favored vineyards, the Reagans did not serve wine from the same vineyard more than three times. In fact, the wines served during Reagan's two terms were the most diverse of any recent administration. It was at Reagan State Dinners, for example, that both California Zinfandel and Merlot wines were first served at the White House.

In selecting this broad array of wines, the president and first lady benefited from the expertise of the Sacramento wine merchant David Berkley, whom Reagan had come to know during his time as governor. Thanks in part to Berkley's guidance, in 1982, John A. DeLuca, the president of the Wine Institute, commented that the Reagans were "the best-informed administration on wine in this century."

Yet for all their knowledge and skill, the Reagans still encountered wine-service dilemmas. What to do, for instance, when the guest of honor at a State Visit is the leader of a major wine-producing country? When French Prime Minister Jacques Chirac visited on March 31, 1987, he and Reagan had by that time known each other for several years, and both shared an interest in promoting the wines of their respective countries. A brilliant diplomatic decision was made when Reagan chose as the centerpiece of the evening wine service 1982 Opus One—a joint venture between Baron Philippe de Rothschild, the innovative leader of France's Château Mouton Rothschild, and Robert

I had grown up believing that wine is good for you, that it's liquid food, and that fine wine can turn a good meal into a feast.
—*Robert Mondavi*

President Ronald Reagan
toasts Soviet leader Mikhail
Gorbachev at a State Dinner
following the signing, earlier in
the day, of a historic treaty to
eliminate intermediate-range
missiles, December 8, 1987.

Wine is the most healthful and hygienic of beverages.

—Louis Pasteur

The Reagans chose a special bottle of Château Margaux 1911, produced the year of the president's birth, to celebrate their thirty-third anniversary in 1985.

Mondavi, the California wine visionary who had helped to propel Napa Valley wines onto the global stage.

Another challenge was one the Reagans inherited. Thanks to Reagan's predecessors, the White House wine cellar contained some of the finest wines from around the world, with a special emphasis on France. They were aged and ready to serve. But the commercial side of diplomacy suggested that only American wines should be served at the White House. To ensure that these foreign treasures did not age beyond drinkability in the White House cellar, the administration served the wines at lower-profile events. One was a September 1985 White House luncheon that took place in the course of a day-long series of briefings for regional editors and reporters from media outlets across the country. The eighty journalists in attendance were served a 1970 Gevrey Chambertin, a premier wine from the Burgundy region of France. Accustomed to the exclusive use of American wines at the White House, the visiting members of the press were surprised. Despite a day of substantive policy briefings from senior administration officials, including President Reagan himself, the main headline of the day was: "French Wine at White House Luncheon Riles California Vintners: Reagan Stirs Tempest in a Bottle."

The Reagans share champagne with staff on board *Air Force One* in a birthday celebration for Deputy Assistant James McKinney, 1988.

Wine was also important to President Reagan in his more private, unofficial moments. An entry in his diary on March 4, 1985—the thirty-third anniversary of his marriage to Nancy Reagan—notes: "At dinner we opened a bottle of Château Margaux 1911." The wine commemorated another milestone in the president's life, as the vintage was the year of his birth.

And when Ronald Reagan visited Prime Minister Margaret Thatcher as a "private citizen" in June 1989, five months after leaving the White House, Mrs. Thatcher wanted to appropriately celebrate their partnership and the man who, in her words, won the decades-long Cold War "without firing a shot." She welcomed the Reagans to No. 10 Downing Street for a formal dinner to toast their friendship and celebrate the triumph of freedom in so many formerly communist countries. To mark the occasion in style, the prime minister directed that the best of her cellars be served for the special dinner, including Château Pétrus 1970, one of the rarest and finest wines produced in the world. Other wines served included a 1987 Matanzas Creek Chardonnay, a tribute to Ronald Reagan's home state, as well as a Bollinger Champagne, Warre's 1945 Port, and an 1878 Grands Fins Bois Cognac. Toasts continued throughout the evening until every bottle had been emptied.

GEORGE H. W. BUSH

Forty-First President of the United States, 1989–1993

Nothing makes the future look so rosy as to contemplate it through a glass of Chambertin.

—*Napoleon Bonaparte*

PRESIDENT GEORGE H. W. BUSH continued the excellent wine service of his predecessor, selecting fine varieties from California vineyards. Bush, too, relied on David Berkley's expertise and served some of the Reagans' favorites throughout his administration. But he also sought out new vineyards and kept his wine service varied—the hallmark of Berkley's approach to wine selection. This sophistication aligned well with the diplomatic experience and nuance that Bush—former director of the Central Intelligence Agency and envoy to China—brought to the White House. These skills were on full display during the May 14, 1991, visit of Queen Elizabeth II, who was served Swanson Reserve Chardonnay 1988, Shafer Hillside Select Cabernet Sauvignon 1986, and Jordan J 1987 at the evening's State Dinner.

President George H. W. Bush drew on his extensive diplomatic experience as he selected wines for the many State Dinners he hosted for world leaders, including Queen Margrethe II of Denmark, 1991.

PUBLIC LAW 102–468—OCT. 23, 1992

Public Law 102–468
102d Congress

Joint Resolution

Designating February 21, 1993, through February 27, 1993, as "American Wine Appreciation Week", and for other purposes.

Whereas wine was produced by our Founding Fathers, including Thomas Jefferson, and winegrape growing and wine production in the United States continue today as a significant agricultural industry in 43 of the States;

Whereas the history of winegrape growing in the world dates back over 7,000 years and it continues as a proud tradition nurtured by the small farmer in all regions of the United States;

Whereas this agricultural industry is comprised of thousands of family-owned farms, many of which are passed on from generation to generation, sustaining responsible preservation of our agricultural resources;

Whereas more than 1,300 wineries and over 8,000 grape and fruit growers around the country work cooperatively to create wine;

Whereas over 85 percent of all wine consumed in the United States is produced by United States winemakers;

Whereas the direct economic impact of the United States wine industry is estimated to account for over $8,000,000,000 in sales annually, including the support of over 200,000 jobs as well as $1,000,000,000 in governmental taxes and fees;

Whereas the United States wine industry contributes to our quality of life by its ongoing contributions to organizations and associations in the health, civic, and educational sectors of the country;

Whereas acclaim for wine produced in the United States has grown internationally for many years and these products account for an increasing percentage of United States exports, helping to reduce the United States trade deficit;

Whereas wine, consumed in moderation, enhances the appetite and provides delicious accompaniment to all types of regional cuisine in the United States, enriching the quality of life for the citizenry of the United States; and

Whereas wine has fulfilled a valued role in a wide variety of the cultural, religious, and familial traditions of the United States: Now, therefore, be it

Resolved by the Senate and House of Representatives of the United States of America in Congress assembled, That—

(1) the Congress commends the winegrape and fruit growers and vintners of the United States for the production of such high quality agricultural products; and

(2) February 21, 1993, through February 27, 1993, is designated as "American Wine Appreciation Week". The President is authorized and requested to issue a proclamation calling upon the people of the United States to observe the week with appropriate programs, ceremonies, and activities.

Approved October 23, 1992.

WILLIAM J. CLINTON
Forty-Second President of the United States, 1993–2001

I'm relieved I never had a craving for [liquor]. I have enough problems without that one.

—*William J. Clinton*

IN RECRUITING DANIEL SHANKS to serve as assistant usher of food and beverage, President Bill Clinton and First Lady Hillary Clinton can be credited with bringing the first wine professional on to the White House staff. Shanks had years of experience working among the vineyards and restaurants of California wine country. With his expertise he carefully selected wines for the White House for the next several administrations. He sought not only to match occasions and menus but to introduce White House guests to fine wines from many different regions of the United States.

The result was a series of well-received diplomatic visits throughout Clinton's time in office. On October 29, 1997, when President Jiang Zemin of China made a State Visit to America, for example, the Clintons' dinner paired excellent American wines with dishes that would be enjoyed by the Chinese delegation. Toasts were exchanged with a 1995 Cuvaison Carneros Chardonnay. Accompanying the meal were a 1995 25th Anniversary Ponzi Pinot Noir from Oregon and a 1991 Iron Horse Blanc de Blancs sparkling wine. After dinner guests enjoyed a performance by the National Symphony Orchestra on the South Lawn.

The Clintons also hosted the legendary South African leader Nelson Mandela. For the special White House welcome on October 4, 1994, the carefully selected food courses were paired with three very different California white wines: a 1993 Joseph Phelps Viognier, a 1991 Peter Michael Chardonnay, and a 1985 Piper Sonoma Tete de Cuvée sparkling wine. As was often the case in the Clinton administration, the celebration reportedly continued late into the evening.

President Bill Clinton shares
State Dinner toasts with
Chinese President Jiang
Zemin (opposite) in 1997 and
with South African President
Nelson Mandela (above)
in 1994.

WINE AND THE WHITE HOUSE

GEORGE W. BUSH
Forty-Third President of the United States, 2001–2009

Wine makes daily living easier, less hurried, with fewer tensions and more tolerance.

—*Benjamin Franklin*

ALTHOUGH PRESIDENT GEORGE W. BUSH had given up alcohol on his fortieth birthday, First Lady Laura Bush ensured that the food and wine served to state visitors represented the best of America. Mrs. Bush hired the first female White House executive chef, Cristeta Comerford, who offered innovative food and wine pairings at official dinners.

In a great example of White House "wine diplomacy," the Bushes skillfully averted a clash between America and the global "superpower of wine" when they hosted French President Nicolas Sarkozy on November 6, 2007. They thoughtfully served the French leader three California wines—all of which were developed by joint Franco-American wine ventures. The evening began with a 2004 HdV Chardonnay, produced through a partnership between Aubert de Villaine, of the world-famous Domaine de la Romanée-Conti, and Californian winemaker Larry Hyde. The entrée was paired with a 2004 Dominus Estate Napa Valley jewel made by Christian Moueix, who was the longtime winemaker at Château Petrus before moving to California. At the end of the evening the Bushes served Chandon Rosé—a Napa Valley sparkling wine launched in 1973 by Frenchman Robert-Jean de Vogüé using traditional methods for producing the finest champagnes of France.

President George W. Bush calls for a toast to French President Nicolas Sarkozy at a State Dinner in Sarkozy's honor, 2007 (opposite). Bush chose to serve three California wines made through Franco-American collaboration for the dinner.

Australia's Prime Minister John Howard toasts his host, President George W. Bush (right), during an official dinner in Howard's honor, 2006.

BARACK OBAMA
Forty-Fourth President of the United States, 2009–2017

Glasses of green champagne are offered on silver trays at President Obama's annual White House St. Patrick's Day reception, 2009.

PRESIDENT BARACK OBAMA and First Lady Michelle Obama left the American people with little doubt as to who in their family had the greater appreciation for wine. Mrs. Obama hosted wine tastings at the White House for her close friends. The president, meanwhile, was not shy about being a "beer man," enjoying his beverage of choice at sporting events and raising a pint in a village pub when visiting Ireland.

President Obama even brewed his own beer in the White House using honey from a beehive in the first lady's garden on the South Lawn. His White House Honey Brown Ale debuted at a 2011 Super Bowl party the Obamas hosted at the Executive Mansion. Once word of the president's special brew got out, the public demanded the recipe. President Obama agreed to release it, saying, "It will be out soon! I can tell you from first hand experience, it is tasty." After more than 12,000 people signed an online petition asking the president to provide the recipe, it was finally released by the White House on September 1, 2012, along with bonus instructions for making a White House Honey Porter.

A man will be eloquent, if you give him good wine.

—*Ralph Waldo Emerson*

President Barack Obama and President Xi Jinping of China share a toast in 2015 (opposite) during the first White House State Dinner at which Chinese wine was served. But President Obama made no secret of his preference for beer, which he enjoyed in 2011 (above) at a pub in Moneygall, Ireland, in front of a banner welcoming him on the visit.

For the Obama administration's formal entertaining, however, beer took a back seat to American wines, following the custom of the previous few decades. But on September 25, 2015, history was made with the first-ever service of Chinese wine at a White House State Dinner. Guests gathered in honor of the visit of President Xi Jinping were served Shaoxing, a Chinese rice wine, along with Penner-Ash Viognier Oregon 2014, Pride Mountain Merlot Vintner Select 2012, and Schramsberg Crémant Demi-Sec 2011.

The final State Dinner of the Obama administration, for Italian Prime Minister Matteo Renzi, took place in a tent on the South Lawn on October 18, 2016. Noted Italian American chef Mario Batali designed a menu featuring traditional Italian dishes that had become ingrained in American cuisine, such as agnolotti and beef braciole. The Obamas were also careful to select American wines associated with Italy, including a 2015 Palmina Vermentino Santa Ynez, a 2012 Villa Ragazzi Sangiovese from Napa, and a 2014 Ridge Vineyards Zinfandel East Bench.

DONALD J. TRUMP
Forty-Fifth President of the United States, 2017–

**Wine is bottled
poetry.**

—*Robert Louis Stevenson*

First Lady Melania Trump, the
Duchess of Cornwall, and the
Honorable John F. W. Rogers
raise their glasses for a toast
during a reciprocal dinner
Tuesday, June 4, 2019, at
Winfield House in London.

ALTHOUGH A NONDRINKER HIMSELF, President Donald J. Trump is the first president to own a full-production commercial winery. Five years before his election as president, Trump purchased a winery originally launched by the wife of billionaire John Kluge in Charlottesville, Virginia. Kluge Estate Winery and Vineyards ended up in bankruptcy, and Trump acquired it at auction, committing to carry on the Kluge legacy of producing high-quality wines in the shadow of Thomas Jefferson's Monticello.

At State Dinners and other important White House events, First Lady Melania Trump has served domestic wines to showcase the best of America. At an elegant May 15, 2019, dinner honoring the work of the White House Historical Association, the Trumps served Stag's Leap Chardonnay Karia 2015, Hartford Zinfandel Fanucchi Wood Road 2014, and Schramsberg Crémant Demi-Sec 2014 to the fifty-four guests seated at a single table spanning the length of the White House East Room.

In a spectacular dinner for the Prime Minister of Australia held in the White House Rose Garden on September 20, 2019, guests enjoyed a Spring Mountain Napa Sauvignon Blanc and a 2016 Argyle Pinot Noir from Oregon's Willamette Valley. They finished the meal with a J Vineyards Demi-Sec sparkling wine while being serenaded by the United States military bands and choruses.

Mrs. Trump, too, has managed to skillfully balance France's heritage and America's vinicultural success. During the April 2018 State Visit of President and Mrs. Emmanuel Macron, in addition to a 2015 Domaine Serene Chardonnay Evenstad Reserve—

produced by American winemakers Ken and Grace Evenstad, who also own a major wine estate in Burgundy, France—the menu included a 2014 Domaine Drouhin Pinot Noir Laurène, named for the oldest daughter of the winemaker Véronique Drouhin at the French-styled Oregon winery. The guests finished the evening with a 2014 Schramsberg Crémant.

The service of fine American wines is now an established tradition at White House dinners and receptions. Guests are welcomed to events with their choice of red, white, or champagne from White House butlers as they mingle through the State Rooms. For gatherings in the State Dining Room, three wineglasses await each diner, hinting at the standard three-wine service during the meal that has endured for many decades. The wines, carefully selected and served, have become much more than a pleasant drink to sip with meals: they play an important role in White House hospitality, the nation's diplomacy, and America's history.

United States military service musicians entertain guests in the East Room at a dinner hosted by President and Mrs. Donald J. Trump in honor of the White House Historical Association on May 15, 2019.

CHAPTER TWO

THE SELECTION, STORAGE, AND SERVICE OF WINE

I enjoy cooking with wine. Sometimes, I even put it in the food.

—*Julia Child*

White House butlers pre-pour white wine in the East Room before a dinner for congressional committee chairs, 2009.

WITH SOME TEN THOUSAND wineries operating in the United States, how does the White House choose which ones—and which of their products—to feature at official events? Though presidents have always had trusted advisers in the cabinet and among their senior staffs, until very recently there was no official position for a designated wine-selection expert. Throughout most of America's history, the chief executive had to seek counsel, or receive unsolicited suggestions, from colleagues or political contemporaries who maintained a personal interest in wine.

Thomas Jefferson was foremost in this role, lending his knowledge of and passion for wine to several presidents. The first beneficiary of his expertise was George Washington, who, in addition to receiving Jefferson's counsel on matters of foreign affairs, could also rely on his judgment on all matters pertaining to wine. In 1790, while in the midst of an important domestic trip with Washington, Jefferson placed a rush order for champagne to stock the president's cellar. In the dispatch to his aide, William Short, Jefferson wrote: "Being just now informed that a vessel sails this afternoon for a port in Normandy, and knowing that the President wished to have some Champagne, and this is the season to write for it, I have been to him, and he desires 40 dozen bottles."

Later that year, Jefferson sent a letter to the United States consul in Bordeaux, Joseph Fenwick, seeking his assistance on a wine order for the president and himself. He asked Fenwick to forward letters to each of the individual vineyards and procure the following quantities from each:

M. la comte de Lur-Saluce	*30 doz Sauterne for the President*
	10 doz do. for myself
M. de Mirosmenil	*20 doz vin de Segur for the President*
Madame de Rozan	*10 doz vin de Rozan for myself*
Monsieur Lambert at Frontignan	*10 doz Frontignan for the President*
	5 doz do. for myself

Jefferson then continued with detailed instructions on shipping his order:

Be so good as to have the wines delivered immediately and forward them by the first safe vessel bound from Bordeaux to Philadelphia. I have directed those for the President to be packed separately and marked G.W. and mine T.I.

**No nation
is drunken where
wine is cheap.**

—*Thomas Jefferson*

Thomas Jefferson (as portrayed by Bill Barker above) advised the early presidents on purchasing fine European wines to serve at the President's House.

On September 6, 1790, Thomas Jefferson wrote, in French, to the Comte de Lur-Saluces at d'Yquem to praise his Sauternes (opposite). He also placed a large order of the wine for himself and President George Washington. As secretary of state with diplomatic responsibilities, Jefferson frequently ordered wine for President Washington during his presidency.

"T.I." was the set of stylized initials Jefferson used for ordinary transactions and shipments of goods, such as wine orders. Always interested in organization and systemization, he used other initials for different purposes throughout his life.

The vineyard owners responded that it was a great honor to supply Jefferson and President Washington with their wine. Jefferson continued to be of service to subsequent presidents, even after his own presidency. Upon the election of America's fifth president, James Monroe, Jefferson sent a message that was brief on congratulations but extensive in its recommendations for the White House wine cellar:

I shall not waste your time in idle congratulations. you know my joy on the commitment of the helm of our government to your hands. I promised you, when I should have received and tried the wines I had ordered from France and Italy, to give you a note of the kinds which I should think worthy of your procurement: and this being the season for ordering them, so that they may come in the mild temperature of autumn, I now fulfill my promise—they are the following.

Vin blanc liqoureux d'Hermitage de M. Jourdan à Tains. this costs about 82½ cents a bottle put on ship-board.

Vin de Ledanon (in Languedoc) something of the Port character, but higher flavored, more delicate, less rough. I do not know it's price, but probably about 25. cents a bottle.

Vin de Roussillon. the best is that of Perpignan or Rivesalte of the crop of M. Durand. it costs 74. cents a gallon, bears bringing in the cask. if put into bottles there it costs 11. cents a bottle more than if bottled here by an inexplicable & pernicious arrangement of our Tariff.

Vin de Nice. the crop called Bellet, of mr Sasserno is best. this is the most elegant every day wine in the world and costs 31. cents the bottle. not much being made it is little known at the genl market.

Jefferson's expertise on wine proved essential to the leaders of a young nation still learning about the wines of the Old World, lacking domestic choices of its own. A century and a half later, as vineyards planted in America began to bear fruit, presidents realized that serving American wines at the White House would send an important message to the world about the quality of the emerging U.S. wine industry. With this commitment to serving American wine, however, came the need for expertise in new and growing wine regions.

In the late 1950s, the Wine Institute, an organization representing America's growing wine industry, sought to supply American wine to the White House. President Dwight D. Eisenhower, eager to showcase America's accomplishments in the post–World War II era, accepted the offer. During his administration, a variety of California wines delivered by the Wine Institute began to appear on White House tables. While

WINE AND THE WHITE HOUSE

Monsieur le comte   à Philadelphie. 6. 7bre. 1790.

Le vin blanc de Sauterne, de vôtre crû, que vous avez eu la bonté
de m'envoyer à Paris au commencement de l'année 1788. a été
si bien approuvé des Americains qui y en ont gouté, que je ne
doute pas que mes compatriotes generalement ne le trouvent
aussi conforme à leur gout. actuellement que je me suis établi
ici, j'ai persuadé à notre President, le General Washington
d'en essayer un echantillon. il vous en demande trente
douzaines, Monsieur, et moi, je vous en demande dix
douzaines pour moi-même, le tout 40. douzaines, de
vôtre meilleur pour la service actuelle. ayez la bonté de
le faire mettre en bouteilles, et bien emballer, separemment,
sur le lieu, en etiquettant les 30. douzaines G.W. et les 10. dou-
-zaines TI. afin d'arranger les malheurs qui peuvent arriver
en voyage. Monsieur Fenwick, Consul des Etats unis
à Bordeaux recevra les emballages, et aura l'honneur de
vous payer le montant, dont il est muni. ayez la bonté
de m'en annoncer l'expedition, ~~pour vous~~ et de m'assurer
qu'ils viennent veritablement de vous.

     J'ai l'honneur d'être avec la consideration la
plus distinguée, Monsieur le comte, vôtre très humble et
très obeissant serviteur

     Th. Jefferson

Monsieur le comte de Lur-Saluces.

JEFFERSON'S ADVICE

On the Purchase of the Finest European Wines

Thomas Jefferson's guidance on wine was not limited to his fellow presidents. His expertise on the subject was well known outside of Washington and Virginia, and he was often asked for recommendations by his associates. For example, Henry Sheaff, a Philadelphia merchant from whom Jefferson had purchased wine in the past, wrote asking for his insights into the quality, prices, and sources of top European wines. What follows is a transcription of Jefferson's extensive response written in 1793— much of which would be of interest to wine consumers today.

LISBON WINES. The best quality of the dry kind is called Termo, and costs 70 dollars the pipe at about 2 years old. At 5 years old it is becoming a fine wine; at 7 years old is preferable to any but the very best Madeira. Bulkeley & son furnish it from Lisbon.

SHERRY. The best dry Sherry costs at Cadiz, from 80 to 90 Dollars the pipe. But when old and fine, such as is sent to the London market it costs £30 sterling the pipe. Mr. Ysnardi, the son, Consul of the US. at Cadiz, at this time in Philadelphia, furnishes it.

The following facts are from my own enquiries in going thro' the different wine cantons of France, examining the identical vineyards producing the first quality of wines, conversing with their owners, and other persons on the spot minutely acquainted with the vineyards, and the wines made on them, and tasting them myself.

BURGUNDY. The best wines of Burgundy are

Montrachet, a white wine. It is made but by two persons, to wit Monsr. de Clermont, and Monsr. de Sarsnet. The latter rents to Monsr. de la Tour. This costs 48 sous the bottle, new, and 3 livres when fit for drinking.

Mersault. A white wine. The best quality of it is called Goutte d'or. It cost 6 sous the bottle new. I do not believe this will bear transportation. But the Montrachet will in a proper season.

Chambertin, Vougeau, Veaune, are red wines, of the first quality, are the only fine red wines of Burgundy which will bear transportation, and even these required to be moved in the best season, and not to be exposed to great heat or great cold. These cost 48 sous the bottle, new and 3 livres old. I think it next to impossible to have any of the Burgundy wines brought here in a sound state.

CHAMPAGNE. The Mousseux or Sparkling Champagne is never brought to a good table in France. The still, or non-mousseaux, is alone drunk by connoisseurs.

Aij. The best is made at Aij, by Monsr. d'Orsay, who makes more than all the other proprietors of the first quality put together. It costs 3 livres the bottle when of the proper age to drink, which is at 5 years old.

The Red Champagne is not a fine year. The best is made by the Benedictine monks at Auvillaij.

The wines of Burgundy and Champagne being made at the head of the Seine, are brought down that river to Havre from whence they are shipped. They should come down in the month of November, so that they may be brought over sea in the winter and arrive here before our warm Spring days. They should be bottled on the spot where they are made. The bottle, bottling, corking, and packing costs 5 sous a bottle. Capt. Cutting Consul of the U.S. at Havre a good person and well informed, to supply the wines of Burgundy and Champagne.

BORDEAUX RED WINES. There are four crops of them more famous than all the rest. These are Chateau-Margau, Tour de Segur, Hautbrion, and de la Fite. They cost 3 livres a bottle, old: but are so engaged before hand that it is impossible to get them. The merchants, if you desire it, will send you a wine by any of those names, and may you pay 3 livres a bottle: but I will venture to affirm that there never was a bottle of those wines sent to America by a merchant. Nor is it worth while to seek for them; for I will defy any person to distinguish them from the wines of the next quality, to wit

Rohan-Margau, which is made by Madame de Rohan. This is what I import for myself, and consider as equal to any of the four

crops. There are also the wines of Dabbadie, la Rose, Quirouen and Durfort which are reckoned as good as Madame de Rozan's. Yet I have preferred hers. These wines cost 40 sous the bottle, when of the proper age for drinking.

BORDEAUX WHITE WINES.

Grave. The best is called Pontac, and is made by Monsr. de Lamont. It costs 18 sous a bottle.

Sauterne. This is the best white wine of France (except Champagne and Hermitage) the best of it is made by Monsr. de Luz-Saluz, and costs at 4 years old (when fit to drink) from 20 to 24 sous the bottle. There are two other white wines made in the same neighborhood called Prignac and Barsac, esteemed by some. But the Sauterne is that preferred at Paris, and much the best in my judgement. They cost the same. A great advantage of the Sauterne is that is becomes higher flavored the day after the bottle has been opened, than it is at first.

Mr. Fenwick, Consul of the US. at Bordeaux, is well informed on the subject of these wines, and has supplied the President and myself with them genuine and good. He would be a proper person to endeavor to get from the South of France some of the wines made there which are most excellent and very cheap, say 10 or 12 sous the bottle. Those of Roussillon are the best. I was not in Roussillon myself, and therefore can give no particular directions about them. At Nismes I drank a good wine, stronger than claret, well flavored, the tavern price of which was 2 sous the

quart. Mr. Fenwick might perhaps be able to get these brought through the Canal of Languedoc.

A good correspondent at Amsterdam might furnish the following wines.

Moselle. The best of these is called Brownberg, being made on a mountain of that name adjoining the village of Dusmond, 15 leagues from Coblentz, to which last place it is brought and stored for sale. The best crop of Brownberg is that of Baron Breidbach Burreasheim. It costs 22 sous the bottle when old enough to drink. It is really a good wine.

Hock. There has been discovered within these 30 years, a finer wine of this quality called Johansberg, now decidedly preferred to Hock. They both cost 5 sterl. a bottle when of the oldest and best quality. It is to be observed of the Hock wines that no body can drink them but Germans or the English who have learnt it from their German kings. Compared with the wines of more Southern climates they are as an olive compared with a pineapple.

Observe that whenever the price of wine by the bottle is mentioned, it means to include the price of the bottle, &c which is 5 sous. Deduct that sum therefore, and it leaves always the price of the wine.

Richard Nixon relied largely on his own knowledge when selecting wine. He is seen here in 1973 as champagne is served to—and spilled by—Leonid Brezhnev, general secretary of the Soviet Union.

The tables are set for a State Dinner during the Dwight D. Eisenhower administration in 1954 (opposite), a time when less formal events would have showcased California wines delivered to the White House by the Wine Institute.

Wine is one of the most civilized things in the world and one of the natural things of the world that has been brought to the greatest perfection.

—Ernest Hemingway

John F. Kennedy declined the Wine Institute's offer during his presidency, his successor, Lyndon B. Johnson, reinstated the arrangement and built a close relationship with the institute as it grew to become an important organization in the nation's capital.

President Richard M. Nixon, his own counsel in many ways, brought his knowledge and appreciation of fine French wines to the White House. Great thought was given to purchasing wine "futures" for selected vintages from Nixon's favorite Bordeaux producers. In procuring wine futures, a buyer purchases yet-to-be-bottled wines directly from the wine *négociants* in France, before they are released for retail sale. This arrangement guarantees the consumer delivery of the wine at a future date—usually two to three years later—at a price often lower than the market price at the official time of release. It also guarantees the wine consumer an allocation of highly popular wines that are in limited supply. Nixon's wine legacy benefited subsequent holders of his office, as some of the orders he placed arrived years later and even then required time in the cellar before reaching maturity. A decade after Nixon's departure, many of these rare bottles of Bordeaux were still aging quietly beneath the White House.

As California wines, and those from other states, gained prominence on the global wine scene, it became important to select the right American wine for each White House occasion. For President Ronald Reagan, this presented an opportunity to draw on his eight years as California's governor to showcase the quality and variety of his state's wines. During his time in Sacramento, Reagan had established a close relationship with specialist David Berkley of the city's Corti Brothers gourmet food and wine shop. Berkley was an important consultant to the Reagan White House on all things vinicultural, and he worked closely with Michael K. Deaver, Reagan's deputy chief of staff, in selecting wines for dinners and other events. After First Lady Nancy Reagan agreed on a menu with White House Chef Henry Haller, Deaver would forward the menu to Berkley for his suggestions. Berkley always strived to recommend wines that were excellent but also that were new or from lesser-known vineyards and may not have

Café
NATOMA

February 9, 1983

Mr. Michael K. Deaver,
Deputy Chief of Staff
The White House
Washington, D.C. 20007

Dear Mike,

The accompanying case of wine should represent a couple of days of enjoyment. I have enclosed samples of several of the suggested wines, and others will be delivered to you either from local distributors or from the White House cellars.

SAN FRANCISCO

Lobster Terrine with Golden Caviar and Dill Sauce

1980 Grgich Hills Chardonnay: a wine Muffy tasted with the preview dinner, and, in her words, "a wine to die over." Certainly consistent with the qualities of Grgich with full rich chardonnay flavor — slightly herbal with buttery flavors. Very good with the terrine, particularly with the dill sauce.

1980 Trefethen Chardonnay: unfortunately Trefethen has seen frequent previous service at the White House; however, not this vintage. Full and unusually opulent for Trefethen, it would also provide successful service. The name Trefethen is Cornish (from Cornwall), and their logo comes from Janet Trefethen's Welsh family.

1981 St. Clement Chardonnay: owned by the Casey's. The name of the winery is in honor of William Casey's ancestral home, "St. Clement's Manor," in Maryland, a seventh-century grant from the English crown. A more elegant styled Chardonnay with fine varietal flavors and with a lighter oak treatment. Clean and crisp with the Lobster Terrine.

During the Ronald Reagan administration, the deputy chief of staff, Michael Deaver (above right), worked with the wine specialist David Berkley to select wines for special events. Although Berkley's advice was generally key to the selection process, his memo (above left) advising the president not to repeat previous selections when hosting Queen Elizabeth II in 1983 was not followed.

been served at the White House previously. He also made his recommendations with an eye toward diplomacy. With knowledge of the type of event and the guests in attendance, Berkley chose wines that would complement the menu and enhance cultural nuances. He sent Deaver detailed descriptions of his recommendations and bottles to sample. Deaver, in turn, sometimes shared the samples with the first lady and members of the White House staff to get their opinions.

A month in advance of a March 1983 dinner hosted in San Francisco for Queen Elizabeth II and Prince Philip, for example, Berkley listed several wines under each proposed dinner course and explained his choices—noting vineyard provenance, tasting notes, and body descriptions. He expressed reservations about two of the wines owing to their frequency of previous service at White House events. But Reagan did not want to take any chances with visiting royalty, so he served the two wines anyway, knowing they would be more certain of success.

Queen Elizabeth II and President Ronald Reagan raise their glasses during a dinner hosted by the president for the queen at the M. H. de Young Memorial Museum in San Francisco, 1983.

While serving as Reagan's vice president, George H. W. Bush had grown to appreciate Berkley's talent, and so, as president, continued to seek Berkley's advice on wines for diplomatic and other special events. During Bill Clinton's presidency, the first wine professional was brought onto the White House staff—Napa Valley veteran Daniel Shanks. Shanks was the first food and beverage usher, a position he held through the Clinton, Bush, and Obama administrations and into the early years of the Trump administration before his retirement in October 2018. Through his decades of service, Shanks defined not only the role of official presidential wine adviser but also the thoughtful approach to wine selection that prevails at the White House today.

White House wine acquisitions are typically made on an event-by-event basis. Gone are the days when presidents stored huge collections of wine for just the right occasion. Even then, the White House wine cellar was never a grand affair. Buckingham Palace has the Royal Cellars of the Queen, and the Élysée Palace has the Cave du President— both vast underground brick facilities lined with racks of wine bottles aging in precisely

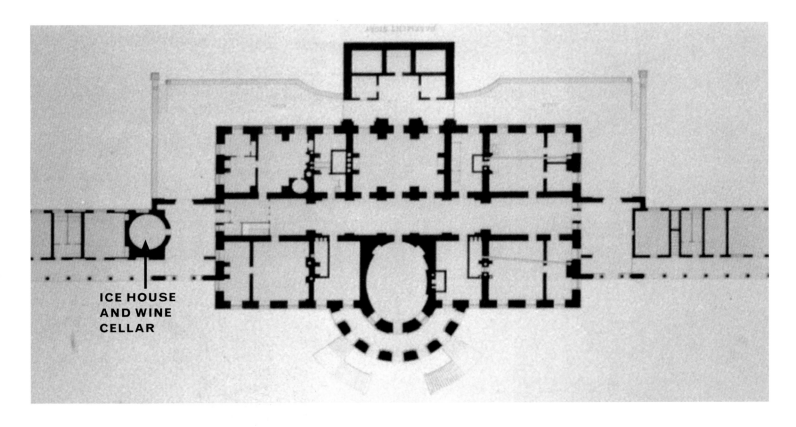

President Thomas Jefferson's architectural plans included a circular ice house and wine cellar within a west wing designed to hold other service areas. Thomas U. Walter's plan of 1853 (above) is the earliest known plan of the White House basement level and wings. It reflects Jefferson's plans for the wing.

ICE HOUSE AND WINE CELLAR

The President's house . . . will be wanting for a cellar to be made adjoining it.

—*Thomas Jefferson*

the right temperature and humidity—but for America's head of state, wine storage has always been much more modest.

In 1801, when Thomas Jefferson moved into the newly built Executive Mansion, he found that the house was not fully finished. Although the incomplete state of the Residence was frustrating to the new president, it did give Jefferson the opportunity to design and construct the White House's first wine cellar. Located under the site of today's West Colonnade, the structure Jefferson designed was made of clay bricks with a wood covering to protect against weather. He called the cellar the "ice house," as wine was racked on a wood floor elevated over ice packed in sawdust, with the ice replaced on a monthly basis. Although the exact dimensions are unknown, the cellar was circular and resembled an inverted flower pot. On a visit to Washington in 1805, the British diplomat Sir Augustus John Foster, likely a frequent dinner guest at the White House, described cellars that "President Jefferson, after experiencing great losses in wines, has been obliged to add at a depth of sixteen feet under ground. These are so cool that the thermometer stood two degrees lower in them than it did in a vacant spot in the ice-house early in July, when in the shade out of doors it was at ninety-six." Foster's account indicates that the oenophile president's creation of a wine cellar was well known.

During the War of 1812, the British burned the White House, damaging Jefferson's prized cellar. By the time Andrew Jackson became president, the wine cellar had been relocated to the basement of the Residence, beneath the State Dining Room. Floored with brick, the room was furnished with barrel and bottle racks along the walls protected with gates to which only the steward had the key. On one occasion, however, President John Tyler is reported to have obtained the key so that he could open the cellar for a guest, with whom he enjoyed some of the locked-away bottles.

Illustrated by Dahl Taylor in 2020, the first White House wine cellar was walled with brick, cooled by regularly replenished ice under the floorboards, and furnished with racks on which Jefferson's collection of fine wines was stored.

White House Head Butler Eugene Allen holds a bottle of champagne in the White House wine storage room during the Ronald Reagan administration (opposite). With storage space for about 300 bottles of wine, the room is surprisingly small, especially when compared with the cellars of other heads of state.

The cellar beneath Élysée Palace in France holds 14,000 bottles, overseen by sommelier Virginie Routis (top right).

England's Government Wine Cellar in Lancaster House holds an estimated 38,000 bottles for Buckingham Palace and other royal residences, overseen by Yeoman of the Royal Cellars Robert Lange (right).

A real connoisseur does not drink wine but tastes of its secrets.
—*Salvador Dalí*

After the wear and tear of thirty presidents, the aging White House went through a major renovation from 1948 to 1952 during the administration of Harry S. Truman. The Truman renovation was extensive and entirely gutted the White House, leaving only the external walls in place. The construction brought the interior of the Residence up to modern mid-twentieth-century standards, updating amenities and adding a new elevator, balcony, theater, and even a bowling alley—but no wine cellar. From then on, the wines of the president were stored in a plain, nondescript space adjoining the kitchen. This modest closet, with the capacity to accommodate 300 bottles, is still used today, as changes in the service of wine mean that presidents no longer require an extensive wine cellar for aging bottles, only a place for wines to rest before their service.

WELCOMING WHITE HOUSE GUESTS WITH WINE

The following memories from First Lady Melania Trump, former First Lady Michelle Obama, and social secretaries who served in earlier administrations reveal the care that goes into the planning of White House wine service and the pleasure the planners take in knowing that guests have enjoyed their White House experience.

MELANIA TRUMP
First Lady
Donald J. Trump Presidency
2017–

"The White House is our home, and our family's appreciation for this extraordinary place grows each day. It is the 'people's house' and a treasured symbol of our nation. When foreign leaders and other special guests visit, the president and I have the great honor and responsibility of showcasing the best of America, while paying tribute to our guests and their home countries. This has always been our goal as we selected the food, entertainment, flowers, decor, settings, and, of course, the wine for the State Dinners and official events. The experience of planning the appropriate complements to each of the dinner's facets is in of itself a celebration of the abundant excellence of America's farmers, artists, and vintners. Successful pairings so often enhance the lasting memories of the evening. We have always treasured giving our guests an unforgettable experience when attending White House celebrations."

First Lady Melania Trump previews the State Dining Room ahead of the Governors' Dinner, February 26, 2017.

MICHELLE OBAMA
First Lady
Barack Obama Presidency
2009–2017

"Since the days of Thomas Jefferson, Americans have used wine as an expression of warmth and hospitality. Whether it's over a family dinner in a Southside Chicago bungalow or a State Dinner at the White House, wine has a way of sparking curiosity and bringing people together in companionship. While hosting guests in the White House, we tried to be thoughtful about the wine we served—choosing varieties that not only complemented the food courses, but also showcased the extraordinary quality of American-made wines. It was always a special moment when an honored guest complimented or asked about a particular wine, giving us a chance to lift up the talent of American wine-makers, each of whom treat their craft with admirable care and consideration. Both Barack and I look back fondly on evenings spent entertaining in the White House, thanks in no small part to the conversations shared about and over wine."

First Lady Michelle Obama raises her glass for a toast during the Governors' Dinner at the White House, February 23, 2014.

MABEL BRANDON CABOT
Social Secretary, 1981–1983
Ronald Reagan Presidency

"The Reagans served their guests the finest of California wines wherever they entertained. The late Michael Deaver was keenly interested in the vineyards of California and was a great wine connoisseur. He and I worked closely together with Mrs. Reagan to provide the best California wines to match the menus.

The Reagan White House served many regional dishes at the Economic Summit at Colonial Williamsburg in 1983. Heads of state from seven nations attended this global economic summit, and the wines were chosen with great care to salute the visitors but, more important, to introduce them to the finest wines of California.

When President and Mrs. Reagan entertained abroad, as they did in Paris to welcome President Mitterrand to the American Embassy, the wines were flown in from California for this very special occasion."

GAHL HODGES BURT
Social Secretary, 1983–1985
Ronald Reagan Presidency

"In the early 1980s, California wineries were just beginning to receive national and international recognition. President and Mrs. Reagan were proud to showcase California wines at every official White House lunch and dinner. Celebrity entertainers like Yehudi Menuhin, Frank Sinatra, and Leontyne Price, as well as world leaders, would autograph and write comments on their menu cards, and we would send them back to the wineries. These efforts helped build the reputation of California wines as some of the best in the world."

Gahl Hodges Burt (far left) walks down the White House Cross Hall with Mrs. Reagan.

LINDA FAULKNER JOHNSON
Social Secretary, 1985–1989
Ronald Reagan Presidency

"President and Mrs. Reagan were always proud to promote glorious California wines during their important dinners, which honored British royals Prince Charles and Princess Diana as well as world leaders such as Prime Minister Margaret Thatcher and General Secretary Mikhail Gorbachev. During my time as social secretary, David Berkley was their California wine consultant. Once Mrs. Reagan had approved the menu, he would assign the perfect wine for the first, second, and third courses."

Linda Faulkner Johnson meets with White House social aides in the Family Dining Room prior to an event.

ANN STOCK
Social Secretary, 1993–1997
William J. Clinton Presidency

"During my time as social secretary in the Clinton White House, we wanted to showcase the American wine industry at State Dinners and other White House events. We hired the first food and beverage usher, Daniel Shanks, to bring wines from all fifty states to the White House.

The toasts from President Nelson Mandela's first State Dinner I will never forget. President Clinton got up and read an excerpt from a letter President Mandela had written from prison to his daughter, Zindzi Mandela-Hlongwane, who was also at the dinner. "'While you have every reason to be angry with the fates for the setbacks you may have suffered from time to time, you must vow to turn those misfortunes into victories. There are few misfortunes in this world you cannot turn into personal triumphs if you have the iron will and necessary skills.' You have shown us the iron will and necessary skills,' President Clinton concluded. Not a dry eye was in the house.

President Mandela thanked the United States and its people for the role they played in ending apartheid. 'We salute you for taking our concerns as your own. It is our heartfelt desire that the bond based on common interests between our two nations will grow ever more diverse and stronger.'

All said with glasses of wine held high in the air."

Ann Stock with President and Mrs. Clinton during a White House event.

LEA BERMAN
Social Secretary, 2005–2007
George W. Bush Presidency

Lea Berman reviews the tables and place settings before guests enter the State Dining Room for an official dinner in honor of Charles, Prince of Wales, and Camilla, Duchess of Cornwall, 2005.

"The White House chief usher, Gary Walters, and the head sommelier, Daniel Shanks, were wonderfully creative in matching wines not only to the meal but to honor the occasion itself. It was a source of delight to see how cleverly they selected charming and apt wines. For a 2005 luncheon in honor of new Chief Justice John Roberts, a Landmark Chardonnay 2002 was served, a whimsical play on the language of the law. At the Cinco de Mayo party in 2005, a raucous Rose Garden dinner with serenading mariachis, a Vine Cliff Chardonnay Bien Nacido 2002 was served.

The White House wine masters always brought their best efforts to State Dinners. The Australian State Dinner in 2006 featured Greg Norman Chardonnay 2004, to honor the great Australian golfer. For the Japanese prime minister in 2006, a Clos Pegase Chardonnay Mitsuko 2004 was selected. The wine choices were a reflection of the Residence staff's desire to make guests feel welcome and honored, through every possible vehicle—food, flowers, menu cards, and always the wines."

AMY ZANTZINGER
Social Secretary, 2007–2009
George W. Bush Presidency

"The beauty of serving wine at the White House is that it celebrates another facet of our country's agricultural abundance. The White House ensures the wine served is sourced from smaller, independent farmers as well as larger, well-known vineyards."

Amy Zantzinger (center) reviews designs for the Bush Official State China Service with Mrs. Bush and White House Curator William Allman, 2008.

JEREMY BERNARD
Social Secretary, 2011–2015
Barack Obama Presidency

"The selection of wines was as important a component of a State Dinner as the food choice. I will never forget my first State Dinner tasting, for Germany in 2011, just months after I started the job. The tastings took place as lunches weeks prior to the dinners. Mrs. Obama, her mother, Mrs. Robinson, and I were sitting in the Yellow Oval Room looking out past the Truman Balcony toward the Washington Monument and beyond on a picture-perfect day. With each course we had a choice of three different American wines, all selected with great consideration of the guests' preferences. It was such fun. President Obama walked in to say hello and I recall how surreal it was. Was I really sitting with the first lady in the Residence as the president stopped by?

The tastings were one of my favorite memories of the many wonderful memories of my more than four years as the White House social secretary."

Jeremy Bernard and Melissa Winter review the decor in the Diplomatic Reception Room with Mrs. Obama ahead of the State Dinner for Prime Minister Shinzō Abe of Japan, 2015.

WHITE HOUSE WINE SERVICE: A CHOREOGRAPHED BALLET

by Daniel Shanks, the First Food and Beverage Usher

Presidential meals and special events are organized by the staff of the White House Usher's Office, a team of highly discreet and professional men and women who have long served in a variety of important roles for the White House and first family. On February 15, 1995, Daniel Shanks—a twenty-year veteran of the Napa Valley wine industry—joined this office as the first White House food and beverage usher. From his earliest conversations with Chief Usher Gary Walters and the Clintons' social secretary, Ann Stock, it became clear that Shanks had an earnest desire to ensure that the president's wine and food service reflected the exciting developments in American cuisine while remaining true to long-standing traditions at the White House. As Shanks describes, the service of wine is a critical part of the success of any White House event. Perhaps the best insight into how Shanks crafted the role of official White House wine adviser—and the best insights into how wine at the White House is selected and served—can be found in his reflections on the subject.

OVER THE YEARS, like David Berkley before me, I worked to build relationships with vintners and owners who consistently produced superior wines that best suited White House cuisine and elegance. With time I began to sense which wineries inevitably brought guests the greatest enjoyment, and it was frequently not a "trophy wine" lauded in the wine press. In some ways the White House is a very different environment from fine dining in a restaurant. Guests come to a White House event with a diversity of life experiences. They do not necessarily arrive with thoughts of food and beverage in the forefront, but always with a great sense of heightened enthusiasm. Like any perceptive wine steward, my task was to find wines that are full in character and commensurate with the atmosphere yet comfortable on the palate.

Many factors contribute to choosing a wine for a specific event. The time of year, for example, needs to be considered: heartier wines are favored in colder months, while more fruit-driven, lighter-bodied wines are favored during the warmer months. Another factor was the guest count: our largest events could not be accommodated by the smaller production wines we like to source. We also considered if the event would be held indoors or outdoors: outdoor events are suited to wine with richer mouth feel, while inside events require wines whose aromas show more fully. The time of day was another factor: luncheons, by White House tradition, usually feature a single wine suitable to pair with a variety of dishes, whereas dinners require multiple wines that each set the stage for a course. For a buffet service, newly released wines offer more vibrant fruit and match better than the elegant wines, which are best suited to a plated meal.

For particular dinners we research previous occasions with the same guests to avoid repeating wines. Religious preferences are also taken into account. We serve kosher-certified wine and beer at events for Jewish or Israeli guests, and we refrain from serving alcohol at events for which the guest of honor is from a nation with religious prohibitions against alcohol. The State Department is always a great resource for guidance on such issues.

If the event honors a foreign country, we look to highlight ties between us. That means considering a winemaker or winery owner whose background is related to the guest's country or a grape varietal native to the guest's country that a winemaker in our country highlights. For a 1996 State Dinner with President Jacques Chirac of France we selected a Beringer Viognier Reserve 1994 and Zaca Mesa Syrah 1993, both French varietals with newfound popularity in America. In a similar manner, for a State Dinner for President Felipe Calderón of Mexico in 2010, we featured Valdez Chardonnay, Herrera Cabernet Sauvignon 2006, and Mumm Napa Carlos Santana Brut—highlighting winemakers who had emigrated from Mexico, started with entry-level jobs in wineries, and evolved to create their own award-winning wines.

All beverages selected for the White House are produced in the United States with the exception of some back-bar alcohols. The wines served are generally full-flavored and easy on the palate with wide appeal. Over the years I noticed that for guests Chardonnay is the preferred white and Pinot Noir the preferred red. Both are comfortable in flavor and weight, and the aroma of the Pinot Noir adds to the enjoyment. Certain menus called for a more robust wine. During President George W. Bush's administration we were asked to serve more beef dishes. Those moments cried for the power of Cabernet Sauvignon.

On occasion, usually when there were vintage changes or a wine was out of inventory, we assembled a few of the Residence staff to taste and comment on new releases for inclusion in our stock. These "tasters" had an interest in our beverage program and came from all departments, a cross section of staff that we hoped would parallel the range of guests we serve. These in-house tastings also gave the staff some "buy-in" on the beverages they would be serving.

When an event came on the social schedule, our chefs would begin creating a menu reflecting the honored guest's profile, using products and spices featured in his or her culture but prepared in the manner served in our country. I would search for any wine associations with the invited group and call on my tasting experience and notes to choose wines to consider.

Could a winery donate wine for use at the White House? This was a question I was frequently asked, but we resisted these generous offers as excitement among the vintners would have resulted in a glut of donated wine that we simply could not use. An equal consideration was that the White

Daniel Shanks inspects a shipment of wine in the White House wine storage room, 2017.

House could not appear to favor any specific winery over others. We prided ourselves as representing all American producers. Regularly changing vendors also helps with the public perception that we do not favor any specific one. Inevitably, a winemaker's pride in having his or her product served at a White House event might be trumpeted in social media in such a way as to hint at an official endorsement, but we cautioned against this practice; if it happened twice, the winery was no longer considered for future service.

Two of the presidents I served did not consume alcohol, and the other two very sparingly. It was the case over my four administrations that the first lady is the source of direction when it comes to beverage service. From Hillary Clinton to Melania Trump, the first ladies I served enjoyed wine with meals, often preferring wines with character and depth that reflect the world they inhabit.

A formal White House dinner is always a special and memorable event. Many months of detailed planning go into balancing the diplomatic protocol, the strategic purpose of the visit, and the entertainment, as well as the cuisine itself. Formal dining in the White House is a choreographed ballet of chefs and servers working in unison, performing a time-restricted event in a fluid environment. The president's tight schedule makes any change of plan a challenge that can jeopardize serving a superior dining experience, our ultimate objective. The greatness of great wine purchased for an event can easily be lost if the service falters. Fortunately, this will not happen at the White House. Working in the Executive Residence and constantly interacting with the president's guests keep us cognizant of the level of performance expected.

Staffing for wine service involves developing a cadre of butlers who replicate service techniques at every meal. We staffed with a lead wine steward who controlled inventory, wrapped white and sparkling wines in bags to protect labels during chilling, monitored wine temperatures, determined the number of bottles to open pre-event, assigned a steward to each station, and oversaw service during the meal. Stations traditionally have three tables of ten, with more servers added if an additional wine is scheduled.

By tradition, we serve only one wine at a luncheon, given the mid-day timing and lighter cuisine. At dinner we offer white, red, and sparkling wines, usually with each accompanying a specific course. White-tie State Dinners, however, are four courses and require the addition of a fourth wine, which can be either white or red, to accompany the in-between course.

The most general rule on consumption for 130 guests (typical State Dining Room numbers) is four cases (forty-eight bottles) of the white and three cases (thirty-six bottles) of the red. Three cases (thirty-six bottles) of the sparkling wine is the rule, unless the wine will continue to be offered during the entertainment.

The serving temperature for wine is crucial, so the timing of pre-pouring is carefully planned. I believe the practice of pre-pouring wine ahead of the guests' arrival is derived from a long-held desire to minimize the time staff is in the room, allowing for privacy in conversation. The white wine chosen must have a flavor profile accommodating temperature changes, as the time guests spend in the receiving line can vary. We chill the wine cooler than the preferred drinking temperature to balance the wait time.

WINE AND THE WHITE HOUSE

Ideally the white wine should be at 50–52°F at the time of consumption. Sparkling wines should be just a bit cooler. Red wine is served at 60–62°F. There is some variability with these guidelines, as wines are served slightly warmer in cold months and cooler during the warmer months.

For the four administrations I served, a timeline for a State Dinner breaks down as follows: white wine is pre-poured at table for guests as they enter from the receiving line, and it is poured again after toasts by both the president and honored head of state. Immediately upon completion of the toasts, the first course is served. Red wine is poured, the main course is served, sparkling wine is poured, the dessert course follows, and coffee service is offered.

I sought to introduce ways of presenting the wine for the guests' benefit. Following in David Berkley's footsteps, I sought to consider small, family-owned wineries when purchasing wine to highlight the range of wine produced in our country. America's breadth of vineyards and range of varietals are unparalleled anywhere in the world. As many of the winery names printed on menus were thus unfamiliar and frequently had little national distribution, we wanted guests who were curious to be aware of them. Knowing that wineries give a lot of thought to the labels they develop, and that the label is usually in keeping with the style and taste profile of the wine, I had the wine stewards pour wine with the front label prominently displayed, facing the guest. Guests can then visually connect with the wines, and the practice became another aspect of our polished service. And to make sure that the labels were presentable, we placed wines needing to be chilled in sealed bags so the labels would not become saturated and disfigured by the ice and water. We also cut the top foil with precision so the artistic packaging designed by the winery was intact when presented to guests.

Because we purchase recently released wines, we initiated decanting the red wine to better show its attributes. Often I would call the winemaker for his or her opinion on optimal decanting time. Tasting the wine prior to decanting and then again at the time we poured showed a noticeable difference, and one that our guests would appreciate.

We made one additional change with the pouring of the wine for the main course, which was usually a red. Instead of pouring it as or after the main course was served, we began pouring it as guests finished their first course, so the service was completed before the main course came out. This practice simplified table service by butlers and stewards, as the space between tables can be tight, and also reduced distraction for guests. More important, it gave the wine the benefit of a little breathing in the glass and the guests a chance to enjoy the red wine on its own merits during the course transition.

Another of the changes I sought was to offer red wine on bars during White House events. Red wine had previously been avoided because the curators were understandably concerned about spills that could damage historic furnishings. Although I fully sympathized with that rationale, I asked for a change in policy that would allow the first family's guests another oft-requested option to heighten their White House experience. Once the red wine was made available, the many guests who asked for it at receptions were pleased and I was relieved, for we quickly found that damage was minimal due both to the demeanor of the guests and to the vigilance of the staff.

These experiences are described to demonstrate the fluidity of each moment at the White House and how we responded "outside the box" to find solutions, always without personal self-gratification but in recognition that we are serving a greater good. Many people in the past have held the positions we were fortunate enough to be offered, and we understand that the day each of us walks out through those gates for the final time, we become a part of White House history.

CHAPTER THREE

FROM FRENCH BEGINNINGS TO VIRGINIA AND BEYOND

An American flag waves above a Napa Valley, California, vineyard—evidence that, as Thomas Jefferson envisioned more than two centuries ago, the United States has succeeded in developing a thriving winemaking industry of its own.

"WE COULD, IN THE UNITED STATES, make as great a variety of wines as are made in Europe: not exactly of the same kinds, but doubtless as good," Thomas Jefferson predicted in 1808. America's third president was a determined advocate for the serious pursuit of viticulture in the United States, and he saw both a need and an opportunity. In 1811, he again stressed this pursuit, writing, "Wine being among the earliest luxuries in which we indulge ourselves, it is desirable it should be made here, and we have every soil, aspect, & climate of the best wine countries."

Jefferson would be proud to note that today every U.S. state produces wine—even Alaska. The wine currently served at the White House is exclusively American and sourced from all over the country, allowing presidents to showcase the richness and breadth of America's wine industry. That industry, however, took more than two centuries to secure the prominence it enjoys today. Along the way White House tables had to be furnished with the very best wines available, and in the eighteenth, nineteenth, and early twentieth centuries, the best were European. The wines that have been served at the White House thus represent an extraordinary array of winemakers and styles from both sides of the Atlantic and, later, from the Pacific Coast as well.

A French Beginning

Come quickly, I am tasting the stars!
—*Dom Pérignon*

The Burgundies, Bordeaux, and champagnes of France have been enjoyed for centuries by world leaders, including many of the presidents of the United States. The presidential affinity for French wine began with George Washington, who offered his guests at the President's House—first in New York and then in Philadelphia—fine French clarets and champagnes, which he imported in large quantities. His successor, John Adams, developed a keen interest in learning about French wine during the years he lived in Paris as America's minister to France. He particularly liked red and white Bordeaux.

The president with the most knowledge on the subject was Thomas Jefferson. He, too, spent time as a diplomat in France, and he traveled extensively through the country's wine regions to observe the process and sample the product of French winemaking. In a memorandum he wrote in April 1788 while living in Paris, he declared, "The best red wines of Burgundy are Chambertin, Vougeau, Romanie, Veaune, Nuys, Beaune, Pommard Voulenay." As a result of his time in France, President Jefferson was more adventurous and discerning in his tastes than was customary even among sophisticated Americans of this era, and the wines he drank included Clos de Vougeau, Chambertin, Sauterne de M. Salus, Château d'Yquem, Château Margaux, and Montrachet, among others.

Presidents Jefferson, James Madison, John Quincy Adams, and Andrew Jackson all had French staff, including chefs, during their time in the White House. It is likely these Frenchmen advised the presidents on suitable vintages from their native country. French wine was considered the best in the world throughout the nineteenth century, and guests of the president at the White House came to expect the service of these fine wines. Even into the twentieth century, French wine reigned supreme and was undoubtedly the first choice on the president's table.

Chassagne-Montrachet ages in barrels in Burgundy, France, as will the grapes above at the Château Margaux. Margaux and Montrachet were among the many French wines enjoyed by Thomas Jefferson.

WINE AND THE WHITE HOUSE

A statue outside the cellars of Moët & Chandon (right) in Épernay, in the Champagne region of France, honors the Benedictine monk Dom Pérignon for his pioneering techniques developed in the seventeenth century, which led to the perfection of the *méthode champenois.*

This *méthode* is seen in the Taittinger Champagne House, in Reims, France (below), where the last stage of fermentation occurs in the bottle.

Presidents Dwight D. Eisenhower, John F. Kennedy, and Richard M. Nixon were the last twentieth-century presidents to serve French wine frequently in the White House. They all had excellent taste in wine, and the events they hosted often featured Château Mouton Rothschild, Château Haut-Brion, Château Margaux, and Dom Pérignon.

President and Mrs. Eisenhower—who lived in Paris twice, from 1928 to 1929 and from 1951 to 1952—primarily served wine from France. Their favorite French selections at State Dinners were Château Climens 1950, Beaune Greves 1952, and Pol Roger 1952. Pol Roger is an especially historic brand that began selling champagne in 1849 and within thirty years was firmly established as one of the world's most renowned champagne producers.

The Kennedys in particular were known for their love of fine French wine, and they served their guests some of the country's best offerings. At their dinner for André Malraux, French minister of cultural affairs, on May 11, 1962, the Kennedys served Corton Charlemagne 1959, Château Gruaud-Larose 1955, and Dom Pérignon 1952.

Although Kennedy's successor, Lyndon B. Johnson, served only American wines, President Nixon returned to the exquisite reds, whites, and champagnes from the lush vineyards of France. Nixon possessed a deep knowledge of and strong interest in wine and even, on occasion, chose the wines for State Dinners himself. His selections showed a particular fondness for Château Margaux 1959, Château Lafite Rothschild 1962, and Taittinger champagne.

Despite Nixon's enthusiasm for French wines, his presidency coincided with the dramatic rise of American winemakers. It was still assumed that White House events would feature the

In 1984, President Ronald Reagan served President François Mitterrand of France a Cabernet Sauvignon from the Clos du Val Winery. The vineyard is a Franco-American collaboration on the Silverado Trail in Napa, California.

very finest wines, but now presidents had a real opportunity to both meet guests' expectations and showcase the quality of American viticulture.

Emphasizing American wines did not require a complete break with the French tradition, however. France's winemakers have had considerable influence on American winemaking since its earliest days. As California's wine industry was taking root, Frenchmen applied their expertise to the region's fertile fields to produce high-quality wines from vineyards such as Paul Masson, Mirassou, and Beaulieu, all of which were pioneers of fine wine production in the lands around San Francisco Bay during the nineteenth century. Since then, scores of winemakers of French descent have established vineyards in America that carry on the traditions of French winemaking. Several French companies have even established vineyards in California to specifically produce sparkling wine made with French champagne techniques, including Moët & Chandon, which opened Domaine Chandon in 1973; Champagne Taittinger, with

Domaine Carneros; and Champagne Mumm, which launched Mumm Cuvée Napa in the late 1970s.

In order to celebrate the success of Franco-American winemakers, wines from French-heritage vineyards have often been featured at State Dinners for visiting leaders from France. For example, on March 22, 1984, President Ronald Reagan served President François Mitterrand Clos du Val Cabernet Sauvignon 1975. Clos du Val was founded in 1972 by a descendant of a successful Bordeaux wine merchant, and the operation was headed by a French-trained winemaker. The winery's inaugural wine, the 1972 Cabernet Sauvignon, was part of the 1976 Judgment of Paris and rated higher than its French equivalent.

Reagan's second official dinner for France was held on March 31, 1987, and honored Prime Minister Jacques Chirac. The event was attended by Philippine de Rothschild and Bernard Arnault, owners of two of France's premier châteaus. At the dinner, three French-style American wines were served: Chardonnay from Sonoma-Cutrer, a vineyard from Sonoma Valley that proudly carries on Burgundian traditions; Opus One 1982, from the legendary collaboration between California's Robert Mondavi and France's Baron Philippe de Rothschild; and Domaine Mumm Cuvée Napa. The Opus One in particular served as a strong symbol of partnership between the American president and the French prime minister, and President Reagan even remarked in his toast: "I hope you all enjoy this evening's dinner wine. You see, it was produced in California as part of a joint French-American venture."

French wine's lasting legacy in the United States is evident in the vineyards around the country that incorporate the practices of winemaking developed in France, imbuing the Grand Cru of the American industry—and their appearances at the White House—with a decidedly French character.

Wine ages in Napa Valley, California, inside rows of French oak barrels at the Opus One Winery, a collaboration between California's Robert Mondavi and France's Baron Philippe de Rothschild. President Reagan chose Opus One for a 1987 dinner in honor of Prime Minister Jacques Chirac, and he acknowledged the legendary Franco-American collaboration with a toast.

PIERRE LURTON
Chief Executive Officer
Château d'Yquem
SAUTERNES, FRANCE

"On my desk at Château d'Yquem is a letter dated 1790 from Thomas Jefferson to Le Comte de Lur-Saluces of the family that produced wines at the estate for two centuries. After praising the quality of Château d'Yquem wines, Thomas Jefferson requests that thirty cases of it be sent to the American President George Washington and that ten cases be sent for Mr. Jefferson's cellar.

For me, it is a powerful reminder of the great work our winemakers have done for centuries in producing exceptional wine enjoyed around the world. It is also a reminder of the long-standing friendship between our countries.

We are honored that an American president two hundred years later served Château d'Yquem to a visiting president of France when Ronald Reagan toasted the friendship between our countries with François Mitterrand in 1981."

Château d'Yquem in Sauternes was visited by future president Thomas Jefferson while he was the U.S. minister to France in 1787.

Vins rouges classés du Départ. de la Gironde

4

Crus	Communes	Propriétaires

Premiers Crus

Château Lafite	Pauillac	Sir Samuel Scott Baronet
Château Margaux	Margaux	Aguado
Château Latour	Pauillac	de Beaumont / de Courtivron / de Flers
Haut Brion	Pessac (Graves)	Eugène Larieu

Seconds Crus

Mouton	Pauillac	Bon. N. de Rothschild
Rauzan { Ségla / Gassies }	Margaux	Comtesse de Castelpers / Vigneau
Léoville	St Julien	Marquis de las Cazes / Baron de Poyferré / Barton
Vivens Durfort	Margaux	de Puységur / de Bethman
Gruau Larose	St Julien	Baron Sarget / de Boisgerard
Lascombe	Margaux	Mademoiselle Hue
Brane	Cantenac	Baron de Brane
Pichon Longueville	Pauillac	Baron de Pichon Longueville
Ducru Beaucaillou	St Julien	Ducru — Ravez
Cos Destournel	St Estèphe	Martyns
Montrose	Cos	Dumoulin

THE 1855 BORDEAUX CLASSIFICATION

An Enduring System for Ranking the Best

WINES CAN BE a source of national pride and an important instrument for promoting a country's cuisine and culture. So when leaders have an opportunity to showcase wines from their country, they naturally want to choose the best. But on a matter as subjective as wine-tasting, what is a reliable measure of "the best"? This is a challenge every White House encounters when selecting from among America's many excellent wines for service at official events.

In 1855, France's Emperor Napoleon III faced the same dilemma. He knew that that year's Exposition Universelle de Paris—a "world's fair" of sorts—would draw influential visitors from across the globe, and he wanted to highlight the quality of French winemaking. He asked the Bordeaux region to contribute an exhibit—which meant coming up with a system for deciding which of the area's many wines merited recognition.

The result was the ranking that, to this day, endures as "The 1855 Bordeaux Classification." It featured fifty-eight wineries, ranked according to the reputation of the château as well as the quality and price of the wine. The highest tier in the classification is "First Growths," or Premiers Crus; the lowest is "Fifth Growths," or Cinquièmes Crus. The wineries in the classification are further ranked within each "growth" tier, listed in order of distinction.

After 150 years, the 1855 classification system still exerts significant influence over the price and popularity of the red wines of Bordeaux in a global wine market. The only official revision of the 1855 rankings came in 1973, when, after a decades-long effort by Baron Philippe de Rothschild, Château Mouton Rothschild was elevated to the exalted Premier Cru status it continues to enjoy today.

The Bordeaux Classification *(as updated in 1973)*

PREMIERS CRUS (FIRST GROWTH)

Château Haut-Brion, Pessac-Léognan
Château Lafite-Rothschild, Pauillac
Château Latour, Pauillac
Château Margaux, Margaux
Château Mouton-Rothschild, Pauillac

DEUXIÈMES CRUS (SECOND GROWTH)

Château Brane-Cantenac, Margaux
Château Cos-d'Estournel, Saint-Estéphe
Château Ducru-Beaucaillou, Saint-Julien
Château Dufort-Vivens, Margaux
Château Gruaud-Larose, Saint-Julien
Château Lascombes, Margaux
Château Léoville-Barton, Saint-Julien
Château Léoville-Las-Cases, Saint-Julien

Château Léoville-Poyferré, Saint-Julien
Château Montrose, Saint-Estéphe
Château Pichon-Longueville-Baron-de-Pichon, Pauillac
Château Pichon-Longueville-Comtesse-de-Lalande, Pauillac
Château Rauzan-Ségla, Margaux
Château Rauzan-Gassies, Margaux

TROISIÈMES CRUS (THIRD GROWTH)

Château Boyd-Cantenac, Margaux
Château Calon-Ségur, Saint-Estéphe
Château Cantenac-Brown, Margaux
Château Desmirail, Margaux
Château Ferriére, Margaux
Château Giscours, Margaux
Château d'Issan, Margaux
Château Kirwan, Margaux
Château Lagrange, Saint-Julien
Château La Lagune, Haut-Médoc

Château Langoa-Barton, Saint Julien
Château Malescot-Saint-Exupéry, Margaux
Château Marquis-d'Alesme, Margaux
Château Palmer, Margaux

QUATRIÈMES CRUS (FOURTH GROWTH)

Château Beychevelle, Saint-Julien
Château Branaire-Ducru, Saint-Julien
Château Duhart-Milon, Pauillac
Château Lafon-Rochet, Saint-Estéphe
Château Marquis-de-Terme, Margaux
Château Pouget, Margaux
Château Prieuré-Lichine, Margaux
Château Saint-Pierre, Saint-Julien
Château Talbot, Saint-Julien
Château La Tour-Carnet, Haut-Médoc

CINQUIÈMES CRUS (FIFTH GROWTH)

Château d'Armailhac, Pauillac
Château Batailley, Pauillac
Château Belgrave, Haut-Médoc
Château Camensac, Haut-Médoc
Château Cantemerle, Haut-Médoc
Château Clerc-Milon, Pauillac
Château Cos-Labory, Saint-Estéphe
Château Croizet-Bages, Pauillac
Château Duzac, Margaux
Château Grand-Puy-Ducasse, Pauillac
Château Grand-Puy-Lacoste, Pauillac
Château Haut-Bages-Libéral, Pauillac
Château Haut-Batailley, Pauillac
Château Lynch-Bages, Pauillac
Château Lynch-Moussas, Pauillac
Château Pédesclaux, Pauillac
Château Pontet-Canet, Pauillac
Château du Tertre, Margaux

PHILIPPE SEREYS DE ROTHSCHILD
Chairman of the Supervisory Board
Baron Philippe de Rothschild, SA
PAUILLAC, FRANCE

"At Château Mouton Rothschild, we are proud of our long association with American presidents. Whether it's Thomas Jefferson praising our wines in 1787, or John F. Kennedy serving them to Nikita Khrushchev, or the other modern presidents who have shared Mouton wines with their visitors, we are pleased to be a part of a fine tradition of presidential entertaining.

For us, this connection is personal. My mother was especially honored to be invited to Washington to attend the White House State Dinner that President and Mrs. Reagan hosted for Prime Minister Jacques Chirac. She was so pleased to see that our Opus One joint venture with Robert Mondavi was chosen as the wine for such an auspicious occasion.

Much like America herself, at Mouton we strive to remain true to our founding principles while always improving from one generation to the next."

A selection of the Château Mouton Rothschild vintages with labels featuring designs by leading artists of the period.

PHYLLOXERA

The Tiny Pest That Devastated French Vineyards

FOR ALL THE RIVALRY between the French and Californian wine industries, the grapes they use are actually closely related. The reason: a tiny pest called phylloxera.

Native to the Americas, phylloxera is a microscopic aphid-like insect that feeds off the sap in grape plants. In the United States, grapevines had, over the years, built up a certain level of resistance to the parasite. But when phylloxera was introduced to Europe in the mid-nineteenth century, vines there had no natural defenses. The result was a disaster for the Continent's vineyards.

Hardest hit was France, where the phylloxera plague was first noticed in Languedoc in 1863. It spread rapidly across the country's wine-growing regions, confounding all attempts to combat it. The French government even offered a reward of 300,000 francs to anyone who could develop an effective cure.

By one estimate, phylloxera killed some 70 percent of the vines in France, all but eliminating the ability to produce fine wine. Vineyards and wineries closed forever; livelihoods were lost; and the entire French economy was shaken.

It was not until the 1890s that French growers began implementing the only known solution to phylloxera. Scientists and vintners of the era noticed that while the phylloxera attacked the roots of European plants, they fed only on the leaves of American vines, causing much less damage. As it turned out, grafting the French vines onto American root stocks, generously provided by California winemakers, was the means by which the great blight was ended and French winemaking was rescued. Today, most French wine—even its finest vintages—comes from American roots.

The pest phylloxera (left) attacked the roots of grapevines by injecting deadly venom through a feeding tube by which it took in vine sap and nutrients. The degree to which the parasite devastated the winemaking regions of France by 1882 is indicated on the map (opposite). The darker the color, the worse the devastation.

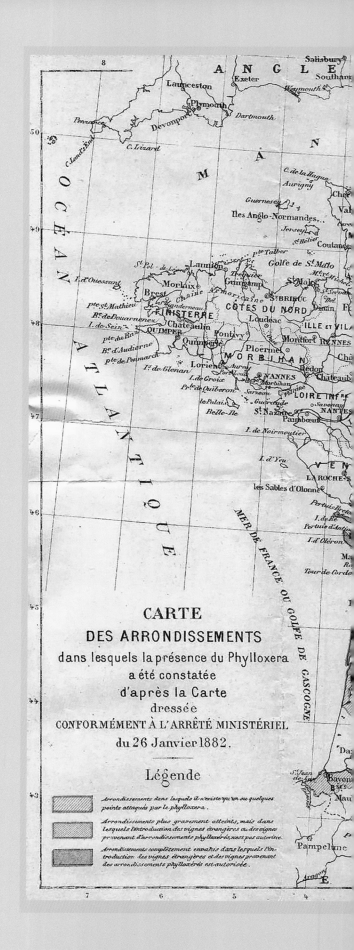

CARTE DES ARRONDISSEMENTS dans lesquels la présence du Phylloxera a été constatée d'après la Carte dressée CONFORMÉMENT À L'ARRÊTÉ MINISTÉRIEL du 26 Janvier 1882.

Légende

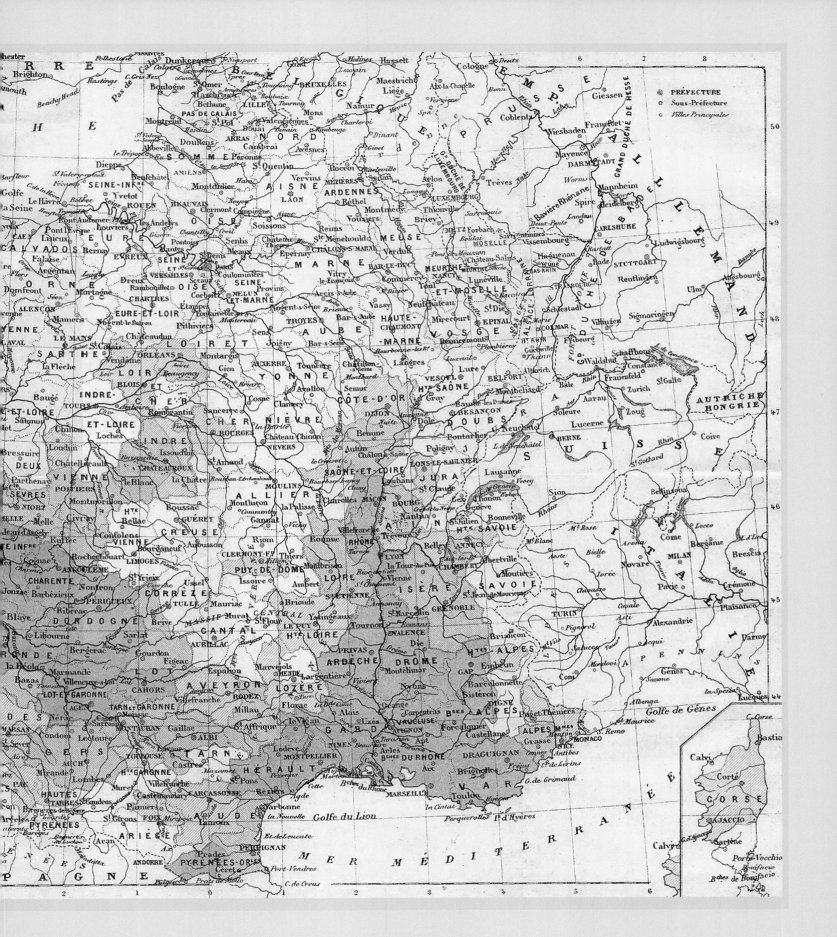

The Italian Influence

For all France's prominence in the wine world, the rich history of Italian wine stretches back farther than any other European viticulture. The ancient Romans are well known for their love of the drink, and Italian wine has been enjoyed around the world for many centuries. Even some of the early presidents of the United States of America served and enjoyed Italian wine in the White House.

Thomas Jefferson first experienced Italian wines during a trip through Northern Italy in 1787 and quickly developed a love for Italian varieties. His daily journal from this trip is filled with detailed observations and comments on the different vintages he sampled and the practices of the vineyards he visited. Upon returning to the United States he imported large quantities of Montepulciano, a Chianti-like red from the region of Florence. Montepulciano was one of Jefferson's personal favorites; at one time, he even said that it was "a necessary of life." The Italian variety also pleased many of his White House guests, and Jefferson sought to ensure that no disappointment would arise from his supply running out. In 1806 he imported 473 bottles of the red wine, claimed it was "truly the best" he had ever tasted, and requested that a friend stationed in Italy continue to send him supplies of four hundred bottles of the wine each year. Jefferson also frequently enjoyed Nebbiolo, a lightly colored red wine from Italy's Piedmonte region, and he imported large quantities of that variety as well.

The next documented service of Italian wine in the White House would not come for another 160 years. At several luncheons for visiting heads of state, President John F. Kennedy and First Lady Jacqueline Kennedy offered their guests Soave Bertani, with the first recorded instance being a private dinner on January 22, 1961, in honor of the president's Inauguration. This wine has a shining yellow color with intense notes of white flowers, gooseberry, peach, and apricot, and claims an impressive pedigree. The Bertani winery has a long history in Quinto di Valpantena, north of Verona, and its wines were popular in many American cities even by the end of the nineteenth century. Bertani's Soave ("soft" in Italian) vintage was one of the first Italian wines to be internationally recognized in the twentieth century.

President Lyndon B. Johnson's first State Dinner on January 14, 1964, was in honor of Italian President Antonio Segni, and he served another Soave—this one from the Bolla winery in the Veneto region in Italy. The Soave-Bolla 1959, a light white wine with delicate floral notes, was presented with the first course to open the meal.

While wine from Italy has been served at the White House by only a few presidents, the importance of Italian winemaking to American vintners is unmistakable. Many American winemakers of Italian ancestry feel a connection to their forebears and have brought Italian varietals and winemaking practices to America. Finding the climates and soil conditions in Napa Valley similar to the vast wine regions of Italy, these Italian Americans produce some of Italy's most beloved varieties with an American twist.

This lineage traces its origins to Philip Mazzei, who, in 1773, emigrated from Poggio a Caiano in the wine region of Tuscany to the hillsides of central Virginia. In 1774, Mazzei formed a partnership with Thomas Jefferson, and the two endeavored to cultivate grapes for wine near Monticello with the goal of establishing the first commercial vineyard in Virginia. With his Old World expertise and a team of thirty Tuscan vineyard workers, Mazzei was Jefferson's best hope for creating a successful Virginia winery. Unfortunately, Mazzei's experiment ultimately proved unsuccessful, as his attention turned to the American colonists' fight for independence leading up to the

A rustic cart at the foot of the medieval hilltop town of Montepulciano in Tuscany, Italy, touts the region's noble red wine.

Produced by Marchesi Mazzei spa Agricola in Chianti, Italy, Philip 2013 is a Cabernet Sauvignon dedicated to Philip Mazzei, the Italian-born winemaker and friend of Thomas Jefferson. The bottle carries his stylized portrait, and the label explains that Mazzei was a passionate grape grower and political thinker.

Revolutionary War. Still, the relationship between Jefferson and Mazzei remained strong, and in later years it became a symbol of the ties between Italy and the United States. The partnership is often referred to by American presidents in toasts honoring Italian heads of state.

Considering that relationship, Italian American–style wines are often showcased and well received at State Dinners for Italy at the White House. At a State Dinner on July 26, 1977, President Jimmy Carter served Italian Prime Minister Giulio Andreotti a Pinot Noir from the California vineyard Sebastiani, which proudly carries on the legacy of its founder, Samuele Sebastiani, who immigrated to Sonoma from Tuscany in 1895.

President William J. Clinton served wines with Italian heritage for both of his official dinners honoring visiting Italian leaders. At the April 2, 1996, State Dinner for Italian President Oscar Luigi Scalfaro, the first course featured Gallo Estate Chardonnay—a nod to one of the most prominent Italian American families in the U.S. wine industry and the winery that brothers Ernest and Julio Gallo founded in Modesto, California, in 1933. On May 6, 1998, the Clinton White House hosted Italian Prime Minister Romano Prodi and served two rare American-made Italian-style wines. One was Arneis, a dry white wine, from Oregon's Ponzi Vineyards, which, thanks to similarities between the climate of the Willamette Valley and Italy's Piedmonte region, is one of the few vineyards in the United States to grow this Italian varietal. The second was a Nebbiolo, one of Thomas Jefferson's favorite Italian wines, from Virginia's Horton Vineyard.

In October 2016, President Barack Obama hosted Italian Prime Minister Matteo Renzi. For this dinner, the Obamas chose to showcase three Italian-style wines from American vineyards. The evening opened with a Vermentino—an aromatic light white wine—from California's Palmina Vineyard, which grows Italian grape varietals in a climate and soil similar to that of Northern Italy. The wine for the salad course came from an Italian American–owned vineyard, Villa Ragazzi, and was a Sangiovese—an Italian-style red wine high in acidity with a fruit-forward taste and earthy aromas. (Villa Ragazzi was in fact the first vineyard to produce Sangiovese grapes—a varietal native to Tuscany—in Napa in 1985.) Accompanying the main course was a Zinfandel from Ridge Vineyards, first cultivated in 1885 as Monte Bello by a prominent member of the San Francisco Italian community.

MASSIMO FERRAGAMO
Owner
Castiglion del Bosco
TUSCANY, ITALY

"As an Italian winemaker with strong ties to America, I am proud of the role Italian wines have had since the earliest days of the United States. It's inspiring today to see so many wines by Italian American winemakers proudly presented at important affairs of state, when world leaders are entertained at the White House.

Salute!"

Grapes on the vine in
Tuscany, Italy.

The Fortified Wines of Portugal

The traditional wooden rabelo boats transport Port wine from the Douro Valley to the cellars near the city of Porto in Portugal.

In 2009, Barack Obama toasted his Inauguration as president with a glass of Madeira in honor of the nation's first president, George Washington, who in 1789 toasted his Inauguration with this fabled wine from the tiny island in the Atlantic. By far the most popular wine in eighteenth-century America, Madeira was a fitting choice for the toast, as George Washington ordered, served, and consumed great quantities of it, drinking, according to one source, a pint a day. As president, he ordered two pipes (about 240 gallons) every few months. At that time, water was unhealthy, and people of all ages drank beer, cider, rum, punch, and spirits throughout the day. But they were especially fond of Madeira. It was the wine that John Hancock tried to smuggle into Boston in 1768, that the Signers drank to toast the Declaration of Independence in 1776, and that was distributed at the polls in the nation's first presidential election in 1789. As a young country, Americans consumed about one-quarter of all Madeira produced.

The island, a port of call since the fifteenth century, began producing white wine for export in the 1640s. This wine had the strength to withstand long sea voyages because it was stabilized, or "fortified," by the addition of grape spirits or brandy during fermentation. While French wines deteriorated, Madeira actually improved in the cask when subjected to the heat and jostling of ships' cargo holds, where it often served as ballast. The added spirits not only sweetened the wine but increased the alcohol content to about 20 percent by volume (as opposed to about 13 percent for standard table wines).

But Madeira and Port, a fortified Portuguese red wine, were also popular because they were cheap. A 1703 trade agreement between England and Portugal kept import taxes on Portuguese wines to one-third less than the rate for French wines, which were prohibited altogether when England and France were at war, as they so often were, and by British trade policy. Just before the Revolution, Madeira constituted three-quarters

A view over the vineyards of the Madeira Wine Company on the island of Madeira.

of the wine imported into colonial America. Thomas Jefferson explained, "The taste of this country [was] artificially created by our long restraint under the English government to the strong wines of Portugal and Spain." Independence ended these restraints, and Jefferson took pride in introducing the lighter wines of France to America.

Madeira gradually dropped out of favor, although it was served at the White House with the fruit and nut course that followed dessert into the late nineteenth century. By that time, however, production on the island was much reduced by disease and the vineyards of Madeira were given over to sugar cane.

MIGUEL AND TOMÁS ROQUETTE
Owners
Quinta do Crasto
SABROSA, PORTUGAL

"As owners of an estate that has been producing wine and Port for four hundred years, we are proud of the role that Portuguese wines have played in the White House and as a bridge between our two countries. It is well known in Portugal that President Thomas Jefferson was a great Port aficionado and that some major moments of American history were celebrated with a bottle of Port.

We are honored that Portuguese wines were enjoyed by the nation's Founding Fathers and remain popular with Americans today."

Portugal's vineyards of Quinta do Crasto have produced wine and Port for four centuries.

Hungarian Tokaji:
"The Wine of Kings, the King of Wines"

Although often overshadowed by other winemaking powerhouses such as France, Italy, and Spain, Hungary—and specifically its famous Tokaji wine—has a loyal following among oenophiles, including in the White House.

The Tokaji region in northeastern Hungary has been producing the rare eponymous dessert wine for many centuries. Located near the Carpathian Mountains, the area's volcanic soil, rich in iron and lime, provides a fertile foundation for growing the six grape varieties approved for use in the production of Tokaji wine. Nearly two-thirds of the grapes planted in this region are of the Furmint variety, which is prone to the fungal infection *Botrytis cinerea*. Known as the "noble rot," *Botrytis* saps moisture from grapes and leaves behind a higher concentration of sugars. In the case of Tokaji, the result is a sweet dessert wine tasting of honey, caramel, apricots, and peaches. Despite the high sugar content, the alcohol level of Tokaji remains low, hovering between 5 and 8 percent.

While perhaps less well known than some of its French cousins, Tokaji has had a prestigious group of devotees across the last three centuries. In the eighteenth century, it achieved great notoriety in the royal courts of Europe. Louis XIV described it as *Vinum Regum, Rex Vinorum*—or "The Wine of Kings, the King of Wines."

In 1700, Hungary's Prince Francis Rákóczi of Transylvania had the vineyards around the Tokaji region's twenty-eight villages classified by the quality of the wines they produced. By 1730, the prince's project was complete, with the vineyards sorted into Great First Growths, First Growths, Second Growths, and Third Growths. Established more than a century before the famous 1855 Bordeaux ranking, the Tokaji system was the first known classification of vineyards in the world.

In the nineteenth century, France's Napoleon III ordered thirty to forty barrels of Tokaji annually, and Russia's Romanovs imported large quantities of the wine each year. Emperor Franz Josef, king of Hungary, sent bottles of Tokaji to England's Queen Victoria for her birthday, with an interesting twist: each year's gift would include one bottle for every month of the queen's life. Victoria, Britain's second-longest-reigning monarch, ended up receiving a total of 972 bottles on her eighty-first, and final, birthday in 1900.

Many of Europe's great nineteenth-century composers, including Ludwig van Beethoven, Franz Schubert, and Johann Strauss, enjoyed Tokaji's sweet nectar. Many consumers of that era felt that Tokaji had health benefits, including "restorative powers." Some doctors dispensed Tokaji medicinally to their seriously ill patients.

With such a devoted following in Europe, it is not surprising that Tokaji enjoyed a warm reception from America's leaders as well. "Tokay," as it was often written, was one of the wines Thomas Jefferson experienced on his discovery tours of Europe, praising its "silky" character. He clearly enjoyed the wine and continued to acquire it while in the White House. Among Jefferson's many wine orders from Europe, one notable purchase was from the merchant J. Erich Bollman, who in 1804 sold Jefferson more than two hundred bottles of Hungarian wine, including thirty-six bottles of Tokay. It was the highest price, per bottle, that Jefferson ever paid for wine.

Jefferson's successor, James Madison, also consumed Tokay, and he wrote to the American winemaker John Adlum expressing his appreciation for two versions of Tokay that Adlum had given him—one made with native-grown Hungarian grapes and the

Nothing more excellent or valuable than wine was ever granted by the gods to man.

—*Plato*

Shriveled fruit on the vine will be used for making the famous Tokaji wine. The Hungarian tradition of using grapes affected by the "noble rot" induced by the *Botrytis* fungus, which concentrates the sugar, dates back centuries.

other with American grapes. Madison wrote, "Your specimen from an American grape . . . has an affinity to the general character of the good Hungarian wines, and that it can scarcely fail to recommend itself to discriminating palates."

The modern growth and production of Tokaji wine can be attributed, in part, to the U.S. presidents who helped win the Cold War. During Hungary's communist era, from 1949 to 1989, the production of high-quality Tokaji wines ceased. The agricultural practices of Soviet communism devastated the Tokaji vineyards. Wineries were pushed to mass-produce cheap wines to satisfy the demands of the Soviets and their other satellite states. It was not until the Iron Curtain fell that the production of fine Tokaji wines resumed.

Today the Tokaji wine industry is thriving, with its products gracing the tables of heads of state and wine enthusiasts across the globe, and with its rarest wines considered among the most desirable in the world. In 2019, a Tokaji winery released a Tokaji Aszú Essencia priced at $40,000 a bottle—perhaps the best tribute to the democratic free-enterprise vision championed by America's presidents.

RAPHAEL REYBIER
Owner
Tokaj-Hétszölö Winery
TOKAJ, HUNGARY

"As the owner of a Hungarian estate that has been producing Tokaj Aszú for more than four hundred years, I am humbled to reflect on those who have enjoyed the wines of our region.

Tokaj has graced the tables of the earliest American presidents as well as the royal palaces of Europe. The heritage of Tokaj Aszú wines and the historical role of those who have enjoyed them inspire us to do our best to produce wines that will have a future as bright as their glorious past."

View of the vineyards at
Tokaj-Hétszölö Winery in
Hungary.

Germany's Riesling Returns

Music and wine are one.

—*Ralph Waldo Emerson*

Although Jefferson is well known for introducing the red wines of Bordeaux to America, he delighted his White House guests with a variety of European wines, including white wines from Germany, most likely Rieslings from the Rhine River Valley. Jefferson had traveled down the Rhine on a return trip from Amsterdam to Paris in 1788, when he was serving as minister to France, and he took detailed notes on the vineyards he visited, their histories and processes, and the tastes of the wines he sampled.

Riesling grapes, cultivated in the Rhine Valley since the fifteenth century, have been described as "the most noble and unique white grape variety in the world." The wine they produce is light (as low as 8 percent alcohol by volume), flavorful, balanced, and transparent, and in the nineteenth century Riesling became the most successful of all German wines. In England, where it was also beloved, it was known as "hock," derived from the town of Hochheim, which Jefferson visited on his tour. Eventually the term "hock" was used to describe all German white wines, and whether the "hock" served at the White House in the nineteenth century was always actually Riesling is not known. White German wines were, however, often poured in "hock" glasses, which, if traditional, had green stems.

The first 100 percent Riesling vineyard was planted in 1720 at Schloss Johannisberg to the west of Wiesbaden, Hesse, in the Rheingau wine-growing region of Germany. Thomas Jefferson visited the winemaker in 1788, observing that the vineyards in this region are south-facing and that the wine is "of the very first quality."

Riesling vineyards were devastated by the wars in the first half of the twentieth century and only slowly replanted. During the administration of Richard M. Nixon, German Riesling was often poured for first courses at White House dinners. President Nixon heavily favored Bernkasteler Doktor and Schloss Johannisberg of the 1967, 1969, and 1970 vintages. President Gerald R. Ford served some of Nixon's leftover Schloss Johannisberg and Bernkasteler Doktor at his first two State Dinners, before he began the practice of serving only American wines.

The Riesling vineyards of Schloss Johannisberg fill the valley leading to Germany's Rhine River. President Richard Nixon especially enjoyed the Riesling produced by Bernkasteler Doktor and Schloss Johannisberg.

DR. KATHARINA PRÜM
Owner
Weingut J. J. Prüm
BERNKASTEL-WEHLEN, GERMANY

"My family has been producing Riesling wine in the Mosel region since the time of George Washington.

The human aspects as well as the culture and history are fundamental to making wine. The production of great wines has always required passion and inspiration. Riesling wines have been served at the White House for more than two centuries. As a long-established family winery, we take pride in continuing the tradition of producing fine Riesling wines that have been enjoyed by presidents."

Vineyards fill the hills above Bernkastel-Kues, along Germany's River Moselle. In 1788, Thomas Jefferson visited this region on a wine-tasting tour.

WINE AND THE WHITE HOUSE

California Arrives

Wine to me is passion. It's family and friends. It's warmth of heart and generosity of spirit. Wine is art. Wine is culture. It's the essence of civilization and the art of living.

—Robert Mondavi

California vineyards have supplied more wine to the nation's presidents and their guests than any other state or foreign nation. American wine is nearly synonymous with California. No other state in the nation cultivates more acreage of grapes or has achieved such an illustrious reputation for such a vast variety of world-class wines. The first commercial winery in California was founded in 1833 by Jean Louis Vignes near what would become Los Angeles. Since then, numerous vineyards have taken shape, dotting the hillsides of Napa and Sonoma and the numerous wine-producing districts of the Golden State.

California's wine story begins in the late eighteenth century. While the Founding Fathers created and shaped the United States on the East Coast, Spanish Franciscans were establishing missions with accompanying vineyards to make sacramental wine on the West Coast—on land that would one day become the state of California. Their missions moved north up the coast, and in 1823 one was established in Sonoma, which by then was a territory of Mexico after that country obtained independence from Spain in 1821.

California was seized by U.S. troops during the Mexican-American War and subsequently saw a high influx of adventurous settlers establishing vineyards during the Gold Rush that began in 1849. California officially entered the Union as a state in 1850. The first winery in Napa is credited to John Patchett, whose excellent wine received the first official review of any California wine, in 1860. (His winemaker was Charles Krug, who quickly rose to prominence in the industry for his own winery.) In the ensuing decades, numerous vineyards throughout California produced top-quality wines that were shipped around the world.

In 1918, on the eve of Prohibition, there were more than 2,500 commercial vineyards operating in the United States. By its repeal in 1933, only 100 of those businesses had survived, chiefly by exploiting loopholes such as shifting to producing fruit juice or

One of America's most influential post-Prohibition winemakers, André Tchelistcheff helped to define the style of California's best wines. He is remembered with a statue (right) at the Beaulieu Vineyard in Rutherford, California, where he served as vice president from 1938 to 1973.

Today Napa Valley (opposite) is one of the world's premier winemaking regions and home to nearly five hundred vineyards.

sacramental wine. Just forty of these enterprises were in California. Prohibition had virtually destroyed America's winemaking industry, and when alcohol became legal again, California winemakers were eager to get back to their craft. Several of the remaining vineyards—such as Beaulieu, under the leadership of André Tchelistcheff—were able to rapidly revive production and reestablish themselves as leaders in America's wine industry during the 1930s.

This growth continued, and in the 1960s, Robert Mondavi became instrumental in the development of the California wine industry. Mondavi not only crafted some of the state's highest-quality wines, he also encouraged tourism to Napa Valley, establishing the region as a destination for all things viticultural. With a sincere desire to see California wine flourish, Mondavi fostered a collegial atmosphere among the state's winemakers, hoping they could pool their knowledge for the sake of the industry. By 1976 the years of hard work were rewarded when two California wines were deemed superior to French counterparts at the Judgment of Paris. The winners of the blind tasting were a 1973 Chardonnay from Chateau Montelena and a 1973 Cabernet Sauvignon from Stag's Leap Wine Cellars. Today California's more than 4,500 vineyards produce 90 percent of American wine, making the United States the fourth largest producer of wine in the world, after Italy, Spain, and France.

California wines first made their way to the White House in the nineteenth century. President Benjamin Harrison, in office from 1889 to 1893, visited the Golden State during his presidency and is even reported to have enjoyed sweet red wine from California during his years in the White House. In July 1938, while visiting San Francisco to tour the preparation for the Golden Gate International Exposition, President Franklin D. Roosevelt was treated to a luncheon that included thirty-three

Winemaker Robert Mondavi, seen here at his Napa Valley vineyard in 2004, was instrumental in bringing global recognition to California wine.

Jim Barrett (right), owner of Chateau Montelena in Calistoga, California (below), holds a bottle of his 1973 Chardonnay. The wine famously won the 1976 Judgment of Paris, a prestigious blind tasting. The win confirmed that the wines of California were on par with those of France and helped transform California's wine industry into the international powerhouse it is today.

Wine is sunlight, held together by water.
—Galileo

California wines. The numerous wines indicated that the wine industry, devastated by Prohibition, was quickly reemerging.

As the fortunes of California's wine industry have risen, so have presidents' appreciation of the Golden State's products, with California wines being favored in the White House throughout the twentieth century and into the present day. Even the Kennedys, despite their well-known fondness for everything French, served wine from historic California vineyards, with Inglenook's Pinot Chardonnay and Almaden's Cabernet Sauvignon ranking among their favorites.

President Lyndon B. Johnson exclusively served California's finest wines while he was in the White House, favoring the historic Beaulieu Vineyard Cabernet Sauvignon for the main courses of his dinners and luncheons. His decision to showcase California wine at the Executive Mansion proved significant, as it provided a crucial boost to California vineyards' reputation.

As the wine industry began to boom in the 1970s, the range of wines from California vineyards greatly increased and provided presidents with more variety in domestic wines than ever before. By the time Ronald Reagan took office, the number of vineyards in the state was the highest it had ever been, allowing the former California governor to serve a wide assortment of Golden State wines in the White House. Although he had his own favorites, his guests could expect offerings from different wineries at almost every White House event. Twenty-two different vineyards were represented during his first ten State Dinners alone.

One California standout is Schramsberg sparkling wine, which has been a top choice of U.S. presidents for decades. Founded in 1862 in Napa, the Schramsberg winery is immensely proud of its consistent service to the White House. The first time its sparkling wine was used at a presidential event was at the historic "Toast to Peace" between President Nixon and Chinese Premier Zhou Enlai at a State Dinner in Beijing on February 25, 1972. The fact that Nixon toasted Zhou with Schramsberg Blanc de Blancs 1969 gave tremendous visibility to California's fledgling sparkling wine industry. Since then, every president has served Schramsberg Blanc de Blancs or Crémant Demi-Sec at a State Dinner, with President Donald J. Trump recently serving Schramsberg Crémant Demi-Sec 2014 at his State Dinner for France on April 24, 2018.

As another means of showcasing the domestic wine industry, presidents have sometimes served American wine while dining abroad at United States Embassies in foreign countries. Though Nixon normally served German, American,

Grapevines (above) thrive on the terraced hillside at Newton Vineyard in Napa Valley.

A display at the Schramsberg Vineyards in Calistoga, California (opposite), tells the story of "The Toast to Peace." President Nixon used Schramsberg sparkling wine to drink to peace with Chinese leader Zhou Enlai in 1972. The display includes a photograph of the leaders as well as their glasses. Schramsberg has been a favorite of many presidents including George W. Bush, who chose Schramsberg Crémant 1999 to serve to Queen Elizabeth II in 2003 during a reciprocal dinner at Winfield House in Great Britain.

and French wines at his State Dinners in the White House, he selected only California wines for his hosted dinners abroad. At his dinner at Spaso House in Moscow for Soviet leaders on May 26, 1972, the menu featured Beaulieu Vineyard Pinot Chardonnay 1969, Louis Martini Cabernet Sauvignon 1967, and Schramsberg Blanc de Blancs 1969. When President Carter hosted a dinner at the American Embassy in Mexico City on February 15, 1979, he served Inglenook Pinot Chardonnay, Louis Martini Cabernet Sauvignon, and Korbel Extra Dry from three well-established California vineyards.

On November 20, 2003, President George W. Bush served Queen Elizabeth II three California wines at his dinner at Winfield House, the U.S. ambassador's residence in London. Two of them were Newton Chardonnay 2000 and Schramsberg Crémant 1999. The third, Peter Michael Les Pavots 1997, was a nod to the Bushes' guest of honor. The winery's owner, Sir Peter Michael, is a British subject who was knighted by the queen in 1989. President Donald Trump, too, showcased California wines during a State Visit to the United Kingdom in June 2019. At the dinner he and First Lady Melania Trump hosted at Winfield House in honor of the Prince of Wales and the Duchess of Cornwall, guests enjoyed three wines from California's Iron Horse Vineyard: Heart of the Vineyard Chardonnay 2016, North Block Pinot Noir 2016, and Joy Brut 2005.

Once a small industry begun by Spanish missionaries, California wines now travel the globe and grace the tables of world leaders—including the U.S. presidents who appreciate them as among the best wines available anywhere.

THE JUDGMENT OF PARIS

A Turning Point for the Industry

TWO HUNDRED YEARS AFTER the Declaration of Independence, a historic contest helped American wines finally come into their own. During the late 1960s and 1970s, serious wine aficionados were giving the wines of Napa and other American vinicultural regions a closer look. But while the California wines' bold, fruit-forward style received accolades from a growing number of wine consumers, the wines of France remained the undisputed champions.

In 1976, the English wine merchant Steven Spurrier decided to put these wines to the test. Because Spurrier spoke English, his Paris wine shop, Les Cave de la Madeleine, was often visited by Napa winemakers, and he knew just how excellent California's wines could be. In the mind of the French wine consumer, however, California did not exist.

Spurrier thought the French wine establishment would enjoy the chance to mark America's Bicentennial with a tasting of California wines. Spurrier himself visited Napa-area wineries and selected some of their finest wines for the tasting. He invited nine of the most respected wine experts in France—including top vineyard owners, French restaurateurs, and heads of wine societies—to participate. Only two of the nine had ever tasted a California wine, and the group came ready for a pleasant afternoon of oenological discovery.

Spurrier asked all of the major French newspapers to send correspondents, but none accepted his invitation. They dismissively assumed the event would be nothing more than an unremarkable tasting of novelty wines. A Paris-based reporter for *Time* magazine, George Taber, told Spurrier, "I'll come if it is a slow news day."

At the last minute, however, Spurrier made a decision that would render the tasting much more dramatic. He decided to serve French wines as well, pulling four of the very best Bordeaux red wines and four top Burgundy white wines from his shop for comparison against their California counterparts, Cabernet Sauvignon and Chardonnay. To intensify the competition, Spurrier decided to serve the wines "blind" so that the judges could not identify which wine they were sampling. The judges would then rank each wine on a 20-point scale, with only taste to guide their decisions.

The "Judgment of Paris," as the showdown came to be known, was held on May 24, 1976, at the Paris Intercontinental Hotel. With Spurrier's wife, Bella, capturing the event on her personal camera, the esteemed panel began to taste the French and American wines without knowing which were in their glasses. The whites were tasted first, and it soon became clear that the judges were struggling to distinguish the French national treasures from the American challengers. They appeared confused over which wines were French Burgundies and which were California Chardonnays, causing what Spurrier later described as "shock" among the judges. As the tasting switched to the red

Alan Rickman (standing center) portrays the wine merchant Steven Spurrier in the 2008 film *Bottle Shock*, which tells the story of how California's Chateau Montelena 1973 Chardonnay ranked first in the 1976 Judgment of Paris blind tasting competition. The scores (below) also put California's Stag's Leap 1973 ahead of the French Cabernet Sauvignons.

THE JUDGMENT OF PARIS
Results

	VINTAGE	SCORE
Chardonnay	Chateau Montelena, 1973 *(California)*	132.0
	Meursault Charmes, 1973 *(France)*	126.5
	Chalone Vineyard, 1974 *(California)*	121.0
	Spring Mountain, 1973 *(California)*	104.0
	Beaune Clos de Mouches, 1973 *(France)*	101.0
	Freemark Abbey, 1972 *(California)*	100.0
	Bâtard-Montrachet, 1973 *(France)*	94.0
	Puligny-Montrachet, 1972 *(France)*	89.0
	Veedercrest, 1972 *(California)*	88.0
	David Bruce, 1973 *(California)*	42.0
Cabernet Sauvignon	Stag's Leap Wine Cellars, 1973 *(California)*	127.5
	Château Mouton Rothschild, 1970 *(France)*	126.0
	Château Haut-Brion, 1970 *(France)*	125.5
	Château Montrose, 1970 *(France)*	122.0
	Ridge Monte Bello, 1971 *(California)*	103.5
	Château Léoville-Las-Cases, 1971 *(France)*	97.0
	Mayacamas, 1971 *(California)*	98.5
	Clos Du Val, 1972 *(California)*	87.5
	Heitz Martha's Vineyard, 1970 *(California)*	84.5
	Freemark Abbey, 1969 *(California)*	78.0

wines, the judges' comments and body language conveyed that they were experiencing similar difficulty in telling the French and California wines apart.

After the judges had completed their ranking forms, Spurrier gathered all of the documents and carefully tabulated the results. In news that would rock the wine world, the California wines had bested their French counterparts. Many of the judges were in a state of disbelief when they heard the outcomes of their own evaluations. One asked to have her tasting notes back, a request Spurrier denied.

Fortunately, *Time* magazine's George Taber decided to attend after all. Though he was the only journalist on hand to witness the contest, it was enough to spread the word of America's victory around the world. "The immediate effect," Spurrier recounted, "was to get California wines into the prestigious wine shops and restaurants on the East Coast. After years of being rebuffed by the Eastern establishment, California wines were now in demand."

The longer-term impact, as Spurrier saw it, was that "intelligent people in the French wine world were in California to explore and invest." The storied 1979 Opus One joint venture between Baron Philippe de Rothschild and Robert Mondavi, Spurrier explained, would otherwise never have happened.

The Judgment of Paris opened the eyes of the world—and U.S. presidents—to the quality of California wines. Seven years after the tasting, President and Mrs. Ronald Reagan celebrated their wedding anniversary aboard the royal yacht *Britannia* with Queen Elizabeth II and Prince Philip. The wine chosen for the special occasion was a 1974 Stag's Leap Wine Cellars Cabernet Sauvignon, the 1973 vintage of which had been the top choice for reds at the Judgment of Paris.

In the years since the epic contest, most of the wines from both the French and American winemakers at the Judgment of Paris have graced the tables at the White House.

With the quality of California wines confirmed to the world, American wines would be chosen more frequently for such special occasions as the wedding anniversary of President and Mrs. Ronald Reagan, which was celebrated on board the royal yacht *Britannia* with Queen Elizabeth II and Prince Philip.

The Judgment of Paris

Americans abroad have been boasting for years about California wines, only to be greeted in most cases by polite disbelief—or worse. Among the few fervent and respected admirers of le vin de Californie in France is a transplanted Englishman, Steven Spurrier, 34, who owns Les Cave de la Madeleine wine shop, one of the best in Paris, and the Académie du Vin, a wine school whose six-week courses are attended by the French Restaurant Association's chefs and sommeliers. Last week in Paris, at a formal wine tasting organized by Spurrier, the unthinkable happened: California defeated all Gaul.

The contest was as strictly controlled as the production of a Château Lafite. The nine French judges, drawn from an oenophile's Who's Who, included such high priests as Pierre Tari, secretary-general of the Association des Grands Crus Classés, and Raymond Oliver, owner of Le Grand Vefour restaurant and doyen of French culinary writers. The wines tasted were transatlantic cousins—four white Burgundies against six California Pinot Chardonnays and four Grands Crus Châteaux reds from Bordeaux against six California Cabernet Sauvignons.

Gallic Gems. As they swirled, sniffed, sipped and spat, some judges were instantly able to separate an imported upstart from an aristocrat. More often, the panel was confused. "Ah, back to France!" exclaimed Oliver after sipping a 1972 Chardonnay from the Napa Valley. "That is definitely California. It has no nose," said another judge—after downing a Bâtard Montrachet '73. Other comments included such Gallic gems as "this is nervous and agreeable," "a good nose but not too much in the mouth," and "this soars out of the ordinary."

When the ballots were cast, the top-soaring red was Stag's Leap Wine Cellars' '73 from the Napa Valley, followed by Mouton-Rothschild '70, Haut-Brion '70 and Montrose '70. The four winning whites were, in order, Chateau Montelena '73 from Napa, French Meursault-Charmes '73 and two other Californians, Chalone '74 from Monterey County and Napa's Spring Mountain '73. The U.S. winners are little known to wine lovers, since they are in short supply even in California and rather expensive ($6 plus). Jim Barrett, Montelena's general manager and part owner, said: "Not bad for kids from the sticks."

George Taber's article in the June 7, 1976, issue of *Time* magazine spread the news of California's groundbreaking victory over French wines in the Judgment of Paris.

MICHAEL MONDAVI
Owner
Michael Mondavi Family Estate
NAPA, CALIFORNIA

"As the third generation of Italian American winemakers, I've grown up with a commitment to producing the finest wines for the enjoyment of Americans and wine enthusiasts around the world.

It would have been in my grandfather's greatest dreams that Mondavi wines would be served by the president of the United States. To see California wines featured on State Dinner menus and enjoyed by the president of the United States and official guests from around the world is the ultimate source of pride to us and to all California growers. The whole objective is to make wonderful wines that are an expression of the soil but also enhance the lifestyle. If the wine doesn't taste good and invite you back to the glass, as my grandmother said, 'Go back to work.' To watch people as they learn about the importance of the soil, the climate, the maturity level of the grapes which give you additional layers of flavor in the wine, it's just really fun to see."

Rows of vines grow in Michael Mondavi's Animo Vineyards in Napa Valley.

Virginia and Beyond

> We could, in the United States, make as great a variety of wines as are made in Europe: not exactly of the same kinds, but doubtless as good.
>
> —*Thomas Jefferson*

While the wine industry in California is perhaps the most well known in the United States, the story of the American wine industry actually began on the East Coast, in colonial Virginia.

The earliest hopes for a successful wine industry in Virginia came from across the Atlantic, where the British were intent that wine produced in America be enjoyed throughout the empire. In 1619, "Acte 12" was signed into law by the Virginia House of Burgesses, requiring every male settler to plant and tend to at least ten grapevines. Although the vines imported by the colonists from Europe failed, native vines held more promise. Jefferson himself experimented with growing grapes at Monticello, and although no wine was produced there during his lifetime, by the end of the nineteenth century Virginia was the fifth largest wine producer in the country. Today there are nearly three hundred wineries throughout Virginia's wine country, sweeping from the north down through the Blue Ridge Mountains into southwestern Virginia, attracting visitors to savor flavorful wines and enjoy the stunning scenery.

Despite its long history, Virginia wine was not served by any presidents until late in the twentieth century. In September 1989, President George H. W. Bush held the dinner for the President's Education Summit at Monticello and served one wine from Virginia in honor of Thomas Jefferson, the Montdomaine Monticello Chardonnay. President William J. Clinton also served wine from Virginia, Horton Nebbiolo 1995, at the State Dinner for Italy in May 1998. President Barack Obama has served the most Virginia

Today wine is made in every U.S. state, from coast to coast. An East Coast vineyard (opposite) grows on the hillside at Monticello, in Charlottesville, Virginia, where Thomas Jefferson first planted grapevines more than two hundred years ago. More than 2,600 miles away, in the Pacific Northwest (above), rows of wine grapes thrive at Sagemoor Vineyards along the Columbia River in Washington State.

wine, offering various sparkling wines from the state at four State Dinners. Thibaut-Janisson Brut was chosen for his first State Dinner in November 2009 in honor of Prime Minister Manmohan Singh of India, and it was served again in March 2012 at a dinner honoring Prime Minister David Cameron of the United Kingdom. Thibaut-Janisson Blanc de Chardonnay was offered at the State Dinner for France in February 2014, and RdV Rendezvous was served at the Nordic Dinner in May 2016.

Although the wine industry in the Pacific Northwest is much younger than Virginia's, wines from Washington and Oregon, too, have often graced dining tables at the White House. With their warm, stable climate and fertile soil—in many ways resembling the Burgundy region of France—these two states offer some of the best wine-growing conditions in the country.

Even though Washington launched its wine industry only after the repeal of Prohibition, it has become the second-largest wine-producing state in the country, with the Columbia Valley its most prolific region. Chateau Ste. Michelle was one of the first vineyards in Washington and was a favorite winery of Presidents Gerald R. Ford and Jimmy Carter. Chateau Ste. Michelle's Chenin Blanc, Semillon Blanc, and Riesling were frequently offered at White House events during those two administrations, often served during the first course.

Wine prepares the heart for love.

—Ovid

Oregon is known for its Pinot Noir, which accounts for more than 53 percent of the state's wine production. Presidents have enjoyed many Oregon Pinot Noirs at the White House, including Domaine Drouhin, Penner-Ash, Ponzi, and Rex Hill, to name a few. Pinot Noir from Domaine Drouhin was served at President Clinton's first State Dinner on June 13, 1994, for Japan, and again at President Donald J. Trump's first State Dinner, for France, on April 24, 2018. President George W. Bush offered Pinot Noir from Penner-Ash Wine Cellar in the Willamette Valley at his 2004 Holiday Dinner.

New York, with its renowned wineries across the Finger Lakes, has supplied several varieties of wine for White House events, including Great Western's Natural Champagne and Gold Seal Pinot Chardonnay and Blanc de Blancs. President Jimmy Carter favored New York's sparkling wine, serving Great Western and Gold Seal champagnes at several State Dinners. These included his dinners for Jordan in April 1977, for Venezuela in June 1977, and for Latin American heads of state in celebration of the signing of the Panama Canal Treaty on September 7, 1977.

Wine from a president's home state is often chosen on special occasions. President Gerald R. Ford, for example, was pleased to serve Vidal Blanc from Michigan's Tabor Hill vineyard at one of his early State Dinners, on November 12, 1974, for Austria. After

More than one hundred wineries operate in the cool climate of New York's Finger Lakes region (opposite), while almost as many thrive in Arizona's semi-arid Sonoita wine-growing region (above). Wines from both regions have been featured on White House menus.

the selection proved a success, President Ford kept wines from Tabor Hill on his wine rotation, proudly offering Michigan wines at several subsequent White House events.

Sometimes presidents choose wines to honor the home state of a distinguished American guest. In 2006, President George W. Bush paid tribute to retiring Supreme Court Justice Sandra Day O'Connor with a dinner at the White House that featured wine from her native Arizona. Guests were served a Dos Cabezas Wineworks Pinot Gris 2004 and Callaghan Vineyards Cuvee 2004, both located in the Sonoita "wine country" in the southern part of Arizona.

With American wine from states in all regions of the country receiving recognition each year, Thomas Jefferson's vision for the industry has been more than fully realized. He may never have imagined that American wine would one day rival the offerings of Europe, or that wine would be produced across such a vast and diverse nation—or that the fruit of two hundred years of hard work would someday grace dinner tables at the White House.

JEAN CASE
Owner
Early Mountain Vineyards
MADISON, VIRGINIA

"It was President Thomas Jefferson who first experimented with planting vines at his Monticello estate in Virginia, and with it came a vision and a hope for great wine made in America. While Jefferson didn't find success in his lifetime, the generations that followed have. Inspired by Jefferson's work, today we join other Virginia vintners in bringing a commitment to fine wine, as each season we listen to what the vine, soil, and climate tell us. Then, under the guidance of talented winemaking teams, elegant wines are crafted that reflect the best the land in Virginia has to offer. In many ways, the growing success of quality wine from Virginia is proof of the promise that Thomas Jefferson saw for wines from Virginia two hundred years ago."

The Blue Ridge Mountains stretch beyond the grapevines of Early Mountain Vineyards in Madison, Virginia.

RUTGER DE VINK
Owner
RdV Vineyards
DELAPLANE, VIRGINIA

"In 2014 Michelle Obama and nine of her friends visited us at RdV. It was such an honor to share with them our story, our wines and the rich history of winemaking in Virginia. Two years later, our Rendezvous 2010 was selected to be the featured wine at a State Dinner honoring the leaders of five Nordic countries. Having our wine poured at such an important evening was a tremendous validation that we are producing world-class wines. Even though we are just an hour from Washington, D.C., I couldn't have imagined that we would develop such a connection to the White House. This is truly is an American dream."

A view over RdV Vineyards in the foothills of Virginia's Blue Ridge Mountains. The vineyard lies at the base of Lost Mountain, adjacent to land once owned by President George Washington.

CHAPTER FOUR

THE WHITE HOUSE COLLECTION

It is better to hide ignorance, but it is hard to do this when we relax over wine.

—Heraclitus

Vermeil wine ewer, 1817–18

This gilded silver wine ewer decorated with grapevines is part of a collection of vermeil serving pieces given to the White House during the Dwight D. Eisenhower administration.

ANCIENT CIVILIZATIONS of both the East and the West drank their wines out of vessels made from clay, bronze, silver, gold, and the earliest forms of glass. The most sophisticated of these cups were often highly decorated; those that have survived across the centuries provide some of the best glimpses we have into those cultures' artistic development, such as the ancient Greek *kylixes* or Chinese *fangyi* that are now preserved in museums around the world. Elaborate bejeweled chalices for sacred wine are some of the most remarkable surviving examples of the art of medieval Europe.

Only much more recently did cosmopolitan wine-drinkers start consuming their libations from crystal-clear glasses resembling the form we are accustomed to today. And only in the nineteenth century did the current practice of having a specialized glass for each type of wine emerge. Today oenophiles can enjoy the perfect merger of form and function, drinking from beautiful glasses designed precisely to concentrate vapors and aromas, keep body heat from raising the liquid's temperature, or allow ethanol to evaporate quickly.

Because of this history, most of America's presidents chose their glassware with aesthetics, rather than utility, in mind. As a result, the White House glassware collection has, over the years, reflected the dinnerware styles and fashions popular among America's trendsetters. And while some of the glassware used in the first four administrations was English, French, or Bohemian, since the presidency of James Monroe, in keeping with the law, it has almost always been American. The surviving glassware pieces in today's collection are therefore impressive artifacts of U.S. art history.

It is unlikely that Congress, for its part, originally saw White House glassware as future museum pieces. Congress provided for these purchases through the "furniture fund," money appropriated at the beginning of each administration. "Furniture" included furnishings of all kinds that a new president and his family might need, and only a small amount of the usual $14,000 to $20,000 appropriation was spent on glassware.

Historic glassware

Glassware from many of the historic services, such as that ordered by the Franklin D. Roosevelt administration (left), are still used on special occasions at the White House, while selections from the full collection are on display in the White House China Room. The cabinet (opposite) holds pieces from the Franklin Pierce administration on the top shelf and the Abraham Lincoln administration on the bottom shelf.

Although breakage meant that replacements were ordered frequently, only seven presidents ordered new glassware patterns—James Monroe, Andrew Jackson, Franklin Pierce, Abraham Lincoln, Benjamin Harrison, Franklin D. Roosevelt, and John F. Kennedy. No pieces of the Monroe State Service or the Jackson order remain, but there are examples of glassware from the other State Services in the White House collection today, together with some glassware purchased for family use and given to the White House because of an association with a president or his family. Although none of the presidents had unlimited means when ordering glassware, the elegance of the remaining examples testifies to the high quality of American glass in the nineteenth century.

From George Washington to John Quincy Adams

1789 to 1829

Sorrow can be alleviated by a good sleep, a bath and a glass of wine.

—Thomas Aquinas

Wine cooler, 1798–1809

One of four silver wine coolers made by French silversmith Jean-Baptiste-Claude Odiot in Paris. James Monroe purchased the wine coolers for himself and later sold them to the White House.

AMERICA'S FIRST OFFICIAL PRESIDENTIAL RESIDENCES were in New York and later in Philadelphia. To equip those homes for formal events, President George Washington commissioned the American diplomat Gouverneur Morris to purchase a variety of wine-serving accoutrements in Paris. The specifics of his order included cut-glass decanters and eight double coolers, each to hold two pint decanters, for serving Madeira and claret with dinner, as well as four more coolers—each to hold four bottles or decanters—for after-dinner use. Washington's instructions to Morris concluded: "One idea . . . I must impress you with and that is . . . to avoid extravagance. For extravagance would not comport with my own inclination, nor with the example which ought to be set." At the end of his time in office, Washington left an accounting of the furnishings of his residence: "Nothing has been said relating to the Table Linnens, Sheeting, China and Glassware which was furnished at the expense of the United States," he explained, "because they have been worn out, broken, stolen and replaced at private expenses over and over again." In 1797 the incoming president, John Adams, used government funds to purchase some of the Washingtons' leftover household furnishings, and the rest was sold at auction.

Adams and his wife, Abigail, had great need for high-quality glassware, as they held frequent official dinners for members of the government and foreign dignitaries. One congressman, writing to his wife about a dinner he attended, said that the table service including "glass tumblers and wineglasses and bone handled knives and forks were the best that we had." Unfortunately for Adams, he did not have much time in the White House to enjoy his acquisitions. He moved into the almost completed mansion on November 1, 1800; learned that he lost his bid for reelection on December 16, 1800; held a New Year's Day reception at the White House on January 1, 1801; and at 4:00 a.m. on March 4, 1801, moved out. Adams's final inventory, dated February 26, 1801, says of glassware only that there was "a plentiful quantity."

Thomas Jefferson moved into a partially furnished mansion. He gave up the levees held by Washington and Adams and did not care for large, formal dinners. Instead he preferred small parties of twelve or fourteen guests, who were impressed by the quantity and quality of the wines he served. He spent more than $10,000 on wine ($201,881 in 2020 dollars) during the eight years of his presidency, and drew praise for his selections. "Never before had such dinners been given in the President's House," one guest recalled, "nor such a variety of the finest and most costly wines." She also observed: "One great reform in dining parties was made by Mr. Jefferson; instead of remaining for hours at table after the ladies had withdrawn, at his parties, the gentlemen after taking two or three glasses of wine, left the table and took their coffee in the drawing room, which custom not only preserved temperance, but promoted the most refined social enjoyment." With these improvements came an investment in glassware; when

No one who has been drinking old wine desires new, for he says, "The old is good."

—Luke 5:39

Jefferson left office, the inventory of the large dining room listed thirty decanters and 120 wineglasses.

When James and Dolley Madison entered the White House in 1809, they entertained much more frequently and lavishly than their predecessor. Mrs. Madison understood the value of entertaining as a means of promoting her husband's policies, and at the couple's Wednesday evening receptions, political rivals could engage each other cordially over wine and whiskey punch. Wineglasses and decanters were purchased regularly, with no intention of matching or forming sets. Some were bought secondhand, and others were purchased at auction.

When British troops burned the White House in 1814, all of these glassware items—and the rest of the mansion's furnishings—were destroyed. The Madisons moved into rented quarters but continued entertaining, purchasing more glassware secondhand and from local merchants. It was at this time that one of the earliest pieces in the White House collection was given to the Madisons by Bakewell, Page & Bakewell of Pittsburgh, the first glass manufacturers to make fine lead-glass tableware profitable. Two beautiful cut-glass decanters came with this letter from the firm:

Sir, convinced that you who have devoted so large a portion of your life to the promotion of the welfare of Independance of our Country, will not look with indifference upon the progress she is making in the Arts and Manufactures, we take the liberty of sending you a pair of decanters made and cut at our manufactory of which we request the favor of your acceptance.

When it is recollected that all the materials for making glassware are found abundantly in our own soil and how large this article contributes to the comforts, conveniences and elegances of life, we flatter ourselves you will derive as much pleasure from receiving this specimen as we in furnishing it.

The decanters were a personal gift to the Madisons and were taken home to Montpelier in 1817. One eventually made its way back to the White House. It is a stunning example of the diamond-cut style then popular, and its engraving of the eagle and shield, taken from the Great Seal of the United States, is the earliest known use of this design as a symbol of the presidency. Some variation of it was used on White House glass and china throughout the nineteenth century and into the twentieth.

James Monroe, inaugurated in March 1817, had to furnish the White House from scratch. His agents purchased most of the furnishings in France, but he sold his own French glassware to the White House for official use, including two pairs of decanters, eighteen claret glasses, and forty-nine wineglasses. In September of that year, Monroe visited Pittsburgh and toured the Bakewell glasshouse. The proprietor presented Monroe with a pair of cut-glass decanters as he had President Madison. Shortly thereafter, Monroe ordered glassware from Bakewell for the White House: "a full set of Decanters, Wine Glasses and Tumblers of various sizes and different models, exhibiting a brilliant specimen of double flint, engraved and cut by Jardelle. This able artist has displayed his best manner, and the arms of the United States on each piece have a fine effect." Although none of this glassware remains, it was likely decorated in the strawberry-diamond motif that was fashionable at the time.

The Monroes entertained on a grand scale. One guest at the New Year's Day reception in 1821 recalled that "wine was handed about in wine-glasses on large silver salvers." At the end of Monroe's term, the inventory recorded twelve large elegant cut wine decanters, thirty-nine champagne glasses, and eighty-nine wineglasses.

When John Quincy Adams and his wife, Louisa, moved into the White House in 1825, they had little need of more glassware. Only one purchase—for two dozen cut wineglasses—is recorded. Although the couple held formal receptions twice a month, President Adams was not an enthusiastic host. In his diary he confided that the gatherings were "very much crowded . . . multitudes of strangers. . . . These parties are becoming more and more insupportable." Perhaps for this reason, Adams sought to govern his household with economy. Yet in 1826 he still needed to ask for an addition to the furniture fund—a request that was not well received by Congress. Following some bitter arguments, Congress granted the request but specified that "all furniture purchased for the use of the President's House shall be as far as practicable of American or domestic manufacture." The act had far-reaching consequences for American glass manufacturers, which thereafter contended with one another to furnish the president's table with wineglasses.

John Quincy Adams's glassware legacy continues to this day, as the current White House collection has two wineglasses that descended through the Adams family. The glasses were made in England and date from sometime between 1765 and 1780, making them the oldest wineglasses in the collection. Both glasses have opaque twists in their stems, achieved by inserting white enameled rods into the mold of molten glass and drawing the rod out to create the pattern. This decoration is typical of English glassware from this period.

Madison decanter, Bakewell, Page & Bakewell, Pittsburgh, 1816

One of a pair, this cut and engraved decanter (opposite) was given to President James Madison by the manufacturer and bears the president's "M" monogram.

Wineglasses, England, c. 1765–80

Descended through the John Quincy Adams family, these wineglasses (above) are the oldest in the White House collection.

Wine coolers, London, England, c. 1806–35

Early nineteenth-century vermeil wine coolers in the White House collection, made by notable silversmiths such as Paul Storr and William Pitts, depict mythological scenes and decorative elements referencing wine (opposite).

Wine cistern, Thomas Farrer, London, England, 1720–21

Once owned by the British ambassador to Russia, this silver wine cistern (above) was brought to the White House collection in 1963.

182   WINE AND THE WHITE HOUSE

From Andrew Jackson to James Buchanan

1829 to 1861

ON MARCH 4, 1829, unprecedented crowds surged on Washington, D.C., to see Andrew Jackson, hero of the Battle of New Orleans, take the Oath of Office at the Capitol. They followed him back to the White House for a public reception that quickly got out of hand. One observer wrote, "Orange punch by barrels full was made but as the waiters opened the door to bring it out, a rush would be made, the glasses broken, the pails of liquor upset and the most painful confusion prevailed. To such a degree was this carried, that wine and ice-cream could not be brought out to the ladies." Another writer described "a rabble . . . scrambling, fighting, romping" and believed that several thousand dollars' worth of cut glass and china had been broken by the crowds that day. To replace the lost inventory, President Jackson soon placed a huge glassware order with Bakewell, Page & Bakewell for 435 pieces, including twelve pairs of decanters and eighteen dozen wineglasses of the "richest cut." The cost of the order, including packing and shipping, was $1,451.75—roughly $40,000 in 2020 dollars. The glassware was ready by July 25, 1829. According to a Pittsburgh newspaper, it was "pellucid as crystal and beautiful cuttings give brilliancy of effect."

The Jackson service was cut in flat panels, a style that soon surpassed the strawberry-diamond cutting that had been popular since the end of the eighteenth century. This service was in use for more than twenty years, and Jackson himself, as well as subsequent presidents, ordered replacements from other manufacturers that did not always exactly match in pattern or shape.

When Jackson's successor, Martin Van Buren, entered the White House in 1837, the mansion was more elaborately finished than it had been for any of his predecessors. Van Buren enjoyed entertaining, and because he was a widower, his daughter-in-law Angelica Singleton Van Buren served as hostess for the president's social events. Their "charming little dinners," as one guest described them, were much admired. The president ordered replacements for the Jackson-pattern wineglasses from various local merchants but was not nearly so extravagant in his spending as Pennsylvania Congressman Charles Ogle made him out to be in the "Gold Spoon Oration."

Van Buren's successor, William Henry Harrison, died a month after taking office and was succeeded by his vice president, John Tyler. Tyler placed several small orders for glassware during his single term. These likely augmented the glassware

Decanter detail

Cut-glass swags and engraved grapevines adorn this Bohemian decanter of the mid-nineteenth century.

Fan the sinking flame of hilarity with the wing of friendship; and pass the rosy wine.

—*Charles Dickens*

sets bought by Jackson and supplemented by Van Buren but were considerably less expensive. Cut tumblers that had been $20 a dozen in 1829 had dropped to $5 or $6 a dozen by 1842. The lower costs probably reflected the growth of the American glass industry, but they may also indicate that the glasses were not engraved. Pressed glass tumblers had recently become available, and they were $1 a dozen. Wineglasses, however, continued to be cut.

When James K. Polk and Sarah Polk moved into the White House in 1845, they evidently found the glassware much depleted, as they made several purchases from Baldwin Gardiner and Ebenezer Collamore, both of New York. It was around this time that wineglasses were beginning to become specialized to the type of wine they would serve. The Polks ordered green-colored hock glasses (glasses for Rhine wine, traditionally green), "straw stem" glasses (glasses with delicate, straight stems), as well as red-colored straw stem clarets (glasses for red wine).

The colored glassware ordered by the Polks reflected the beginning of the popularity of colored glass during the middle of the nineteenth century. The White House collection has several pieces of such colored glassware, including an English-made green decanter from sometime between 1820 and 1840. With its unembellished, flat-cut sides, the decanter would have likely have been used for informal dining at the White House.

Zachary Taylor, in office for slightly more than a year before he died in 1850, purchased four dozen rose-colored clarets, another eight dozen wineglasses, and forty-one hock glasses. Some of the rose claret glasses are still in the White House collection, along with smaller rose-colored wineglasses that would have been used for dessert wine. These were probably ordered in 1849, 1850, or 1853 as supplements. Also still in today's collection are a colorless panel-cut decanter and two matching wineglasses owned by Taylor before his election as president. During his years as a general in the army, Taylor earned the nickname "Old Rough and Ready." The simple design of this glassware is in keeping with his relatively Spartan style and is typical of American glassware of that period.

Following Taylor's death, Vice President Millard Fillmore acceded to the presidency. His purchases included eighteen cut-glass decanters, a dozen cut cordials, a dozen hock glasses, thirty-seven wineglasses, and two dozen cut champagne glasses. Also in the White House collections from the period is a wineglass cut in the Ashburton pattern. Most common in pressed glass, the Ashburton pattern was named after Alexander Baring, Lord Ashburton, one of the most popular English diplomats ever to come to the United States. It was a simple pattern with large facets that imitated the fashionable panel cutting.

Franklin Pierce took office in March 1853, and although he and his wife were in mourning for their 11-year-old son, killed in a railroad accident two months earlier, they continued the customary weekly morning and evening receptions while Congress was in session and the weekly formal dinners for thirty-six guests. In July, President Pierce traveled to New York to open the Crystal Palace Exhibition of the Industry of All Nations, modeled after the Crystal Palace Exhibition in London of 1851. There he saw fine china and glassware displayed by New York retailers Haughwout & Dailey, and when he returned he ordered French porcelain china, decorated at Haughwout's atelier, and a very large amount of cut glassware; both served sixty people. Haughwout employed talented English and Irish glasscutters, and the glass cutting may have been done in Brooklyn, probably on the premises of the Brooklyn Flint Glass Company.

Pierce's glassware order included five dozen each of champagnes, Pomona green hocks, ruby clarets, Irving wines, Lammartine wines (Irving and Lammartine may have

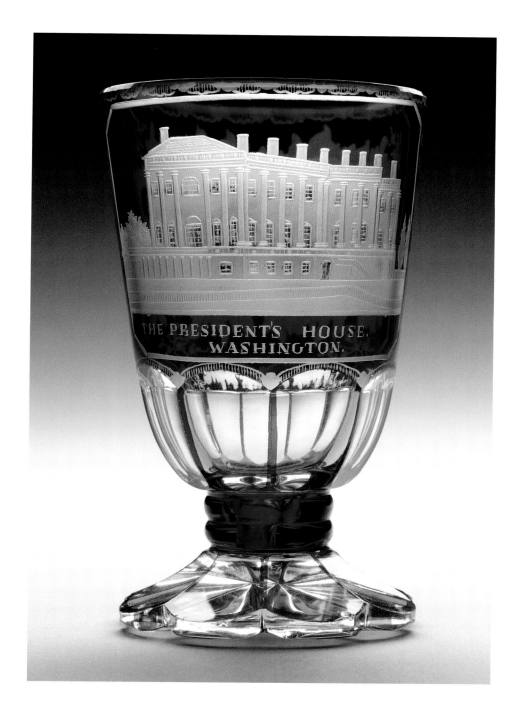

been pattern designations), hocks, "Eng." Wines, four dozen wine coolers, four dozen cordials, six pairs of quart decanters, six pairs of pint decanters, and two dozen handled flagons (wine or water pitchers). This complex order makes it clear that by mid-century it was customary to serve each wine in a wineglass specially designed for it. Nineteenth-century rules for table setting are instructive:

At the right hand of every plate place a tumbler, and one or more wineglasses, according to the variety of wines that are to be brought to the table, it being customary to drink different wines out of different sorts of glasses; the fashionable glass for each wine varying so frequently, that it is difficult in this respect to give any rules. The decanters are to stand near the corners. It is now usual at many tables to have a small water-bottle (holding about a pint) placed by the side of every plate, that each person may pour out water for himself.

The White House collection today reflects Pierce's influence, both in the pieces he ordered and in items subsequently purchased to supplement his original set of cut glass. These include two decanters (one with an elaborate handle), wineglass rinsers, and a variety of different wineglasses for dinner and dessert wines. The pieces are engraved with an elaborate motif of grapevines and leaves and have an American eagle insignia. Some of the supplemental wineglasses ordered later feature varying designs on their stems; some are straight with simple disk connections to the bowls, while others have multifaceted knobs at the bases of the bowls. There are even a few colored pieces that display the grapevine, leaf, and eagle motif.

America's fifteenth president, James Buchanan, a bachelor, took office in 1857, with his niece Harriet Lane serving as his hostess. He made frequent but small purchases of wineglasses, including sherry and Madeira glasses, replacements for the Pierce service or possibly for the Jackson service. Despite restrictions on her spending, Harriet Lane gave brilliant dinners and receptions.

Goblet, c. 1840–60

Though likely used for water, this Bohemian engraved ruby-stained goblet featuring the southwest view of the President's House reflects the popularity of colored glass in the mid-nineteenth century, as seen in other examples from the Polk and Pierce presidencies.

Decanter, probably English, c. 1820–40

Colored glass increased in popularity during the administration of James K. Polk. This decanter with its unadorned flat sides would have been used for informal dining (above).

Decanter and wineglasses, United States, c. 1830–50

President Zachary Taylor's colorless panel-cut decanter and matching wineglasses (opposite), owned before his presidency, are typical of American glassware of the period.

Wineglass, United States, c. 1844–55

An example of the Ashburton pressed-glass pattern, common during the period of President Millard Fillmore's administration, this wineglass has large facets imitating panel cutting.

Wineglasses, possibly Haughwout & Dailey, New York, 1853, or later reorder

President Franklin Pierce placed a large order for glassware after seeing a display at the New York Crystal Palace Exhibition in 1853 (opposite). Supplemental pieces of the same pattern were ordered by five later administrations.

WINE AND THE WHITE HOUSE

Wineglasses and rinser, possibly Haughwout & Dailey, New York, 1853, or later reorder

The Pierce glassware set was engraved with a grapevine motif with leaves and an American eagle insignia. Supplemental pieces ordered later featured more elaborately designed stems.

Pierce decanter detail

The eagle and shield engraving appears on the Pierce decanter (above).

Cordial glass, wineglass, decanter, rinser, possibly Haughwout & Dailey, New York, 1853, or later reorder

The service ordered by President Pierce was for sixty people and included 564 individual pieces of glassware. By the mid-nineteenth century, each wine was served in a wineglass specifically designed for it (opposite).

just three months into his term of office, he was fatally shot. Vice President Chester A. Arthur of New York became president, and he found the Executive Mansion, which had not been redecorated since Grant's first term, to be in need of extensive work. In preparation for the most elaborate program of redecoration since the White House burned in 1814, Arthur sent twenty-four wagonloads of furnishings to a mammoth sale in April 1882, including thirty barrels of china and glass. Yet an inventory taken the following month indicates that much glassware remained. Among other pieces were 91 champagne glasses, 278 wineglasses, 157 claret glasses, 169 green and 108 pink hock glasses, 54 decanters, 49 liqueur and brandy glasses, 45 sherry glasses, and 49 Sauterne glasses.

While the White House was being improved, President Arthur, a widower, spent the summer at the presidential retreat on the grounds of the Soldiers' Home in Northwest Washington. He returned with his children to a White House ready for the formal entertaining on the grand scale that he enjoyed. His sister, Mary McElroy, acted as his hostess. The administration's first formal dinner was in honor of former President Grant and his wife. According to one account, "Dinner was served in fourteen courses, with which there were served eight varieties of wine, each variety having an appropriate wine glass." Evidently Arthur was content with the existing glassware, as he made only a few minor purchases.

Grover Cleveland began his first term as president on March 4, 1885. During his first eighteen months in the White House, his sister, Rose Cleveland, served as hostess. In July, Colonel John Wilson, commissioner of public buildings, placed a glassware order with Thomas G. Hawkes, a Corning glasscutter, who publicized this commission in articles reprinted in newspapers:

> *The fifty dozen pieces ordered include for the most part what is called stem ware, i.e., goblets, tumblers, decanters, liqueurs, lemonades, etc. The light glasses are for the most part gold, ruby, or amber ware. No pains have been spared to make each piece as perfect as possible. The slightest flaw that only a trained eye can see dooms the most valuable piece, so that its only use thereafter is as broken glass to be remelted. Of the 100 men in the shop only twenty of the best ones are employed on this order. The design engraved . . . consists of an American eagle perched on a shield above the words "E Pluribus Unum." It is the design that has always ornamented ware for the White House. . . . The work for the White House in the blowing room was done entirely by hand, no molds being used. There was included in it some gold-ruby ware, which requires unusual skill in manufacturing. The patterns on the glassware consist of sets of parallel lines, crossing at different angles, and forming many-sided diamonds and stars which are changed by additional complex cuts.*

The order included two dozen champagnes, three dozen clarets, five dozen Madeiras (red), three dozen sherries, and one dozen white wine (red), all in the Lincoln pattern. A contemporary description of Cleveland's first State Dinner in 1886 states, "At each plate were set six Bohemian wine glasses, a cut-glass carafe, tumbler and champagne glass."

In June 1886, the 49-year-old Cleveland married 21-year-old Frances Folsom in the White House Blue Room. Although the new first lady had never before managed a household, she proved to be a skilled hostess. When Cleveland lost the election of 1888 to Benjamin Harrison, she is supposed to have predicted correctly that she would be back in four years.

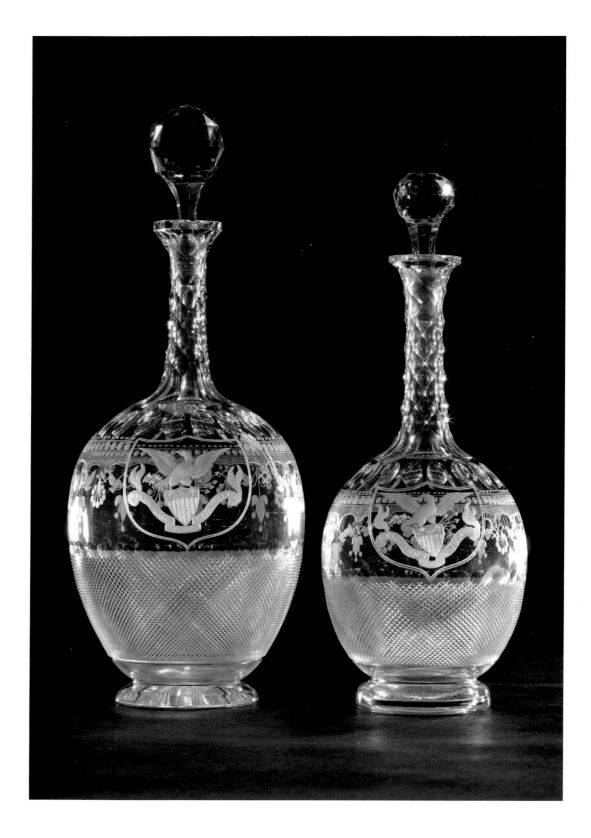

Decanters, Christian Dorflinger's Greenpoint Glass Works, Brooklyn, New York, 1861

The Lincoln glassware departed from the traditional heavy cut glass in favor of thin glassware with a band of fine diamond cutting and copper-wheel engraving (left). The central insignia on the decanter features an eagle carrying arrows in its left talon and an olive branch in its right talon (detail opposite).

Cordial glass, two dessert wineglasses, two wineglasses, and champagne glass, Christian Dorflinger's Greenpoint Glass Works, Brooklyn, New York, 1861, or later reorder

The Lincoln service was reordered at least seven times and used at the White House until the Benjamin Harrison presidency.

**Wineglasses,
United States, c. 1865–75**

A set of wineglasses with
cut stems and engraved
vines is thought to have been
ordered in 1873 by President
Ulysses S. Grant.

**Bottle coasters:
(left) J. Dixon & Sons,
England, c. 1850,
silverplate; (middle)
Martin-Guillaume Biennais,
Paris, France, c. 1809–19,
silver; (right) United States,
c. 1881, silver**

Coasters in the White House
collection were used to hold
wine bottles. The middle
coaster was used during the
Andrew Jackson presidency
and has "President's House"
engraved on the bottom.

From Benjamin Harrison to Woodrow Wilson

1889 to 1921

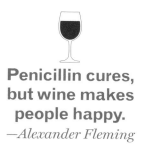

Penicillin cures, but wine makes people happy.

—*Alexander Fleming*

BENJAMIN HARRISON, the grandson of President William Henry Harrison, took office in March 1889. By this time the Lincoln-pattern glassware had been in use more than twenty-five years and reordered in quantity at least seven times. First Lady Caroline Harrison, a skilled china painter, designed a new china service. At the same time, she invited the retailer M. W. Beveridge to furnish the Executive Mansion with new glassware.

The design for this new set was to be "the straight shape and the Russian cut, with the coat of arms of the United States engraved in medallion." This Russian pattern had been designed in 1882 by Philip McDonald, a cutter for Hawkes, in Corning, and so many other glass-cutting firms began to adopt it that it became the industry standard. Departing from the motifs of diamonds and hobnails, the Russian pattern was star-cut, and the glass blank—the unfinished starting piece—was much thicker and heavier than the one used for the Lincoln-pattern service to allow for the complex and deeply cut pattern. The insignia shows the eagle facing its left shoulder, toward the arrows in its talon, instead of looking right, and rather than sitting on a shield, this eagle bears the shield across its breast. For the service produced for the Harrisons, the engraving was done by Joseph Haselbauer, a Bohemian-born craftsman. The design was ordered and reordered for the White House from 1891 through 1917.

The Harrison order, for five dozen place settings of goblets and saucer champagne glasses, claret glasses, Sauterne (white) glasses, and sherry glasses, and eight quart decanters, indicates some changes in the customs of service at table. The number of glasses per person was smaller than in orders of the Lincoln pattern, and there was no colored glass. The newspapers announced that "guests at the state dinners next winter will have the pleasure of eating off the new set of china . . . [and] a full service of cut glass ware. . . . A variety of new patterns were submitted to the President and Mrs. Harrison's inspection a month or two ago, and they selected many novel and beautiful shapes. In the new collection there will be water goblets, claret, champagne and brandy glasses. The shield and eagle is cut deeply in each one."

In the spring of 1893, the Clevelands returned to the White House, making Grover Cleveland both the twenty-second and twenty-fourth president of the United States. The first lady, finding the Harrisons' new china and glass in use, decided to purchase additional items. A comparison of the shapes ordered in 1891 and the replacements ordered in 1896 shows that the size formerly called "sauterne glasses" became wineglasses.

The Clevelands left the White House for the second time with the Inauguration of William McKinley in 1897. First Lady Ida Saxton McKinley was an invalid who took little part in the social life of the administration. Access to White House receptions was

Harrison decanter detail

The Coat of Arms engraved on the Benjamin Harrison glassware shows the eagle facing its left shoulder, toward the arrows in its talon, instead of looking right.

If wine tells the truth, and so have said the wise / It makes me laugh to think how brandy lies.

—*Oliver Wendell Holmes*

more restricted than it had been in the Cleveland administration, but they were still crowded. The McKinleys ordered replacements for the Russian-pattern glassware but also ordered green glasses for white wines and ruby Burgundy glasses that must have been in the Lincoln pattern. It is interesting that Lincoln-pattern glassware continued to be ordered through the end of the nineteenth century and once again in the early twentieth century.

In 1901 President McKinley was assassinated and was succeeded by his vice president, Theodore Roosevelt. The Roosevelts were a large and lively family, and almost immediately the new president and first lady ordered a major renovation of the White House that included a reallocation of space within the mansion and a new West Wing for the president's office. They entertained frequently and celebrated important family occasions in the Executive Mansion. The older daughter, Alice, was married at the White House with great ceremony in 1906, and the younger daughter, Ethel, made her debut with a dance at the White House in 1908. For both occasions much glassware was required. While an order for replacement glassware in 1901 included Lincoln-pattern wineglasses, it was the Russian pattern that Mrs. Roosevelt ordered in quantity. Again the engraver was Haselbauer, and the Corning newspaper reported:

> *Joseph F. Haselbauer and son Frederick . . . are engaged in engraving a number of pieces of glassware, belonging to what is known as the "President Harrison set" at the White House, the engraving of the original set having been done in Corning. Since coming to this country, about 40 years ago, Joseph Haselbauer has worked on nearly every order for cut glass that has gone to the White House.*

Mrs. Roosevelt was keenly aware of the prominence and prestige attached to the White House and every object within it. Rather than selling chipped china and glass at auction, as her predecessors had, she instructed her husband's aide, Major Archibald Butt, to smash it. She believed selling the items "cheapens the White House." As Butt reported:

> *In former years it was regarded as the property of the mistress of the White House, who would give it away . . . but Mrs. R. thinks that it should never be given away. . . . If it were sold by private bids it would create an awful howl in the press should it become known, and so I convinced all concerned that it should be broken up and scattered in the river, which will be done. When I think how I should value even one piece of it, it hurts to smash it, but I am sure it is the only right thing to do.*

William Howard Taft, inaugurated in 1909, entertained as often as the Roosevelts had, but First Lady Helen Herron Taft thought it was ridiculous to change china and glass patterns frequently. She used the Harrison glassware, and replacement orders during her husband's administration were small.

The election of Woodrow Wilson, inaugurated in 1913, saw many changes in social style. First Lady Ellen Axson Wilson was a reserved woman who attached little importance to public position or glamorous entertaining. The once elaborate White House dinners and receptions now became small, sedate affairs. But in August 1914, Mrs. Wilson died, and White House entertaining was curtailed. Late in 1915, Wilson married Edith Bolling Galt, and in 1916 social life returned to the White House.

In 1917 the president and Mrs. Wilson decided to purchase new china and glassware of American manufacture. But the designs for glassware supplied by Tiffany &

WINE AND THE WHITE HOUSE

Glasses, c. 1890–1900

Wineglasses are seen arranged in a semicircle around the top of a plate from the Grover Cleveland service as they would have been set for a formal dinner in the late nineteenth century.

Co. were not deemed satisfactory, and glassware in the Russian pattern was reordered for, as it turned out, the last time. The United States had entered World War I, and all White House receptions and dinners were canceled. They were not resumed after the Armistice in 1918 owing to the Wilsons' travels to the peace conference in Paris, followed by President Wilson's illness. The ratification in January 1919 of the Eighteenth Amendment, which proscribed the manufacture, importation, and sale of alcoholic beverages within the United States, also diminished the demand for glassware in the White House.

1901 WHITE HOUSE GLASSWARE INVENTORY
A Snapshot in Time

AS NEW ACQUISITIONS have been made and old acquisitions broken or discontinued, the White House glassware collection has been in constant evolution. But a detailed inventory made in 1901 provides a fascinating snapshot of the vast quantities and varied types of wineglasses in use at the White House at that time. The original inventory included attributions to the presidents who added the glassware to the collection. No invoice has been found, however, for the set of stemware designated "Roman border," so it is unclear which administration ordered the set between 1890 and the 1901 inventory. Considering the pared-down design of the Roman border set, it could be that the McKinleys were responsible for ordering the glassware, since during their term the Victorian taste for extravagant furnishings began to fade in favor of more simple, delicate styles. Regardless of who purchased them, the Roman border glasses remain an exquisite part of the White House collection today.

Included in the Roman border set listed in the inventory are twenty-five romer, or Roemer, glasses. A romer was an unusual type of European wineglass, a seventeenth-century designation that was rarely applied to American glass. This example was made c. 1750–1810 in the Netherlands and is engraved with vines and leaves.

PURCHASED DURING THE ADMINISTRATION OF PRESIDENT BENJAMIN HARRISON, COAT-OF-ARMS ENGRAVED

83	glasses, sherry, stem	92	glasses, claret
85	bowls, champagne	81	glasses, burgundy
69	tumblers, champagne	7	decanters
8	claret jugs, silver topped	4	decanters, cut glass

COAT OF ARMS ENGRAVED ON SAME
[MOST LIKELY THE LINCOLN PATTERN]

63	glasses, burgundy, ruby	19	glasses, liqueur
7	glasses, Rhine wine	28	glasses, claret
19	decanters, tall	81	glasses, sauterne, green
12	glasses, sauterne, green	24	glasses burgundy, ruby
60	glasses, sherry	54	glasses, madeira, ruby
63	glasses, port		

ENGRAVED WITH VINE
[SETS ORDERED BY PIERCE AND GRANT]

16	glasses, sherry, odd	13	glasses, sauterne, stem
18	glasses, sauterne, stem	4	glasses, Rhine wine
22	glasses, claret	6	decanters with handles
1	decanter, old	26	glasses, liqueur, stem, odd
11	glasses, sauterne, stem	64	glasses, white wine
25	glasses, claret	27	glasses, burgundy

ROMAN BORDER

24	glasses, liqueur, engraved, Roman border, old
64	glasses, sherry, engraved, Roman, old
43	glasses, champagne, engraved, Roman, old
14	glasses, claret, engraved, Roman border
35	glasses, burgundy, engraved, Roman border
25	romers, engraved with border

Claret glass, champagne glass, decanter, wineglass, and sherry glass, engraved by Joseph Haselbauer, C. Dorflinger & Sons, White Mills, Pennsylvania, 1891

The glass ordered during Benjamin Harrison's presidency was thicker and heavier to allow for the deeply cut Russian pattern, also called the "brilliant" style, a new industry standard, replacing the diamond or hobnail motif.

Wineglasses and champagne glass, United States, c. 1890–1900

A set of glasses in the White House collection is engraved with a hexagon pattern.

WINE AND THE WHITE HOUSE

**Wine bottle holder,
Meriden Britannia Co.,
Meriden, Connecticut,
c. 1904, silverplate**

Used by President Theodore
Roosevelt, the wine bottle
holder in the White House
collection is lined with
red velvet and inscribed
"President's House."

From Warren G. Harding to Donald J. Trump

1921 to the Twenty-First Century

Wine gave a sort of gallantry to their own failure.

—*F. Scott Fitzgerald*

DURING WORLD WAR I the American glass factories that had made fine tableware suffered from shortages of lead, a crucial ingredient in fine glass. Heavily cut glass had gone out of fashion, and lighter-weight glass, with less elaborate cutting and engraving, had gained popularity. As a result, companies had less work for their cutters and engravers and were forced to close. Prohibition brought new problems to the glass industry, as the market for expensive stemware sets nearly disappeared.

Although Warren G. Harding was known to serve liquor at private parties in the White House, no new glassware was ordered. First Lady Florence Kling Harding, however, did receive a gift set of gilded glassware in the "Dragon" pattern from the Central Glass Works of Wheeling, West Virginia. A trade publication described the set as "etched and filled in with gold. It is gold-rimmed and gold-stemmed, and each piece has a 35-point star on the bottom." The Hardings did a great deal of entertaining, and the gilded service was used at State Dinners, which were even larger than they had been in the past—sometimes hosting more than one hundred guests. The glassware was Mrs. Harding's personal property, however, and returned with her to Ohio after President Harding died in 1923. Some pieces have since been donated to the White House.

Following Harding's death, his vice president, Calvin Coolidge, acceded to the presidency. Prohibition was strictly observed in his administration, as well as during the presidency of his successor, Herbert Hoover. Both administrations maintained active schedules of formal dinners but ordered no new glassware, ensuring that the Harrison Russian-pattern glassware remained in use. The Hoovers did order some inexpensive open-stock glassware cut in a diamond pattern by Bryce Brothers of Mount Pleasant, Pennsylvania. It was repeatedly reordered and used daily at the White House until the mid-1950s.

Franklin D. Roosevelt took office in 1933 in the depths of the Great Depression. The glass service ordered by the Harrisons in 1891 was still in use, but First Lady Eleanor Roosevelt found that the Russian-pattern decanters had been sent to storage because of Prohibition. When the Eighteenth Amendment was repealed that same year, the Roosevelts began to serve wine at State Dinners, using the Russian- and Lincoln-pattern sets together.

Mrs. Roosevelt reordered the Hoover glassware for family use, and for State events she ordered a pattern by T. G. Hawkes that was first marketed as "Venetian" and then later renamed "White House," adding a Coat of Arms. Henrietta Nesbitt, the White House housekeeper, recalled that Hawkes had trouble finding experienced engravers. The first samples were not faithful to the design that the Roosevelts had

Cocktail glass detail

The American eagle insignia surrounded by stars was engraved on the set of glasses ordered for the presidential yacht USS *Williamsburg* in 1945.

requested, so the president sent them back. The insignia that was finally engraved was a simplified version of the one designed for the Lincolns in 1861. According to Nesbitt, President Roosevelt had intended to spend no more than $60 a dozen for stemware, so the choices were limited. Ultimately, the Roosevelts decided to forgo more expensive hollow stemware in favor of plain saucer champagne glasses. Cordial, sherry, and wineglasses were also purchased.

In 1940, when the 1939 New York World's Fair closed, the White House acquired more glassware free of charge. The Libbey Glass Company had made a set of glassware specially for the Federal Building at the fair in a shape called "Embassy." The stems for this set were pressed, and the glass was acid-etched with a stylized version of the Great Seal. The Libbey Company felt the White House was the most appropriate home for the Great Seal–emblazoned glassware and provided a set that included eight sizes of stemware and three sizes of tumblers, with nine to ten dozen pieces of each size. The delicate pieces were mostly used at formal luncheons at the White House during the ensuing years.

Vice President Harry S. Truman became president upon Roosevelt's death in 1945, and, during his administration, obtaining replacements for the Hawkes set became difficult. In the 1930s, when the glass had first been ordered, only a few firms were producing hand-cut and specially engraved stemware, in contrast to the several hundred that were doing such work when the Russian-pattern set was ordered in the 1890s. After World War II only Steuben Glass and T. G. Hawkes & Company, both in Corning, were producing highest-quality hand-blown lead-glass stemware with special cutting and engraving. As demand dropped, the glass became much more expensive, leading to a further decline in demand and eventually to a reduced supply. In 1955 replacements were ordered from Hawkes — the last to be purchased from the firm.

The last of the eagle-engraved sets of glasses was ordered in 1945 for the presidential yacht USS *Williamsburg*. Steuben Glass filled the special order. Champagne glasses in two shapes, white wine glasses, cordials, old-fashioneds, cocktail glasses, highball

Wine basket, American, silver, c. 1957

Woven with silver wire, this wine basket was likely used during the Eisenhower presidency to hold bottles of wine on the table during informal meals. The wine bottle would have been placed on its side and secured by two loops over the basket opening. The handle at the top would have facilitated pouring.

WINE AND THE WHITE HOUSE

glasses, pilsners, jiggers, decanters, cocktail shakers, and other items were all engraved with an American eagle surrounded by stars. When the *Williamsburg* was decommissioned in 1953, the U.S. Navy gave three of the remaining glasses to the White House and disposed of the rest.

Dwight D. Eisenhower began his first term in January 1953. When replacements for the Roosevelt set of glassware were needed in 1955, they were supplied by Hawkes. But by 1958, Hawkes no longer had engravers who could do the work, so the White House ordered the replacements through an importing firm, Royal York China. They were made in West Germany—marking the first time since President Monroe's term that the White House had purchased European glass for a State Service. The order included four dozen each of champagne, red wine, white wine, and sherry glasses, and the insignia was acid etched rather than copper-wheel engraved.

When the Kennedys entered the White House in January 1961, they acquired new glassware. Grateful to the voters of West Virginia who had given Kennedy a big win in the Democratic primary, they ordered glass made in that state. For the first time in White House history, a pattern with no engraving was ordered for State Dinners. The Morgantown Glassware Guild filled the order, which included six dozen each of red and white wineglasses and tulip-shaped champagne glasses. To a suggestion that more elaborate glassware would have been better suited to the White House, Mrs. Kennedy replied, "I really love my West Virginia wineglasses. . . . Also, I really don't mind having plain glasses without a seal. It is almost a relief. Our flatware and china are all engraved."

At $11.60 a dozen, the pieces were an inexpensive State Service. The glass itself contained no lead and was machine-made rather than hand-blown, two factors that accounted for the low price. (Lead glass, commonly advertised as "crystal" and used in all the previous White House services, is finer in quality and sparkles more than non-lead glass.) The basic design of the new set was simple, relying on clean lines rather than decoration for its appeal.

Both the Morgantown Glassware Guild and Fostoria—a Moundsville, West Virginia, firm that purchased the Morgantown molds and patterns when the guild went out of business in 1971—marketed the pattern as "President's House." Fostoria, too, eventually closed down, but not before it supplied replacements to the set in 1974, during the Nixon administration.

President Richard M. Nixon ordered a small set of glassware for his family's use in the Family Dining Room at the White House. The set was made in France at the Compagnie des Cristalleries de Saint Louis in 1969. The goblets, along with the red wine, white wine, and liqueur glasses, are in the "Chantilly" pattern selected by Mrs. Nixon. They have round bases, and the bowls are cut with a stylized sunburst pattern.

In 1981, during the administration of Ronald Reagan, the White House received as a gift 131 pieces of Steuben's "Strawberry Mansion" glassware. The ornate set, made sometime between 1931 and 1939, stands in striking contrast to the West Virginia glass. It is used for private lunches and dinners.

Recent administrations have chosen not to order official glassware sets, instead relying on modern glassware that is not part of the White House collection. The historic glassware, unable to be replaced, is used sparingly for smaller dinners or lunches. Because there is no complete glassware service in the White House collection today, State Dinners and other large official functions must showcase America's fine wines in glasses rented from catering services—until another president decides to add to the collection.

There comes a time in every woman's life when the only thing that helps is a glass of champagne.

*—Bette Davis
as Kit Marlowe*

Wineglass and champagne glass, Central Glass Works, Wheeling, West Virginia, 1921

A gilded glassware set decorated in the "Dragon" pattern with a stylized "H" integrated into the design was gifted to First Lady Florence Kling Harding by the maker (opposite).

Champagne glass and cordial glass, Bryce Brothers, Mount Pleasant, Pennsylvania, 1933–34

First ordered during the Hoover presidency in 1929, the glassware (above) was later reordered by First Lady Eleanor Roosevelt in 1933 and used daily at the White House until the mid-1950s.

WINE AND THE WHITE HOUSE

Champagne glass and wineglass, T. G. Hawkes & Company, Corning, New York, 1937; cordial glass and dessert wineglass, West Germany, 1959

For official State functions, First Lady Eleanor Roosevelt ordered a set of glasses in the "Venetian" pattern, later renamed the "White House" pattern (opposite), with a detailed copper-engraved American eagle insignia (right top). When replacements were needed during President Dwight D. Eisenhower's second term, U.S. engravers could no longer do the work. Instead the glasses were made in West Germany with a less detailed acid-etched insignia (right bottom) and imported through the Royal York China company.

WINE AND THE WHITE HOUSE

Cordial glass, sherry glass, dessert wineglass, dinner wineglass, and cocktail glass, Libbey Glass Company, Toledo, Ohio, 1939

Libbey made this glassware for the Federal Building at the 1939 New York World's Fair in the "Embassy" shape, reminiscent of architecture. The company donated the glasses to the White House at the end of the fair. They were used for formal luncheons.

Dessert wineglass detail

The "Embassy" shape of the World's Fair glassware, made in the Art Deco style, has pressed-glass stemware and a stylized version of the Great Seal.

Sherry glass, cocktail glass, and champagne glass, Steuben Glass, Corning, New York, 1945

A set of glasses ordered for the presidential yacht USS *Williamsburg* was given by the U.S. Navy to the White House collection when the yacht was decommissioned in 1953.

Cocktail glass detail

The eagle insignia and stars were engraved on the glassware ordered for the presidential yacht.

Champagne glass and wineglasses, Morgantown Glass Guild, Morgantown, West Virginia, or Fostoria Glass Company, Moundsville, West Virginia, 1961–71

For the first time a set of completely unadorned glassware was ordered for State Dinners by First Lady Jacqueline Kennedy.

Liqueur glass and wineglasses, Compagnie des Cristalleries de Saint Louis, France, 1969

Glassware in the "Chantilly" pattern was selected by First Lady Pat Nixon for informal family use.

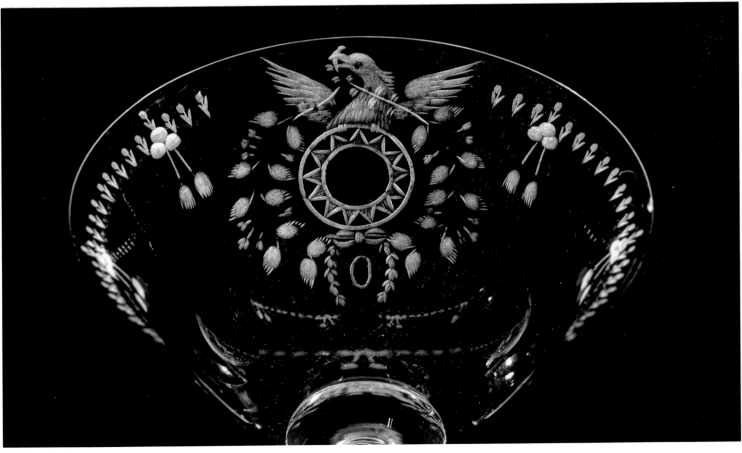

WINE AND THE WHITE HOUSE

Sherry glass, cordial glass, wineglass, and champagne glass, Steuben Glass, Corning, New York, 1931–39

Given as a gift to the White House during the Reagan presidency, this set of 131 pieces of "Strawberry Mansion" pattern glassware was used for private lunches and dinners (opposite).

Rented glassware

Rather than ordering new glassware, late twentieth- and early twenty-first-century presidents have preserved historic collections and relied instead on caterers to supply glassware for large functions. Elegant gold-banded glassware adorned the table at the State Dinner hosted by President Donald J. Trump for French President Emmanuel Macron in 2018 (right).

CHAPTER FIVE

PRESIDENTIAL TOASTS

A HIGH POINT of any State Dinner or diplomatic event is the exchange of toasts between the president and his foreign counterpart. Today, most toasts are a delicate balance of pleasantries, tributes to the other country, and, perhaps, a brief reference to the purpose of the meeting, following scripts that are carefully prepared and thoroughly vetted. But while these moments are now highly orchestrated, they have emerged from a long—and often surprisingly unrefined—tradition.

The custom of drinking to another's health dates back to antiquity, when the practice was employed to pay tribute to present company, absent friends, legendary heroes, and ancient gods. As Homer recounts in the *Iliad*, Odysseus raised a cup of wine to the health of Achilles. In ancient Rome, banquet guests would pass a large drinking cup around the table wishing good health to the person receiving it. The Roman Senate even passed a law stipulating that all diners had to drink to the health of Caesar Augustus at every meal.

It was from Roman custom that the term "toast" evolved—a reference to the practice of placing a piece of burnt bread in the communal wine goblet to absorb impurities and improve flavor. As the Romans' empire expanded, the toasting custom was adopted and spread through much of their territory, including Britain.

Though toasting was a hallmark of civilization for the Romans, it was also practiced by their barbarian enemies. As he prepared an attack to plunder Roman territory in the fifth century, Attila the Hun reportedly offered multiple toasts with each course of a long meal. Toasting was even more brutal in the Scottish Highlands, where, until the eleventh century, triumphant warriors would drink from the skulls

President Ronald Reagan makes a State Dinner toast to Australian Prime Minister Malcolm Fraser, 1981.

of their fallen enemies. This is believed to be the origin of the Scandinavian toasting term "Skoal!"

By the seventeenth century, toasting in England had become so commonplace that imbibing without toasting the health of another was considered, in the words of one contemporary, an uncivilized form of "drinking on the sly." Toasting became so prevalent—and eventually so excessive—that concerns arose in the eighteenth century that toasts were getting out of hand and distracting from meals. The solution was to establish the role of a "toastmaster"—a person whose responsibility it was to preside over important events, guiding and proposing toasts while preserving an atmosphere of gentility and ensuring that all guests had an opportunity to participate.

Meanwhile, on the other side of the Atlantic, the response to over-the-top toasting was more heavy-handed. In 1634, Massachusetts officials, alarmed by the colonists' alcohol consumption, passed a law banning toasts. It proved largely ineffective and was repealed just over a decade later.

Following the Revolutionary War, a tradition took hold whereby official events would honor the thirteen states with thirteen separate toasts. These verbal tributes were often followed by cannon volleys or patriotic songs. At a banquet marking the conclusion of his presidency, George Washington took the custom one step further by adding a fourteenth toast to "sufficient powers to Congress for general purposes," a phrase he sometimes invoked when expressing his preference for a robust federal government.

Formal gatherings during Thomas Jefferson's presidency, by contrast, were marked by a conspicuous lack of toasting. As one of his guests wrote, "The dinners are neat and plentiful, and no healths are drunk at table, nor are any toasts or sentiments given after dinner." Once he was out of office, however, Jefferson relaxed his rule against toasting. At a dinner in the unfinished Rotunda of the University of Virginia, during the traditional thirteen toasts to the original colonies, Jefferson downed two glasses of wine during the tribute to his—and the university's—home state.

What was perhaps America's "golden age" of toasting arrived in the late nineteenth century, when public officials and dinner hosts were judged by the eloquence of their tableside remarks. Magazine articles and even books were written highlighting outstanding toasts and offering tips to aspiring toast-makers. But the passage of the Eighteenth Amendment brought an end to this era, as Prohibition outlawed the open consumption of alcohol. Plenty still took place underground, however, and when toasts did occur, they were often criticisms of Prohibition itself. One popular anti-Volstead Act toast went:

Here's to Prohibition,
The devil take it!
They've stole our wine,
So now we make it!

In the era of the modern presidency, ceremonial toasts have generally been brief and warm tributes to begin or conclude official events. But not every leader has seen fit to follow this custom. During his 1975 State Visit, Zambian President Kenneth Kaunda responded to President Gerald R. Ford's short, gracious toast with an extensive summary of his nation's foreign-policy positions that lasted more than twenty minutes. Three years later, Yugoslavia's Marshal Josip Broz Tito offered up what the popular historian Paul Dickson describes as "a rambling forty-minute dissertation on his views of the international political scene." And in 1979, during Jimmy

Carter's visit to Mexico City, the toasts devolved into what some guests perceived as an exchange of insults. President José López Portillo began with a wide-ranging indictment of the United States; President Carter responded with a reference to Montezuma's revenge.

Eventually the State Department had seen enough. In order to avoid incoherent or unfriendly toasts, and to establish parity in duration, in the early 1980s the department's Office of Protocol began recommending that State Dinner toasts not exceed three minutes.

Until 1979, the exchange of toasts at State Dinners occurred at the end of the meal. But at a White House dinner honoring the president of Mexico, President Carter apparently jumped the gun, beginning his toast at the start of the evening. The wine had not yet been poured, so the president used his water glass. As the service staff scrambled to pour the wine for the assembled guests, President Carter returned to the podium with his wineglass in hand to, in his words, "make sure that the toast is authenticated."

Although this adjustment to toasting's place in the State Dinner sequence of events may have been accidental, presidents starting with William J. Clinton have adhered to the custom. As President Carter said of the switch, "When the toast comes first you don't have to sit through the dinner worrying about the speech you have to give afterward." Presidents have reason to be nervous. Even though their toasts have long been the careful work of speechwriters, gaffes do happen. In a toast to Egyptian President Anwar Sadat in 1975, for example, President Ford raised his glass to pay tribute to the "great people and the government of Israel. . . . Egypt, excuse me." And when President Ronald Reagan visited President João Figueiredo of Brazil during a trip to South America in 1982, he replied to his host's remarks by raising his glass to the "people of Bolivia."

On the positive side, President Reagan's seven-hundred-word toast at a 1984 dinner honoring Chinese Premier Zhao Ziyang led to a nuclear cooperation treaty between China and the United States. Opponents of the agreement criticized President Reagan for practicing "diplomacy by dinner toast." Yet the reality is that all presidential toasts serve a crucial diplomatic function, setting the tone for State and Official Visits and the important conversations with foreign leaders that are the centerpiece of these exchanges. As the words and images of historic White House toasts reveal, how America's leaders choose to carry on this long-standing tradition can have significant influence over their presidential legacies.

This is the last time I shall drink to your health as a public man. I do it with sincerity, wishing you all possible happiness.

—*George Washington*

**George Washington
The President's House
Philadelphia**

Though his toasts were not captured by an image made in his own time, President Washington was later imagined raising a glass to his successor John Adams by an illustrator for *Harper's Weekly* in 1899 (above). Entitled "Washington's Farewell Dinner: His Toast to the President Elect," the drawing depicts Washington standing opposite John Adams as he gives his toast.

**George Washington
Mount Vernon, Virginia**

A *Harper's Weekly* illustration (opposite) published a century after Washington's death captures the first president on his last birthday, February 22, 1799, which coincided with the day his wife's granddaughter, Eleanor ("Nelly") Parke Custis, married Lawrence Lewis. Washington and his guests are seen raising their wineglasses to the bride and groom in the celebration held in the dining room of Washington's home at Mount Vernon.

Andrew Jackson
Indian Queen Hotel, Washington, D.C.
April 13, 1830

"Our Federal Union, it must be Preserved," was given at a Jefferson Day Dinner in 1830. A toast to the president himself was included in a list of ten patriotic toasts distributed in a broadside the same year: "Andrew Jackson, President of the United States. Honest in heart, firm in purpose, fearless in patriotic acts, and true to the best interests of his country—while he asserts the rights of American citizens, he will never compromise our National honor, his name as the Patriot, the Sage and the Hero will be held in grateful remembrance in all coming time."

Our Federal Union, it must be Preserved.

—Andrew Jackson

DRINK TO YOUR FAVORITES.

Election of 1884

A caricature of the 1884 presidential candidates invites the viewer to "Drink to Your Favorites." Democrat Grover Cleveland (far right toasting his running mate, Thomas A. Hendricks) defeated Republican James G. Blaine (far left toasting his running mate, John A. Logan) in the election.

William McKinley
November 1900

A cartoon published in the November 1900 issue of *Puck* magazine depicts President McKinley celebrating his reelection by thanking his opponent, a dejected William Jennings Bryan. The caption reads: "Let us conclude our Thanksgiving Dinner with a toast to the man who made it so easy for us!" The illustration shows President William McKinley standing beside his vice president, Theodore Roosevelt.

A toast to the man who made it so easy for us!

—*William McKinley*

The years in front of us are going to be just as dramatic and are going to witness the same kind of changes we have in the past twenty. And yet, with all of these changes certain to come upon us, we must keep a steady mind and a steady heart.

—*Dwight D. Eisenhower*

Dwight D. Eisenhower
The Philippines, June 15, 1960

At a dinner given in his honor, President Eisenhower proposed a toast to his host, President Carlos P. Garcia, recalling, "There are some of you at this dinner that attended a somewhat similar occasion in this very spot just a bit over 20 years ago. There was a *despedida* given to my wife and me by President Quezon. Europe was at war . . . I think we should stop and recognize how this pace, let's say the curve of civilization—has leaped forward in leaps and bounds in these very few years. Even if we go back to the beginning of the Industrial Revolution, we still have a pace that, compared to the prior years, was like taking a race horse and comparing it to a snail. This means, I think, that the years in front of us are going to be just as dramatic and are going to witness the same kind of changes we have in the past twenty. And yet, with all of these changes certain to come upon us, we must keep a steady mind and a steady heart."

**John F. Kennedy
The White House
April 17, 1961**

In a luncheon toast to the long-serving Prime Minister Constantine Karamanlis of Greece, President Kennedy observed, "Someone once said everyone is either an Athenian or a Spartan—in any case, we are all Greeks in the great sense of recognizing the wellspring from which all of our efforts began. I am sure that sometimes the Greeks get tired of hearing about ancient history, because they are concerned with making history today. But we look to ancient Greece for inspiration, and we look to modern Greece for comradeship." President and Mrs. Kennedy are seen greeting Prime Minister Karamanlis and his wife Amalia Karamanlis.

We look to ancient Greece for inspiration, and we look to modern Greece for comradeship.
—John F. Kennedy

John F. Kennedy
Paris, France
May 31, 1961

In a toast to President Charles de Gaulle at Élysée Palace, President Kennedy observed, "It is naturally a great honor for any President of the United States to come to Paris. . . . As Frenchmen, I know that you take satisfaction that people around the world invoke your great motto of Liberty, Equality and Fraternity. What counts, of course, is not merely the words, but the meaning behind them. We believe in liberty, equality and fraternity. We believe in life and liberty and the pursuit of happiness. . . . We believe in the significance behind these great ideas. Therefore, I think it quite natural that in the most difficult decade of the 1960s, France and the United States should be once again associated together."

We believe in liberty, equality and fraternity. We believe in life and liberty and the pursuit of happiness.

—*John F. Kennedy*

This is becoming a sort of eating place for artists. But they never ask us out!

—*John F. Kennedy*

**John F. Kennedy
The White House
May 11, 1962**

In toasting President Charles de Gaulle at a dinner in honor of André Malraux, the French minister of cultural affairs, President Kennedy reflected, "This is becoming a sort of eating place for artists. But they never ask us out! . . . You know, one of the great myths of American life is that nothing is pleasanter or easier than lying around all day and painting a picture or writing a book and leading a rather easy life. In my opinion, the ultimate in self-discipline is a creative work. Those of us who work in an office every day are actually the real gentle livers of American society."

**While geography
has made
us neighbors,
tradition has made
us friends.**

—*John F. Kennedy*

**John F. Kennedy
Mexico City, Mexico
June 29, 1962**

Before sharing a toast with President Adolfo López Mateos of Mexico, President Kennedy remarked: "It is with great pleasure and high regard that I have crossed the peaceful border which separates our two nations. For Mexico and the United States share more than a common frontier. We share a common heritage of revolution, a common dedication to liberty, a common determination to preserve in these great days the blessings of freedom and to extend its fruits to all. While geography has made us neighbors, tradition has made us friends."

**Lyndon B. Johnson
The White House
February 14, 1967**

Raising a State Dinner toast to Haile Selassie I, emperor of Ethiopia, President Johnson reflected, "It is a high privilege tonight to honor one of this century's most courageous, farsighted, and respected statesmen who has earned an indelible place in the hearts of men everywhere. Monarch of the oldest Christian kingdom and an ancient civilization, you, Your Majesty, personify to us the eternal spirit of devotion to freedom and independence of your Ethiopian people. The essence of the Ethiopian character was put in your stirring words many years ago: 'With God's help, we have always stood proud and free upon our native mountains.'"

It is a high privilege tonight to honor one of this century's most courageous, farsighted, and respected statesmen who has earned an indelible place in the hearts of men everywhere.
—*Lyndon B. Johnson*

252

Clink!

AS TOASTS ARE MADE at White House dinners, guests typically turn to the dinner companions seated next to them to gently touch wineglasses. This "clinking" lends a festive air to presidential gatherings, but where did the practice come from?

There are three main theories about the origins of the clinking custom. The first supposes that, centuries ago, Europeans thought the sound from the tap of glasses resembled the pealing of church bells, and so clinking was a means of banishing the Devil from celebratory events.

The second theory also claims that clinking is a centuries-old custom, the product of an era when warring foes would use feasts as opportunities to "off" their enemies. Tapping glasses, the thinking goes, was a means of ensuring that some contents of one party's glass would splash into the other's—providing a deterrent against poisoning a rival's drink.

The third theory—perhaps more popular with oenophiles—is that clinking emerged as a way to enrich the wine experience. A wine's color appeals to our sense of sight; bouquet engages smell; and flavor appeals to taste. The clink is wine-drinking's offering to the ear.

Whatever the reason, the gentle ringing of wine-filled glasses has become the traditional sound of welcome for guests at White House social events.

We drink to your health, having in mind . . . the desire of the two strongest nations in the world . . . to work together for peace.

—Richard M. Nixon

Observe good faith and justice toward all nations. Cultivate peace and harmony with all.

—Richard M. Nixon quoting George Washington

**Richard M. Nixon
Beijing, China
February 25, 1972**

Toasting Chinese Premier Zhou Enlai on his historic trip to China, President Nixon remarked, "Mr. Prime Minister, you have noted that the plane which brought us here is named the *Spirit of '76*. Just this week, we have celebrated in America the birth of George Washington . . . our first President. He bade farewell at the close of his term with these words to his countrymen: 'Observe good faith and justice toward all nations. Cultivate peace and harmony with all.'"

**Richard M. Nixon
Soviet Embassy,
Washington, D.C.
June 21, 1973**

Offering a dinner toast to Leonid Brezhnev, general secretary of the Central Committee of the Communist Party of the Soviet Union, President Nixon said, "As we drink to your health, we drink to it not simply in the casual way that one raises a glass of champagne, be it California or New York or French or, in this case, Russian champagne, but we drink to your health, having in mind what you have said and what I have tried to reaffirm: the desire of the two strongest nations in the world, through their top leaders, to work together for peace."

**Gerald R. Ford
Imperial Palace
Tokyo, Japan
November 19, 1974**

In offering a toast to his host Emperor Hirohito, President Ford began, "I am honored to be the guest of Your Imperial Majesties. . . .The first state visit of an American President to Japan is an occasion of very great importance to all Americans. . . . Though separated by the broadest of oceans, Your Majesty, we have achieved between our two nations the closest of friendships."

Though separated by the broadest of oceans, Your Majesty, we have achieved between our two nations the closest of friendships.
—*Gerald R. Ford*

**Ronald Reagan
The White House
December 8, 1987**

In his State Dinner toast to General Secretary Mikhail Gorbachev of the Soviet Union, President Reagan observed, "In our public statements and in our meetings together, Mr. General Secretary, we've always paid each other the compliment of candor. . . . Man's most fundamental beliefs about the relationship of the citizen to the state and of man to his creator lie at the core of the competition between our two countries. History has indeed endowed our relationship with a profound meaning. . . . There is more work to be done, and time and history are marching on. . . . To your health. *Za vashe zdorovye.*"

History has indeed endowed our relationship with a profound meaning. . . . There is more work to be done, and time and history are marching on. . . . To your health.
—*Ronald Reagan*

We honor your courage and celebrate the new possibilities now open to us.
—*George H. W. Bush*

George H. W. Bush
The White House
March 6, 1990

In a State Dinner toast to his guest, Prime Minister Giulio Andreotti of Italy, President Bush reflected, "I am reminded of a story concerning America's national pastime. It seems that great Italian tenor, Enrico Caruso, was asked by a group of American reporters what he thought of Babe Ruth. Caruso, ever polite, replied that he didn't know, because unfortunately he had never heard her sing. . . . But most important of all, there is perhaps the toughest issue between our two nations, a meeting which will take place this summer in Italy. And our side has already made bold advances against other nations involved, but we must be allowed to compete on a level playing field. And that's right, I'm talking about the 1990 World Cup in soccer."

George H. W. Bush
The White House
June 16, 1992

In offering a State Dinner toast to President Boris Yeltsin of Russia, President Bush said, "Mr. President, you've been described many times as a maverick, a word coined in the American heartland to capture the independent streak that sets some individuals apart from the crowd. Well, I think our fellow Texans Jim Baker and Bob Strauss would agree you possess a certain spirit that you find on the plains of the West. And tonight we honor your courage and celebrate the new possibilities now open to us."

**William J. Clinton
London, England
November 29, 1995**

In toasting his host, Prime
Minister John Major of the
United Kingdom, President
Clinton explained, "We have
a relationship that is enduring
and very special. If I might
paraphrase one of my very
favorite British citizens, 007,
our relationship can never
be stirred nor shaken. It will
always be there; it will always
be strong."

**Our relationship
can never be stirred
nor shaken. It will
always be there;
it will always be
strong.**

—*William J. Clinton*

**William J. Clinton
The White House
December 31, 1999**

President Clinton gave three toasts on the eve of the Millennium—the first to his dinner guests, the second to his wife, Hillary, and the third toast, he said, "is, in a way, the most daunting, because I'm supposed to say something profound to a thousand years of history in two or three minutes. In the State of the Union I get a whole hour to talk about a single year, and usually I run over. Tonight we rise to the mountaintop of a new Millennium. Behind us we see a great expanse of American experience and before us vast frontiers of possibility still to be explored."

Tonight we rise to the mountaintop of a new Millennium. Behind us we see a great expanse of American experience and before us vast frontiers of possibility still to be explored.

—*William J. Clinton*

William J. Clinton
The White House
November 9, 2000

At a gala evening celebrating the two-hundredth anniversary of the White House, President Clinton toasted the former presidents and first ladies who joined him for dinner. "Good evening, Mrs. Johnson, President and Mrs. Ford, President and Mrs. Carter, President and Mrs. Bush, distinguished guests. It has been said that an invitation to the White House to dinner is one of the highest compliments a President can bestow on anyone. Tonight Hillary and I would amend that to say that an even higher compliment has been bestowed on us by your distinguished presence this evening. In the entire two hundred years of the White House's history, never before have this many former Presidents and First Ladies gathered in this great room. . . . In ways both large and small, each and every one of you has cast your light upon this house and left it and our country brighter for it. For that, Hillary and I and all Americans owe you a great debt of gratitude. I salute you and all those yet to grace these halls with the words of the very first occupant of the White House, John Adams, who said, 'I pray to heaven to bestow the best of blessings on this house and all that shall hereafter inhabit it. May none but the honest and wise rule under this roof.' Ladies and gentlemen, I ask you to join me in a toast to Mrs. Johnson, President and Mrs. Ford, President and Mrs. Carter, President and Mrs. Bush for their honest and wise service to the people while they inhabited this house."

Every one of you has cast your light upon this house and left it and our country brighter for it.

—William J. Clinton

**George W. Bush
The White House
November 2, 2005**

Raising a toast to Charles, Prince of Wales, President Bush began, "Your visit is a reminder of the unique and enduring bond between the United Kingdom and the United States. Americans know that we have no greater friend than the United Kingdom. . . . Nowhere are those shared values more nobly expressed than in our common commitment to expanding freedom in this world."

Americans know that we have no greater friend than the United Kingdom. . . . Nowhere are those shared values more nobly expressed than in our common commitment to expanding freedom in this world.
—George W. Bush

George W. Bush
The White House, February 25, 2007

In offering a toast to the nation's governors at an annual dinner in their honor, President Bush, a former governor of Texas, began, "This is really one of the dinners that we look forward to the most. And we welcome the governors and their spouses. . . . There's life after being a governor."

There's life after
being a governor.
—George W. Bush

Barack Obama
The White House
April 28, 2015

President Obama toasted Prime Minister
Shinzō Abe of Japan with a lighthearted
reference to the wine. "On my last visit to
Tokyo, the Prime Minister and I went to what
is reputed to be the best sushi place in Tokyo.
And I have to confess that you could not have
the sushi if you did not have some excellent
sake to go with it. . . . So tonight we're breaking
with tradition a little bit and serving sake from
Shinzō's home Prefecture of Yamaguchi. And
please enjoy yourselves, but not too much."

We're breaking with
tradition a little
bit and serving sake.
. . . Please enjoy
yourselves, but not
too much.

—*Barack Obama*

**Barack Obama
The White House
March 10, 2016**

In toasting Prime Minister
Justin Trudeau of Canada
at a State Dinner in his honor,
President Obama recalled
a previous toast. "Now, we
intend to have fun tonight.
But not too much. If things
get out of hand, remember
that the Prime Minister
used to work as a bouncer.
This is true. . . . Forty-four
years ago, President Nixon
made a visit to Ottawa. And
he was hosted by Prime
Minister Pierre Trudeau. . . .
'Tonight we'll dispense with
the formalities,' President
Nixon said. 'I'd like to propose
a toast to the future Prime
Minister of Canada, Justin
Pierre Trudeau.' He was four
months at the time."

**We intend to have
fun tonight.**

—Barack Obama

May our friendship grow even deeper, may our kinship grow even stronger, and may our sacred liberty never die.

—Donald J. Trump

Donald J. Trump
The White House
April 24, 2018

Offering a State Dinner toast to President Emmanuel Macron of France, President Trump observed, "Tonight we celebrate nearly two-and-a-half centuries of friendship between the United States and France. . . . The veins that link our nations are forged in battle, strengthened through trial, and defined by the timeless principles that make us who and what we are: respect for life, love for our neighbors, pride in our traditions, defense of our heritage, and reverence for the rights bestowed on us through grace and the glory of God. . . . May our friendship grow even deeper, may our kinship grow even stronger, and may our sacred liberty never die."

**Donald J. Trump
The White House
September 20, 2019**

Raising a State Dinner toast to the prime minister of Australia, Scott Morrison, President Trump began, "Tonight we celebrate more than a century of loyal and devoted friendship between the United States and Australia. . . . Our two countries were born out of a vast wilderness, settled by the adventurers and pioneers whose fierce self-reliance shaped our destiny. . . . May our heroes forever inspire us, may our heritage always guide us, may our values always unite us, and may our nations always remain the home of the proud and the brave and the free."

Tonight we celebrate more than a century of loyal and devoted friendship. . . . May our nations always remain the home of the proud and the brave and the free.
—Donald J. Trump

Dinner

in honor of His Excellency

Nicolas Sarkozy

President of the French Republic

Maine Lobster Bisque

Vermouth Cream

HDV CHARDONNAY "CARNEROS" 2004

Elysian Farm Lamb

with Heirloom Tomato Fondue

Ragoût of Green Beans, Chanterelles

and Caramelized Shallots

Sweet Potato Casserole

DOMINUS "NAPA VALLEY" 2004

Salad of White and Green Asparagus

Peppercress and Mâche

White Balsamic Vinaigrette

La Fayette's Legacy

THE WHITE HOUSE

CHAPTER SIX

ON THE MENU

THE FOLLOWING PROGRESSION OF WHITE HOUSE dinner menus—more than one hundred spanning more than one hundred years—offers a wealth of interesting insights. One is the diminishing amount and array of foods served, from eight courses (some with multiple dishes) down to four or three. Another is the introduction of hand-lettered menu cards, souvenirs that guests may take with them after dinner. Today these are prepared in the White House Calligraphy Office, a descendant of the Office of Social Entertainments established in 1881. Since the mid-1960s, menu cards have been embossed, in gold, with the Presidential Seal, but before that menu cards were infrequent or have not survived. Other phenomena that can be observed are the enduring influence of French cuisine (the Kennedys even wrote their menus in French) and the persistence of Brie cheese, bibb lettuce, and, in the early years, especially, celery.

But the relevance of the menus for this book is in what they reveal about the wines that were selected for special guests, whether heads of state, heads of government, or individuals—both international and American—who are honored for their achievements. The menus reproduced here are by no means comprehensive of all the official dinners at the White House, just a representative selection. Nevertheless, it seems apparent that until the 1950s wine did not get much attention on menus at all. Even for a dinner honoring Winston Churchill in 1949 (for which there is only a typed working list), sherry, white wine, and champagne are penciled in, almost as an afterthought. Printed menus became standard in President Dwight D. Eisenhower's administration. For his first State Dinner, October 28, 1953, sherry, white wine, and champagne are listed. Later, vineyard and vintage are named. For President John F. Kennedy's dinner for Nobel Prize winners, the three wines—all French—set a high standard, and from this time the menus almost always show three wines served with three courses.

With President Lyndon B. Johnson, California wines make their appearance. They almost disappear during the years of President Richard M. Nixon, who much preferred French wines, though he did serve California wines when hosting dinners overseas. California wines return in abundance with President Ronald Reagan, the former governor of California who took a special interest in wines from his home state, and he began the practice of seeking advice on wine selections from specialists. The number of State Dinners declined following the Reagan years, even as the care with which wines were selected and served—even showcased—remained important.

As the following pages attest, some of the wines at White House events were selected to please the guests and some to please the president. Collectively, the menus portray changing fashions for foods and wines and their presentation in the President's House.

Embossed with a gold Presidential Seal, a hand-calligraphed menu is placed to welcome the president's guests to their seats at State Dinners. For the dinner for President Nicolas Sarkozy of France in November 2007, President and Mrs. George W. Bush selected three California wines made by French winemakers.

Dîner du 19 Avril.

Consommé printanier à la royale.

Petites bouchées à la Cardinale.

Filets de bass à la Normande.

Filets de bœuf à la Richelieu.

Pains de volaille à l' Impériale.
Côtelettes d'agneau aux petits-pois.
Cimbales d'Olives garnies de filets de pigeons.
Cerrines de foies-gras à la Lucullus.

Punch au Kirsch.

Faisans piqués garnis de bécasses aux cressons.
Salade de laitue.

Asperges en branches, sauce à la crème.
Ramequins de dijon au parmesan.

Crèmes diplomate au marasquin.
Gelées d'Oranges garnies de fraises.

Déssert.

Café.

April 19, 1877

During the nineteenth-century temperance movement, President and Mrs. Rutherford B. Hayes generally abstained from alcohol but the service of wine remained an important element of official hospitality. For the sake of diplomacy, the customary six wines were served at the State Dinner for the Grand Duke Alexis, son of the Russian czar, although they are not listed on the menu card.

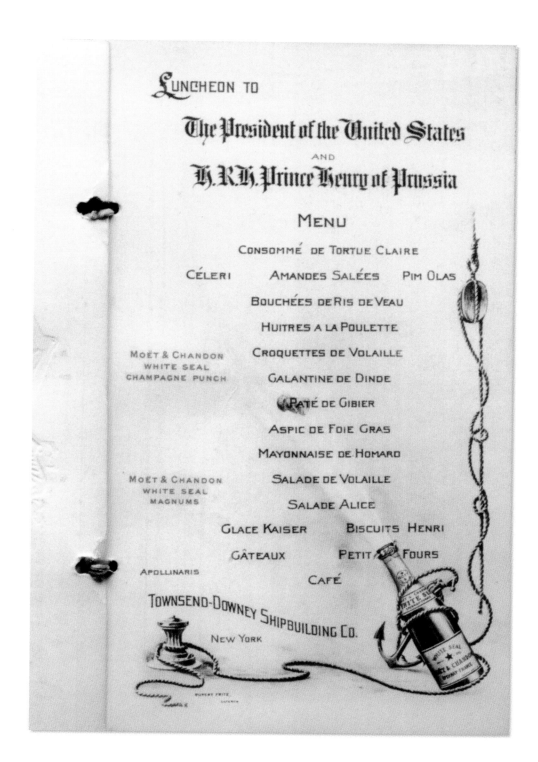

LUNCHEON TO

The President of the United States

AND

H.R.H. Prince Henry of Prussia

MENU

CONSOMMÉ DE TORTUE CLAIRE

CÉLERI   AMANDES SALÉES   PIM OLAS

BOUCHÉES DE RIS DE VEAU

HUITRES A LA POULETTE

MOËT & CHANDON
WHITE SEAL
CHAMPAGNE PUNCH

CROQUETTES DE VOLAILLE

GALANTINE DE DINDE

PATÉ DE GIBIER

ASPIC DE FOIE GRAS

MAYONNAISE DE HOMARD

MOËT & CHANDON
WHITE SEAL
MAGNUMS

SALADE DE VOLAILLE

SALADE ALICE

GLACE KAISER   BISCUITS HENRI

GÂTEAUX   PETITS FOURS

APOLLINARIS

CAFÉ

TOWNSEND-DOWNEY SHIPBUILDING CO.

NEW YORK

February 25, 1902

The U.S. importer of Moët & Chandon sponsored this menu for a lavish luncheon in honor of President Theodore Roosevelt and Prince Henry of Prussia in the loft of the Townsend-Downey Shipyards in New York. Before the luncheon, Alice Roosevelt had the honor of christening the kaiser's new yacht with a bottle of Moët & Chandon, which was also the only champagne served at the luncheon. A bottle of Moët & Chandon is also prominently illustrated on the menu.

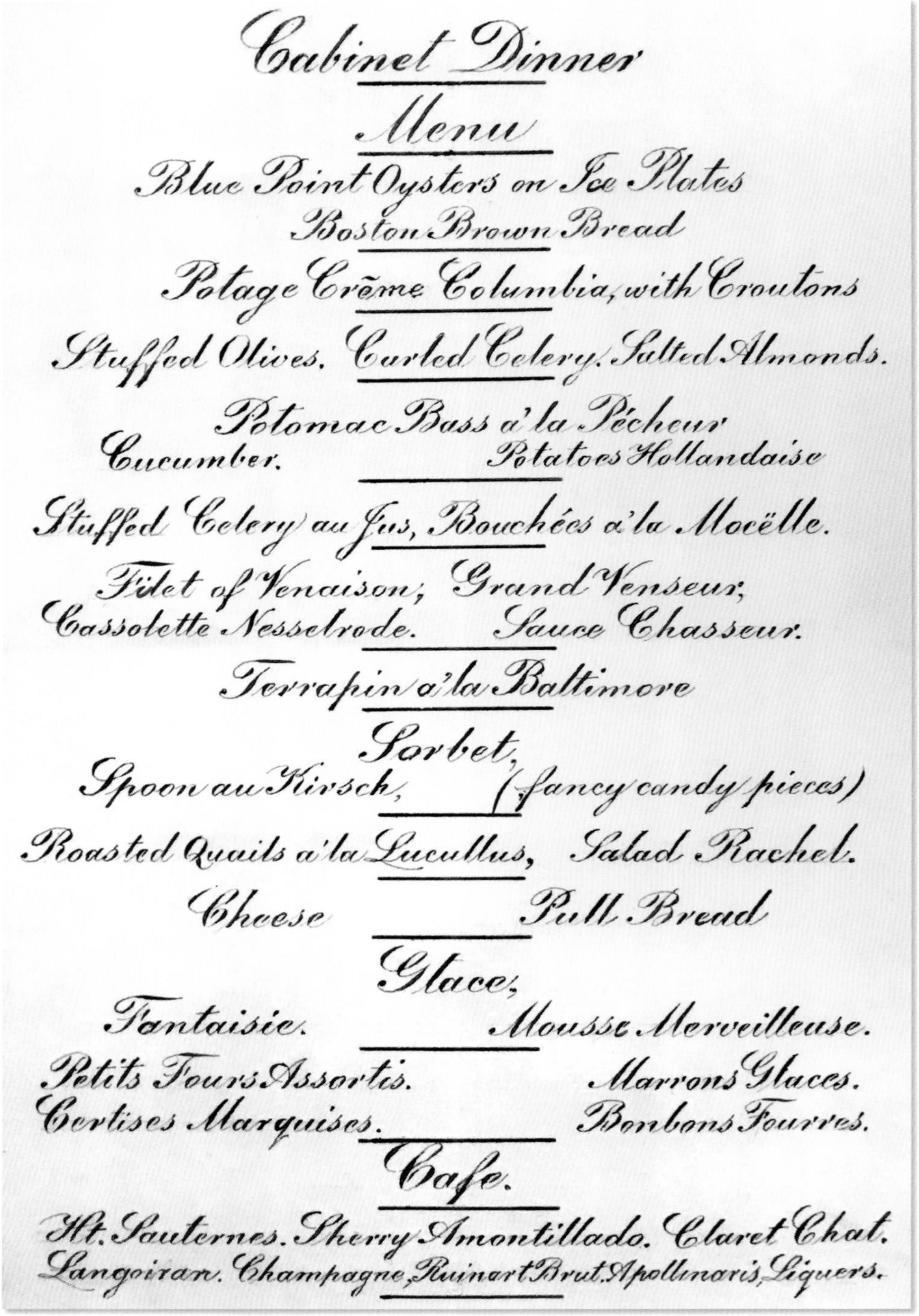

Cabinet Dinner
Menu
Blue Point Oysters on Ice Plates
Boston Brown Bread
Potage Crême Columbia, with Croutons
Stuffed Olives. Curled Celery. Salted Almonds.

Potomac Bass à la Pêcheur
Cucumber.   Potatoes Hollandaise

Stuffed Celery au Jus, Bouchées à la Mocëlle.

Filet of Venaison; Grand Venseur;
Cassolette Nesselrode.   Sauce Chasseur.

Terrapin à la Baltimore

Sorbet,
Spoon au Kirsch,   (fancy candy pieces)

Roasted Quails à la Lucullus,   Salad Rachel.

Cheese   Pull Bread

Glace,
Fantaisie.   Mousse Merveilleuse.
Petits Fours Assortis.   Marrons Glaces.
Cerises Marquises.   Bonbons Fourres.
Café.

Ht. Sauternes. Sherry Amontillado. Claret Chat.
Langoiran. Champagne Ruinart Brut. Apollinaris, Liquers.

December 17, 1903

President Theodore Roosevelt served three French wines—Haut Sauterne, Claret Château Langoiran, and Champagne Ruinart Brut—and a Spanish sherry amontillado at a 1904 dinner for his cabinet members.

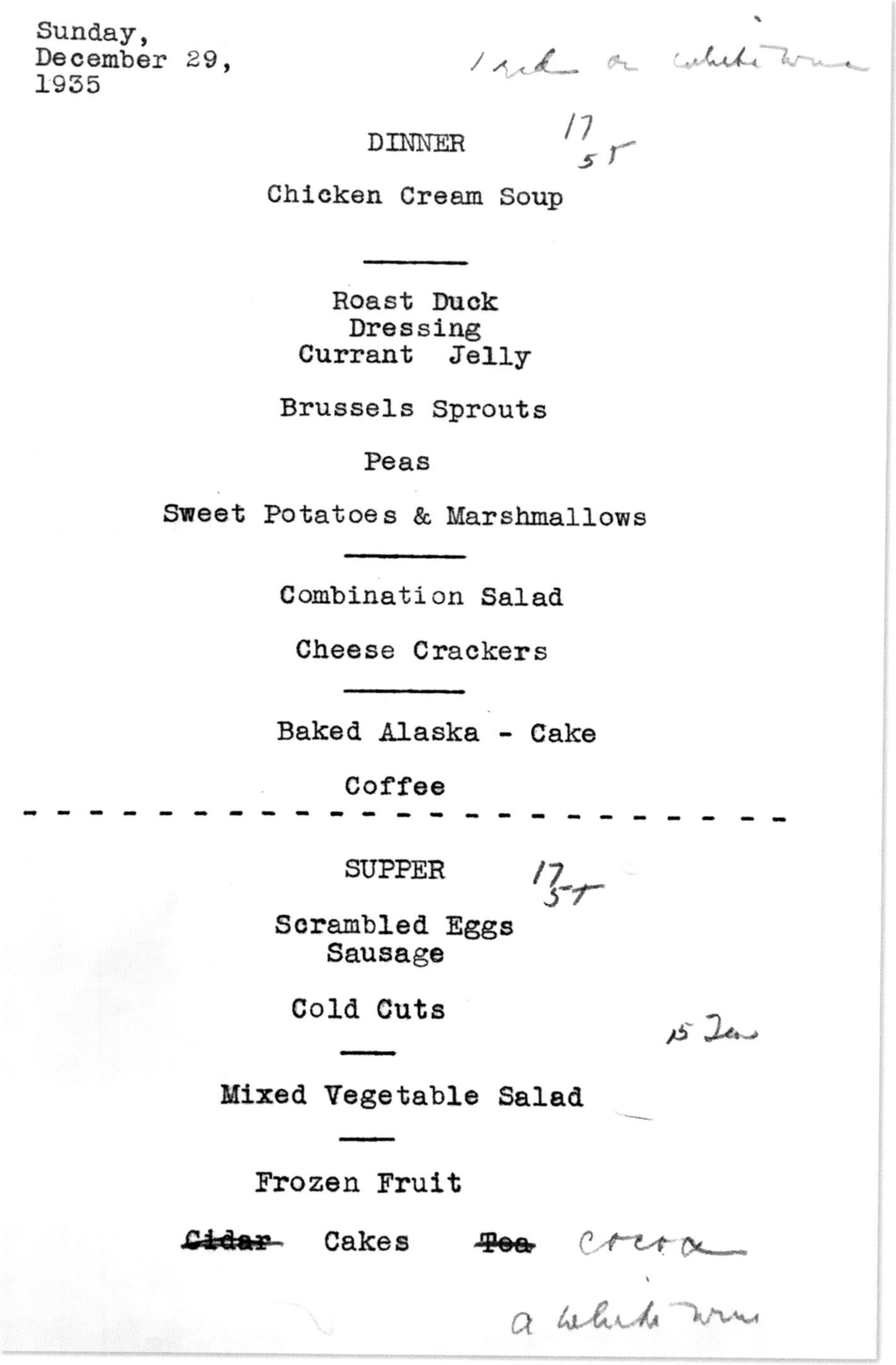

Sunday,
December 29,
1935

1 red or white wine

DINNER   *17 / 55*

Chicken Cream Soup

———

Roast Duck
Dressing
Currant   Jelly

Brussels Sprouts

Peas

Sweet Potatoes & Marshmallows

———

Combination Salad

Cheese Crackers

———

Baked Alaska - Cake

Coffee

- -

SUPPER   *17 / 55*

Scrambled Eggs
Sausage

Cold Cuts   *15 Jan*

———

Mixed Vegetable Salad

———

Frozen Fruit

~~Cidar~~   Cakes   ~~Tea~~   *cocoa*

a white wine

December 29, 1935

White House dinner menu cards were not printed during the Depression years in order to conserve paper, but typed drafts of menus can be found in presidential libraries and archives. Red and white wine is added in pencil on this example made for a Sunday dinner and supper during Franklin D. Roosevelt's presidency in 1935.

June 8–9, 1939

Although it detailed the musical program, no dinner menu or wine list was included in the booklet (above left) printed for the State Dinner hosted by President and Mrs. Franklin D. Roosevelt in honor of King George VI and Queen Elizabeth during their State Visit in 1939. The menu was not released to the public. In March 1939 as the visit was being planned, however, FDR received a letter (right) from his ambassador to France, William C. Bullitt, detailing the preferences of the royal visitors for French champagne and noting that he planned to procure one-hundred bottles of Pommery & Greno 1928 for the visit.

> I may add that it has been indicated to me by the Government of the French Republic that the preferences of Their Majesties in the way of wines do not go beyond Veuve Clicquot and Pommery-Greno champagne of the best years. I have, therefore, prepared against the arrival of Their Majesties in Washington, one hundred bottles of Pommery-Greno, 1928, which I shall be glad to place at your disposal provided the situation in Europe should seem to indicate that there may be some chance of Their Royal Majesties going to America. My parsimony is motivated by the fact that the grand smash seems fairly imminent. I prefer, therefore, to restrain the departure of these bottles until my next departure for the United States in the hope that we may drink them together.
>
> With my profound obeisances, I am,
> Your humble and obedient servant,
>
> *William C. Bullitt*

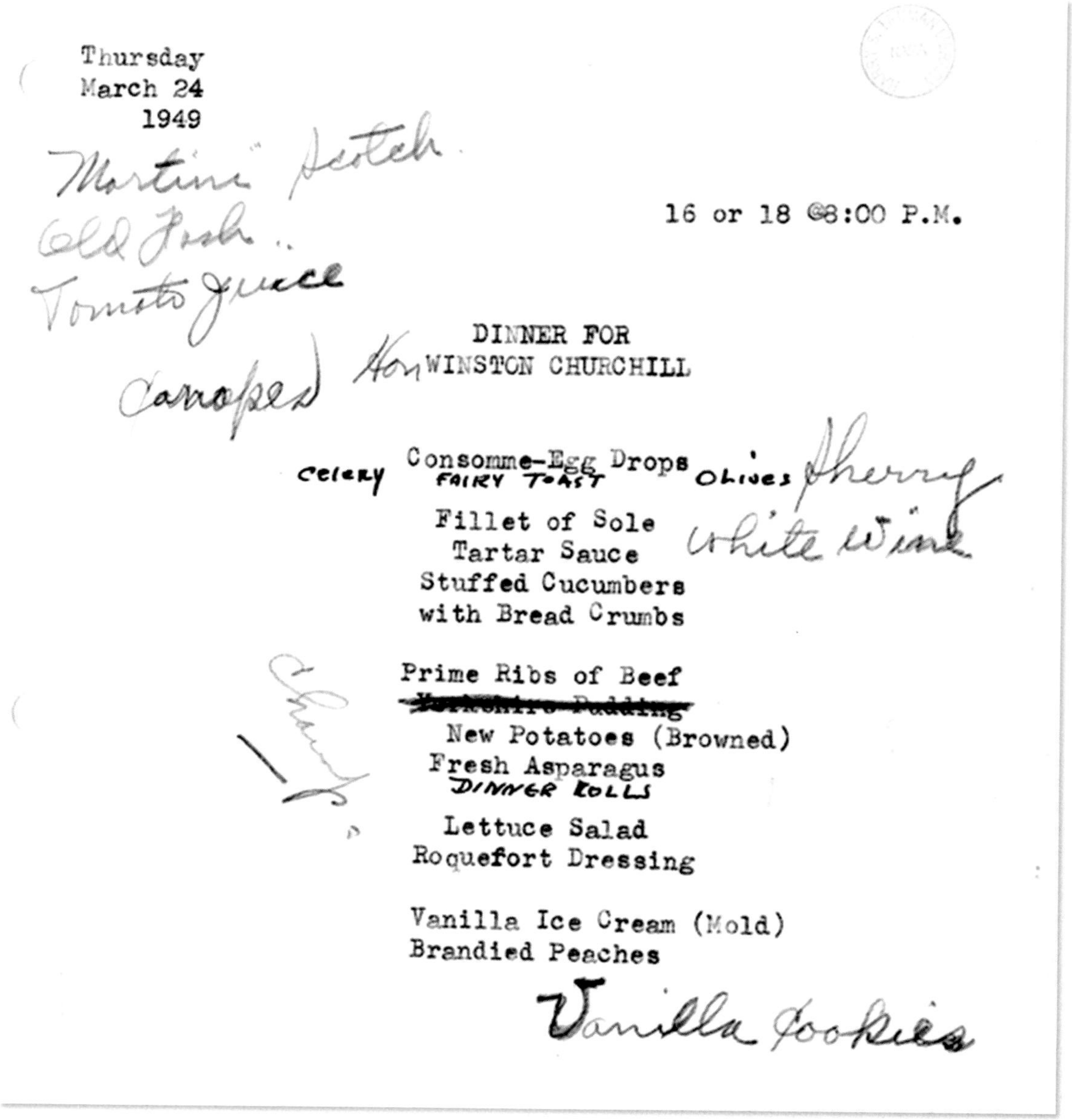

Thursday
March 24
1949

Martini Scotch
Old Fash..
Tomato Juice

Canapes

16 or 18 @8:00 P.M.

DINNER FOR
Hon. WINSTON CHURCHILL

Celery Consomme-Egg Drops *Olives* *Sherry*
FAIRY TOAST
Fillet of Sole *White Wine*
Tartar Sauce
Stuffed Cucumbers
with Bread Crumbs

Prime Ribs of Beef
~~Yorkshire Pudding~~
New Potatoes (Browned)
Fresh Asparagus
DINNER ROLLS

Lettuce Salad
Roquefort Dressing

Vanilla Ice Cream (Mold)
Brandied Peaches

Vanilla Cookies

March 24, 1949

Sherry, white wine, and, most important, champagne are added by hand to the menu created for a dinner honoring former British Prime Minister Winston Churchill during Harry S. Truman's presidency.

8/8/49

STAG DINNER FOR
THE PRESIDENT OF THE PHILIPPINES

Crab Meat Cocktail
Saltines

Clear Soup
Curled Celery   Assorted Olives
Melba Toast
Dry Sherry

Broiled Pampano
Cucumbers & Sour Cream
Sauterne

Fillet of Beef
Mustard Sauce
Corn Pudding
Asparagus
~~Champagne~~ *RED WINE*

Green Salad
Blue Cheese   *CHAMPAGNE*
French Dressing
Assorted Crackers

Vanilla Ice Cream Mold
Fresh Crushed Peaches
Sponge Drops *CHAMPAGNE*

Demi Tasse

Nuts   Candy   Dinner Rolls

Brandy & Liquors

August 8, 1949

The champagne was moved from the main course to the salad course and deleted from the dessert course in this edited draft of a menu created for President Truman's Stag Dinner honoring President Elpidio Quirino of the Philippines. Stag Dinners were traditionally working occasions, and only men were invited.

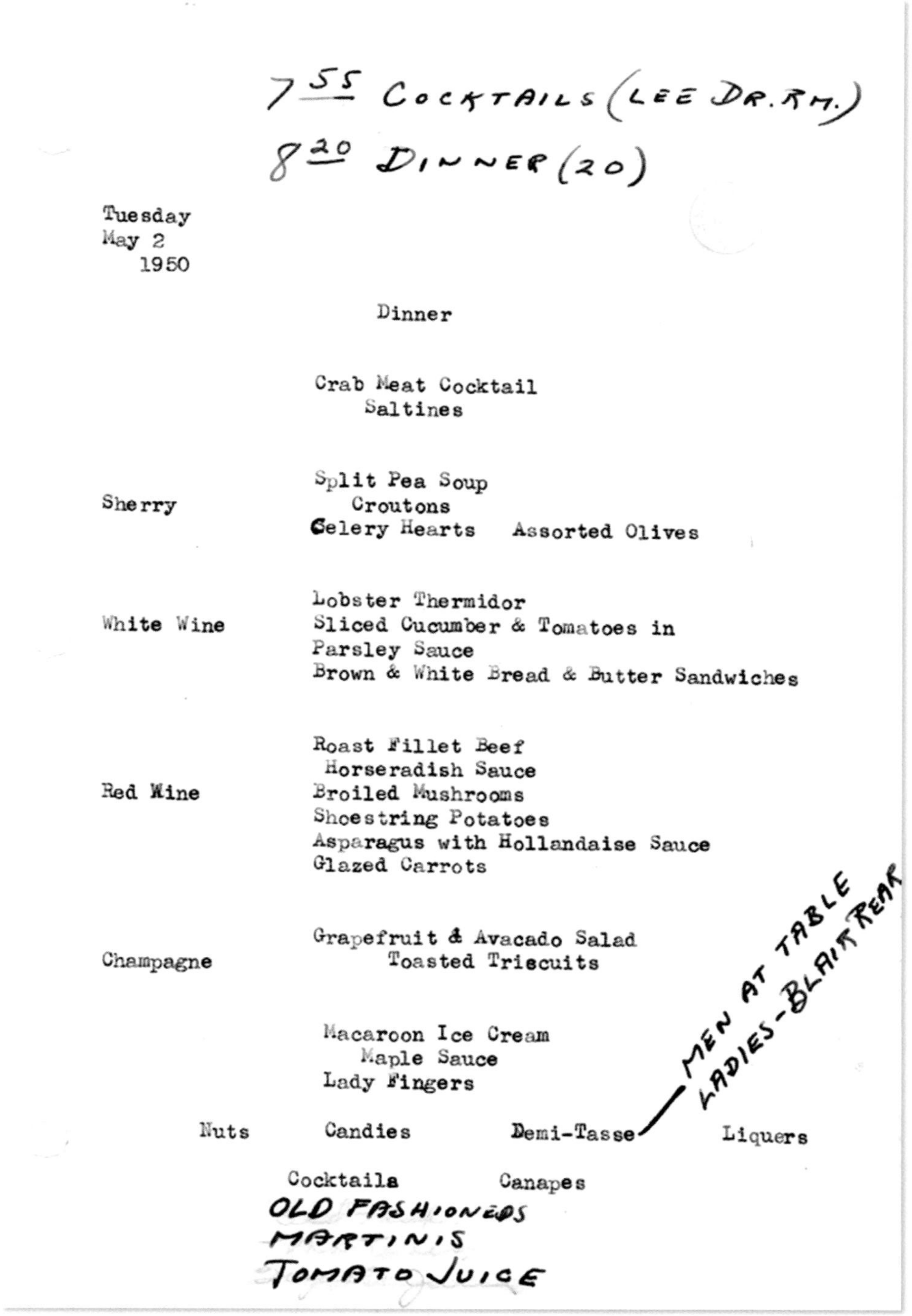

7:55 COCKTAILS (LEE DR. RM.)
8:20 DINNER (20)

Tuesday
May 2
1950

Dinner

Crab Meat Cocktail
Saltines

Sherry
Split Pea Soup
Croutons
Celery Hearts   Assorted Olives

White Wine
Lobster Thermidor
Sliced Cucumber & Tomatoes in
Parsley Sauce
Brown & White Bread & Butter Sandwiches

Red Wine
Roast Fillet Beef
Horseradish Sauce
Broiled Mushrooms
Shoestring Potatoes
Asparagus with Hollandaise Sauce
Glazed Carrots

Champagne
Grapefruit & Avacado Salad
Toasted Triscuits

Macaroon Ice Cream
Maple Sauce
Lady Fingers

Nuts   Candies   Demi-Tasse   Liquers

MEN AT TABLE
LADIES—BLAIR REAR

Cocktails   Canapes
OLD FASHIONEDS
MARTINIS
TOMATO JUICE

May 2, 1950

During the renovation of the White House from 1948 to 1952, President Truman hosted some of his official dinners at Blair House, his temporary residence just across the street. For this dinner in 1950, the men remained in the Lee Dining Room for coffee while the women retreated to another room at the rear of the house. Old-fashioneds and martinis were served before dinner.

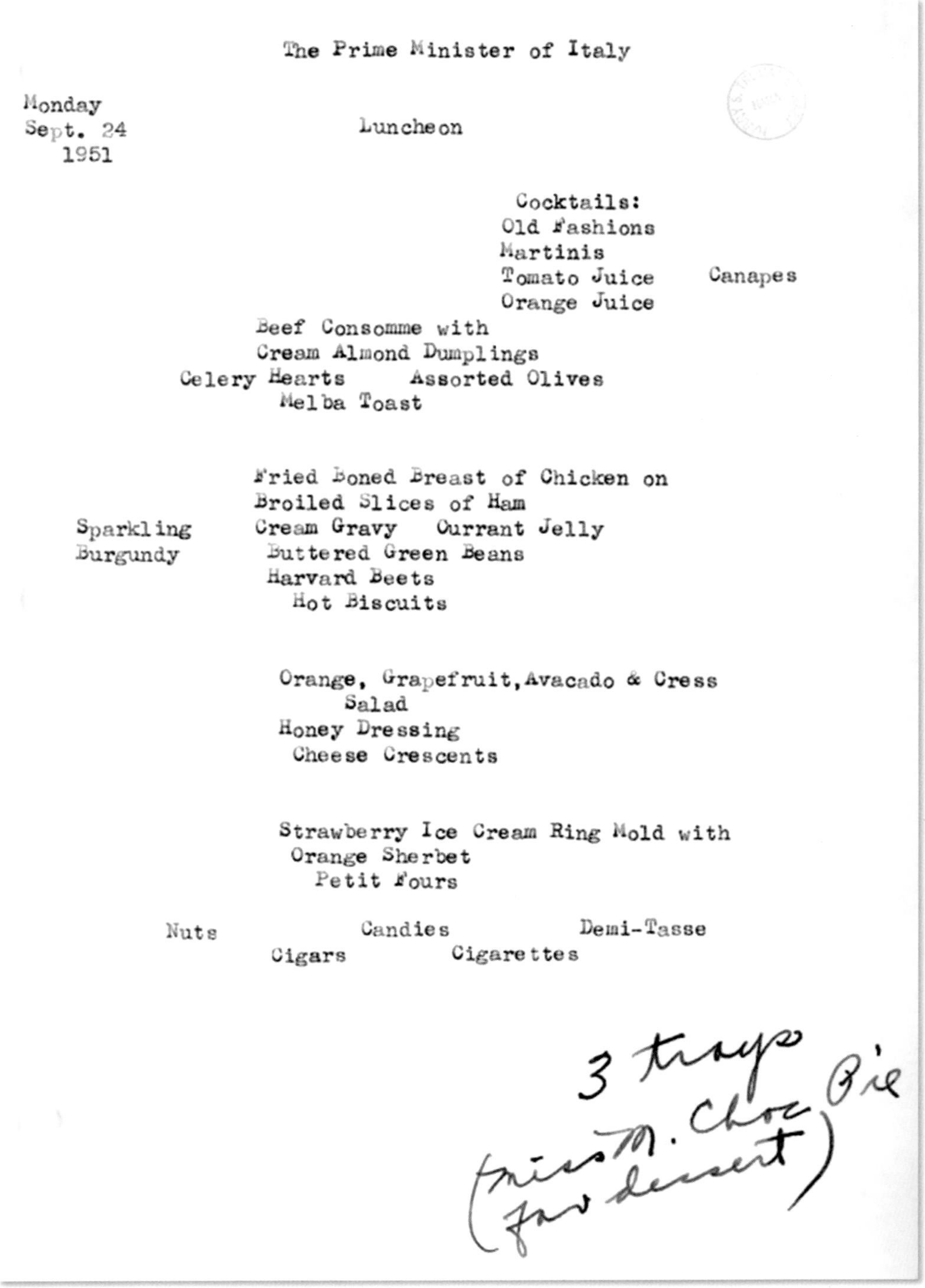

The Prime Minister of Italy

Monday
Sept. 24   Luncheon
1951

                                    Cocktails:
                                    Old Fashions
                                    Martinis
                                    Tomato Juice   Canapes
                                    Orange Juice

                        Beef Consomme with
                        Cream Almond Dumplings
              Celery Hearts   Assorted Olives
                        Melba Toast

                        Fried Boned Breast of Chicken on
                        Broiled Slices of Ham
    Sparkling   Cream Gravy   Currant Jelly
    Burgundy   Buttered Green Beans
                        Harvard Beets
                        Hot Biscuits

                        Orange, Grapefruit, Avacado & Cress
                                Salad
                        Honey Dressing
                        Cheese Crescents

                        Strawberry Ice Cream Ring Mold with
                        Orange Sherbet
                        Petit Fours

        Nuts   Candies   Demi-Tasse
                    Cigars   Cigarettes

3 trays
(miss M. Choc Pie
for dessert)

September 24, 1951

Old-fashioneds, martinis, and sparkling Burgundy are included on the menu for President and Mrs. Truman's luncheon honoring the prime minister of Italy, Alcide De Gasperi.

DINNER

Shrimp Cocktail
Cocktail Sauce   Saltine Crackers

Sherry

Clear Consomme
Sliced Lemon
Celery Hearts   Assorted Olives
Fairy Toast

White Fish in Cheese Sauce
Coleslaw
Boston Brown Bread Sandwiches

White Wine

Crown Roast of Lamb
Stuffed With Spanish Rice
Mint Jelly
French Peas   Braised Celery
Bread Sticks

Orange and Roquefort Cheese Salad Bowl
French Dressing
Toasted Triscuits

Champagne

Caramel Cream Mold
Burnt Caramel Sauce
Lemon Iced Diamond Shaped Cakes

Nuts   Candies   Demitasse

THE WHITE HOUSE
Wednesday, October 28, 1953

October 28, 1953

The White House Kitchen was not yet fully operational when President Truman returned to live in the house following the renovation, and thus the last State Dinner of his presidency was held at the Carlton Hotel. The first State Dinner at the White House after the renovation was hosted by Truman's successor, President Dwight D. Eisenhower, in honor of King Paul of Greece with a menu that included sherry, white wine, and champagne. Prior to 1956, President Eisenhower's menus did not identify wines in detail.

DINNER

Prosciutto Ham and Melon

Dry Sack

Cream of Water Cress Soup
Melba Toast
Celery Hearts   Assorted Olives

Chateau
Climens
1950

Seafood Newburg
Vol-au-Vent
Cucumber Sandwiches

Beaune
Greves
1952

Roast Stuffed Long Island Duckling
Applesauce
Casserole of Eggplant
French String Beans Almondine

Tossed Greens in Salad with Anchovy
Cheese Crusts

Pol Roger
1952

Frosted Mint Delight
Lady Fingers

Assorted Nuts   Bon Bons   Demitasse
Mints

THE WHITE HOUSE
Tuesday, March 17, 1959

March 17, 1959

The typical menu during President Eisenhower's presidency included Dry Sack, a Spanish sherry; Château Climens, a French Sauterne; Beaune Grèves, a French Pinot Noir; and Pol Roger, a French champagne, as seen on this menu for the dinner honoring President Seán O'Kelly of Ireland.

DINNER

Aspic of Pate de Foie Gras
Chippers and Melbas

Cream of Almond Soup
Dry Sack   Fairy Toast
Hearts of Celery   Queen and Ripe Olives

Chateau   Baked Florida Red Snapper
Coutet   Parslied New Potatoes
a Barsac   Hot Tartare Sauce
1937   Cucumber Sandwiches

Delmonico Roast of Beef
Artichoke Bottoms
Beaune   with Sauteed Mushroom Garnish
Greves   Horseradish Sauce
1952   Southern Corn Pudding
New Asparagus with Pimento
Bread Sticks

Tossed Bibb Lettuce Parmesan
French Dressing
Cheese Crusts
Pol Roger
1952   Frozen Rum Pudding
Butterscotch Sauce
Sponge Drops

Salted Nuts   Candies   Demitasse

THE WHITE HOUSE
Friday, April 22, 1960

April 22, 1960

The Eisenhowers departed from their typical French Sauterne for the 1960 State Dinner in honor of President Charles de Gaulle of France. Possibly a favorite wine of their guest of honor, they served Château Coutet a Barsac 1937 for the second course, and returned to their favorites for the main and dessert courses, Beaune Grèves 1952 and Pol Roger 1952.

DEJEUNER

————

Turbot Grille Sauce Bearnaise

Carre d'Agneau Persille Favorite

Haricots Verts au Beurre

Fromages

Savarin Parisienne

Chablis Valmur 1959

Chateau Gruaud Larose 1950

Mumm Cordon Rouge 1952

11 Juillet 1961

July 11, 1961

Written in French, the menu for President and Mrs. John F. Kennedy's luncheon honoring President Mohammad Ayub Khan of Pakistan includes three French wines, Chablis Valmur 1959, Château Gruaud-Larose 1950, and Mumm Cordon Rouge 1952.

DINNER

Inglenook Pinot
Chardonnay

Filet de sole Verdi

Grands
Echézeaux
1959

Pièce de boeuf Rochambeau
Petits pois au beurre
Pommes Anna

Salade Mimosa
Fromage Brie

Dom Pérignon
1952

Bombe Glacée Jeanneton

The White House
Tuesday, February 19, 1963

February 19, 1963

President and Mrs. Kennedy featured the California white wine Inglenook Pinot Chardonnay for the first course of their dinner honoring President Rómulo Betancourt of Venezuela. They completed the menu with two French wines, Grands Echézeaux 1959 and Dom Pérignon 1952.

DINNER

Inglenook
Pinot
Chardonnay

Aspic of salmon Dorian
Sauce Vincent

Château
Haut-Brion
1955

Roast spring lamb
Rice à l'Orientale
Spinach à la crème

Green Salad
Brie Cheese

Piper Heidsieck
1955

Bombe glacé aux pêches
Petits-fours sec

The White House
Monday, June 3, 1963

June 3, 1963

For the Kennedys' dinner
honoring President Sarvepalli
Radhakrishnan of India,
they chose Inglenook Pinot
Chardonnay, Château
Haut-Brion 1955, and Piper
Heidsieck 1955.

DINNER

Soave-Bolla 1959	*Délices of Maryland*
Beaulieu, Beaumont Pinot Noir	*Filet of beef Wellington* *Waffle potatoes* *String beans amandine*
	Endive and watercress salad *Brie cheese*
Dom Pérignon 1959	*Bavarois Ceylan*

The White House
Tuesday, January 14, 1964

January 14, 1964

President Lyndon B. Johnson's first State Dinner was held for Italian President Antonio Segni. In his honor, the Italian wine Soave-Bolla 1959 was chosen, as well as a California red wine, Beaulieu Vineyard Beaumont Pinot Noir, and the French champagne Dom Pérignon 1959. President Johnson used the Italian and French wines left over from the Kennedys, but soon promoted American wine by serving only domestic wines at the White House.

DINNER

Inglenook,
Pinot   Crabmeat crépes Maryland
Chardonnay

Beaulieu,   Filet of beef White House
Beaumont   Green beans amandine
Pinot Noir,
1960
                    Green salad
                    Brie cheese
Almaden,
Blanc de Blancs
1959   Chocolate mousse

    The White House
Tuesday, July 6, 1965

July 6, 1965

Three wines produced by historic California vineyards were on the menu for President and Mrs. Johnson's State Dinner honoring Prime Minister Robert Menzies of Australia: Inglenook founded in 1878, Beaulieu founded in 1900, and Almaden founded in 1852.

Luncheon

Sherry · Green turtle soup

Beaulieu Vineyard Cabernet Sauvignon · Tournedos Melba
Rice and broccoli Florence

Almaden Blanc de Blancs 1959 · Greens and grapefruit salad

Peppermint glacé

The White House
Friday, December 17, 1965

December 17, 1965

The luncheon for Prime
Minister Harold Wilson
of Great Britain was one of
seventy-four occasions at
which President and Mrs.
Johnson served Almaden
Blanc de Blancs, their
sparkling wine of choice.

DINNER

Beaulieu Pinot
Chardonnay — Filet of Sole Washington

Great Western
Vin Rouge — Roast Prime Rib of Beef
Braised Lettuce
Potatoes Rissoles

Garden Salad
Cheese Mousse

Almaden
Blanc de Blancs — Pears Glacées Sara

THE WHITE HOUSE
Wednesday, October 2, 1968

October 2, 1968

President Johnson's interest in American wines extended beyond California. He also served wines from New York's wine region, the Finger Lakes, from vineyards Great Western and Gold Seal. At this dinner honoring President François Tombalbaye of Chad, Great Western Vin Rouge complemented the main course.

Dinner

Puligny Montrachet
1964   Coquille Saint-Jacques

           Filet of Beef Wellington
Château Haut-Brion
1961   Bouquetière of Vegetables

Bibb Lettuce
Brie Cheese

Cuvée Dom Pérignon
1961   Marrons Glacés

The White House
Friday, March 14, 1969

March 14, 1969

A group of approximately fifty presidents and chairs of major American companies joined President Richard M. Nixon for cocktails in the Blue Room and Red Room in March 1969 before adjourning to the State Dining Room for a black-tie dinner, where only premium French wines were served.

DINNER

Bernkasteler Doktor
1967   *Filet of Halibut Royale*

Louis Martini
Cabernet Sauvignon   *Entrecôte Mirabeau*
1957   *Potatoes Persillées*
           Asparagus Hollandaise

            Cucumber Mousse

Cuvée Dom Pérignon
1961   *Strawberry Vacherin*

THE WHITE HOUSE
Tuesday, April 8, 1969

April 8, 1969

President and Mrs. Nixon served a combination of a German Riesling, a California Cabernet Sauvignon, and a French champagne for the State Dinner honoring King Hussein I of Jordan.

LUNCHEON

Crabe à l'Andalouse

Corton-Charlemagne
1964

Médaillons de Veau Bruxelloise
Endives à la Meunière

Château Margaux
1959

Petits Pois

Salade Panachée

Paul Ruinart
Blanc de Blancs
1961

Fromage de Edam

Mousse Fabiola

THE WHITE HOUSE
Tuesday, May 20, 1969

May 20, 1969

President Nixon's personal preference was for French wine, as often seen in his selections for special events. Written in French, the luncheon menu for King Baudouin I of Belgium features three great French wines: Corton-Charlemagne 1964, Château Margaux 1959, and Paul Ruinart Blanc de Blancs 1961.

DINNER

Corton Charlemagne 1964

Château Margaux 1959

Dom Pérignon 1961

Suprême of Turbot Impériale

Tournedos Sauté Béarnaise
Potatoes Anna
Fresh Artichokes

Caesar Salad
Brie Cheese

Peaches Cardinale
Petits Fours Sec

The White House
Tuesday, July 8, 1969

July 8, 1969

The Nixons served three French wines at the State Dinner honoring Emperor Haile Selassie I of Ethiopia—Corton-Charlemagne 1964, Château Margaux 1959, and Dom Pérignon 1961.

DINNER
In honor of the
Apollo 11 Astronauts

Wente Brothers Pinot Chardonnay

Supreme of Salmon Commodore

Filet of Beef Perigourdine

Inglenook Cabernet Sauvignon Cask

Artichauds Columbia

Carottes Des Indes

Limestone Lettuce

Fromages de Brie, Bel Paese,
Roquefort

Korbel Natural

Clair de Lune

CENTURY PLAZA
Los Angeles, California
Wednesday, August 13, 1969

August 13, 1969

Celebrating the *Apollo 11* voyage to the moon, President and Mrs. Nixon hosted a dinner honoring the astronauts at the Century Plaza Hotel in Los Angeles. They served only California wines—Wente Brothers Pinot Chardonnay, Inglenook Cabernet Sauvignon Cask, and Korbel Natural. However, three months later, at a more private White House dinner for the *Apollo 11* crew and their wives, the Nixons went back to serving his favorite French wine. The centerpiece of the November 5, 1969, dinner was Château Mouton Rothschild 1966.

DINNER

Schloss
Johannisberger
1967

Château Margaux
1959

Dom Pérignon
1961

Coquille of Crabmeat Impérial

Breast of Pheasant Smitane
Wild Rice
Broccoli Polonaise

Bibb Lettuce Salad
Carré de L'Est Cheese

Brandied Peach en Surprise
Petits Fours

The White House
Tuesday, September 16, 1969

September 16, 1969

A month after the *Apollo 11* dinner in California, President and Mrs. Nixon returned to serving a German Riesling, Schloss Johannisberg 1967, as well as French wines, Château Margaux 1959 and Dom Pérignon 1961, at the White House dinner honoring Prime Minister Keith Holyoake of New Zealand.

DINNER

Pouilly
Fuissé
1967

Château
Lafite-Rothschild
1962

Suprême of Sole Véronique

Châteaubriand Bérnaise

Potatoes Persillées
Celery Braisés

Cucumber Mousse

Taittinger
1961

Charlotte Revivim
Sauce Sabayon

THE WHITE HOUSE
Thursday, September 25, 1969

September 25, 1969

A departure from their usual pattern, the Nixons chose to serve only French wines at the State Dinner honoring Prime Minister Golda Meir of Israel. Instead of German Riesling with the first course, the dinner began with the French Pouilly Fuissé 1967, which was followed by Château Lafite Rothschild 1962 and Taittinger 1961.

DINNER

Corton
Charlemagne
1964

Supréme of Lobster en Bellevue

Château
Mouton
Rothschild
1964

Royal Squab Farcie Périgueux
Brussels Sprouts au Beurre
Chestnuts Glaces

Garden Salad
Bel Paese Cheese

Dom Pérignon
1961

Soufflé au Grand Marnier
Sauce Noisette

THE WHITE HOUSE
Tuesday, October 7, 1969

October 7, 1969

While President and
Mrs. Nixon often served
German and American
wines, they recognized the
international prestige of
certain French wines and
would strategically serve
them to world leaders. They
chose Corton Charlemagne
1964, Château Mouton
Rothschild 1964, and
Dom Pérignon 1961 for a
dinner in honor of Prince
Souvanna Phouma, prime
minister of Laos.

DINNER

Suprême of Salmon Farcie Impériale

Liebfrauenmilk 1965

Contre-Filet of Beef Bordelaise
Pommes Macaire
Bouquetière of Vegetables

Château LaTour 1962

Bibb Lettuce
Camembert Cheese

Louis Reoderer Christal Brut 1962

Poires Flambées Par-Le-Duc
Sauce Sabayon

The White House
Tuesday, October 21, 1969

October 21, 1969

The menu for President and Mrs. Nixon's dinner for Mohammad Reza Pahlavi, the shah of Iran, featured a semisweet German white wine, Liebfrauenmilch 1965, Château Latour 1962, one of the First Growth French wines, as well as the French champagne Louis Roederer Cristal Brut 1962.

DINNER

Puligny
Montrachet
1966

Tronçon of Striped Bass White House

Médaillons of Veal Périgourdine

Château
Mouton Rothschild
1966

Timbale of Spinach

Jardinière de Légumes

Riverside Salad
Roquefort Mousse

Piper Heidsieck
1962

Charlotte de Pommes

Sauce Sabayon

THE WHITE HOUSE
Wednesday, November 19, 1969

November 19, 1969

French wines, exclusively,
were served at the Nixons'
State Dinner honoring Prime
Minister Eisaku Satō of
Japan, including Château
Mouton Rothschild 1966.

DINNER

Le Saumon La Fayette

Puligny-Montrachet
1966

Le Contre-filet de boeuf aux Cèpes
Les Pommes nouvelles

Château Ausone
1962

Les Asperges fraîches Hollandaise

La Laitue du Kentucky

Le Fromage de Camembert

Louis Roederer
Cristal
1962

Le Melon glacé à la Vigneronne
Les Petits Fours

THE WHITE HOUSE
Tuesday, February 24, 1970

February 24, 1970

President and Mrs. Nixon
selected only French wines
for their State Dinner
honoring President Georges
Pompidou of France. The
menu, written in French,
includes Puligny-Montrachet
1966, Château Ausone 1962,
and Louis Roederer Cristal
1962.

DINNER

Bernkasteler
Doktor
1967

Le Saumon Froid Windsor
La Sauce Verte

Les Supremes de Pigeons Véronique

Château Margaux   Le Riz Sauvage
1959
Les Artichauts Saint-Germain

Le Fromage de Brie
Les Feuilles de Laitue du Kentucky

Taittinger,
Blanc de Blancs
1961

Le Soufflé Duchesse
La Sauce Sabayon

THE WHITE HOUSE
Saturday, April 4, 1970

April 4, 1970

President Nixon selected
his favorite wine, Château
Margaux 1959, for the dinner
honoring the Duke of Windsor,
formerly King Edward VIII,
and Wallis Simpson,
the Duchess of Windsor.
He began the dinner with
Bernkasteler Doktor 1967 and
finished with Taittinger Blanc
de Blancs 1961.

DINNER

Schloss Johannisberger 1967	Lobster en Bellevue Sauce Rémoulade Paillettes Dorées
Beaulieu Vineyard Cabernet Sauvignon 1965	Contre Filet of Beef Rôti Artichokes Béarnaise Mushrooms Provençale
Dom Pérignon 1962	Soufflé au Grand Marnier Sauce Sabayon

THE WHITE HOUSE
Thursday, November 5, 1970

November 5, 1970

President and Mrs. Nixon began including more California wines during the later years of the Nixon presidency. This menu for the dinner honoring Louis Mountbatten, the first Earl of Burma, reflects this change with Beaulieu Vineyard Cabernet Sauvignon 1965 served with the main course. The California wine was complemented with Schloss Johannisberger 1967 and Dom Pérignon 1962.

DINNER

Concannon
Johannisberg
Riesling

Coquille of Seafood Neptune
Paillettes Dorées

Beaulieu Vineyard
Cabernet Sauvignon
1966

Roast Prime Rib of Beef
Pommes Mascotte
Zucchini Sauté Ménagère

Bibb Lettuce Salad
Port du Salut Cheese

Dom Pérignon
1962

Gâteau Glacé Alabama
Sauce Melba

THE WHITE HOUSE
Tuesday, June 29, 1971

June 29, 1971

President and Mrs. Nixon's
dinner for the Postmaster
General Winston M. Blount
included two wines from
California, Concannon
Johannisberg Riesling and
Beaulieu Vineyard Cabernet
Sauvignon 1966. French Dom
Pérignon 1962 finished the
meal.

DINNER

Beaulieu
Pinot Chardonnay
1969

Chatka Crab Mousse

Louis Martini
Cabernet Sauvignon
1967

Roast Filet of Beef
Yorkshire Pudding
Bouquet of Garden Vegetables

Hearts of Palm Salad

Schramsberg
Blanc de Blancs
1969

Wisconsin Cheddar Cheese

Pikantnyi Surprise Flambé

SPASO HOUSE, Moscow
Friday, May 26, 1972

May 26, 1972

While visiting Moscow, President Nixon showcased the quality of American wine by serving three California wines—Beaulieu Pinot Chardonnay 1969, Louis Martini Cabernet Sauvignon 1967, and Schramsberg Blanc de Blancs 1969—at the dinner he hosted for Soviet leaders in the ballroom of Spaso House.

LUNCHEON

Delice of Lobster in Aspic

Roast Breast of Capon Printanière
Wild Rice Amandine

Beaulieu Pinot
Chardonnay Bouquet of Garden Vegetables
1969

Boston Lettuce with Cherry Tomatoes

Schramsberg
Blanc de Blancs   Sherbet Cardinal
1969

Demi-tasse

SAAD-ABAD PALACE, Tehran
Wednesday, May 31, 1972

May 31, 1972

While visiting Iran,
President and Mrs. Nixon
hosted a luncheon for Shah
Mohammad Reza Pahlavi
at the Saad-Abad Palace in
Tehran. As they did a few
days before in Moscow, the
Nixons chose to serve only
California wines.

DINNER

Robert Mondavi
Fumé Blanc
1972

Striped Bass Supreme

Mirassou
Pinot Noir
1969

Roast Prime Sirloin of Beef
Almond Potatoes
Bouquet of Garden Vegetables

Hearts of Palm Salad
Brie Cheese

Schramsberg
Blanc de Blancs
1971

Grand Marnier Mousse
Petits Fours

SPASO HOUSE, Moscow
Tuesday, July 2, 1974

July 2, 1974

President and Mrs. Nixon hosted a second dinner at Spaso House in Moscow in July 1974. It would be the last official dinner they would host before President Nixon's resignation on August 9. As they had done two years earlier, they chose to serve only California wines to the Soviet leaders.

DINNER

Tabor Hill
Trebbiano
1971

Turtle Soup

Cold Smoked Rainbow Trout

Freemark Abbey
Cabernet
Sauvignon
1969

Breast of Pheasant
Wild Rice
Chestnut Purée

Bibb Lettuce Salad
Brie Cheese

Schramsberg
Blanc de Blancs
Reserve
1970

Chocolate Delight

Demitasse

THE WHITE HOUSE
Tuesday, November 12, 1974

November 12, 1974

President and Mrs. Gerald R. Ford selected Tabor Hill Vidal Blanc 1971 from their home state of Michigan for a dinner held in honor of Chancellor Bruno Kreisky of Austria. The wine was mistakenly identified as Trebbiano on the menu. It was the first time a wine from the Midwest was served at the White House.

DINNER

Gazpacho

Robert Mondavi
Cabernet
Sauvignon
1971

Filet of Beef
Bouquet of Vegetables

Bibb Lettuce Salad
with Watercress
Bel Paese Cheese

Vanilla Ice Cream
with Strawberries Flambé

Mirassou
Brut
1970

Demitasse

THE WHITE HOUSE
Thursday, May 8, 1975

May 8, 1975

President and Mrs. Ford
served only two wines at the
State Dinner honoring Prime
Minister Lee Kuan Yew of
Singapore: Robert Mondavi
Cabernet Sauvignon 1971 and
Mirassou Brut 1970, both from
California.

DINNER

Cold Cucumber Soup

Freemark Abbey
Cabernet
Sauvignon
1969

Tenderloin of Beef
Bouquet of Vegetables

Hearts of Lettuce Salad
Brie Cheese

Schramsberg
Blanc de Blancs
1972

Hazelnut Ice Cream Ring
with Chocolate Sauce

Petits Fours

Demitasse

THE WHITE HOUSE
Wednesday, May 14, 1975

May 14, 1975

The Fords served Freemark Abbey Cabernet Sauvignon 1969 and Schramsberg Blanc de Blancs 1972 at the dinner for Prime Minister Joop den Uyl of the Netherlands. Freemark Abbey, from Napa Valley, became a staple vineyard of the Ford presidency.

DINNER

Saint Michelle
Semillon
1973

Lobster en Bellevue

Robert Mondavi
Pinot Noir
1971

Medaillons of Veal
Wild Rice
Green Beans Niçoise

Endive and Watercress Salad
Port-Salut Cheese

Schramsberg
Blanc de Noir
1971

Fresh Raspberry Mousse
Petits Fours

Demitasse

THE WHITE HOUSE
Thursday, October 2, 1975

October 2, 1975

President and Mrs. Ford selected wines from Washington and California for the State Dinner honoring Emperor Hirohito of Japan: Ste. Michelle Semillon 1973, Robert Mondavi Pinot Noir 1971, and Schramsberg Blanc de Noir 1971. The Fords often served wines from Washington's Ste. Michelle during his presidency.

Luncheon

Dry Creek
Dry Chenin Blanc
1974

Chappellet
Cabernet Sauvignon
1971

Schramsberg
Blanc de Blancs
1973

Lobster with Rémoulade Sauce

Roast Saddle of Lamb
Almond Potatoes
Parmesan Asparagus

Bibb Lettuce Salad
Danish Bleu Cheese Mousse

Glace Praliné
Petits Fours

Demitasse

THE WHITE HOUSE
Tuesday, May 11, 1976

May 11, 1976

President and Mrs. Ford chose three California wines for the luncheon held for Queen Margrethe II of Denmark—Dry Creek Dry Chenin Blanc 1974, Chappellet Cabernet Sauvignon 1971, and Schramsberg Blanc de Blancs 1973.

DINNER

Sterling
Chenin
Blanc
1972

New England Lobster en Bellevue
Sauce Rémoulade

Beaulieu
Vineyard
Cabernet
Sauvignon
1968

Saddle of Veal
Rice Croquettes
Broccoli Mornay

Garden Salad
Trappist Cheese

Schramsberg
Blanc de Blancs
1973

Peach Ice Cream Bombe
with Fresh Raspberries
Petits Fours

Demitasse

THE WHITE HOUSE
Wednesday, July 7, 1976

July 7, 1976

To celebrate America's
Bicentennial, President and
Mrs. Ford served excellent
American vintages at the
State Dinner in honor of
Queen Elizabeth II and Prince
Philip of Great Britain.

DINNER

Saint Michelle
Chenin
Blanc
1975

Filet of Red Snapper Meunière

Louis
Martini
Cabernet
Sauvignon
1970

Suprême of Rock Cornish Hen
Wild Rice Croquettes
Zucchini with Mushrooms

Watercress and
Hearts of Palm Salad
Trappist Cheese

Beaulieu
Extra Dry
1970

Chocolate Soufflé
Vanilla Sauce

Demitasse

The White House
Monday, December 6, 1976

December 6, 1976

The last State Dinner of the
Ford presidency was held
in honor of Prime Minister
Giulio Andreotti of Italy and
featured Ste. Michelle Chenin
Blanc 1975, Louis M. Martini
Cabernet Sauvignon 1970,
Beaulieu Extra Dry 1970.

宴 会

海鲜百花卷
烧烤小牛腿
芷红花香饭 翡翠甘兰花
生拌苣荬西洋芽
计 司

奶油栗子冻
巧克力点心

咖 啡

白宫
一九七九年一月廿九日

DINNER

Paul
Masson
Pinot
Chardonnay
1976
   Timbale of Seafood
   Fleurons

Simi
Rosé
Cabernet
Sauvignon
1976
   Roast Stuffed Loin of Veal
   Saffron Rice
   Broccoli Spears

Endive and Watercress Salad
Hanns
Kornell
Champagne
   Trappist Cheese

Chestnut Mousse
Chocolate Truffles

Demitasse

THE WHITE HOUSE
Monday, January 29, 1979

January 29, 1979

President and Mrs. Jimmy Carter served only California wines for the State Dinner honoring Vice Premier Deng Xiaoping of China. The dinner menu was specially formatted with Chinese on the left and English on the right.

DINNER

Poached Striped Bass
with Shrimp Sauce

Filet of Beef Choron
Wild Rice
Zucchini Stuffed with Creamed Spinach
Baby Carrots

Avocado and Papaya Salad
Trappist and Bel Paese Cheeses

Strawberry Crêpes
Grand Marnier Sauce

Demitasse

Petits Fours

Inglenook
Pinot Chardonnay

Louis Martini
Cabernet Sauvignon

Korbel Extra Dry

The American Embassy
Mexico City, Mexico
Thursday, February 15, 1979

February 15, 1979

While on a State Visit,
President and Mrs. Carter
served all California wines
at a reciprocal dinner for
President and Mrs. José
López Portillo of Mexico held
at the American Embassy
in Mexico City. Departing
from the custom of previous
administrations, menus from
the Carter era rarely included
vintage years for the wines.

Luncheon

Cold Lobster
Sauce Rémoulade
Golden Twists

Medaillons of Veal
Garden Vegetables

Coconut Ice Cream
in Hibiscus Shell
Petits Fours

Demitasse

Beaulieu Vineyard
Pinot Chardonnay

Simi Rosé
Cabernet Sauvignon
Korbel Natural Champagne

The White House
Tuesday, April 22, 1980

April 22, 1980

President and Mrs. Carter
served California wines for
a luncheon honoring King
Baudouin I of Belgium. They
selected Beaulieu Vineyard
Pinot Chardonnay, Simi Rosé
Cabernet Sauvignon, and
Korbel Natural Champagne.

DINNER

Lobster en Belle-vue
Sauce Rémoulade

Roulade of Veal Farcie
Chablis Wine Sauce

Vegetables Printanière

Birthday Cake

Assorted Sorbet

Ventana Chardonnay 1979
Inglenook Cabernet Sauvignon 1974
Schramsberg Blanc de Blancs

THE WHITE HOUSE
Friday, February 6, 1981

February 6, 1981

First Lady Nancy Reagan surprised President Ronald Reagan with a dinner in the East Room to celebrate his seventieth birthday—his first birthday in the White House. Only California wines were served, including Inglenook Cabernet Sauvignon 1974, produced the last year Reagan was governor of California and considered as one of the best years for California wines.

DINNER

Fresh Asparagus
and Crab Mousse in Aspic
Fine Herb Sauce
Cheese Twists

Saddle of Lamb Farcie
in Golden Crust
Fresh Mint Sauce
Braised Fennel
Green Beans

Crown of Sorbet Prince of Wales
Petits Fours Sec

McDowell Valley Vineyard
Fume Blanc 1980

Beaulieu George de Latour
Private Reserve
Cabernet Sauvignon 1970

Schramsberg
Blanc de Noirs 1975

THE WHITE HOUSE
Saturday, May 2, 1981

May 2, 1981

The first dinner to be
hosted following President
Reagan's recovery from an
assassination attempt
was a private event for
Charles, Prince of Wales,
at which only premium
California wines were served.

DINNER

Poached Halibut in Dill Sauce
Fleurons

Sliced Tenderloin of Beef
Sauce Choron
Soufflé Potatoes
Broiled Tiny Tomatoes
Artichokes St. Germain

Bibb Lettuce Salad
Brie Cheese

Chestnut Bombe
Acorn Petits Fours

Château Montelena
Chardonnay 1979

Jordan
Cabernet Sauvignon 1976

Schramsberg
Crémant Demi-sec 1979

THE WHITE HOUSE
Monday, November 2, 1981

November 2, 1981

Only California wines were served at President and Mrs. Reagan's State Dinner honoring King Hussein I of Jordan, including Chateau Montelena Chardonnay 1979, Jordan Cabernet Sauvignon 1976, and Schramsberg Crémant Demi-Sec 1979. Jordan was a newly launched wine that became a favorite of President Reagan. The 1973 vintage of the Chateau Montelena famously finished first in the historic Judgment of Paris five years earlier.

LUNCHEON

Lobster Bisque
Cheese Twists

Medallion of Veal
in Chablis
Wild Rice
Fresh Asparagus in Lemon Butter

Pineapple Sorbet
Petits Fours

Jordan
Valley
Chardonnay
1979

THE WHITE HOUSE
Friday, March 12, 1982

H.E. The President of the French Republic

March 12, 1982

President and Mrs. Reagan showcased a single California wine, Jordan Valley Chardonnay 1979, rather than a French wine, at their luncheon for President François Mitterrand of France.

DINNER

Poached Filet of Pompano Beatrix
Fleurons

Roast Beef Tenderloin Hearts
Sauce Béarnaise
Soufflé Potatoes
Artichokes Printanière

Bibb Lettuce Salad
Brie Cheese-Fines Herbes

Sugar Tulip Basket
with Orange Sorbet
Petits Fours

Trefethen
Chardonnay 1979
Jordan
Cabernet Sauvignon 1976
Schramsberg
Crémant Demi-Sec 1979

THE WHITE HOUSE
Monday, April 19, 1982

Her Majesty the Queen
and His Royal Highness Prince Claus
of the Netherlands

April 19, 1982

President and Mrs. Reagan served Jordan Cabernet Sauvignon 1976, his favorite wine, to world leaders and royalty including Queen Beatrix of the Netherlands. The inclusion of this wine on White House menus contributed to an increase in its popularity.

DINNER

Loup de mer flambé au fenouil
Riz au safran

Selle d'agneau Richelieu
Bouquetière de légumes

Salade à l'estragon
Brillat-savarin

Bavarois Plombière Coulis de framboise

Grgich Hills
Chardonnay 1979

Martha's Vineyard
Heitz
Cabernet Sauvignon 1974

Domaine Chandon
Brut Special Reserve

AMERICAN EMBASSY RESIDENCE
Paris, France
Thursday, June 3, 1982

Le Président de la République Française
and Madame Mitterrand

June 3, 1982

President and Mrs. Reagan featured American wines exclusively at a reciprocal dinner held at the U.S. Embassy in Paris for President François Mitterrand. Included was Heitz Martha's Vineyard Cabernet Sauvignon 1974 one of the all-time great California wines. The 1970 vintage of this wine was among those featured at the Judgment of Paris.

DINNER

Maryland Crab and Lobster in Aspic
Fine Herb Sauce
Sesame Seed Twists

Suprême of Capon
in Flamed Brandy Sauce
Wild Rice
Cauliflower and Green Beans

Spinach Salad
Port Salut Cheese

Sugar Basket filled with
Fresh Fruit Sorbet
Petits Fours Sec

Stags' Leap
Chenin Blanc 1981

ZD Chardonnay 1979   **THE WHITE HOUSE**
                                        Thursday, September 16, 1982
Schramsberg
Crémant 1979

H.E. The President of the Republic of the Philippines
and Mrs. Marcos

September 16, 1982

The Reagans often served lesser-known wines and those not previously served at the White House, such as Stags' Leap Chenin Blanc 1981 and ZD Chardonnay 1979 seen on the State Dinner menu honoring President Ferdinand E. Marcos of the Philippines. Schramsberg Crémant 1979, also served at this dinner, was one of the Reagans' favorite sparkling wines.

LUNCHEON

Cold Maine Lobster
in Champagne Sauce
Rémoulade Sauce
Cheese Twists

Noisettes of Lamb in Fine Herbs
Saffron Rice
Artichokes Florentine

Pear Sorbet
Petits Fours

Jekel
Chardonnay 1980

Jordan
Cabernet Sauvignon 1976

Schramsberg
Crémant 1979

THE WHITE HOUSE
Friday, October 1, 1982

Members of The Supreme Court

October 1, 1982

President Reagan chose
Jordan Cabernet Sauvignon
1976, one of his favorite
wines, for a luncheon
honoring the members
of the Supreme Court.

LUNCHEON

Hot Madrilene
Sesame Seed Twists

Baked Country Ham
Gruyere Cheese Soufflé
Bibb Lettuce Salad

Fresh Fruit Compote
Petits Fours

Joseph Phelps
Johannisberg Riesling
1981

Korbel
Blanc de Noirs

THE WHITE HOUSE
Monday, November 15, 1982

H.E.The Chancellor of the Federal Republic of Germany

November 15, 1982

President and Mrs. Reagan selected the German-style Joseph Phelps Johannisberg Riesling 1981 from California to serve at this luncheon for Chancellor Helmut Kohl of the Federal Republic of Germany.

DINNER

Lobster Terrine
with Golden Caviar and Dill Sauce

Double Consommé of Pheasant
Quenelles of Goose Liver
Cheese Straws

Loin of Veal
with Morel Mousse
Sauce with Essence of Balsam
Spring Season's First Vegetables
Truffle Potato

Kentucky Limestone Salad
with Goat Cheese
Walnut Dressing

Aurora Pacifica

Demitasse

Trefethen
Chardonnay 1980

Jordan
Cabernet Sauvignon 1976

Piper Sonoma
Brut 1980

The M.H. de Young Memorial Museum
of the Fine Arts Museums of San Francisco
Golden Gate Park
San Francisco, California

Thursday, March 3, 1983

Her Majesty Queen Elizabeth II
His Royal Highness The Prince Philip
Duke of Edinburgh

March 3, 1983

The wines served at a dinner held in San Francisco for Queen Elizabeth II and Prince Philip of Great Britain were chosen a month in advance of the event. The wine specialist David Berkley cautioned against the Trefethen Chardonnay 1980 and Jordan Cabernet Sauvignon 1976 because they were served frequently at the White House, but his selections were overridden by President and Mrs. Reagan. Piper Sonoma Brut 1980, however, was served for the first time.

LUNCHEON

Chesapeake Crab Bisque
Sesame Seed Twists

Suprême of Royal Squab
Rice Pilaf
with Artichokes
Tiny Minted Peas

Mocha Glacé
Petits Fours

Jordan
Cabernet Sauvignon
1976

THE WHITE HOUSE
Thursday, April 28, 1983

The Prime Minister of Canada

April 28, 1983

The only wine on the menu
for the Reagans' luncheon for
Prime Minister Pierre Trudeau
of Canada was Jordan
Cabernet Sauvignon 1976.
Trudeau reportedly bought
a case of this wine for himself
after tasting it at the White
House luncheon.

Dinner

Honoring
His Excellency
The Premier of the State Council
of the People's Republic of China

Poached Turbot
Sauce Aurora
Sesame Seed Twists

Beef Farci en Croûte
Truffle Sauce
Potatoes Soufflé
Carrot Ring

Garden Green Salad with Walnuts

Pomegranate Sorbet with Fresh Fruit
Petits Fours Sec

Pine Ridge Chardonnay 1981
Silver Oak Cabernet Sauvignon 1978
Schramsberg Crémant Demi-Sec 1981

THE WHITE HOUSE
Tuesday, January 10, 1984

January 10, 1984

A well-regarded California wine, Silver Oak Cabernet Sauvignon 1978 was served during the Reagans' State Dinner honoring Zhao Ziyang, the premier of the State Council of the People's Republic of China.

DINNER

Honoring
His Excellency
The President of the French Republic
and Mrs. Mitterrand

Columbia River Smoked Salmon
Cucumber Sauce
Sesame Seed Twists

Tenderloin of Veal en Croûte
Truffle Sauce
Saffron Rice
Garden Asparagus

Bibb Lettuce with Endive
Brie Cheese

Springtime Sorbet
Petits Fours Sec

Robert Mondavi Fumé Blanc Reserve 1981
Clos du Val Cabernet Sauvignon 1975
Domaine Chandon Blanc de Noirs

THE WHITE HOUSE
Thursday, March 22, 1984

March 22, 1984

At the State Dinner for Prime Minister François Mitterrand of France, President and Mrs. Reagan served Cabernet Sauvignon 1975 from Clos du Val, a winery in Napa Valley launched in 1972 by a Frenchman descended from famed Bordeaux wine merchants. The Cabernet Sauvignon rivaled French wines and took first place at the French Culinary Institute tasting in 1986.

DINNER

Honoring
The New Members of Congress

Rainbow Trout in Lobster Sauce
Fleurons

Suprême of Cornish Hen
Wild Rice
Braised Fennel with Red Peppers

Hearts of Romaine & Endive Salad
Cheddar Cheese Mousse
Corn Sticks

Strawberry Bombe
Petits Fours

Vichon Chardonnay 1980
Robert Mondavi Pinot Noir 1978
Schramsberg Blanc de Blancs 1980

THE WHITE HOUSE
Tuesday, January 29, 1985

January 29, 1985

Robert Mondavi Pinot
Noir 1978 was one of three
California wines served
at President and Mrs.
Reagan's dinner honoring
new members of Congress.

DINNER

Honoring
His Excellency
The President of the People's Republic of China
and Madame Lin Jiamei

Lobster en Belle-vue
Tarragon Mayonnaise
Sesame Seed Twists

Tenderloin of Veal in Golden Crust
Morel Sauce
Tomato Cups with Minted Peas
Summer Squash

Romaine Lettuce and Jicama Root
Pine Nut Dressing

Peach and Strawberry Sorbet
Lime Sabayon
Petits Fours

Balverne Chardonnay 1981
Caymus Cabernet Sauvignon 1977
Schramsberg Cuvée de Pinot

THE WHITE HOUSE
Tuesday, July 23, 1985

July 23, 1985

Caymus Vineyards in Napa Valley produced its first vintage in 1972 and was still relatively new when President and Mrs. Reagan served its Cabernet Sauvignon 1977 at a dinner honoring President Li Xiannian of the People's Republic of China. The winery would gain acclaim in the following years.

Luncheon

Regional Editors and Broadcasters

Cold Curry Soup
Cheese Twists

Tenderloin of Veal with Mushrooms
Fine Noodles
Zucchini Provençale

Macédoine of Fresh Fruit
Ladyfingers

Gevrey Chambertin 1970

The White House
Monday, September 16, 1985

September 16, 1985

At a luncheon for regional editors and broadcasters, President Reagan selected a French wine, Gevrey Chambertin 1970, rather than an American choice, causing great controversy.

DINNER
Honoring
Their Royal Highnesses
The Prince and Princess of Wales

Lobster Mousseline
with Maryland Crab
Horseradish Sauce

Glazed Chicken Capsicum
Brown Rice
Garden Vegetables

Jicama Salad
Herbed Cheese
Croutons

Peach Sorbet Basket
Champagne Sauce
Petits Fours

Quail Ridge Chardonnay 1981
Conn Creek Cabernet Sauvignon 1979
Schramsberg Cuvée de Pinot 1982

THE WHITE HOUSE
Saturday, November 9, 1985

November 9, 1985

The Reagans served
California wines to Prince
Charles and Princess
Diana of Wales at a dinner
in their honor. Included on
the menu are Quail Ridge
Chardonnay 1981, Conn
Creek Cabernet Sauvignon
1979, and Schramsberg
Cuvée de Pinot 1982.

Luncheon

HONORING
The Members of The Supreme Court
of the United States

Shrimp and Watercress Salad
Herbed Toast Rounds

Medallions of Veal in Marsala
Pasta with Gruyère Cheese
Fresh Asparagus Polonaise

Mango Mousse with Baked Apple

BALVERNE Chardonnay 1981
JORDAN Cabernet Sauvignon 1976

THE WHITE HOUSE
Tuesday, November 25, 1986

November 25, 1986

President Reagan again chose
one of his favorite wines,
Jordan Cabernet Sauvignon
1976, at his luncheon honoring
members of the Supreme
Court.

Luncheon

HONORING
His Excellency
The President of the Republic of Zaire

Fruit Compote

Broiled Salmon
Parslied Rice
Buttered Broccoli

Fresh Garden Salad

White Chocolate Mousse
Coffee

CAKEBREAD Chardonnay 1984

THE WHITE HOUSE
ROOSEVELT ROOM · Tuesday, December 9, 1986

December 9, 1986

One of President Reagan's favorite luncheon selections was Cakebread Chardonnay 1984, as seen on this menu for President Mobutu Sese Seko of the Republic of Zaire.

DINNER

HONORING
His Excellency
The Prime Minister of the French Republic
and Mrs. Chirac

Lobster Mousse
Fines Herbes Sauce
Gruyère Bow Ties

Médaillons of Veal Périgueux
Barquettes of Vegetables
Asparagus in Hazelnut Butter

Endive and Chicory Salad
Coulommiers & Saint Paulin Cheese

Gin Parfait with Honey Grapefruit
Petits Fours

Sonoma-Cutrer Chardonnay 1984

Opus One 1982
Robert Mondavi / Baron Philippe de Rothschild

Domaine Mumm, Cuvée Napa

THE WHITE HOUSE
Tuesday, March 31, 1987

March 31, 1987

French-style wines were chosen for the Reagans' State Dinner in honor of French Prime Minister Jacques Chirac. Sonoma-Cutrer Chardonnay 1984 is a California Chardonnay made in the Burgundian style. Domaine Mumm Cuvée Napa is a sparkling wine made in California by a French champagne company. The centerpiece of the meal was Opus One 1982 from the joint venture between California's Robert Mondavi and Baron Philippe de Rothschild of Château Mouton Rothschild of France. President Reagan highlighted the wine as a symbol of the enduring friendship between the United States and France with an end-of-the-meal toast.

DINNER

Honoring
His Excellency
The Prime Minister of Japan
and Mrs. Nakasone

Columbia River Smoked Salmon
Horseradish Sauce
Fennel Twists

Champagne Chicken Tarragon
Wild Rice in Turnips
Early Spring Zucchini

Field Salad with Walnut Dressing
Bel Paese Cheese
Melba Toast

Orange Surprise
Petits Fours Sec

JORDAN *Chardonnay* 1984
SCHUG CELLARS *Pinot Noir* 1984
CHÂTEAU ST. JEAN 1983

THE WHITE HOUSE
Thursday, April 30, 1987

April 30, 1987

Three California wines are included on this menu for President and Mrs. Reagan's State Dinner for Prime Minister Yasuhiro Nakasone of Japan: Jordan Chardonnay 1984, Schug Cellars Pinot Noir 1984, and Chateau St. Jean 1983.

DINNER
Honoring The Right Honorable
The Prime Minister of the United Kingdom
of Great Britain and Northern Ireland
and Mr. Thatcher

Baby Lobster Bellevue
Caviar Yogurt Sauce
Curried Croissant

Roasted Saddle of Veal Périgourdine
Jardinière of Vegetables
Asparagus with Hazelnut Butter

Autumn Mixed Salad
Selection of Cheese

Chestnut Marquise
Pistachio Sauce
Orange Tuiles and Ginger Twigs

SAINTSBURY *Chardonnay 1987*
STAG'S LEAP WINE CELLARS *Cabernet Sauvignon 1978*
SCHRAMSBERG *Crémant Demi-Sec 1984*

THE WHITE HOUSE
Wednesday, November 16, 1988

November 16, 1988

The menu for the last State Dinner hosted by President and Mrs. Reagan was for Prime Minister Margaret Thatcher of the United Kingdom. It included three California wines—Saintsbury Chardonnay 1987, Stag's Leap Wine Cellars Cabernet Sauvignon 1978, and Schramsberg Crémant Demi-Sec 1984.

May 22, 1989

One of the first official dinners hosted by President and Mrs. George H. W. Bush featured Saintsbury Chardonnay 1987, Robert Mondavi Cabernet Sauvignon 1985, and Domaine Ste. Michelle Columbia Valley Brut. The Domaine Ste. Michelle, produced in Washington, was a change from the typical California champagne chosen by the Reagans.

DINNER
Honoring
The Governors of the States and Territories

Coquille of Maryland Crabmeat
Dilled Mayonnaise
Cheese Twists

Beef Tenderloin with Truffle Sauce
Potato Macaire & Broiled Cherry Tomato
Spinach Ring with Glazed Parsnips

Mesclun Salad and
Tuscan Olive Oil Dressing
Cheddar & Blue Cheese

Biscuit Glacé Cotes des Nuits
with Frosted Grapes
Sabayon

SAINTSBURY *Chardonnay 1987*
ROBERT MONDAVI *Cabernet Sauvignon 1985*
DOMAINE STE. MICHELLE *Columbia Valley Brut*

THE WHITE HOUSE
Monday, May 22, 1989

Dinner

Honoring His Excellency
The President of
the Union of Soviet Socialist Republics
and Mrs. Gorbachev

Maine Lobster en Gelée
Aurora Sauce
Corn Sticks

Roasted Filet of Beef Mascotte
Green Peppercorn Sauce
Asparagus, Sauce Aveline

Mixed Spring Salad
Lemon & Olive Oil Dressing
Saint Paulin Cheese

Lime Turban with Iced Raspberries
Friandises

FLORA SPRINGS *Barrel Fermented Chardonnay 1987*
HEITZ CELLARS MARTHA'S VINEYARD *Cabernet Sauvignon 1974*
S. ANDERSON *Blanc de Noirs Cuvée Extraordinaire 1985*

THE WHITE HOUSE
Thursday, May 31, 1990

May 31, 1990

At the State Dinner for Soviet President Mikhail Gorbachev, President and Mrs. Bush served the blockbuster Heitz Cellars Martha's Vineyard Cabernet Sauvignon 1974, the same wine that President Reagan had served to the French president at a reciprocal dinner in Paris eight years earlier.

DINNER
Honoring Her Majesty
Queen Margrethe II of Denmark
and His Royal Highness Prince Henrik of Denmark

Lobster Médaillons & Cucumber Mousse
Caviar Sauce
Gruyère Bow Ties

Crown Roast of Lamb, Jalapeño Mint Sauce
Croquette Potatoes
Carrot Timbale with Snow Peas

Endive, Watercress & Mushroom Salad
Native Chèvre Cheese
Melba Toast

Hot Raspberry Soufflé
Custard Sauce
Petits Fours

SANFORD *Chardonnay Barrel Select 1988*
ROBERT MONDAVI *Pinot Noir Reserve 1988*
VICHON *Sémillion Botrytis 1987*

THE WHITE HOUSE
Wednesday, February 20, 1991

February 20, 1991

President and Mrs. Bush
often chose California wines
for official dinners, including
Robert Mondavi Pinot Noir
Reserve 1988 served at
the dinner honoring Queen
Margrethe II of Denmark.

DINNER

Honoring Her Majesty
The Queen of Thailand

Lobster Bisque with Quenelles
Pesto Galettes

Crown Roast of Lamb
Château Potatoes
Acorn Squash, Baby Corn & Snow Peas

Autumn Salad
Almond Brie Cheese

Fruit Sorbets Surprise
with Sabayon Sauce
Petits Fours

SANFORD *Chardonnay 1989*
STAR HILL *Pinot Noir 1988*
DOMAIN CHANDON *Brut*

THE WHITE HOUSE
Monday, October 28, 1991

October 28, 1991

President and Mrs. Bush sought new wine selections, such as California's Star Hill, which provided a 1988 Pinot Noir for the State Dinner honoring Queen Sirikit of Thailand.

DINNER

Honoring His Excellency
Constantinos Stephanopoulos
President of the Hellenic Republic

Roasted Tomato with Smoked Basil Shrimp,
Fava Beans and Eggplant Salad
Potato Garlic Sauce

Grilled Lamb Tenderloin with Spinach Orzo,
Spicy Olive Slivers and Crispy Beets
Yellow Pepper Reduction

Marinated Young Greens,
Warm Kefalotiri Cheese and Baked Figs
Orange Saffron Dressing

Lemon Honey Marbleized Dome
Black Raspberry Sauce with Seasonal Fruit
Baklava, Pine Nut Macaroons
and Kourabiedes

LOLONIS *Chardonnay "Reserve" 1994*
TOPOLOS *Zinfandel "Piner Heights" 1994*
PINDAR *Brut "Long Island" 1989*

The White House
Thursday, May 9, 1996

Wilson Service Plate · Franklin D. Roosevelt Dinner Service

May 9, 1996

Wines selected by President and Mrs. William J. Clinton for official White House events were often chosen as tributes to the guests of honor. The menu for the dinner in honor of President Constantinos Stephanopoulos of Greece lists three American wineries established by Greek immigrants and their descendants.

Dinner

Honoring His Excellency
Jiang Zemin
President of the People's Republic of China
and Madame Wang Yeping

Chilled Lobster with Corn Leek Relish
Marinated Butternut Squash
Lobster Tarragon Sauce

Pepper Crusted Oregon Beef
Yukon Gold Whipped Potatoes
Roasted Root Vegetables
Shallot Marmalade
Pinot Noir and Chanterelle Sauce

Salad of Mache, Endive and Arugula
Tomato Asiago Custard
Balsamic and Chive Dressing

Orange Blossom Surprise
Pomegranate Sauce
Mandarin Tea Tartlet
Chocolate Tea Candy
Crystallized Ginger

CUVAISON "Carneros" Chardonnay 1995
PONZI "25th Anniversary" Pinot Noir 1995
IRON HORSE Blanc de Blanc (L.D.) 1991

The White House
Wednesday, October 29, 1997

October 29, 1997

At the Clintons' State Dinner in honor of Chinese President Jiang Zemin, the guests enjoyed Cuvaison Carneros Chardonnay 1995 from California, Ponzi 25th Anniversary Pinot Noir 1995 from Oregon, and Iron Horse Blanc de Blanc 1991 from California. Ponzi Vineyards, founded in the 1960s, set out to create Pinot Noir in the Willamette Valley in the Burgundian tradition.

DINNER

Honoring Their Majesties
King Juan Carlos I
of Spain
and Queen Sofia

Pheasant and Morel Consommé
Dumplings of Foie Gras and Confit

Lobster and Maine Shrimp
Saffron Risotto and Chorizo

Grilled Rack of Lamb
Blood Orange and Rosemary Sauce
Braised Winter Vegetables with Parsnip Purée

Pear and Bleu Cheese Terrine
Bouquet of Lettuces
25 Year Old Sherry Dressing

Topiary Valencia
Glazed Kumquat Sauce
Caramel Walnut Candy
Butter Raspberry Ginger Cookies

MIRAMAR TORRES *Chardonnay 1997*
ARTESA *Pinot Noir "Bien Nacido" 1997*
GLORIA FERRER *"Royal Cuvée" Brut 1991*

The White House
Wednesday, February 23, 2000

February 23, 2000

Three California wines from wineries established by families with Spanish connections were served at the Clintons' State Dinner honoring King Juan Carlos I and Queen Sofía of Spain. The founder of Miramar Torres was from Barcelona, Spain; Artesa Vineyards was established by Spain's oldest winemaking family; and the founders of the Gloria Ferrer winery are descended from Spanish winemakers.

DINNER

In celebration of
The 200th Anniversary
of The White House

Truffle and Duck Consommé
Roasted Vegetables and Madeira
Seared Striped Bass
Corn and Crab Fricassee
Chive and Oyster Sauce

Grapefruit and Gin Sherbet
Smoked Loin of Lamb
Heirloom Apples, Butternut Squash and Salsify
Terrine of Pears, Figs and Wild Ripened Cheese
Winter Greens
Fig Dressing
Abigail Adams' Floating Island
Raisin Biscuits
Lemon Bars

Kistler *Chardonnay* "Cuvee Cathleen" 1996
Landmark *Pinot Noir* "Kastania Vineyard" 1997
Bonny Doon *"Vin Glaciere Muscat"* 1999

The White House
Thursday, November 9, 2000

November 9, 2000

In 2000 President and Mrs. Clinton celebrated the White House's two-hundredth anniversary with a special dinner at which three California wines were served: Kistler Chardonnay Cuvee Cathleen 1996, Landmark Pinot Noir Kastania Vineyard 1997, and Bonny Doon Vin Glaciere Muscat 1999.

DINNER
in honor of

THE RIGHT HONORABLE
JEAN CHRÉTIEN, P.C., M.P.
PRIME MINISTER of CANADA

Maine Lobster
Applewood Smoked Bacon and Leeks
Lewis Cellars Chardonnay "Reserve" 1997

Pan Seared Bison Loin with Madeira Sauce
Wild Mushroom Flan
Crispy Potato Cake
Joseph Phelps "Insignia" 1994

Salad of Winter Greens
Avocado · Maytag Bleu Cheese · Sherry Dressing

Chocolate Hazelnut Terrine
Vanilla Sauce

THE WHITE HOUSE
Monday, February 5, 2001

February 5, 2001

President and Mrs. George W. Bush selected two California wines, Lewis Cellars Chardonnay Reserve 1997 and Joseph Phelps Insignia 1994, for the dinner in honor of Canadian Prime Minister Jean Chrétien. There was no dessert champagne served at this dinner.

DINNER

Honoring
The Governors of the States and Territories

Maine Lobster with Carrot Soup
Infused Risotto
Llano Estacado "Cellar Select" Chardonnay 1999 (Texas)

Grilled Yearling Beef with Truffled Potatoes
Roasted Onions and Herbed Vegetable Ragoût
Rex Hill "Jacob Hart" Pinot Noir 1998 (Oregon)

Winter Greens with Maytag Bleu Cheese in Brioche
Sherry Dressing

Chocolate Tumbleweed
Honey Parfait
Poached Pear in Pomegranate Sauce
Linden Vineyards "Late Harvest" 1999 (Virginia)

THE WHITE HOUSE
Sunday, February 25, 2001

February 25, 2001

White House guests were introduced to the geographically diverse fine wines of the United States at President Bush's dinner for the Governors of the States and Territories. The menu lists Llano Estacado Cellar Select Chardonnay 1999 from Texas, Rex Hill Jacob Hart Pinot Noir 1998 from Oregon, and Linden Vineyards Late Harvest 1999 dessert wine from Virginia.

Dinner celebrating
The Spirit of Special Olympics

Rosemary-scented Grilled Blue Prawns
Saffron Risotto with Tasso Ham
Citrus Sauce
PAUL HOBBS CHARDONNAY "DINNER VINEYARD" 1999

Herb-crusted Lamb
Corn and Chive Timbale
Shallot Jus
TALLEY PINOT NOIR "ROSEMARY'S VINEYARD" 1997

Salad of Mâche and Chicory
Oven-roasted Beets
Soft-ripened Blue Cheese
Balsamic Vinaigrette

Special Olympics Snow Ball
Raspberry Sauce · Chocolate Sauce
WOLFFER "CHRISTIAN CUVEE" BRUT 1995

The White House
Thursday, December 13, 2001

December 13, 2001

President and Mrs. Bush served a wine by one of America's most highly regarded winemakers, Paul Hobbs Chardonnay Dinner Vineyard 1999, at the 2001 dinner honoring the Special Olympics.

Dinner in honor of
Her Majesty Queen Elizabeth II
and His Royal Highness The Prince Philip
Duke of Edinburgh

Corn Soup with Avocado
Fried Tortilla
NEWTON CHARDONNAY 2000

Mixed Leaf and Citrus Salad
Parmesan Wafer

Herb-crusted Canon of Lamb
Mushroom Sauce
Dauphinoise Potatoes
Yellow and Green Zucchini with Basil
Medley of Beans and Bacon
PETER MICHAEL "LES PAVOTS" 1997

Fudge Brownie Pudding
Kahlúa Sauce
Mascarpone Ice Cream
SCHRAMSBERG "CRÉMANT" 1999

WINFIELD HOUSE   LONDON, ENGLAND
THURSDAY, NOVEMBER 20, 2003

November 20, 2003

Newton Chardonnay 2000, Peter Michael Les Pavots 1997, and Schramsberg Crémant 1999, all California wines, were chosen for President and Mrs. Bush's reciprocal dinner held for Queen Elizabeth II at Winfield House in London. Newton and Peter Michael were both founded by English winemakers.

Valentine's Day Dinner

"Oysters and Pearls"
Oyster Stew garnished with Osetra Caviar
Ancien Chardonnay "Carneros" 2002

Tenderloin of Buffalo

Hudson River Foie Gras

Asparagus, Carrots and
Grilled Vegetable Bundles
Duckhorn "Paraduxx" 2001

Butterhead, Red Oak and Arugula Salad

Raspberry Crème Brûlée
Chocolate Flourless Cake
Vanilla Sugared Beignet
"J" Brut Rosé, n/v

The White House
Monday, February 14, 2005

February 14, 2005

President and Mrs. Bush's
White House Valentine's
Day dinner menu features
three California wines—
Ancien Chardonnay
Carneros 2002, Duckhorn
Paraduxx 2001, and J Brut
Rosé.

DINNER
in honor of
THEIR ROYAL HIGHNESSES
THE PRINCE OF WALES
and
THE DUCHESS OF CORNWALL

Celery Broth with Crispy Rock Shrimp
NEWTON CHARDONNAY "UNFILTERED" 2002

Medallions of Buffalo Tenderloin
Roasted Corn

Wild Rice Pancakes

Glazed Parsnips and Young Carrots
PETER MICHAEL PINOT NOIR "LE MOULIN ROUGE" 2002

Mint Romaine Lettuce
Blood Orange Vinaigrette
Vermont Camembert Cheese and Spiced Walnuts

Petits Fours Cake
Chartreuse Ice Cream Red and Green Grape Sauce
IRON HORSE "WEDDING CUVÉE" 2002

THE WHITE HOUSE
Wednesday, November 2, 2005

November 2, 2005

On the occasion of the visit of Prince Charles of Wales and Camilla, Duchess of Cornwall, to the White House, President and Mrs. Bush served Newton and Peter Michael wines—the same two wineries featured on the reciprocal dinner menu for Britain's Queen Elizabeth II in 2003. They also served Iron Horse Wedding Cuvee 2002 in honor of the couple's recent marriage.

Dinner
in honor of
The Governors of
the States and Territories

Maryland Blue Crab
and Meyer Lemon Soup
Spinach Spaetzle
BECKER VINEYARDS CHARDONNAY "RESERVE" 2004 (TEXAS)

Alaska Honey-glazed Venison
Parsnips and Sweet Potatoes
Grilled Asparagus with Bearnaise Sauce
CARDINALE 2001 (CALIFORNIA)

Ohio Field Lettuces
Citrus Avocado Dressing

"Shining City on a Hill"
Crispy Caramel Cake · Raspberry Sherbet
Hawaiian Kona Coffee
SHELDRAKE POINT RIESLING "ICE WINE" 2004 (NEW YORK)

The White House　　　　　*Sunday, February 26, 2006*

February 26, 2006

Wines from Texas, California, and New York were served at President and Mrs. Bush's 2006 dinner for the Governors of the States and Territories.

Dinner honoring
The Right Honourable
Tony Blair, M.P.
Prime Minister of the United Kingdom
of Great Britain and Northern Ireland

Summer Pea Soup
Maine Shrimp and Pike Quenelle
SELBY CHARDONNAY "RUSSIAN RIVER" 2004

Roasted Veal Loin
Port and Red Wine Essence
Fava Bean, Minted Carrots
and Crushed Fingerling Potatoes
GRACE FAMILY CABERNET "NAPA" 2002

Baby Greens
Grapefruit Fillets, Marinated Hearts of Palm
Hazelnut Oil Dressing

Warm Apples in Country Bread
Vanilla Ice Cream · Caramel Sauce

THE WHITE HOUSE   THURSDAY, MAY 25, 2006

May 25, 2006

President and Mrs. Bush chose top California wines, Selby Chardonnay Russian River 2004 and Grace Family Cabernet Napa 2002, for their State Dinner for Prime Minister Tony Blair of the United Kingdom.

Dinner
in honor of
Her Majesty Queen Elizabeth II
and His Royal Highness The Prince Philip
Duke of Edinburgh

Spring Pea Soup with Fernleaf Lavender
Chive Pizzelle with American Caviar
NEWTON CHARDONNAY "UNFILTERED" 2004

Dover Sole Almondine
Roasted Artichokes, Pequillo Peppers and Olives

Saddle of Spring Lamb
Chanterelle Sauce
Fricassee of Baby Vegetables
PETER MICHAEL "LES PAVOTS" 2003

Arugula, Savannah Mustard
and Mint Romaine
Champagne Dressing · Trio of Farmhouse Cheeses

"Rose Blossoms"
SCHRAMSBERG BRUT ROSÉ 2004

The White House   Monday, May 7, 2007

May 7, 2007

When President and Mrs. Bush hosted their third dinner for Queen Elizabeth II and Prince Philip, they repeated the excellent wine selections made for their previous dinners with the British royal family—Newton and Peter Michael. Schramsberg Brut Rosé 2004 was served for dessert.

Dinner
in honor of His Excellency
Nicolas Sarkozy
President of the French Republic

Maine Lobster Bisque
Vermouth Cream
HDV CHARDONNAY "CARNEROS" 2004

Elysian Farm Lamb
with Heirloom Tomato Fondue
Ragoût of Green Beans, Chanterelles
and Caramelized Shallots
Sweet Potato Casserole
DOMINUS "NAPA VALLEY" 2004

Salad of White and Green Asparagus
Peppercress and Mâche
White Balsamic Vinaigrette

La Fayette's Legacy
CHANDON "ROSÉ" N/V

THE WHITE HOUSE   TUESDAY, NOVEMBER 6, 2007

November 6, 2007

For the State Dinner honoring President Nicolas Sarkozy of France, President and Mrs. Bush selected three California wines made by French winemakers—HdV Chardonnay Carneros 2004, Dominus Napa Valley 2004, and Chandon Rosé, a sparkling wine launched in 1973 by Frenchman Robert-Jean de Vogüé.

Dinner Menu

Wild Mushroom Soup with Black Truffle
Shaoxing Wine

Butter Poached Maine Lobster with Spinach, Shiitake
and Leek Rice Noodle Rolls
Penner-Ash Viognier "Oregon" 2014

Grilled Cannon of Colorado Lamb with Garlic Fried
Milk and Baby Broccoli
Pride Mountain Merlot "Vintner Select" 2012

Poppyseed Bread and Butter Pudding
with Meyer Lemon Curd Lychee Sorbet
Schramsberg Cremant Demi-Sec 2011

September 25, 2015

President and Mrs. Barack Obama were the first to serve a Chinese wine at the White House. Shaoxing, a traditional Chinese wine, is included on the menu for the 2015 State Dinner for President Xi Jinping of the People's Republic of China.

DINNER

Salt-cured Ahi Tuna
Pickled Young Radish
Watermelon-Juniper Granite

TRISAETUM DRY RIESLING "ESTATES" 2014

Tomato Tartare
Cardamom Yogurt
Micro Lettuce
Citrus Vinaigrette

GRGICH HILLS FUMÉ BLANC "ESTATE" 2013

Red Wine Braised Short Ribs
Hot Kale Salad
Thyme Dumplings

RdV "RENDEZVOUS" 2010

Caramel Almond Mille Feuille
Vanilla Bean Chantilly
Lingonberry Cream

May 13, 2016

President and Mrs. Obama served a variety of wines at their State Dinner for the leaders of the Nordic counties of Sweden, Norway, Finland, Denmark, and Iceland. They served Trisaetum Dry Riesling Estates 2014 from Oregon, Grgich Hills Fumé Blanc Estate 2013 from California, and concluded the evening with RdV Rendezvous 2010, a spectacular new wine from Virginia.

Dinner Menu

First Course
Sweet Potato Agnolotti with Butter and Sage
Palmina Vermentino "Santa Ynez" 2015

Salad Course
Warm Butternut Squash Salad with Frisee
and Pecorino di New York
Villa Ragazzi Sangiovese 'Napa" 2012

Main Course
Beef Braciole Pinwheel with Horseradish Gremolata
and Broccoli Rabe
A vegetarian version of this dish will be available
Ridge Vineyards Zinfandel "East Bench" 2014

Dessert
Green Apple Crostata with Thyme Caramel
and Buttermilk Gelato

"Celebrating Autumn's Harvest"
Petits Four Display:
Sweet Corn Crema and Blackberry Cup
Concord Grape Bittersweet Chocolate Leaf
Orange Fig Slice
Pumpkin Cranberry Tart
Tiramisu

October 18, 2016

President and Mrs. Obama's last State Dinner at the White House, which honored Prime Minister Matteo Renzi of Italy, showcased three Italian-style wines from American vineyards: Vermentino Santa Ynez 2015 from California's Palmina vineyard, which grows Italian grape varietals, Sangiovese Napa 2012 from the Italian American–owned Napa vineyard Villa Ragazzi, and Zinfandel East Bench 2014 from Ridge Vineyards, a historic vineyard first cultivated in 1985 by Italian immigrants.

April 24, 2018

Two American wines made in the French style were served by President and Mrs. Donald J. Trump at their first State Dinner, which honored President Emmanuel Macron of France. Domaine Serene Chardonnay Evenstad Reserve 2015 and Domaine Drouhin Pinot Noir Laurène 2014 are produced by Oregon vineyards owned by French American families who use French winemaking traditions. Schramsberg Crémant 2014 was also served.

Dinner
IN HONOR OF
His Excellency
Emmanuel Macron
PRESIDENT OF THE FRENCH REPUBLIC
and Mrs Brigitte Macron

Goat Cheese Gateau
Tomato Jam
Buttermilk Biscuit Crumbles
Young Variegated Lettuces
DOMAINE SERENE CHARDONNAY "EVENSTAD RESERVE" 2015

Rack of Spring Lamb
Burnt Cipollini Soubise
Carolina Gold Rice Jambalaya
DOMAINE DROUHIN PINOT NOIR "LAURÈNE" 2014

Nectarine Tart
Crème Fraîche Ice Cream
SCHRAMSBERG "CRÉMANT" 2014

The White House   *Tuesday, April 24, 2018*

May 15, 2019

California wines were chosen for a White House dinner President and Mrs. Trump hosted in honor of the White House Historical Association. They served Stag's Leap Chardonnay Karia 2015, Hartford Zinfandel Fanucchi-Wood Road 2014, and Schramsberg Crémant Demi-Sec 2014. Schramsberg, served with dessert, was a favorite on White House menus for more than fifty years.

The Presidential Seal

Dinner
IN HONOR OF
The Honorable
Scott Morrison MP
Prime Minister of Australia
and Mrs. Jennifer Morrison

Sunchoke Ravioli
Reggiano Cream
Late Summer Shaved Vegetables
SPRING MOUNTAIN SAUVIGNON BLANC "NAPA" 2017

Dover Sole
Zucchini Squash Blossoms
Fennel Mousseline
ARGYLE PINOT NOIR "RESERVE" 2016

Lady Apple Tart
Calvados Ice Cream
J VINEYARDS DEMI-SEC NV

The White House   *Friday, September 20, 2019*

September 20, 2019

At the beautiful Rose Garden State Dinner honoring Prime Minister Scott Morrison of Australia, President and Mrs. Trump served Spring Mountain Sauvignon Blanc Napa 2017, Argyle Pinot Noir Reserve 2016, and J Vineyards Demi-Sec. Oregon's Argyle Winery was co-founded by Australian winemaker Brian Coser.

Sa tendre volonté séduit le plus rebelles.

Dessin inédit   de Matta

1962   1962

Cette récolte a produit :
149.266 Bordelaises et ½ B^{es} de 1 à 149.266
1.708 Magnums de M 1 à M 1.708
34 Grands Formats de GF 1 à GF 34
double-magnums, jéroboams, impériales
2000 Réserve du Château "marquées R.C.
Ci.

Philippe de Rothschild

Château
Mouton Rothschild

BARON PHILIPPE DE ROTHSCHILD PROPRIÉTAIRE A PAUILLAC

APPELLATION PAUILLAC CONTRÔLÉE

TOUTE LA RÉCOLTE MISE EN BOUTEILLES AU CHÂTEAU

CHAPTER SEVEN

THE WINES SERVED
A Catalog of Vintages

Wine and cheese are ageless companions, like aspirin and aches, or June and moon, or good people and noble ventures.

—M.F.K. Fisher

The 1962 Château Mouton Rothschild served by President Reagan in 1986 at a private dinner for supporters of the Reagan Presidential Foundation bore a label painted by the Chilean-born artist Roberto Matta. Since Baron Philippe de Rothschild established the tradition in 1945, a different artist has been invited to paint a unique label each year.

FORMAL DINNERS AND LUNCHEONS at the White House are usually diplomatic events, opportunities to welcome world leaders by showcasing American hospitality at its best. Other official dinners honor the achievements of Americans, such as Nobel Prize winners and Olympic athletes, or those in high office, such as the governors of the states and the justices of the Supreme Court. Even when the events are described as working luncheons or dinners, the wines are always most carefully chosen, often making a connection to a guest's homeland or home state. The wines listed here include those served since the administration of President Dwight D. Eisenhower, when menu cards began to be regularly presented to guests at their tables and menus made public. The names of the vintner, grape, and vintage have been compiled from these menus, and the list is as comprehensive as these sources allow. Such a list naming the wines on the president's table across more than half a century has never before been published. The images of wine bottles and labels that illustrate the list have been contributed by the winemakers themselves.

French wines dominate in the 1950s, and then, starting in the 1960s, wines from California appear on the menu. By the 1970s and 1980s the wines are predominately American, but on occasion selections from France, Germany, Italy, Portugal, and Spain appear as well. To date, wines from nearly two dozen U.S. states have been served in the White House. Presidential preferences are clear throughout, with favorites often served at a dozen or more events.

Astute readers will note variations, often from one administration to the next, in the way the name of the honored guest is presented, the practice of identifying vintages, and even whether a dinner is called "State," "official" or "working." Administrations have had different preferences, and the format for the menus has changed over the years. In short, the catalog reflects information on the menus for which wines are named.

Château Climens 1950

Château Climens is a First Growth Sauterne from the Bordeaux region that began production of its wine in the seventeenth century. Along with Beaune Grèves and Pol Roger, Château Climens was a staple wine of the Eisenhower presidency. The 1942 or 1950 vintages were served for the second course at ten dinners.

Dwight D. Eisenhower Presidency
1953–1961

1953

October 28
State Dinner in honor of King Paul of Greece
Sherry
White Wine
Champagne

1954

May 26
State Dinner in honor of Emperor Haile Selassie I of Ethiopia
Sherry
Sauterne
Red Burgundy
Champagne

July 26
State Dinner in honor of President Rhee of Korea
Sherry
Sauterne
Red Burgundy
Champagne

October 18
State Dinner in honor of President Tubman of Liberia
Sherry
Sauterne
Red Burgundy
Champagne

1956

May 16
Luncheon in honor of President Sukarno of Indonesia
Pol Roger Dry Special, France

1957

May 8
State Dinner in honor of President Diem of Vietnam
Dry Sack, Spain
Château Climens 1942, France
Beaune Greves 1952, France
Pol Roger 1945, France

May 27
Luncheon in honor of Chancellor Adenauer of Germany
Beaune Greves 1952, France

October 17
State Dinner in honor of Queen Elizabeth II of the United Kingdom
Dry Sack, Spain
Château Climens 1943, France
Beaune Greves 1952, France
Charles Heidsieck 1949, France

November 25
State Dinner in honor of King Mohammed V of Morocco
Dry Sack, Spain
Château La Tour Blanc 1949, France
Faisca Rosé, Portugal
Pol Roger Dry Special, France

1958

June 17
State Dinner in honor of President Garcia of the Philippines
Dry Sack, Spain
Château Climens 1942, France
Saint-Julien 1949, France
Pol Roger 1945, France

1959

January 20
State Dinner in honor of President Frondizi of Argentina
Dry Sack, Spain
Château Climens 1950, France
Beaune Greves 1952, France
Pol Roger 1952, France

March 10
State Dinner in honor of President Lemus of El Salvador
Dry Sack, Spain
Château Climens 1950, France
Beaune Greves 1952, France
Pol Roger 1952, France

March 17
State Dinner in honor of President O'Kelly of Ireland
Dry Sack, Spain
Château Climens 1950, France
Beaune Greves 1952, France
Pol Roger 1952, France

May 6
Dinner in honor of Winston Churchill
Dry Sack, Spain
Château Lafite Rothschild 1953, France
Pol Roger 1952, France

May 11
State Dinner in honor of King Baudouin of Belgium
Dry Sack, Spain
Château Climens 1950, France
Beaune Greves 1952, France
Pol Roger 1952, France

September 15
State Dinner in honor of Premier Nikita Khrushchev of the Soviet Union
Dry Sack, Spain
Château Climens 1950, France
Beaune Greves 1952, France
Pol Roger 1952, France

September 30
Luncheon in honor of Prime Minister Segni of Italy
Dry Sack, Spain
Puligny-Montrachet Pucelles 1952, France

1960

January 19
Luncheon in honor of Prime Minister Kishi of Japan
Dry Sack, Spain
Beaune Greves 1952, France

March 15
Luncheon in honor of Chancellor Adenauer of Germany
Dry Sack, Spain
Berncastler Doctor 1958, Germany
Pol Roger 1952, France

April 5
State Dinner in honor of President Lleras of Colombia
Dry Sack, Spain
Château Climens 1950, France
Beaune Greves 1952, France
Pol Roger 1952, France

April 22
State Dinner in honor of President Charles de Gaulle of France
Dry Sack, Spain
Château Coutet a Barsac 1937, France
Beaune Greves 1952, France
Pol Roger 1952, France

April 27
State Dinner in honor of King Mahendra of Nepal
Dry Sack, Spain
Château Climens 1950, France
Beaune Greves 1952, France
Pol Roger 1952, France

October 26
Luncheon in honor of Prime Minister Rahman of Malaya
Dry Sack, Spain
Almaden Pinot Noir, California

Pol Roger 1952

Pol Roger Brut was the champagne most often served by the Eisenhowers during the dessert course of their State Dinners. During the last two years of the administration, they served the 1952 vintage at every dinner including that for Winston Churchill, knowing that it was his favorite champagne.

Dom Pérignon 1952

Dom Pérignon was one of the most popular brands of champagne in the 1960s. The Kennedys served the 1952 vintage of the wine on fifteen occasions, including the May 1961 luncheon for Prince Rainier and Princess Grace of Monaco.

John F. Kennedy Presidency
1961–1963

1961

January 22
Private Dinner with the Honorable and Mrs. Franklin D. Roosevelt Jr., William Walton, Mrs. Ned Russell, and Joseph W. Alsop
Soave Bertani 1953, Italy
Château Haut-Brion 1955, France

February 1
Private Dinner with Attorney General and Mrs. Robert F. Kennedy, Mr. Billings, and Mrs. McEvoy
Dry Sack, Spain
La Bernardine Châteauneuf du Pape 1947, France
Dom Pérignon 1952, France

February 10
Private Luncheon with Mr. and Mrs. Arthur Hays Sulzberger, Mr. and Mrs. James B. Reston, Dr. Howard Rusk, and Vice President Johnson
Maximin Gruhauser Harrenberg 1958, Germany

February 14
Luncheon in honor of Prime Minister Kampmann of Denmark
Lancers Vin Rosé 1957, Portugal

February 20
Luncheon in honor of Prime Minister Diefenbaker of Canada
Corton-Charlemagne 1952, France
Beaune Greves 1955, France

March 15
Dinner for Prince and Princess Stanisław Radziwill
Pouilly Fuisse 1959, France
Château Haut-Brion 1955, France
Bollinger 1953, France

April 5
Luncheon in honor of Prime Minister Macmillan of Great Britain
Puligny-Montrachet Pucelles 1958, France
Corton-Grancey 1955, France
Dom Pérignon 1952, France

April 12
Luncheon in honor of Chancellor Konrad Adenauer of Germany
Puligny-Montrachet Pucelles 1958, France
Corton-Grancey 1955, France
Dom Pérignon 1952, France

April 17
Luncheon in honor of Prime Minister Karamanlis of Greece
Riesling 1955, Germany
Château Beychevelle 1947, France
Mumm Cordon Rouge 1953, France

May 3
State Dinner in honor of President Bourguiba of Tunisia
Corton-Charlemagne 1957, France
Château Haut-Brion 1953, France
Perriet-Jouet 1952, France

May 9
Luncheon for Florida Editors
Beaune Greves 1952, France

May 23
Senate Ladies' Luncheon
Almaden Grenache Rosé, California

May 24
Luncheon for Prince Rainier and Princess Grace of Monaco
Puligny-Montrachet 1958, France
Château Corton-Grancey 1955, France
Dom Pérignon 1952, France

June 8
Luncheon in honor of President Youlou of Congo
Vin Rosé, France
Piper-Heidsieck 1953, France

June 12
Luncheon in honor of Prime Minister Fanfani of Italy
Soave Bertani 1955, Italy
Château Haut-Brion 1953, France
Dom Pérignon 1952, France

June 21
Luncheon in honor of Prime Minister Ikeda of Japan
Soave Bertani 1955, Italy
Château Haut-Brion 1955, France
Dom Pérignon 1952, France

July 11
State Dinner at Mount Vernon in honor of President Ayub Khan of Pakistan
Château Haut-Brion Blanc 1958
Moët & Chandon Imperial Brut, 1955

July 12
Luncheon in honor of Governors
Almaden Pinot Chardonnay, California

July 20
Luncheon in honor of General MacArthur
Christian Brothers Cabernet, California
Moët & Chandon 1953, France

July 25
Luncheon in honor of Prime Minister Balewa of Nigeria
Inglenook Pinot Chardonnay, California
La Bernardine Châteauneuf du Pape 1955, France
Moët & Chandon Imperial Brut 1955, France

July 31
Luncheon in honor of Vice President Chen Cheng of China
Soave Bertani 1955, Italy
Almaden Cabernet Sauvignon, California
Moët & Chandon Dry Imperial Brut, France

September 13
Luncheon in honor of President Sukarno of Indonesia and President Modibo Këita of Mali
Wente Brothers White Pinot, California
Château Haut-Brion 1953, France
Piper Heidsieck 1953, France

September 15
Luncheon in honor of Western Foreign Ministers
Pouilly Fuisse 1957, France
Bonnes Mares 1945, France
Pommery 1952, France

September 19
State Dinner in honor of President Prado of Peru
Puligny-Montrachet Pucelles 1958, France
Almaden Pinot Noir, California
Dom Pérignon 1952, France

October 4
State Dinner in honor of President Abboud of Sudan
Inglenook Pinot Chardonnay, California
Château Haut-Brion 1953, France
Dom Pérignon 1952, France

October 16
Luncheon in honor of President Kekkonen of Finland
Mersault Genevrieres 1952, France
Château Richon Lelande 1952, France
Roederer 1955, France

October 19
Luncheon in honor of President Tubman of Liberia
Soave Bertani 1955, Italy
Almaden Pinot Noir, California
Piper Heidsieck 1953, France

Almaden Pinot Noir

Almaden Pinot Noir made history as the first American wine served at a State Dinner at the dinner in honor of President Prado of Peru, September 19, 1961. Almaden was established in California in 1852 and is recorded as first served at the White House by the Eisenhowers at a luncheon in 1960. The Kennedys would continue to serve it at six more luncheons and dinners.

Soave Bertani

Thomas Jefferson served many Italian wines at the White House in the early nineteenth century, but Soave Bertani was the first Italian wine to be served at a president's table in the twentieth century. This light white wine from Verona was served at eight luncheons and dinners with the first course, including two luncheons for Italian Prime Minister Amintore Fanfani in 1961 and 1963.

November 1
Dinner in honor of President and Mrs. Truman
Puligny-Montrachet Pucelles 1958, France
Château Gruaud-Larose 1955, France
Dom Pérignon 1952, France

November 3
Luncheon in honor of President Senghor of Senegal
Inglenook Pinot Chardonnay, California
Dom Pérignon 1952, France

November 7
State Dinner in honor of Prime Minister Jawaharlal Nehru of India
Almaden Pinot Blanc, California
Château Haut-Brion 1953, France
Dom Pérignon 1952, France

November 13, 1961
Dinner in honor of Governor Luis Muñoz Marín of Puerto Rico
Inglenook Pinot Chardonnay, California
Almaden Cabernet Sauvignon, California
Piper Heidsieck 1953, France

November 21
Luncheon in honor of Chancellor Adenauer of Germany
Wachenheimer Gerumpel Kabinet 1953, Germany
Almaden Pinot Noir, California
Moët & Chandon Imperial Brut 1955, France

1962

January 18
Private Dinner in honor of Mr. and Mrs. Igor Stravinsky
Château Haut-Brion 1958, France
Corton-Grancey 1955, France
Dom Pérignon 1952, France

February 5
Luncheon in honor of Prime Minister Adoula of Congo
Almaden Grenache Rosé, California
Piper Heidsieck 1953, France

February 9
Private Dinner for Mr. and Mrs. Stephen Smith
Puligny-Montrachet Pucelles 1959, France
Château Haut-Brion 1958, France
Piper Heidsieck 1953, France

February 20
Dinner in honor of the Vice President, the Speaker of the House, and the Chief Justice
Inglenook Pinot Chardonnay, California
La Tache Grand Cru 1957, France
Piper Heidsieck 1955, France

March 13
Luncheon in honor of President Ahidjo of Cameroon
Inglenook Pinot Chardonnay, California
Château Haut-Brion 1958, France
Piper Heidsieck 1953, France

March 20
Luncheon in honor of President Olympio of Togo
Almaden Grenache Rosé, California
Moët & Chandon Dry Imperial 1955, France

April 3
Luncheon in honor of President Goulart of Brazil
Puligny-Montrachet Pucelles 1958, France
Inglenook Pinot Noir, California
Piper Heidsieck 1955, France

April 11
State Dinner in honor of the Shah of Iran
Chevalier Montrachet 1959, France
Château Haut-Brion 1957, France
Moët & Chandon 1955, France

April 29
*Dinner in honor of Nobel
Prize Winners*
Puligny Montrachet Combetter
1er Cru 1959, France

Château Mouton Rothschild
1955, France

Piper Heidsieck 1955, France

May 3
*Luncheon in honor of Chancellor
Gorbach of Austria*
Almaden Grenache Rosé, California

Piper Heidsieck 1955, France

May 9
*Luncheon in honor of Prime
Minister Gerhardsen of Norway*
Inglenook Pinot
Chardonnay, California

Château Gruaud-Larose 1955, France

Piper Heidsieck 1955, France

May 11
*Dinner in honor of André
Malraux, French Minister
of Cultural Affairs*
Corton Charlemagne 1959, France

Château Gruaud-Larose 1955, France

Dom Pérignon 1952, France

May 22
*State Dinner in honor
of President Houphouët-
Boigny of the Ivory Coast*
Almaden Pinot Blanc, California

Château Haut-Brion 1955, France

Piper Heidsieck 1955, France

June 1
*Private Dinner-Dance with
the French Ambassador and
Friends of the Kennedys*
Soave Bertani 1955, Italy

Château Haut-Brion 1955, France

Piper Heidsieck 1955, France

June 5
*Luncheon in honor of President
Archbishop Makarios of Cyprus*
Inglenook Pinot
Chardonnay, California

Château Talbot St. Julien 1957, France

Piper Heidsieck 1955, France

June 12
*Luncheon in honor of
President Chiari of Panama*
Almaden Grenache Rosé, California

Piper Heidsieck 1955, France

June 18
*Luncheon in honor of Prime
Minister Menzies of Australia*
Soave Bertani 1955, Italy

Almaden Pinot Noir, California

Paul Ruinart Blanc de
Blancs 1953, France

June 25
*Luncheon in honor of President-
Elect Valencia of Colombia*
Puligny Montrachet 1959, France

Louis M. Martini Red
Pinot, California

Paul Ruinart Blanc de
Blancs 1953, France

July 23
*Luncheon in honor of President
Arosemena of Ecuador*
Wente Brothers White
Pinot, California

Château Gruaud-Larose 1955, France

Paul Ruinart Blanc de
Blancs 1955, France

July 27
*Luncheon in honor of
Prime Minister Souvanna
Phouma of Laos*
Puligny Montrachet 1959, France

Paul Ruinart Blanc de
Blancs 1953, France

Château Haut-Brion 1957

A premier First Growth wine from
Bordeaux, Château Haut-Brion was a
favorite of the Kennedys, who served
different vintages at twenty official and
private dinners. The 1957 vintage was
served at a State Dinner in honor of the
shah of Iran, April 11, 1962.

Château Gruaud-Larose 1955

The Kennedys served Château Gruaud-Larose, a Second Growth wine from France's Saint-Julien appellation, at seven dinners and luncheons. The 1955 vintage was chosen to accompany the main course of the glamorous dinner on May 11, 1962, for French Minister of Cultural Affairs André Malraux.

October 2
Luncheon in honor of Chancellor Konrad Adenauer of Germany
Inglenook Pinot Chardonnay, California
Château Haut-Brion 1955, France
Paul Ruinart Blanc de Blancs 1953, France

October 23
Private Dinner in honor of the Maharaja of Jaipur
Château Margaux 1957, France
Château Haut-Brion 1955, France
Piper Heidsieck 1955, France

November 14
Luncheon in honor of Chancellor Konrad Adenauer of Germany
Bernkasteler Schwanen Spatlese 1959, Germany
Almaden Pinot Noir, California
Paul Ruinart Blanc de Blancs 1953, France

November 27
Luncheon in honor of Prime Minister Abdirashid of Somalia
Almaden Grenache Rosé, California
Paul Ruinart Blanc de Blancs 1953, France

December 11
Luncheon in honor of President Alessandri of Chile
Inglenook Pinot Chardonnay, California
Château Haut-Brion 1955, France
Moët & Chandon Imperial Brut 1955, France

1963

January 16
Luncheon in honor of Prime Minister Fanfani of Italy
Soave Bertani 1959, Italy
Almaden Pinot Noir, California
A. Salon Mesnil 1955, France

January 21
Dinner in honor of the Vice President, Speaker of the House, and the Chief Justice
Inglenook Pinot Chardonnay, California
Château Gruaud-Larose 1959, France
Piper Heidsieck 1955, France

February 19
State Dinner in honor of President Betancourt of Venezuela
Inglenook Pinot Chardonnay, California
Grands Echézeaux 1959, France
Dom Pérignon 1952, France

February 25
Luncheon in honor of King Savang Vatthana of Laos
Inglenook Pinot Chardonnay, California
Château Haut-Brion 1955, France
Moët & Chandon 1955, France

February 26
Luncheon in honor of Prince Albert of Belgium
Inglenook Pinot Chardonnay, California
Grands Echézeaux 1959, France
Piper Heidsieck 1955, France

March 8
Private Dinner-Dance for Friends of the Kennedys
Pouilly Fuisse 1961, France
Charmes-Chambertin 1955, France
Dry Monopole Brut 1955, France

March 27
State Dinner in honor of King Hassan II of Morocco
Inglenook Pinot Chardonnay, California
Château Latour 1953, France
Dom Pérignon 1955, France

March 28
State Dinner in honor of Prime Minister Gandhi of India
Charles Krug Johannisberg Riesling, California

Beaulieu Cabernet Sauvignon California

Almaden Blanc de Blancs, California

March 30
Business Council Dinner
Inglenook Pinot Noir, California

Almaden Blanc de Blancs, California

April 13
Women Doers Luncheon hosted by Mrs. Johnson
Almaden Blanc de Blancs, California

April 27
Dinner in honor of Prime Minister Jens Otto Krag of Denmark
Charles Krug Johannisberg Riesling, California

Louis M. Martini Pinot Noir, California

Almaden Blanc de Blancs, California

May 16
Dinner in honor of Ambassador Henry Cabot Lodge
Inglenook Pinot Chardonnay, California

Almaden Blanc de Blancs, California

June 9
Luncheon in honor of President Schick of the Republic of Nicaragua
Beaulieu Cabernet Sauvignon, California

Almaden Blanc de Blancs, California

June 21
State Dinner in honor of King Faisal of Saudi Arabia
Charles Krug Johannisberg Riesling, California

Inglenook Pinot Noir, California

Almaden Blanc de Blancs, California

June 29
Luncheon in honor of Prime Minister Holt of Australia
Inglenook Gamay, California

Almaden Blanc de Blancs, California

July 14
Luncheon in honor of Prime Minister Holt of Australia
Beaulieu Cabernet Sauvignon, California

Almaden Blanc de Blancs, California

July 20
Luncheon in honor of President-elect Barrientos of Bolivia
Inglenook Gamay, California

Almaden Blanc de Blancs, California

July 21
Luncheon in honor of Prime Minister Forbes Burnham of Guyana
Inglenook Pinot Noir, California

Almaden Blanc de Blancs, California

July 29
Luncheon in honor of Prime Minister Harold Wilson of Great Britain
Beaulieu Pinot Chardonnay, California

Almaden Blanc de Blancs, California

August 2
Dinner in honor of President Zalman Shazar of Israel
Wente Pinot Chardonnay, California

Almaden Blanc de Blancs, California

August 23
Dinner in honor of three children of Cabinet Members, Robert A. Humphrey, Margaret McNamara, and Richard Wirtz
Wente Pinot Chardonnay, California

Beaulieu Cabernet Sauvignon, California

Almaden Blanc de Blancs, California

Wente Pinot Chardonnay

Founded in 1883, Wente Vineyards was a leader in California's rise to prominence in the wine industry during the mid-twentieth century. A favorite of the Johnsons, its wines were served at twenty-two dinners and luncheons. Wente Pinot Chardonnay was paired with the first course at twenty events.

Beaulieu Georges de Latour Private Reserve 1964

Founded by Frenchman Georges de Latour in 1900, the Beaulieu Vineyard was regularly featured on White House menus. Its landmark Cabernet Sauvignon was served twenty-five times during the Johnson administration. The 1960 vintage was served at the dinner in honor of Princess Margaret of Great Britain, November 17, 1965.

September 8
State Dinner in honor of General Ne Win, Chairman of the Revolutionary Council of Burma
Charles Krug Johannisberg Riesling, California

Martin Ray Pinot Noir, California

Almaden Blanc de Blancs, California

September 14
State Dinner in honor of President Marcos of the Philippines
Inglenook Pinot Chardonnay, California

Beaulieu Cabernet Sauvignon, California

Almaden Blanc de Blancs, California

September 26
Dinner in honor of Chancellor Erhard of Germany
Wente Pinot Chardonnay, California

Beaulieu Cabernet Sauvignon, California

Almaden Blanc de Blancs, California

September 28
Luncheon in honor of President Senghor of Senegal
Almaden Cabernet Sauvignon, California

1967

January 26
Luncheon in honor of President-elect Artur da Costa e Silva of Brazil
Beaulieu Cabernet Sauvignon, California

Almaden Blanc de Blancs, California

February 9
Dinner in honor of King Hassan II of Morocco
Wente Pinot Chardonnay, California

Beaulieu Cabernet Sauvignon, California

Almaden Blanc de Blancs, California

February 14
State Dinner in honor of Emperor Haile Selassie I of Ethiopia
Paul Masson Emerald Dry, California

Inglenook Pinot Noir, California

Almaden Blanc de Blancs, California

February 20
Luncheon for Farm Leaders
Paul Masson Emerald Dry, California

March 14
Luncheon in honor of Prime Minister Chung of Korea
Beaulieu Cabernet Sauvignon, California

Almaden Blanc de Blancs, California

March 18
Dinner for Governors
Wente Pinot Chardonnay, California

Great Western Vin Rouge, New York

Almaden Blanc de Blancs, California

March 28
Luncheon in honor of Prime Minister Maiwandwal of Afghanistan
Wente Pinot Chardonnay, California

Almaden Blanc de Blancs, California

April 3
State Dinner in honor of President Sunay of Turkey
Charles Krug Johannisberg Riesling, California

Great Western Vin Rouge, New York

Almaden Blanc de Blancs, California

April 27
Beautification Luncheon hosted by Mrs. Johnson
Charles Krug Pinot Chardonnay, California

Almaden Blanc de Blancs, California

May 9
Luncheon in honor of Vice President Yen of China
Concannon Cabernet Sauvignon, California

Almaden Blanc de Blancs, California

June 8
Luncheon in honor of
President Banda of Malawi
Inglenook Pinot
Chardonnay, California
Almaden Blanc de Blancs, California

June 27
State Dinner in honor of
King Adulyadej of Thailand
Charles Krug Johannisberg
Riesling, California
Beaulieu Cabernet
Sauvignon, California
Almaden Blanc de Blancs, California

July 11
Luncheon in honor of former
Chancellor Erhard of Germany
Paul Masson Emerald Dry, California

July 18
Luncheon in honor of President
Ásgeirsson of Iceland
Beaulieu Cabernet
Sauvignon, California
Almaden Blanc de Blancs, California

August 15
State Dinner in honor of
Chancellor Kiesinger of Germany
Charles Krug Pinot
Chardonnay, California
Great Western Vin Rouge, New York
Almaden Blanc de Blancs, California

August 17
Luncheon in honor of
President Houphouët-
Boigny of the Ivory Coast
Charles Krug Johannisberg
Riesling, California
Almaden Blanc de Blancs, California

September 12
Private Dinner aboard the
Presidential Yacht Sequoia
Gold Seal Fournier Nature, New York
Beaulieu Cabernet
Sauvignon, California
Almaden Blanc de Blancs, California

September 19
State Dinner in honor of
President Saragat of Italy
Wente Sauvignon Blanc, California
Charles Krug Pinot Noir, California
Almaden Blanc de Blancs, California

September 26
State Dinner in honor of
President Diori of Niger
Paul Masson Emerald Dry, California
Beaulieu Cabernet
Sauvignon, California
Almaden Blanc de Blancs, California

October 10
Luncheon in honor of General
Ankrah, Chairman of the
National Libertation Council
of the Republic of Ghana
Beaulieu Cabernet
Sauvignon, California
Almaden Blanc de Blancs, California

October 17
State Dinner in honor of Prime
Minister Lee of Singapore
Paul Masson Emerald Dry, California
Mirassou Cabernet
Sauvignon, California
Almaden Blanc de Blancs, California

October 20
Luncheon in honor of
Prime Minister Souvanna
Phouma of Laos
Gold Seal Fournier Nature, New York

October 24
Luncheon in honor of President
Ahidjo of Cameroon
Beaulieu Cabernet
Sauvignon, California

October 26
State Dinner in honor of
President Díaz Ordaz of Mexico
Wente Sauvignon Blanc, California
Louis M. Martini Pinot
Noir, California
Almaden Blanc de Blancs, California

Paul Masson Emerald Dry

Paul Masson, a French immigrant, founded his winery in California in 1905. Emerald Dry, marketed simply as a "white table wine," was another wine frequently seen at the first course of President Johnson's dinners and luncheons. Emerald Dry was served at President Johnson's final State Dinner on December 11, 1968, in honor of the amir of Kuwait.

Gold Seal Champagne

President Johnson, an enthusiastic supporter of the American wine industry, introduced sparkling wine from Gold Seal Vineyards in Hammondsport, New York, to the White House late in his administration. Breaking with precedent, the sparkling wine from the Finger Lakes was chosen for first courses or was the only wine served at five events. It was the first course selection for the State Dinner in honor of Prime Minister Errol Barrow of Barbados, September 11, 1968.

November 1
*State Dinner in honor of
King Mahendra of Nepal*
Wente Pinot Chardonnay, California

Beaulieu Cabernet
Sauvignon, California

Almaden Blanc de Blancs, California

November 9
*Luncheon in honor of Crown
Prince Vong Savang of Laos*
Beaulieu Cabernet
Sauvignon, California

Almaden Blanc de Blancs, California

November 14
*State Dinner in honor of Prime
Minister Satō of Japan*
Wente Pinot Chardonnay, California

Beaulieu Cabernet
Sauvignon, California

Almaden Blanc de Blancs, California

1968

January 18
*Women Doers Luncheon
hosted by Mrs. Johnson*
Gold Seal Fournier Nature, New York

February 8
*Dinner in honor of Prime Minister
Harold Wilson of Great Britain*
Wente Pinot Chardonnay, California

Almaden Blanc de Blancs, California

March 14
*State Dinner in honor of Prime
Minister Egal of the Somali Republic*
Louis M. Martini Pinot
Noir, California

Almaden Blanc de Blancs, California

March 20
*State Dinner in honor of President
Stroessner of Paraguay*
Charles Krug Johannisberg
Riesling, California

Beaulieu Cabernet
Sauvignon, California

Almaden Blanc de Blancs, California

March 27
*State Dinner in honor of
President Tubman of Liberia*
Wente Pinot Chardonnay, California

Great Western Vin Rouge, New York

Almaden Blanc de Blancs, California

April 10
*State Dinner in honor of
Chancellor Klaus of Austria*
Paul Masson Emerald Dry, California

Beaulieu Cabernet
Sauvignon, California

Almaden Blanc de Blancs, California

April 25
*State Dinner in honor of
King Olav V of Norway*
Charles Krug Johannisberg
Riesling, California

Great Western Vin Rouge, New York

Almaden Blanc de Blancs, California

April 26
Private Dinner Party
Inglenook Pinot
Chardonnay, California

Mirassou Cabernet
Sauvignon, California

Almaden Blanc de Blancs, California

May 8
*State Dinner in honor of
Prime Minister Thanom
Kittikachorn of Thailand*
Wente Pinot Chardonnay, California

Beaulieu Cabernet
Sauvignon, California

Almaden Blanc de Blancs, California

May 14
*Dinner in honor of Mrs. Imelda
Marcos of the Philippines*
Charles Krug Johannisberg
Riesling, California

Great Western Vin Rouge, New York

Almaden Blanc de Blancs, California

May 15
*State Dinner in honor of
President Bourguiba of Tunisia*
Beaulieu Pinot Chardonnay,
California

Inglenook Cabernet
Sauvignon, California

Almaden Blanc de Blancs,
California

May 27
*State Dinner in honor of Prime
Minister Gorton of Australia*
Paul Masson Emerald Dry,
California

Beaulieu Cabernet
Sauvignon, California

Almaden Blanc de Blancs,
California

June 4
*State Dinner in honor of
President Trejos of Costa Rica*
Beaulieu Pinot Chardonnay,
California

Inglenook Gamay, California

Hanns Kornell Brut, California

June 11
*Dinner in honor of
the Shah of Iran*
Gold Seal Fournier Nature,
New York

Beaulieu Cabernet
Sauvignon, California

Almaden Blanc de Blancs, California

September 11
*State Dinner in honor of Prime
Minister Barrow of Barbados*
Gold Seal Fournier Nature,
New York

Beaulieu Cabernet
Sauvignon, California

Almaden Blanc de Blancs, California

October 2
*State Dinner in honor of
President Tombalbaye of Chad*
Beaulieu Pinot Chardonnay,
California

Great Western Vin Rouge, New York

Almaden Blanc de Blancs, California

October 9
*State Dinner in honor of Prime
Minister Holyoake of New Zealand*
Paul Masson Emerald Dry, California

Beaulieu Cabernet
Sauvignon, California

Almaden Blanc de Blancs, California

December 5
*State Dinner in honor of Prime
Minister Hoveyda of Iran*
Beaulieu Pinot Noir, California

Inglenook Cabernet
Sauvignon, California

Almaden Blanc de Blancs, California

December 11
*State Dinner in honor of
the Amir of Kuwait*
Paul Masson Emerald Dry, California

Charles Krug Pinot Noir, California

Almaden Blanc de Blancs, California

Richard M. Nixon Presidency
1969–1974

1969

March 14
Businessmen's Dinner
Puligny Montrachet 1964, France

Château Haut-Brion 1961, France

Dom Pérignon 1961, France

March 24
*State Dinner in honor of Prime
Minister Trudeau of Canada*
Bernkasteler Doktor 1967, Germany

Martin Ray Pinot Noir, California

Dom Pérignon 1961, France

Puligny-Montrachet 1964

Puligny-Montrachet, a dry white wine made of Chardonnay grapes from Burgundy, is considered one of the best dry white wine in the world. Various vintages of the wine saw service at the White House by both the Kennedys and the Nixons. President Nixon enjoyed the 1964 and 1966 vintages at five occasions early in his presidency, including the State Dinner in honor of French President Georges Pompidou on February 19, 1970.

Schloss Johannisberg 1967

While President Nixon favored French wines for the main and dessert courses, he preferred to open a meal with a German Riesling. Schloss Johannisberg, from the Rheingau region of Germany, was served at twenty-three dinners. Nixon frequently paired this with another of his favorite wines, Château Mouton Rothschild.

April 8
State Dinner in honor of King Hussein of Jordan
Bernkasteler Doktor 1967, Germany
Louis M. Martini Cabernet Sauvignon 1957, California
Dom Pérignon 1961, France

April 11
Dinner in honor of NATO Representatives
Charles Krug Johannisberg Riesling, California
Château St. Roseline, France
Pol Roger 1961, France

May 6
State Dinner in honor of Prime Minister Gorton of Australia
Puligny Montrachet 1964, France
Château Ausone 1961, France
Pol Roger 1961, France

May 19
Senate Ladies' Luncheon
Charles Krug Johannisberg Riesling, California

May 20
Luncheon in honor of King Baudouin of Belgium
Corton-Charlemagne 1964, France
Château Margaux 1959, France
Paul Ruinart Blanc de Blancs 1961, France

June 12
State Dinner in honor of President Lleras of Colombia
Bernkasteler Doktor 1967, Germany
Château Lafite Rothschild 1962, France
Dom Pérignon 1961, France

July 8
State Dinner in honor of Emperor Haile Selassie I of Ethiopia
Corton-Charlemagne 1964, France
Château Margaux 1959, France
Dom Pérignon 1961, France

August 7
State Dinner in honor of Chancellor Kiesinger of Germany
Bernkasteler Doktor Ausles 1967, Germany
Louis M. Martini Cabernet Sauvignon 1958, California
Pol Roger 1961, France

August 13
Dinner in Los Angeles in honor of the Apollo 11 Astronauts
Wente Brothers Pinot Chardonnay, California
Inglenook Cabernet Sauvignon Cask, California
Korbel Natural, California

August 21
State Dinner in San Francisco in honor of President Park of Korea
Inglenook Pinot Chardonnay, California
Beaulieu Georges de Latour, California
Almaden Blanc de Blancs, California

September 16
State Dinner in honor of Prime Minister Holyoake of New Zealand
Schloss Johannisberg 1967, Germany
Château Margaux 1959, France
Dom Pérignon 1961, France

September 25
State Dinner in honor of Prime Minister Meir of Israel
Pouilly Fuissé 1967, France
Château Lafite-Rothschild 1962, France
Taittinger 1961, France

October 7
State Dinner in honor of Prince Souvanna Phouma, Prime Minister of Laos
Corton-Charlemagne 1964, France
Château Mouton Rothschild 1964, France
Dom Pérignon 1961, France

October 21
*State Dinner in honor
of the Shah of Iran*
Liebfrauenmilk 1965, Germany

Château Latour 1962, France

Louis Roederer Cristal
Brut 1962, France

November 5
*Dinner in honor of the Apollo 11
Astronauts and Their Wives*
Soave Bertani 1963, Italy

Château Mouton Rothschild
1966, France

Taittinger Blanc de
Blancs 1961, France

November 19
*State Dinner in honor of Prime
Minister Satō of Japan*
Puligny Montrachet 1966, France

Château Mouton Rothschild
1966, France

Piper Heidsieck 1962, France

December 20
*Dinner in honor of the
Apollo 12 Astronauts*
Puligny-Montrachet 1966, France

Château Mouton Rothschild
1966, France

Taittinger Blanc de
Blancs 1961, France

1970

January 27
*State Dinner in honor of
Prime Minister Harold
Wilson of Great Britain*
Schloss Johannisberg 1967, Germany

Château Mouton Rothschild
1966, France

Taittinger Blanc de
Blancs 1961, France

February 19
*Dinner in honor of Artist
Andrew Wyeth*
Schloss Johannisberg 1967, Germany

Château Latour 1964, France

Dom Pérignon 1962, France

February 24
*State Dinner in honor of
President Pompidou of France*
Puligny-Montrachet 1966, France

Château Ausone 1962, France

Louis Roederer Cristal 1962, France

March 23
*Dinner for Ambassadors of the
Organization of African Unity*
Schloss Johannisberger
1967, Germany

Château Latour 1966, France

Pol Roger Brut 1961, France

April 4
*Dinner in honor of the Duke
and Duchess of Windsor*
Bernkasteler Doktor 1967, Germany

Château Margaux 1959, France

Taittinger Blanc de
Blancs 1961, France

April 10
*State Dinner in honor of
Chancellor Brandt of Germany*
Schloss Johannisberg 1966, Germany

Château Lafite Rothschild
1962, France

Louis Roederer Cristal 1962, France

April 14
*State Dinner in honor of Prime
Minister Baunsgaard of Denmark*
Schloss Johannisberger
1966, California

Château Lafite Rothschild
1962, France

Louis Roederer Cristal 1962, France

May 22
Senate Red Cross Luncheon
Charles Krug Johannisberg
Riesling, California

May 26
*State Dinner in honor of
President Suharto of Indonesia*
Bernkasteler Docktor 1967, Germany

Château Latour 1962, France

Louis Roederer Cristal 1962, France

Château Margaux 1959

Château Margaux is one of the original
four Bordeaux Premiers Crus from the 1855
ranking. The 1959 vintage appeared at one
luncheon and three dinners at the Nixon
White House. President Nixon selected
this wine, one of his favorites, for the main
course at a dinner in honor of the Duke and
Duchess of Windsor on April 4, 1970.

Château Latour 1962

A First Growth Bordeaux wine, Château Latour was often enjoyed by President Nixon and his guests. The estate has produced wine since the fourteenth century and was named for a fort built on the land during the Hundred Years' War. The 1962 vintage, served at six presidential events, was featured at the dinner in honor of the *Apollo 13* astronauts on June 9, 1970, following their historic mission.

May 27
*Luncheon in honor of
Speaker McCormack*
Bernkasteler Docktor 1967, Germany

Château Lafite Rothschild
1962, France

Paul Ruinart Blanc de
Blancs 1961, France

June 2
*State Dinner in honor of
President Caldera of Venezuela*
Bernkasteler Docktor 1967, Germany

Château Latour 1962, France

Louis Roederer Cristal 1962, France

June 9
*Dinner in honor of the
Apollo 13 Astronauts*
Schloss Johannisberger
1967, Germany

Château Latour 1962, France

Dom Pérignon 1962, France

July 10
*Dinner in recognition of the 25th
Anniversary of the United Nations*
Bernkasteler Doktor 1967, Germany

Château Latour 1962, France

Dom Pérignon 1962, France

July 23
*State Dinner in honor of
President Kekkonen of Finland*
Johannisberger Klaus 1966, Germany

Château Ausone 1962, France

Louis Roederer Cristal 1962, France

August 4
*State Dinner in honor President
Mobutu of the Democratic
Republic of the Congo*
Johannisberger Klaus 1966, Germany

Château Ausone 1962, France

Louis Roederer Cristal 1962, France

October 26
*State Dinner in honor of President
Ceausescu of Romania*
Bernkasteler Doktor 1967, Germany

Louis M. Martini Pinot
Noir 1962, France

Louis Roederer Cristal 1964, France

November 5
*Dinner in honor of the First
Earl Mountbatten of Burma*
Schloss Johannisberger
1967, Germany

Beaulieu Cabernet Sauvignon
1965, California

Dom Pérignon 1962, France

November 18
*Dinner for the Attorney
General and Businessmen*
Bernkasteler Doktor 1967, Germany

Louis M. Martini Cabernet
Sauvignon 1958, California

Pol Roger 1961, France

November 19
*Dinner for members of the
President's Advisory Council
on Executive Organization*
Johannisberger Klaus 1967, Germany

Beaulieu Cabernet Sauvignon
1965, California

Dom Pérignon, 1964, France

November 20
*Luncheon for the Committee for the
Preservation of the White House*
Wente Brothers Sauvignon
Blanc 1967, Germany

December 8
*Dinner in honor of King
Hussein of Jordan*
Bernkasteler Doktor 1967, Germany

Louis M. Martini Cabernet
Sauvignon 1958, California

Taittinger Blanc de
Blancs 1961, France

December 17
State Dinner in honor of Prime Minister Heath of Great Britain
Schloss Johannisberger 1967, Germany

Louis M. Martini Cabernet Sauvignon, California

Louis Roederer Cristal 1964, France

1971

January 26
Dinner in honor of Prince Juan Carlos I of Spain
Schloss Johannisberg 1967, Germany

Château Mouton Rothschild 1966, France

Taittinger Blanc de Blancs 1961, France

February 18
State Dinner in honor of Prime Minister Colombo of Italy
Schloss Johannisberg 1967, Germany

Louis M. Martini Cabernet Sauvignon, California

Taittinger Blanc de Blancs, France

February 23
Dinner in honor of Governors
Bernkasteler Doktor 1967, Germany

Louis M. Martini Cabernet Sauvignon, California

Piper Heidsieck 1964, France

March 25
Businessmen's Dinner
Johannisberger Klaus 1969, Germany

Louis M. Martini Cabernet Sauvignon, California

Pol Roger Brut 1964, France

April 6
Dinner in honor of the Chiefs of Mission of the Americas
Schloss Johannisberger 1967, Germany

Louis M. Martini Cabernet Sauvignon, California

Piper Heidsieck 1964, France

May 3
Luncheon for Members of Congress
Wente Brothers Pinot Chardonnay, California

June 24
Luncheon for the Committee for the Preservation of the White House
Llords & Elwood Johannisberg Riesling, California

June 29
Dinner in honor of Postmaster General and Mrs. Winston M. Blount
Concannon Johannisberg Riesling, California

Beaulieu Cabernet Sauvignon 1966, California

Dom Pérignon 1962, France

September 10
Dinner in honor of Members of the Japanese Cabinet
Schloss Johannisberger 1969, Germany

Louis M. Martini Cabernet Sauvignon, California

Louis Roederer Cristal 1964, France

September 16
Dinner in honor of the Apollo 15 Astronauts and Their Wives
Bernkasteler Doktor 1967, Germany

Louis M. Martini Cabernet Sauvignon 1962, California

Taittinger Blanc de Blancs 1964, France

October 28
State Dinner in honor of President Tito of Yugoslavia
Bernkasteler Doktor 1967, Germany

Louis M. Martini Cabernet Sauvignon 1967, California

Louis Roederer Cristal 1962, France

November 2
Dinner in honor of Prime Minister McMahon of Australia
Bernkasteler Docktor 1967, Germany

Château Latour 1962, France

Louis Roederer Cristal 1962, France

Louis M. Martini Cabernet Sauvignon 1962

Louis M. Martini was President Nixon's preferred Cabernet Sauvignon during the latter half of his administration. He served several vintages at thirty-three dinners and luncheons and paired the 1967 vintage with the main course at the dinner in honor of Soviet leaders at Spaso House in Moscow on May 26, 1972.

Schramsberg Blanc de Blancs 1969

Founded in 1862, Schramsberg Vineyards was the first California winery to produce sparkling wines to rival the quality of French champagnes. Nixon brought the Schramsberg Blanc de Blancs overseas for important reciprocal dinners with heads of state and chose the 1969 vintage for his "Toast to Peace" with Chinese Premier Zhou Enlai on February 25, 1972.

November 4
State Dinner in honor of Prime Minister Gandhi of India
Bernkasteler Docktor 1967, Germany
Château Latour 1962, France
Louis Roederer Cristal 1962, France

December 6
Dinner in honor of Prime Minister Trudeau of Canada
Johannisberger Klaus Riesling 1969, Germany
Louis M. Martini Cabernet Sauvignon 1967, California
Piper Heidsieck 1964, France

December 7
State Dinner in honor of President Médici of Brazil
Bernkasteler Doktor 1969, Germany
Louis M. Martini Cabernet Sauvignon 1967, California
Louis Roederer Cristal 1964, France

1972

February 14
Dinner in honor of André Malraux
Bernkasteler Doktor 1969, Germany
Louis M. Martini Cabernet Sauvignon 1962, California
Taittinger Blanc de Blancs 1961, France

March 21
State Dinner in honor of Prime Minister Erim of Turkey
Schloss Johannisberg 1967, Germany
Château Mouton Rothschild 1966, France
Taittinger Blanc de Blancs 1961, France

March 28
Dinner in honor of King Hussein of Jordan
Johannisberger Klaus 1969, Germany
Louis M. Martini Cabernet Sauvignon 1967, California
Piper Heidsieck Brut 1964, France

May 8
Senate Ladies' Luncheon
Freemark Abbey Pinot Chardonnay, California

May 26
Dinner given at Spaso House, Moscow, honoring Soviet Leaders
Beaulieu Pinot Chardonnay 1969, California
Louis M. Martini Cabernet Sauvignon 1967, California
Schramsberg Blanc de Blancs 1969, California

May 31
Luncheon given at Saad-Abad Palace, Tehran, in honor of the Shah of Iran
Beaulieu Pinot Chardonnay 1969, California
Schramsberg Blanc de Blancs 1969, California

June 15
State Dinner in honor of President Echeverría of Mexico
Schloss Johannisberger Klaus 1970, Germany
Louis M. Martini Cabernet Sauvignon 1967, California
Louis Roederer Cristal 1964, France

June 30
Needlepoint Luncheon hosted by Julie Nixon Eisenhower
Napa Valley Pinot Chardonnay, California

August 31
Dinner in Kahuku, Oahu, Hawaii, in honor of Prime Minister Tanaka of Japan
Wente Pinot Chardonnay 1968, California
Louis M. Martini Cabernet Sauvignon 1967, California
Almaden Blanc de Blancs 1967, California

1973

February 1
State Dinner in honor of Prime Minister Heath of the United Kingdom
Schloss Johannisberg 1967, Germany

Château Mouton Rothschild 1966, France

Taittinger Blanc de Blancs 1961, France

February 6
Dinner in honor of King Hussein of Jordan
Schloss Johannisberger 1970, Germany

Louis M. Martini Cabernet Sauvignon 1968, California

Taittinger Blanc de Blancs 1964, France

February 28
Dinner in honor of U.S. Governors
Berncasteler Doctor 1970, Germany

Louis M. Martini Cabernet Sauvignon 1968, California

Pol Roger 1964, France

March 1
Dinner in honor of Prime Minister Meir of Israel
Schloss Johannisberg 1967, Germany

Château Mouton Rothschild 1966, France

Taittinger Blanc de Blancs 1961, France

March 6
Private Dinner for Business and Community Leaders
Louis M. Martini Cabernet Sauvignon 1968, California

Pol Roger 1964, France

April 10
Dinner in honor of Prime Minister Lee of Singapore
Johannisberger Klaus 1970, Germany

Louis M. Martini Cabernet Sauvignon 1968, California

Bollinger Brut 1966, France

April 17
State Dinner in honor of Prime Minister Andreotti of Italy
Schloss Johannisberg 1967, Germany

Château Mouton Rothschild 1966, France

Taittinger Blanc de Blancs 1961, France

May 1
State Dinner in honor of Chancellor Brandt of Germany
Berncasteler Doctor 1969, Germany

Louis M. Martini Cabernet Sauvignon 1968, California

Taittinger Blanc de Blancs 1964, France

May 15
State Dinner in honor of Emperor Haile Selassie I of Ethiopia
Schloss Johannisberg 1967, Germany

Château Mouton Rothschild 1966, France

Taittinger Blanc de Blancs 1961, France

May 24
Dinner honoring Returned Prisoners of War
Wente Brothers Grey Riesling, California

Louis M. Martini Cabernet Sauvignon 1968, California

Korbel Natural Champagne, California

June 5
Dinner in honor of President Tolbert of Liberia
Johannisberger Klaus 1970, Germany

Louis M. Martini Cabernet Sauvignon 1968, California

Dom Pérignon 1964, France

June 18
State Dinner in honor of General Secretary Brezhnev of the Soviet Union
Schloss Johannisberg 1970, Germany

Louis M. Martini Cabernet Sauvignon 1968, California

Louis Roederer Cristal 1967, France

Berncasteler Doctor

Berncasteler Doctor was another German Riesling very often selected for the first course of President Nixon's dinners and luncheons. The Riesling was served more than twenty times, with the 1967 vintage on sixteen menus. The 1969 vintage was selected for the State Dinner in honor of German Chancellor Willy Brandt on May 1, 1973.

Château Mouton Rothschild

One of President Nixon's favorites, Château Mouton Rothschild, is renowned as one of the world's finest wines. The rich French blend of Cabernet Sauvignon, Merlot, Cabernet Franc, and Petit Verdot grapes was featured at fourteen events during the Nixon presidency. The 1964 vintage was first served at the State Dinner in honor of Prince Souvanna Phouma of Laos on October 7, 1969. Subsequently only the 1966 vintage was served.

July 24
State Dinner in honor of the Shah of Iran
Schloss Johannisberg 1967, Germany
Château Mouton Rothschild 1966, France
Taittinger Blanc de Blancs 1961, France

July 31
State Dinner in honor of Prime Minister Tanaka of Japan
Schloss Johannisberg 1967, Germany
Château Mouton Rothschild 1966, France
Taittinger Blanc de Blancs 1961, France

September 18
State Dinner in honor of Prime Minister Bhutto of Pakistan
Schloss Johannisberg 1967, Germany
Château Mouton Rothschild 1966, France
Taittinger Blanc de Blancs 1961, France

September 27
State Dinner in honor of Prime Minister Kirk of New Zealand
Schloss Johannisberg 1967, Germany
Château Mouton Rothschild 1966, France
Taittinger Blanc de Blancs 1961, France

October 9
State Dinner in honor of President Houphouët-Boigny of the Ivory Coast
Johannisberger Klaus 1970, Germany
Louis M. Martini Cabernet Sauvignon 1968, California
Taittinger Blanc de Blancs 1966, France

December 4
State Dinner in honor of President Ceaușescu of Romania
Schloss Johannisberg 1969, Germany
Louis M. Martini Cabernet Sauvignon 1968, California
Dom Pérignon 1964, France

1974

February 26
Dinner in honor of the Directors of the U.S.-Soviet Union Trade and Economic Council
Johannisberger Klaus 1971, Germany
Louis M. Martini Cabernet Sauvignon 1968, California
Dom Pérignon 1964, France

March 1
Private Dinner for Congressional Supporters and Their Wives
Bernkasteler Doktor 1969, Germany
Louis M. Martini Cabernet Sauvignon 1968, California
Piper Heidsieck 1966, France

March 26
Dinner in honor of Secretary of Defense Melvin Laird
Johannisberg Klaus 1970, Germany
Louis M. Martini Cabernet Sauvignon 1968, California
Dom Pérignon 1964, France

May 13
Senate Ladies' Luncheon
Almaden Grenache Rosé, California

June 6
Luncheon in honor of Prince Fahd of Saudi Arabia
Johannisberg Klaus 1971, Germany
Louis M. Martini Cabernet Sauvignon 1968, California
Louis Roederer Brut 1967, France

July 2
Dinner given at Spaso House, Moscow, in honor of Soviet Leaders
Robert Mondavi Fumé Blanc 1972, California
Mirassou Pinot Noir 1969, California
Schramsberg Blanc de Blancs 1971, California

Gerald R. Ford Presidency

1974–1977

August 16
State Dinner in honor of King Hussein of Jordan
Schloss Johannisberg 1969, Germany

Louis M. Martini Cabernet Sauvignon 1968, California

Louis Roederer Cristal 1967, California

September 12
State Dinner in honor of Prime Minister Rabin of Israel
Bernkasteler Doktor 1971, Germany

Louis M. Martini Cabernet Sauvignon 1962, California

Dom Pérignon 1964, France

September 25
State Dinner in honor of President Leone of Italy
Inglenook Pinot Chardonnay 1972, California

Louis M. Martini Cabernet Sauvignon 1962, California

Almaden Blanc de Blancs 1971, California

October 8
State Dinner in honor of First Secretary Gierek of Poland
Louis M. Martini Johannisberger Riesling, California

Charles Krug Cabernet Sauvignon, California

Korbel Natural, California

November 12
State Dinner in honor of Chancellor Kreisky of Austria
Tabor Hill Vidal Blanc 1971, Michigan

Freemark Abbey Cabernet Sauvignon 1969, California

Schramsberg Blanc de Blancs Reserve 1970, California

December 4
State Dinner in honor of Prime Minister Trudeau of Canada
Robert Mondavi Pinot Noir 1971, California

Mirassou au Natural 1970, California

December 5
State Dinner in honor of Chancellor Schmidt of Germany
Robert Mondavi Fumé Blanc 1972, California

Robert Mondavi Pinot Noir 1970, California

Mirassou au Natural 1970, California

1975

January 30
State Dinner in honor of Prime Minister Wilson of the United Kingdom
Robert Mondavi Pinot Noir 1970, California

Schramsberg Blanc de Blancs 1972, California

February 5
State Dinner in honor of Prime Minister Bhutto of Pakistan
Freemark Abbey Cabernet Sauvignon 1969, California

Schramsberg Blanc de Blancs 1972, California

April 19
Dinner in honor of President Kaunda of Zambia
Freemark Abbey Johannisberg Riesling 1970, California

Freemark Abbey Pinot Chardonnay 1972, California

Schramsberg Blanc de Blancs 1972, California

April 29
Dinner in honor of King Hussein of Jordan
Sterling Cabernet Sauvignon 1969, California

Schramsberg Blanc de Blancs 1972, California

Louis M. Martini 1968

Only seven days after becoming president, Gerald Ford hosted a State Dinner in honor of King Hussein of Jordan. The 1968 vintage of Louis M. Martini Cabernet Sauvignon, a Nixon favorite, was served with the main course.

Robert Mondavi Cabernet Sauvignon 1971

After Robert Mondavi left his family's Charles Krug winery to establish his own venture during the 1960s, his wines soon became presidential favorites. The Fords served Mondavi's Cabernet Sauvignon 1971 at a dinner in honor of Prime Minister Lee Kuan Yew of Singapore on May 8, 1975, and on four other occasions.

May 1
State Dinner in honor of Prime Minister Nouira of Tunisia
Sterling Merlot 1969, California
Schramsberg Blanc de Blancs 1972, California

May 5
Senate Ladies' Red Cross Luncheon
Schramsberg Blanc de Blancs 1972, California

May 8
Dinner in honor of Prime Minister Lee Kuan Yew of Singapore
Robert Mondavi Reserve Cabernet Sauvignon 1971, California
Mirassou Brut 1970, California

May 14
Dinner in honor of Prime Minister den Uyl of the Netherlands
Freemark Abbey Cabernet Sauvignon 1971, California
Schramsberg Blanc de Blancs 1972, California

May 15
Luncheon in honor of the Shah of Iran
Freemark Abbey Johannisberg Riesling 1970, California
Robert Mondavi Reserve Cabernet Sauvignon 1971, California
Schramsberg Blanc de Blancs 1972, California

June 11
State Dinner in honor of Prime Minister Rabin of Israel
Robert Mondavi Fumé Blanc 1973, California
Charles Krug Cabernet Sauvignon, Vintage Selection 1969, California
Schramsberg Blanc de Noir 1970, California

June 16
State Dinner in honor of President Scheel of Germany
Robert Mondavi Chenin Blanc 1973, California
Charles Krug Cabernet Sauvignon 1969, California
Sonoma Vineyards Brut Cuvée, California

September 25
State Dinner in honor of President López of Colombia
Dry Creek Chenin Blanc 1973, California
Louis M. Martini Cabernet Sauvignon 1970, California
Schramsberg Blanc de Blancs 1973, California

October 2
State Dinner in honor of Emperor Hirohito of Japan
Ste. Michelle Semillon 1973, Washington
Robert Mondavi Pinot Noir 1971, California
Schramsberg Blanc de Noir 1971, California

October 3
Working Luncheon in honor of Chancellor Helmut Schmidt of Germany
Ste. Michelle Chenin Blanc 1974, Washington
Charles Krug Cabernet Sauvignon 1969, California
Mirassou au Natural 1970, California

October 27
State Dinner in honor of President Sadat of Egypt
Dry Creek Dry Chenin Blanc 1973, California
Buena Vista Burgundy 1969, California
Schramsberg Blanc de Noir 1971, California

November 12
*State Dinner in honor of
Prime Minister Gaston
Thorn of Luxembourg*
Dry Creek Dry Chenin
Blanc 1973, California

Wente Brothers Pinot
Chardonnay 1973, California

Mirassou au Natural 1970, California

November 24
*Dinner honoring Chief
Justice Warren E. Burger
and the Judiciary*
Ste. Michelle Semillon
1972, Washington

Robert Mondavi Reserve Cabernet
Sauvignon 1971, California

Beaulieu Extra Dry 1970, California

1976

January 27
*Luncheon in honor of Prime
Minister Rabin of Israel*
Paul Masson Dry Sherry, California

Louis M. Martini Pinot
Chardonnay 1972, California

Schramsberg Blanc de
Blancs 1973, California

February 23
Dinner in honor of Governors
Gold Seal Pinot Chardonnay
1974, New York

Beringer Cabernet Sauvignon
1970, California

The Thompson Pere
Marquette, Illinois

March 17
*State Dinner in honor of Prime
Minister Cosgrave of Ireland*
Chappellet Johannisberg
Riesling 1973, California

Ste. Michelle Cabernet
Sauvignon 1968, Washington

Schramsberg Blanc de
Blancs 1973, California

March 30
*State Dinner in honor of
King Hussein of Jordan*
Ste. Michelle Chenin Blanc
1974, Washington

Louis M. Martini Cabernet
Sauvignon 1970, California

Almaden Blanc de Blancs
1973, California

May 11
*Luncheon in honor of Queen
Margrethe II of Denmark*
Dry Creek Dry Chenin
Blanc 1974, California

Chappellet Cabernet
Sauvignon 1971, California

Schramsberg Blanc de
Blancs 1973, California

June 2
*State Dinner in honor of King
Juan Carlos I of Spain*
Ste. Michelle Chenin Blanc
1974, Washington

Charles Krug Gamay 1972, California

Schramsberg Blanc de
Blancs 1973, California

July 7
*State Dinner in honor of Queen
Elizabeth II of the United Kingdom*
Sterling Chenin Blanc 1972, California

Beaulieu Cabernet Sauvignon
1968, California

Schramsberg Blanc de
Blancs 1973, California

July 15
*State Dinner in honor
of Chancellor Helmut
Schmidt of Germany*
Beaulieu Beaufort Pinot
Chardonnay 1973, California

Louis M. Martini Cabernet
Sauvignon 1970, California

Beaulieu Champagne de
Chardonnay 1971, California

Ste. Michelle Chenin Blanc 1974

First served by President Ford at a State
Dinner in honor of King Hussein of Jordan,
on March 30, 1976, Ste. Michelle's Chenin
Blanc from Washington State was featured
at six subsequent White House events.
President Carter selected the light wine for
the first course of his dinner in honor of the
leaders signing the Panama Canal Treaty,
September 7, 1977.

Sebastiani Pinot Noir 1972

For his July 26, 1977, State Dinner in honor of Italian Prime Minister Giulio Andreotti, President Carter honored his guest by serving a California Pinot Noir produced by the Italian American Sebastiani family. Wines from Sebastiani have frequently been served at the White House.

July 27
*State Dinner in honor of
Prime Minister Malcolm
Fraser of Australia*

Wente Brothers Sauvignon
Blanc 1974, California

Mirassou Premier Gamay
Beaujolais 1975, California

Beaulieu Extra Dry 1970, California

August 3
*State Dinner in honor of
President Kekkonen of Finland*

Beaulieu Beaufort Pinot
Chardonnay 1973, California

Louis M. Martini Cabernet
Sauvignon 1971, California

Schramsberg Blanc de
Blancs 1973, California

September 21
*State Dinner in honor of
President Tolbert of Liberia*

Ste. Michelle Semillon Blanc
1975, Washington

Almaden Cabernet Sauvignon
1971, California

Beaulieu Extra Dry 1970, California

October 14
*Dinner in honor of
Martha Graham*

Wente Brothers Sauvignon
Blanc 1973, California

Louis M. Martini Mountain Zinfandel
Private Reserve 1966, California

Schramsberg Blanc de
Blancs 1973, California

December 6
*State Dinner in honor of Prime
Minister Andreotti of Italy*

Ste. Michelle Chenin Blanc
1975, Washington

Louis M. Martini Cabernet
Sauvignon 1970, California

Beaulieu Extra Dry 1970, California

Jimmy Carter Presidency

1977–1981

1977

February 14
*State Dinner in honor of President
López Portillo of Mexico*

Paul Masson Rare Sherry, California

Charles Krug Gamay
Beaujolais, California

Schramsberg Blanc de
Blancs, California

February 21
*State Dinner in honor of Prime
Minister Trudeau of Canada*

Ste. Michelle Chenin
Blanc, Washington

Louis M. Martini Cabernet
Sauvignon, California

Beaulieu Extra Dry, California

March 7
*Working Dinner in honor of
Prime Minister Rabin of Israel*

Charles Krug Johannisberg
Riesling, California

Almaden Blanc de Blancs, California

March 10
*State Dinner in honor of
Prime Minister Callaghan
of Great Britain*

Ste. Michelle Cabernet
Sauvignon, Washington

Schramsberg Blanc de
Blanc 1974, California

March 21
*State Dinner in honor of Prime
Minister Fukuda of Japan*

Ste. Michelle Chenin
Blanc, Washington

New York Taylor
Champagne, New York

April 4
*State Dinner in honor of
President Sadat of Egypt*
Dry Creek Chenin Blanc, California
Almaden Blanc de Blancs, California

April 25
*State Dinner in honor of
King Hussein of Jordan*
Wente Brothers Pinot
Chardonnay, California
Great Western Natural
Champagne, New York

May 24
*Dinner in honor of Crown
Prince Fahd of Saudi Arabia*
Wente Brothers Pinot
Blanc, California
Louis M. Martini Cabernet
Sauvignon, Califonia
Schramsberg Blanc de
Blancs, California

June 28
*State Dinner in honor of
President Pérez of Venezuela*
Beaulieu Pinot Chardonnay
1975, California
Ste. Michelle Cabernet
Sauvignon 1974, Washington
Great Western Natural
Champagne, New York

July 13
*State Dinner in honor of
Chancellor Schmidt of Germany*
Simi Cabernet Rosé, California
Korbel Natural, California

July 26
*State Dinner in honor of Prime
Minister Andreotti of Italy*
Ste. Michelle Dry Semillon,
Washington
Sebastiani Pinot Noir 1972,
California
Gold Seal Blanc de Blancs, New York

August 4
*Working Dinner for President
Nyerere of Tanzania*
Louis M. Martini Cabernet
Sauvignon 1974, California
Almaden Blanc de Blancs
1972, California

September 7
*Dinner in honor of the Leaders
Signing the Panama Canal Treaty*
Ste. Michelle Dry Chenin
Blanc, Washington
Simi Rosé Cabernet
Sauvignon, California
Gold Seal Blanc de Blancs, New York

October 11
*State Dinner in honor
of Lieutenant General
Obasanjo of Nigeria*
Simi Rosé Cabernet
Sauvignon, California
Hanns Kornell Champagne, California

November 15
*State Dinner in honor
of the Shah of Iran*
Sebastiani Pinot Chardonnay
1976, California
Charles Krug Cabernet
Sauvignon 1973, California
Hanns Kornell Brut, California

1978

March 7
*State Dinner in honor of
President Tito of Yugoslavia*
Beaulieu Pinot Chardonnay
1975, California
Simi Michelle Cabernet
Sauvignon 1973, California
Schramsberg Blanc de
Blancs 1974, California

Charles Krug Cabernet Sauvignon 1973

Charles Krug wines were a popular choice
for White House events during the Carter
administration. Its 1973 Cabernet Sauvignon
was selected for the State Dinner in honor
of the shah of Iran, November 15, 1977.

Dry Creek Dry Chenin Blanc 1973

Founded in 1972, Dry Creek Vineyard first appeared on a White House menu in September 1975. Its Dry Chenin Blanc was served at the White House at seven dinners. The 1973 vintage was served at four of those events.

April 12
State Dinner in honor of President Ceauşescu of Romania
Dry Creek Chenin Blanc 1973, California

Beaulieu Gamay Beaujolais 1975, California

Korbel Natural Champagne, California

November 14
State Dinner in honor of King Hassan II of Morocco
Paul Masson Pinot Chardonnay, California

Simi Cabernet Sauvignon, California

Beaulieu Extra Dry Champagne, California

1979

January 29
State Dinner in honor of Vice Premier Deng of China
Paul Masson Pinot Chardonnay 1976, California

Simi Rosé Cabernet Sauvignon 1976, California

Hanns Kornell Champagne, California

February 6
State Dinner in honor of Prime Minister Kriangsak of Thailand
Ste. Michelle Chenin Blanc, Washington

Mirassou Gamay Beaujolais, California

Almaden Chardonnay Nature, California

February 15
Dinner at the U.S. Embassy in Mexico City in honor of President and Mrs. López Portillo
Inglenook Pinot Chardonnay, California

Louis M. Martini Cabernet Sauvignon, California

Korbel Extra Dry, California

March 26
Dinner honoring President Sadat and Prime Minister Begin Following the Signing of Egyptian-Israeli Peace Treaty
Louis M. Martini Pinot Chardonnay, California

Paul Masson Cabernet Sauvignon, California

Almaden Blanc de Blancs, California

May 2
State Dinner in honor of Prime Minister Ōhira of Japan
Dry Creek Dry Chenin Blanc, California

Louis M. Martini Cabernet Sauvignon, California

Chandon Brut Champagne, California

September 28
State Dinner in honor of President López Portillo of Mexico
Simi Johannesburg Riesling, California

Louis M. Martini Cabernet Sauvignon, California

Schramsberg Blanc de Blancs, California

December 17
State Dinner in honor of Prime Minister Thatcher of the United Kingdom
Beaulieu Pinot Chardonnay, California

Mirassou Gamay Beaujolais, California

Schramsberg Blanc de Blancs, California

1980

January 24
State Dinner in honor of Prime Minister Cossiga of Italy
Robert Mondavi Johannisberg Riesling, California

Simi Cabernet Sauvignon, California

Hanns Kornell Extra Dry, California

February 20
*State Dinner in honor of
President Moi of Kenya*
Simi Rosé Cabernet
Sauvignon, California

Dry Creek Dry Chenin
Blanc, California

Chandon Blanc de Noirs, California

March 5
*State Dinner in honor of
Chancellor Schmidt of Germany*
Almaden Dry Sherry, California

Mirassou Gamay
Beaujolais, California

Schramsberg Blanc de
Blancs, California

April 8
*State Dinner in honor of
President Sadat of Egypt*
Louis M. Martini Johannisberg
Riesling, California

Simi Cabernet Sauvignon, California

Schramsberg Blanc de
Blancs, California

April 22
*Luncheon in honor of the
King and Queen of Belgium*
Beaulieu Pinot Chardonnay,
California

Simi Rosé Cabernet
Sauvignon, California

Korbel Natural Champagne,
California

June 9
*Luncheon in honor of Recipients
of the Presidential Medal
of Freedom*
Beaulieu Pinot Chardonnay,
California

June 17
*State Dinner in honor of
King Hussein of Jordan*
Ste. Michelle Chenin
Blanc, Washington

Robert Mondavi Reserve Cabernet
Sauvignon, California

Chandon Blanc Brut
Champagne, California

December 7
*Dinner in honor of the
Kennedy Center Honorees*
Ste. Michelle Johannisberg
Riesling, Washington

Simi Cabernet Sauvignon, California

Great Western Natural
Champagne, New York

Ronald Reagan
Presidency
1981–1989

1981

January 28
*Luncheon in honor of Prime
Minister Seaga of Jamaica*
Simi Rosé Cabernet
Sauvignon, California

February 2
*Luncheon in honor of President
Chun Doo-hwan of Korea*
Charles Krug Cabernet
Sauvignon, California

February 6
*President Ronald Reagan's
70th Birthday Party*
Ventana Chardonnay 1979, California

Inglenook Cabernet
Sauvignon, California

Schramsberg Blanc de
Blancs, California

February 26
*State Dinner in honor of
Prime Minister Thatcher
of the United Kingdom*
Beaulieu Pinot Chardonnay, California

Inglenook Cabernet Sauvignon
1974, California

Schramsberg Blanc de
Noirs, California

Jordan Cabernet Sauvignon 1976

The California wine industry took off in the
1970s, and many new vineyards appeared on
White House menus. Jordan Vineyard and
Winery, founded in 1972, became a favorite
of President Reagan and he served its
wines more often than any others. Jordan
Cabernet Sauvignon was enjoyed at eleven
events, with the 1976 vintage served at
seven of them.

Grgich Hills Chardonnay 1979

Vineyard founder Mike Grgich, the vintner behind Chateau Montelena's award-winning 1973 Chardonnay, took his expertise to his own vineyard, where he produced a Chardonnay that, too, became world renowned. The Reagans selected Grgich Hills 1979 Chardonnay to represent the best of American wine for a dinner at the United States Embassy in Paris in honor of French President François Mitterrand on June 3, 1982.

May 2
Private Dinner for Prince Charles of Wales
McDowell Valley Fumé Blanc 1980, California

Beaulieu George de Latour Private Reserve Cabernet Sauvignon 1970, California

Schramsberg Blanc de Noirs 1975, California

May 7
State Dinner in honor of Prime Minister Suzuki of Japan
Firestone Chardonnay 1979, California

Jordan Cabernet Sauvignon 1976, California

Schramsberg Crémant Demi-Sec, California

May 21
State Dinner in honor of Chancellor Schmidt of Germany
Balverne Healdsburger 1980, California

Inglenook Cabernet Sauvignon 1974, California

Johannisberg Riesling 1979, California

June 9
Luncheon in honor of President Portillo of Mexico
Silkwood Cellars Chardonnay 1979, California

Buena Vista Cabernet Sauvignon 1974, California

Schramsberg Crémant Demi-Sec, California

June 30
State Dinner in honor of Prime Minister Malcolm Fraser of Australia
Trefethen Chardonnay 1978, California

Robert Mondavi Reserve Cabernet Sauvignon 1974, California

Schramsberg Crémant, California

September 9
State Dinner in honor of Prime Minister Begin of Israel
Hagafen Johannisberg Riesling 1980 (Kosher), California

Christian Brothers Chardonnay 1978 (Kosher), California

Schramsberg Crémant Demi-Sec 1979, California

September 16
Luncheon in honor of Hispanic Heritage Week
Pinot Chardonnay 1980, California

September 24
Luncheon for Supreme Court Justices
Inglenook Pinot Chardonnay 1978, California

September 25
Luncheon in honor of President Moi of Kenya
Simi Pinot Noir, California

October 6
Luncheon in honor of Prime Minister Tinsulanonda of Thailand
Robert Mondavi Pinot Chardonnay, California

October 9
Luncheon in honor of Recipients of the Presidential Medal of Freedom
Ventana Chardonnay, 1979, California

Robert Mondavi Pinot Noir, California

October 13
State Dinner in honor of King Juan Carlos I of Spain
Grgich Hills Chardonnay 1979, California

Chalone Pinot Noir Vin Gris 1980, California

Schramsberg Crémant Demi-Sec 1979, California

October 18
Dinner at the Governor's Palace in Williamsburg, Virginia, in honor of President François Mitterrand of France
Aburdarham Sercial Madeira 1950, Portugal

Freemark Abbey-Bosche Cabernet Sauvignon 1970, California

Château d'Yquem 1970, France

November 2
State Dinner in honor of King Hussein of Jordan
Chateau Montelena Chardonnay 1979, California

Jordan Cabernet Sauvignon 1976, California

Schramsberg Crémant Demi-Sec 1979, California

November 17
State Dinner in honor of President Herrera Campins of Venezuela
Kenwood Dry Chenin Blanc 1980, California

Simi Cabernet Sauvignon Reserve 1974, California

Papagni Spumante d'Angelo, California

December 4
Private Dinner
Silkwood Cellars Chardonnay, California

Schramsberg Crémant, California

1982

February 3
State Dinner in honor of President Mubarak of Egypt
Chalk Hill Blanc Fumé Pellegrini 1980, California

Acacia Chardonnay 1980, California

Schramsberg Blanc de Blancs 1979, California

March 12
Luncheon in honor of President Mitterrand of France
Jordan Valley Chardonnay 1979, California

March 17
Luncheon in honor of Prime Minister Haughey of Ireland
Silkwood Cellars Chardonnay 1979, California

March 25
State Dinner in honor of President Pertini of Italy
Jekel Chardonny 1980, California

Louis M. Martini Special Selection Cabernet Sauvignon 1968, California

Schramsberg Crémant Demi-Sec 1979, California

April 19
State Dinner in honor of Queen Beatrix of the Netherlands
Trefethen Chardonnay 1979, California

Jordan Cabernet Sauvignon 1976, California

Schramsberg Crémant Demi-Sec 1979, California

April 21
Luncheon with Vice President George H. W. Bush
Chateau St. Jean Chardonnay 1980, California

May 12
State Dinner in honor of President Oliveira Figueiredo of Brazil
Chateau Montelena Chardonnay 1979, California

Souvertain Merlot Vintage Selection 1978, California

Korbel Sec, California

June 3
Dinner at the U.S. Embassy, Paris in honor of President Mitterrand of France
Grgich Hills Chardonnay 1979, California

Heitz Martha's Vineyard Cabernet Sauvignon 1974, California

Domaine Chandon Brut Special Reserve, California

Chateau Montelena Chardonnay 1979

Chateau Montelena made history when its 1973 Chardonnay took first place over French wines at the 1976 Judgment of Paris. Its internationally recognized Chardonnay was featured at two of President Reagan's State Dinners, first in 1981 in honor of King Hussein of Jordan, and again in 1982 at the dinner for President João Oliviera Figueiredo of Brazil.

Chateau d'Yquem 1970

Chateau d'Yquem 1970 was selected by the Reagans to be served at the dinner at the Governor's Palace in Williamsburg, Virginia, in honor of President François Mitterrand of France.

June 21
Working Luncheon with Prime Minister Begin of Israel
Trefethen Chardonnay 1978, California

July 26
Working Luncheon with President Ahidjo of Cameroon
Hacienda Dry Chenin Blanc 1981, California
Schramsberg Cuvée de Pinot 1979, California

July 29
State Dinner in honor of Prime Minister Gandhi of India
Shafer Chardonnay 1980, California
Beringer Knights Valley Estate Cabernet Sauvignon 1976, California
Korbel Blanc de Noirs, California

September 8
Luncheon in honor of President Finnbogadóttir of Iceland
Trefethen Chardonnay 1979, California
Schramsberg Blanc de Blancs, California

September 16
State Dinner in honor of President Marcos of the Philippines
Stags' Leap Chenin Blanc 1981, California
ZD Chardonnay 1979, California
Schramsberg Crémant 1979, California

October 1
Luncheon for Supreme Court Justices
Jekel Chardonnay 1980, California
Jordan Cabernet Sauvignon 1976, California
Schramsberg Crémant 1979, California

October 12
State Dinner in honor of President Suharto of Indonesia
Ventana Chardonnay 1981, California
Ridge Amador Zinfandel 1980, California
Almaden Eye of the Partridge Cuvée 1979, California

November 15
Working Luncheon with Chancellor Kohl of Germany
Joseph Phelps Johannisberg Riesling 1981, California
Korbel Blanc de Noirs, California

December 7
State Dinner in honor of President Zia-ul-Haq of Pakistan
Girard Chenin Blanc 1981, California
Robert Mondavi Pinot Noir 1978, California
Schramsberg Crémant Demi-Sec 1980, California

1983

January 27
Working Luncheon with President Mubarak of Egypt
Jordan Chardonnay 1979, California
Schramsberg Cuvée de Pinot 1979, California

February 3
Working Luncheon with Chancellor Kreisky of Austria
Beringer Cabernet Sauvignon 1976, California
Chandon Blanc de Noirs, California

February 23
Luncheon in honor of Recipients of the Presidential Medal of Freedom
Raymond Chardonnay 1980, California

February 27
Dinner in honor of U.S. Governors
Edna Valley Chardonnay 1981, California
Schramsberg Crémant Demi-Sec 1980, California

March 3
*Dinner in San Francisco in
honor of Queen Elizabeth II
of the United Kingdom*
Trefethen Chardonnay
1980, California

Jordan Cabernet Sauvignon
1976, California

Piper Sonoma Brut 1980, California

March 30
*Working Luncheon with
President Kaunda of Zambia*
Jekel Chardonnay 1980, California

April 12
*State Dinner in honor of Sultan
Qaboos bin Said of Oman*
Zaca Mesa American State
Chardonnay 1980, California

Mill Creek Merlot 1979, California

Domaine Chandon Blanc
de Noirs, California

April 19
*Private Dinner in honor of
Princess Alexandra and Angus
Ogilvy of the United Kingdom*
Raymond Chardonnay
1980, California

Schramsberg Crémant Demi-
Sec 1980, California

April 20
*Luncheon in honor of Supporters
of the 1980 Campaign*
Saintsbury Pinot Noir 1981,
California

April 28
*Working Luncheon with Prime
Minister Trudeau of Canada*
Jordan Cabernet Sauvignon
1976, California

June 7
*State Dinner in honor
of President Houphouët-
Boigny of the Ivory Coast*
Napa Valley Sauvignon
Blanc 1980, California

Silver Oak Cabernet Sauvignon
1977, California

Chandon Blanc de Noirs, California

July 19
*State Dinner in honor of Amir Isa
bin Salman Al Khalifa of Bahrain*
Stephens Sauvignon Blanc
1981, California

Edna Valley Chardonnay
1981, California

Schramsberg Crémant Demi-
Sec 1980, California

September 15
*State Dinner in honor of President
Santos Ramalho Eanes of Portugal*
Grand Cru-Dry Chenin
Blanc 1981, California

Fetzer Cabernet Sauvignon
1980, California

Chandon Blanc de Noirs, California

October 1
*Private Dinner in honor
of Princess Margaret of
the United Kingdom*
Hanzell Chardonnay 1978, California

Schramsberg Crémant Demi-
Sec 1979, California

October 4
*State Dinner in honor of
President Carstens of Germany*
Vichon Chardonnay 1981, California

Jordan Cabernet Sauvignon
1979, California

Schramsberg Blanc de
Blancs 1980, California

December 7
*State Dinner in honor of
King Birendra Bir Bikram
Shah Dev of Nepal*
Trefethen Chardonnay
1980, California

Jordan Cabernet Sauvignon
1979, California

Korbel Blanc de Noir, California

Trefethen Chardonnay 1980

Another favorite of President Reagan,
Trefethen Vineyards Chardonnay was
served at six events during the his
presidency, including at the dinner in San
Francisco in honor of Queen Elizabeth II,
March 3, 1983.

Chandon Blanc de Noirs

Owned by the esteemed French Champagne house, Moët & Chandon, Domaine Chandon's California wines became a regular feature on White House menus. Domaine Chandon Blanc de Noirs accompanied dessert at six dinners during the Reagan presidency.

1984

January 10
Official Dinner in honor of Premier Zhao Ziyang of China
Pine Ridge Chardonnay 1981, California
Silver Oak Cabernet Sauvignon 1978, California
Schramsberg Crémant Demi-Sec 1981, California

January 18
Working Luncheon with Prime Minister Mahathir of Malaysia
Stags' Leap Chenin Blanc 1981, California

February 16
State Dinner in honor of President Kirchschläger of Austria
Gundlach-Bundschu Kleinberger 1983, California
Far Niente Chardonnay 1981, California
Scharffenberger Brut 1981, California

March 16
Luncheon in honor of Prime Minister FitzGerald of Ireland
Concannon Estate Sauvignon Blanc 1981, California

March 22
State Dinner in honor of President Mitterrand of France
Robert Mondavi Fumé Blanc Reserve 1981, California
Clos du Val Cabernet Sauvignon 1975, California
Domaine Chandon Blanc de Noirs, California

April 10
State Dinner in honor of President Salvador Jorge Blanco of the Dominican Republic
Carmenet Sauvignon Blanc 1982, California
Jordan Cabernet Sauvignon 1979, California
Schramsberg Crémant Demi-Sec 1981, California

April 13
Working Luncheon with Prime Minister Prem of Thailand
Pendleton Chardonnay 1981, California

May 8
Luncheon Commemorating the Centennial of the Birth of President Harry S. Truman
Sanford Pinot Noir Vin Gris 1983, California

May 15
State Dinner in honor of President de la Madrid Hurtado of Mexico
Franciscan Chardonnay Estate 1982, California
Buena Vista Pinot Noir Special Selection 1981, California
Schramsberg Crémant Demi-Sec 1981, California

June 18
State Dinner in honor of President Jayewardene of Sri Lanka
Paulsen Muscat Canelli 1983, California
Matanzas Creek Chardonnay 1981, California
Korbel Blanc de Noirs, California

October 9
Working Luncheon with Prime Minister Peres of Israel
Sonoma-Cutrer Chardonnay 1982, California

November 13
State Dinner in honor of the Grand Duke of Luxembourg
Kendall-Jackson Chevriot du Lac 1983, California
Kistler Dutton Ranch Chardonnay 1982, California
Schramsberg Cuvée de Pinot 1982, California

December 4
State Dinner in honor of
President Lusinchi of Venezuela

Lambert Bridge Chardonnay
1981, California

Chateau Julien Merlot
1982, California

Schramsberg Crémant Demi-
Sec 1982, California

1985

January 29
Dinner for Freshman
Members of Congress

Vichon Chardonnay 1980, California

Robert Mondavi Pinot
Noir 1978, California

Schramsberg Blanc de
Blancs 1980, California

February 11
State Dinner in honor of
King Fahd bin 'Abd al-'Aziz
Al Sa'ud of Saudi Arabia

Cakebread Chardonnay
1981, California

Saintsbury Pinot Noir 1982,
California

Schramsberg Blanc de
Blancs 1981, California

February 25
Issues Briefing Luncheon

Buehler White Zinfandel
1984, California

March 5
Working Luncheon with Prime
Minister Craxi of Italy

David Bruce Pinot Noir
1981, California

March 11
Private Dinner in honor of
Queen Sirikit of Thailand

Trefethen White Riesling
1982, California

Sanford Pinot Noir Vin
Gris 1983, California

Schramsberg Crémant Demi-
Sec 1980, California

March 12
Working Luncheon with
President Mubarak of Egpyt

Louis M. Martini Pinot
Noir 1971, California

March 19
State Dinner in honor of
President Alfonsín of Argentina

Stony Hill Chardonnay
1982, California

Edna Valley Pinot Noir
1981, California

Domaine Chandon Blanc
de Noirs, California

April 17
State Dinner in honor of
President Bendjedid of Algeria

Robert Mondavi Fumé
Blanc 1981, California

Boeger Merlot 1982, California

Van der Kamp Brut Rosé
1982, California

June 12
Official Dinner in honor of Prime
Minister Rajiv Gandhi of India

Bacigalupi Chardonnay
1982, California

Saintsbury Garnet 1983, California

Schramsberg Crémant
Demi-Sec, California

July 23
State Dinner in honor of
President Li Xiannian of China

Balverne Chardonnay 1981, California

Caymus Cabernet Sauvignon
1977, California

Schramsberg Cuvée de
Pinot, California

September 10
Official Dinner in honor of Prime
Minister Schlüter of Denmark

Byron Chardonnay 1984, California

Saintsbury Pinot Noir 1983, California

Van der Kamp Brut Rosé, California

Saintsbury Garnet 1983

In the 1980s, Saintsbury became one of California's leading Pinot Noir producers. Its 1983 Garnet was featured with the main course at the dinner in honor of Prime Minister Rajiv Gandhi of India on June 12, 1985.

Conn Creek Cabernet Sauvignon 1979

Conn Creek, a small Napa Valley winery, is known for its Bordeaux-style wines. Its 1979 Cabernet Sauvignon appeared on two Reagan administration menus—first on November 9, 1985, at the dinner in honor of Prince Charles and Princess Diana of Wales, and again at the luncheon in honor of recipients of the Presidential Medal of Freedom on May 12, 1986.

September 16
Luncheon with Regional Editors and Broadcasters
Gevrey Chambertin 1970, France

September 30
Dinner in honor of King Hussein of Jordan
Bacigalupi Chardonnay 1983, California
Silver Oak Cabernet Sauvignon 1977, California
Schramsberg Crémant Demi-Sec 1981, California

October 8
Official Dinner in honor of Prime Minister Lee Kuan Yew of Singapore
Jordan Chardonnay 1982, California
Austin Cellars Pinot Noir 1982, California
Van der Kamp Brut 1981, California

November 9
Dinner in honor of Prince Charles and Princess Diana of Wales
Quail Ridge Chardonnay 1981, California
Conn Creek Cabernet Sauvignon 1979, California
Schramsberg Cuvée de Pinot 1982, California

1986

January 14
State Dinner in honor of President Febres-Cordero Ribadeneyra of Ecuador
Clos du Bois Calcaire 1984, California
Carneros Creek Pinot Noir 1983, California
Schramsberg Crémant Demi-Sec 1982, California

February 7
Private Dinner in honor of President Reagan's 75th Birthday
Sarah's Vineyard Chardonnay 1982, California
Jordan Cabernet Sauvignon 1979, California
Schramsberg Crémant Demi-Sec 1979, California

March 18
Official Dinner in honor of Prime Minister Martin Brian Mulroney of Canada
Sonoma-Cutrer Chardonnay 1983, California
Leardini Pinot Noir 1983, California
Schramsberg Crémant Demi-Sec 1982, California

May 12
Luncheon in honor of Recipients of the Presidential Medal of Freedom
Conn Creek Cabernet Sauvignon 1979, California

June 17
State Dinner in honor of President Julio María Sanguinetti of Uruguay
Adler Fels Fumé Blanc 1985, California
Calera Pinot Noir 1983, California
Schramsberg Crémant Demi-Sec 1983, California

July 4
Luncheon on Governors Island, New York, in honor of the Statue of Liberty Centennial
Sonoma-Cutrer Chardonnay 1983, California

July 16
Official Dinner in honor of Prime Minister Mohammed Khan Junejo of Pakistan
Saintsbury Chardonnay 1984, California
Charles F. Shaw Napa Valley Gamay 1985, California
Culbertson Cuvée de Frontignan Demi-Sec, California

August 13
*Working Luncheon with President
de la Madrid of Mexico*
Carneros Creek Pinot Noir
1983, California

September 10
*State Dinner in honor of President
José Sarney Costa of Brazil*
Grgich Hills Fumé Blanc
1984, California

Simi Zinfandel 1978, California

Culbertson Cuvée de Frontignan
Demi-Sec, California

September 17
*Working Luncheon with President
Aquino of the Philippines*
Carneros Creek Pinot Noir
1983, California

October 19
*Private Dinner for
Supporters of the Reagan
Presidential Foundation*
Hacienda Dry Chenin
Blanc 1985, California

Château Mouton Rothschild
1962, France

Chateau St. Jean Muscat
Canelli 1980, California

October 21
*Official Dinner in honor of
Chancellor Kohl of Germany*
Monticello Chardonnay
1984, California

Jordan Cabernet Sauvignon
1979, California

Schramsberg Crémant
1983, California

October 27
*Private Dinner for
Supporters of the Reagan
Presidential Foundation*
Sarah's Vineyard Chardonnay
1982, California

Château Mouton Rothschild
1966, France

Château d'Yquem Lur-
Salices 1970, France

November 15
*Working Luncheon at Camp David
with Prime Minister Margaret
Thatcher of the United Kingdom*
Cakebread Chardonnay
1984, California

November 25
*Luncheon in honor of
Supreme Court Justices*
Balverne Chardonnay 1981, California

Jordan Cabernet Sauvignon
1976, California

December 4
*Working Luncheon with
President Arias of Costa Rica*
Cakebread Chardonnay
1984, California

December 9
*Working Luncheon with
President Mobutu of Zaire*
Cakebread Chardonnay
1984, California

1987

February 22
Dinner in honor of Governors
Llano Estacado Chardonnay
1985, Texas

Ste. Chapelle Cabernet
Sauvignon 1981, Idaho

Schramsberg Crémant Demi-
Sec 1983, California

February 23
Issues Briefing Luncheon
Buehler White Zinfandel
1984, California

March 31
*Official Dinner in honor of Prime
Minister Chirac of France*
Sonoma-Cutrer Chardonnay
1984, California

Opus One 1982 Robert
Mondavi–Baron Philippe de
Rothschild, California

Domaine Mumm Cuvée
Napa, California

Opus One 1982

Opus One is the product of the joint
venture between Robert Mondavi and
Baron Philippe de Rothschild, who sought
to create a blend of Old and New World
winemaking styles. The 1982 vintage of
Opus One was selected for President
Reagan's dinner in honor of French Prime
Minister Jacques Chirac on March 31, 1987,
to symbolize the friendship between the
United States and France.

Jordan Chardonnay 1984

From one of President Reagan's favorite California vineyards, Jordan Chardonnay was offered at the White House on five occasions during that presidency. The 1984 vintage was served at the dinner in honor of General Secretary Mikhail Gorbachev of the Soviet Union on December 8, 1987.

April 3
Luncheon with Supporters of the Reagan Presidential Foundation
Leardini Pinot Noir 1983, California

April 7
Luncheon for Corporate Sponsors of the Commemoration of the Bicentennial of the United States Constitution
Sterling Chardonnay 1984, California

April 30
Official Dinner in honor of Prime Minister Yasuhiro Nakasone of Japan
Jordan Chardonnay 1984, California
Schug Pinot Noir 1984, California
Chateau St. Jean 1983, California

June 30
Luncheon for Recipients of the President's Volunteer Action Awards
Stephens Sauvignon Blanc 1981, California

September 9
Official Dinner in honor of Prime Minister Carlsson of Sweden
Jordan Chardonnay 1984, California
St. Francis Merlot 1983, California
Domaine Chandon Blanc de Noirs, California

October 14
State Dinner in honor of President José Napoleón Duarte Fuentes of El Salvador
Clos du Bois Chardonnay 1986, California
Saintsbury Garnet 1985, California
Schramsberg Crémant 1982, California

November 10
State Dinner in honor of President Herzog of Israel
Hagafen Chardonnay 1984 (Kosher), California
Gan Eden Beaujolais 1986 (Kosher), California
Kedem Extra Dry (Kosher), California

December 8
Official Dinner in honor of General Secretary Gorbachev of the Soviet Union
Jordan Chardonnay 1984, California
Stags' Leap Cabernet Sauvignon Lot 2 1978, California
Iron Horse Brut Summit Cuvée 1984, California

1988

January 28
State Dinner in honor of President Mohammed Hosni Mubarak of Egypt
Navarro Gewurztraminer 1985, California
Carneros Pinot Noir 1985, California
Schramsberg Crémant Demi-Sec 1984, California

April 11
Dinner in honor of King Carl XVI and Queen Silvia of Sweden
Ferrari-Carano Chardonnay 1985, California
Tubal Cabernet Sauvignon 1983, California
Iron Horse Brut Rosé 1984, California

April 27
Official Dinner in honor of Prime Minister Martin Brian Mulroney of Canada
Silverado Chardonnay 1986, California
Williams Selyem Pinot Noir 1985, California
S. Anderson Blanc de Noirs 1983, California

June 27
State Dinner in honor of President Kenan Evren of Turkey
Boyer Chardonnay 1986, California
Domaine Michel Cabernet Sauvignon 1984, California
Van der Kamp Brut Rosé 1985, California

October 6
*State Dinner in honor of
President Moussa Traoré of Mali*

Chateau St. Jean Chardonnay
1986, California

Sterling Winery Lake Pinot
Noir 1986, California

Schramsberg Crémant Demi-
Sec 1984, California

November 16
*Official Dinner in honor of Prime
Minister Margaret Thatcher
of the United Kingdom*

Saintsbury Chardonnay
1987, California

Stag's Leap Wine Cellars Cabernet
Sauvignon 1978, California

Schramsberg Crémant Demi-
Sec 1984, California

George H. W. Bush
Presidency
1989–1993

1989

February 2
*Luncheon in honor of Prime
Minister Toshiki Kaifu of Japan*

Chimney Rock Fumé Blanc
1986, California

Boeger Merlot 1982, California

April 4
*Official Dinner in honor
of President Mohammed
Hosni Mubarak of Egypt*

La Crema Reserve Chardonnay
1987, California

Shafer Hillside Select Cabernet
Sauvignon 1984, California

Iron Horse Brut Rosé 1985,
California

April 6
*Official Dinner in honor of Prime
Minister Yitzhak Shamir of Israel*

Hagafen Johannisberg Riesling
1988 (Kosher), California

Hagaden Chardonnay 1988
(Kosher), California

Domaine Chandon Blanc
de Noirs, California

May 22
Dinner in honor of Governors

Saintsbury Chardonnay
1987, California

Robert Mondavi Reserve Cabernet
Sauvignon 1985, California

Ste. Michelle Columbia
Valley Brut, California

June 6
*Official Dinner in honor
of Prime Minister Benazir
Bhutto of Pakistan*

Talbott Chardonnay 1986, California

Jordan Cabernet Sauvignon
1985, California

Schramsberg Crémant Demi-
Sec 1985, California

September 1
*Luncheon in honor of Prime
Minister Toshiki Kaifu of Japan*

Raymond Chardonnay
1987, California

September 27
*Dinner at Monticello for the
President's Education Summit
with U.S. Governors*

Montdomaine Monticello
Chardonnay 1986, Virginia

Monticello Pinot Noir 1987, California

Domaine Cheurlin Brut, France

**Robert Mondavi Reserve Cabernet
Sauvignon 1985**

Robert Mondavi's wines were served
five times during the George H. W.
Bush presidency. In consideration of
Mondavi's Italian heritage, his 1985
Reserve Cabernet Sauvignon was included
on the menu for the State Dinner in honor
of Italian President Francesco Cossiga on
October 11, 1989.

Quady Essensia Orange Muscat 1987

In 1980 Quady Winery utilized the underappreciated Orange Muscat grape, known in Italy as Moscato Fior d'Arancio, to make one of California's highly regarded sweet wines. Essensia, named for how the wine captures the essence of the grapes, is a full-bodied dessert wine. It was served with the dessert course, replacing traditional champagne, during the George H. W. Bush presidency at two dinners. It was first introduced at the State Dinner in honor of President Corazon Aquino of the Philippines, November 9, 1989.

October 3
State Dinner in honor of President Carlos Salinas de Gortari of Mexico
Ferrari-Carano Fumé Blanc 1987, California

Jordan Cabernet Sauvignon 1981, California

Schramsberg Crémant Demi-Sec, California

October 11
State Dinner in honor of President Francesco Cossiga of Italy
Louis M. Martini Chardonnay 1987, California

Robert Mondavi Reserve Cabernet Sauvignon 1985, California

Chandon Brut, California

November 9
State Dinner in honor of President Corazon Aquino of the Philippines
Davis Bynum Reserve Chardonnay 1987, California

St. Francis Merlot Reserve 1985, California

Quady Essensia California Orange Muscat 1987, California

1990

January 24
State Dinner in honor of President 'Ali 'Abdallah Salih of Yemen Arab Republic
McDowell Fumé Blanc 1988, California

Clos du Val Cabernet Sauvignon 1985, California

Dusinberre Cellars Brut 1987, California

February 12
State Dinner in honor of President Sassou-Nguesso of the Republic of Congo
Talbott Chardonnay 1987, California

Jordan Cabernet Sauvignon 1985, California

Firestone Johannisberg Riesling Select Harvest 1986, California

February 27
Luncheon in honor of Prime Minister Charles Haughey of Ireland
MacRostie Chardonnay 1988, California

March 2
Dinner in Palm Springs in honor of Prime Minister Toshiki Kaifu
McDowell Fume Blanc 1988, California

Clos du Val Cabernet Sauvignon 1985, California

Dusinberre Cellars Brut 1987, California

March 6
State Dinner in honor of Prime Minister Andreotti of Italy
Viansa Chardonnay 1987, California

Cosentino Cabernet Franc 1986, California

Robert Mondavi Sauvignon Blanc, California

March 21
Official Dinner in honor of Prime Minister Mazowiecki of Poland
Stag's Leap Wine Cellars Chardonnay Reserve 1986, California

York Mountain Pinot Noir Reserve 1987, California

Quady Essensia California Orange Muscat 1987, California

March 27
Luncheon in Recognition of the Centennial of the Birth of President Dwight E. Eisenhower
Ferrari-Carano Chardonnay 1987, California

April 26
State Dinner in honor of President Pérez of Venezuela
Matanzas Creek Chardonnay 1988, California

Saintsbury Pinot Noir 1988, California

Gabriele y Caroline Riesling 1982, California

May 8
*Luncheon in honor of President
Jaime Paz Zamora of Bolivia*
Matanzas Creek Chardonnay
1988, California

May 15
*State Dinner in honor of President
Zine El Abidine Ben Ali of Tunisia*
DeLoach Chardonnay 1988,
California
Shafer Hillside Select Cabernet
Sauvignon 1984, California
Quady Elysium Black
Muscat 1988, California

May 17
*Luncheon in honor of Chancellor
Helmut Kohl of Germany*
La Crema Reserve Chardonnay
1987, California
Simi Cabernet Sauvignon
1976, California

May 31
*Dinner in honor of President
Gorbachev of the Soviet Union*
Flora Springs Barrel Fermented
Chardonnay 1987, California
Heitz Cellars Martha's Vineyards
Cabernet Sauvignon 1974, California
S. Anderson Blanc de Noirs Cuvée
Extraordinair 1985, California

June 6
*Luncheon in honor of Prime
Minister Konstantinos
Mitsotakis of Greece*
Shafer Chardonnay 1988, California

June 25
*Luncheon in honor of
Nelson Mandela*
DeLoach Chardonnay 1988,
California

September 24
*Luncheon in honor of
President Frederik Willem
de Klerk of South Africa*
Flora Springs Chardonnay
1987, California
Beaulieu Reserve Cabernet
Sauvignon 1970, California

September 25
*Luncheon in honor of
President Özal of Turkey*
Shafer Chardonnay 1988, California

October 18
*Official Dinner in honor of Prime
Minister Antall of Hungary*
Shafer Chardonnay 1988, California
Kendall-Jackson Proprietors Reserve
Cabernet Sauvignon 1985, California
Schramsberg Crémant
1985, California

1991

February 20
*State Dinner in honor of Queen
Margrethe II of Denmark*
Sanford Chardonnay Barrel
Select 1988, California
Robert Mondavi Pinot Noir
Reserve 1988, California
Vichon Semillon Botrytis
1987, California

March 7
*Dinner on the Occasion
of the Presentation of the
Presidential Medal of Freedom
to Margaret Thatcher*
Swanson Chardonnay 1988, California
Jordan Cabernet Sauvignon
1986, California
Roederer Estate Brut, California

March 20
*State Dinner in honor of President
Lech Wałęsa of Poland*
Stag's Leap Wine Cellars
Riesling 1990, California
Clos Pegase Cabernet
Sauvignon 1986, California
Scharffenberger Crémant, California

May 7
*Luncheon in honor of President
Mauno Koivisto of Finland*
Sanford Chardonnay 1988, California

**Shafer Hillside Select Cabernet
Sauvignon 1986**

Created in 1983, Shafer was soon producing
some of California's most highly rated
wines. Both white and red varieties were
served throughout the George H. W.
Bush presidency. Shafer's Hillside Select
Cabernet Sauvignon was served three
times, most notably with the main course at
the State Dinner for Queen Elizabeth II on
May 14, 1991.

Sanford Chardonnay 1989

Sanford was introduced to White House menus by President George H. W. Bush. The vineyard's hand-crafted Chardonnay was served at five dinners and luncheons, with the 1989 vintage paired with the first course of the dinner in honor of Queen Sirikit of Thailand on October 28, 1991.

May 14
State Dinner in honor of Queen Elizabeth II of the United Kingdom
Swanson Reserve Chardonnay 1988, California
Shafer Hillside Select Cabernet Sauvignon 1986, California
Jordan J 1987, California

July 2
State Dinner in honor of President Roh Tae-woo of South Korea
Far Niente Chardonnay 1989, California
Star Hill Pinot Noir 1988, California
Joseph Phelps Delice du Semillon 1989, California

July 24
Luncheon in honor of President Robert Mugabe of Zimbabwe
MacRostie Chardonnay 1989, California
Robert Mondavi Pinot Noir 1988, California

September 10
State Dinner in honor of President Abdou Diouf of Senegal
Flora Springs Soliloquy 1989, California
Kendall-Jackson Proprietor's, Reserve Merlot 1987, California
Renaissance Special Select Late Harvest White Riesling 1985, California

September 26
Official Dinner in honor of King Hassan II of Morocco
ZD Chardonnay 1989, California
Chateau St. Jean Cabernet Sauvignon 1987, California
Frog's Leap Le Baiser Magique 1989, California

October 22
State Dinner in honor of President Václav Havel of Czechoslovakia
Edna Valley Chardonnay 1990, California
Caymus Special Select Pinot Noir 1986, California
Ferrari-Carano Eldorado Gold 1989, California

October 28
Dinner in honor of Queen Sirikit of Thailand
Sanford Chardonnay 1989, California
Star Hill Pinot Noir 1988, California
Domaine Chandon Brut, California

November 14
State Dinner in honor of President Carlos Menem of Argentina
Ferrari-Carano Chardonnay 1989, California
Signorello Pinot Noir 1989, California
Jordan J 1987, California

1992

March 24
Dinner in honor of Prime Minister Michael Manley of Jamaica
Boyer Chardonnay 1990, California
Clos Pegase Cabernet Sauvignon 1986, California
Late Leap Sauvignon Blanc 1989, California

April 2
Luncheon in honor of President Felipe González Márquez of Spain
Talbott Chardonnay 1988, California
Simi Zinfandel 1978, California

April 29
State Dinner in honor of President von Weizsäcker of Germany
Merryvale Starmont Chardonnay 1990, California
Beringer Knights Valley Cabernet Sauvignon 1982, California
Joseph Phelps Delice du Semillon 1989, California

May 6
Luncheon in honor of President Robert Mugabe of Zimbabwe

Talbott Chardonnay 1988, California

Jordan Cabernet Sauvignon 1985, California

May 19
Dinner in honor of Premier Swan of Bermuda

Saintsbury Chardonnay 1990, California

Shafer Cabernet Sauvignon 1986, California

Scharffenberger Blanc de Blancs, California

May 20
Luncheon in honor of Prime Minister Brian Mulroney

Sanford Chardonnay 1989, California

June 3
Luncheon in honor of the Ladies of the Senate

Joseph Phelps Chardonnay 1990, California

June 16
State Dinner in honor of President Boris Yeltsin of Russia

Cakebread Sauvignon Blanc 1990, California

Sanford Barrel Select Pinot Noir 1989, California

Gabriele y Caroline Late Harvest Riesling 1982, California

December 11
Luncheon in honor of the Recipients of the Presidential Medal of Freedom

Sanford Chardonnay 1990, California

William J. Clinton Presidency
1993–2001

1993

November 23
Official Dinner in honor of Kim Young-sam of South Korea

ZD Chardonnay 1991, California

Newton Merlot 1990, California

Bonny Doon Malvasia Bianca Vin de Glaciere 1991, California

1994

June 13
State Dinner in honor of Emperor Akihito of Japan

Kistler Sand Hill Chardonnay 1992, California

Domaine Drouhin Pinot Noir 1992, Oregon

Roederer Estate Extra Dry White House Cuvée, California

July 25
Dinner in honor of King Hussein I of Jordan and Prime Minister Rabin of Israel

Mount Madrona Chardonnay 1992, California

Hagaden Cabernet Sauvignon 1988, California

Baron Herzog Brut, California

September 27
State Dinner in honor of President Boris Yeltsin of Russia

Dehlinger Reserve Chardonnay 1992, California

William Selyem Rochioli Pinot Noir 1990, California

Iron Horse Demi-Sec 1989, California

Roederer Estate Brut

Roederer Estate, the California endeavor of the famous French champagne house Louis Roederer, created a White House Cuvée specially for service at the White House. The White House blend is a slightly sweeter version of Roederer's signature Brut. The Clintons served the special Cuvée at five events, including at their first State Dinner on June 13, 1994, in honor of Emperor Akihito of Japan.

Rex Hill Pinot Noir 1994 Reserve

Beginning as a fruit farm in the 1920s, Rex Hill has been producing Pinot Noir in Oregon since 1982. The winery's 1994 Pinot Noir Reserve was served at a State Dinner in honor of President Kim Dae-jung of South Korea, June 9, 1998.

October 4
State Dinner in honor of President Nelson Mandela of South Africa
Joseph Phelps Viognier 1993, California
Peter Michael Chardonnay 1991, California
Piper Sonoma Tête de Cuvée 1985, California

November 22
State Dinner in honor of President Kuchma of Ukraine
Selene Sauvignon Blanc 1993, California
Talbott Chardonnay 1992, California
Schramsberg Crémant 1989, California

1995

February 9
Official Dinner in honor of Chancellor Kohl of Germany
Solitude Chardonnay 1993, California
La Boheme Pinot Noir 1992, California
Schramsberg Crémant Demi-Sec 1991, California

March 15
State Dinner in honor of King Hassan II of Morocco
Oak Knoll Pinot Gris 1993, Oregon
Beaulieu Tapestry 1990, California
Scharffenberger Crémant Extra Dry, California

April 5
Luncheon in honor of President Mubarak of Egypt
Flora Springs Chardonnay 1991, California

April 11
Luncheon in honor of Prime Minister Bhutto of Pakistan
Joseph Phelps Viognier 1993, California

April 20
State Dinner in honor of President Cardoso of Brazil
Horton Viognier 1993, Virginia
Fiddlehead Pinot Noir 1993, California
Chandon Brut Reserve, California

July 27
State Dinner in honor of President Kim Young-sam of South Korea
Kendall-Jackson Viognier 1993, California
Kistler Pinot Noir Cuvée Catherine 1992, California
Mumm Napa Valley Blanc de Noirs, California

October 10
State Dinner in honor of President Zedillo of Mexico
Caymus Conundrum 1994, California
El Molino Pinot Noir 1992, California
Domaine Carneros Blanc de Blancs, California

1996

February 1
State Dinner in honor of President Jacques Chirac of France
Beringer Viognier 1994, California
Zaca Mesa Syrah 1993, California
Roederer Estates L'Ermitage 1990, California

April 2
State Dinner in honor of President Scalfaro of Italy
Gallo Estate Chardonnay 1993, California
Robert Mondavi Reserve Cabernet Sauvignon 1990, California
Silvan Ridge Early Muscat 1994, California

May 9
State Dinner in honor of President Stephanopoulos of Greece

Lolonis Chardonnay Reserve 1994, California

Topolos Zinfandel Piner Heights 1994, California

Pindar Brut Long Island 1989, New York

June 13
State Dinner in honor of President Mary Robinson of Ireland

Murphy Goode Sonoma Chardonnay 1995, California

Mahoney Estate Carneros Pinot Noir 1994, California

Flynn Oregon Brut 1988, Oregon

1997

February 26
State Dinner in honor of President Frei of Chile

Franciscan Cuvée Sauvage 1994, California

Murrieta's Well Vendimia 1992, California

Robert Mondavi Malvasia Bianca 1995, California

April 8
State Dinner in honor of Prime Minister Chrétien of Canada

Signorello Estate Chardonnay 1995, California

Kalin DD Pinot Noir 1992, California

Schramsberg Crémant 1992, California

September 29
Dinner for the Recipients of the National Medal of Arts and Humanities

Clos Pegase Mitsuko Vineyard Chardonnay 1995, California

Hess Collection Cabernet Sauvignon 1992, California

Schramsberg Crémant 1992, California

October 29
State Dinner in honor of President Jiang Zemin of China

Cuvaison Carneros Chardonnay 1995, California

Ponzi 25th Anniversary Pinot Noir 1995, Oregon

Iron Horse Blanc de Blancs LD 1991, California

1998

February 5
Official Dinner in honor of Prime Minister Tony Blair of the United Kingdom

Newton Chardonnay Unfiltered 1996, California

Swanson Sangiovese Estate 1995, California

Mumm Napa Valley DVX 1993, California

May 6
Official Dinner in honor of Prime Minister Prodi of Italy

Ponzi Arneis 1996, California

Horton Nebbiolo 1995, Virginia

Pecota Moscato d'Andrea 1997, California

Roederer White House Cuvée 1991, California

June 9
State Dinner in honor of President Kim Dae-jung of South Korea

Shafer Chardonnay Red Shoulder 1996, California

Rex Hill Pinot Noir Reserve 1994, Oregon

Roederer L'Ermitage White House Cuvée 1991, California

September 16
State Dinner in honor of President Havel of the Czech Republic

Lewis Chardonnay Reserve 1996, California

Archery Summit Pinot Noir 1994, California

Roederer White House Cuvée 1991, California

Horton Nebbiolo 1995

The wines selected by the Clintons for the dinner in honor of Italian Prime Minister Romano Prodi on May 6, 1998, were chosen for their connection to Italy. Served with the main course was an Italian-style 1995 Nebbiolo from Horton, a Virginia winery. Nebbiolo, a grape from the Piedmonte region of Italy, is one of many diverse varietals Horton cultivates, demonstrating the versatility of wines produced in Virginia.

Artesa Pinot Noir 1997

Artesa Winery in Napa Valley has been owned and operated since 1991 by Spain's oldest winemaking family. The name "Artesa" means "handcrafted" in Catalan. Artesa's 1997 Pinot Noir was paired with the main course for the State Dinner in honor of King Juan Carlos I of Spain on February 23, 2000.

October 28
State Dinner in honor of President Andrés Pastrana Arango of Colombia
Talbott Sleepy Hollow Chardonnay 1996, California
Shafer Hillside Select Cabernet Sauvingnon 1993, California
Roederer White House Cuvée 1991, California

1999

January 11
State Dinner in honor of President Menem of Argentina
Sanford Chardonnay Estate 1996, California
Beaux Freres Pinot Noir 1995, California
Mumm Cuvée Napa DVX 1993, California

February 24
State Dinner in honor of President Rawlings of Ghana
Etude Pinot Blanc 1997, Califonia
Wild Horse Pinot Noir 1997, California
Domaine Carneros Le Reve 1992, California

April 8
Official Dinner in honor of Premier Zhu Rongji of China
Macari Chardonnay Estate 1997, California
Talley Rosemary's Pinot Noir 1996, California
Jordan J 1994, California

April 23
North Atlantic Treaty Organization 50th Anniversary Dinner
Ancien Chardonnay 1997, California
Flowers Pinot Noir Camp Meeting Ridge 1996, California
Paumanok Late Harvest Sauvignon Blanc 1997, New York

May 3
Official Dinner in honor of Prime Minister Keizō Obuchi of Japan
St. Clement Chardonnay Abbots 1997, California
Ridge Cabernet Sauvignon Monte Bello 1991, California
Iron Horse Millennium Cuvée 1994, California

May 18
Dinner in honor of King Abdullah II of Jordan
Chalone Chardonnay 1997, California

June 8
State Dinner in honor of President Árpád Göncz of Hungary
Chalone Chardonnay 1997, California
Rabbit Ridge Zinfandel Estate Reserve 1996, California
Paumanok Late Harvest Sauvignon Blanc 1997, New York

December 31
Millennium New Year's Celebration
Sterling Chardonnay Winery Lake 1998, California
Dehlinger Pinot Noir Estates 1997, California

2000

February 23
State Dinner in honor of King Juan Carlos I of Spain
Miramar Torres Chardonnay 1997, California
Artesa Pinot Noir Bien Nacido 1997, California
Gloria Ferrer Royal Cuvée Brut 1991, California

May 22
State Dinner in honor of President Thabo Mbeki of South Africa
Long Vineyard Pinot Grigio 1999, California
Chimney Rock Elevage 1996, California
S. Anderson Blanc de Noirs 1995, California

June 20
*State Dinner in honor of King
Mohammed VI of Morocco*
Ste. Michelle Reserve
Chardonnay 1997, California

Justin Isoscles 1997, California

Argyle Julia Lee's Block Blanc
de Blancs 1996, California

September 17
*State Dinner in honor of
Prime Minister Atal Behari
Vajpayee of India*
Wolffer Chardonnay Estate
1997, California

Callaghan Buena Suerte
Cuvée 1997, California

Tualatin Estate Semi Sparking
Muscat 1999, California

November 9
*Dinner Commemorating the
200th Anniversary of
the White House*
Kistler Chardonnay Cuvée
Cathleen 1996, California

Landmark Pinot Noir
Kastania 1997, California

Bonny Doon Vin Glaciere
Muscat 1999, California

George W. Bush Presidency
2001–2009

2001

January 26
*Luncheon in honor of Freshman
Members of Congress*
Lewis Cellars Reserve
Chardonnay 1997, California

February 5
*Working Dinner with Prime
Minister Jean Chrétien of Canada*
Lewis Cellars Chardonnay
Reserve 1991, California

Joseph Phelps Insignia
1994, California

February 6
*Dinner in honor of the
Commanders in Chief*
Talley Chardonnay Oliver's
Vineyard 1998, California

Duckhorn Merlot Estate
1997, California

February 23
*Working Luncheon at Camp
David with Prime Minister Tony
Blair of the United Kingdom*
Willakenzie Estate Pinot
Gris 1999, Oregon

March 7
*Working Luncheon with President
Kim Dae-jung of South Korea*
MacRostie Chardonnay
1999, California

March 19
*Working Luncheon with Prime
Minister Yoshirō Mori of Japan*
Clos Pegase Mitsuko's Vineyard
Chardonnay 1999, California

March 30
*Luncheon in honor of the Members
of the Baseball Hall of Fame*
Fess Parker Chardonnay
1999, California

June 26
*Working Luncheon with President
Thabo M. Mbeki of South Africa*
Lewis Cellars Chardonnay
Reserve 1997, California

September 5
*State Dinner in honor of
President Vicente Fox of Mexico*
Mi Sueño Chardonnay
Carneros 1999, California

Shafer Hillside Select Cabernet
Sauvignon 1994, California

Schramsberg Crémant
1997, California

September 10
*Working Luncheon with
Prime Minister John
Howard of Australia*
Geyser Peak Chardonnay
1999, California

Ponzi Chardonnay 1999

One of the first wineries in Oregon's
Willamette Valley, Ponzi Vineyards was
established by Dick Ponzi, the son of Italian
immigrants. His Chardonnay was served
several times during the George W. Bush
presidency and was especially favored for
luncheons, including three luncheons with
Italian Prime Minister Silvio Berlusconi.

Dos Cabezas Pinot Gris 2000

Dos Cabezas WineWorks, named for the Dos Cabezas Mountains in southeast Arizona's Sonoita wine region, appeared on two menus during the George W. Bush presidency. Its 2000 Pinot Gris vintage was first served at a dinner in honor of the nation's governors, February 24, 2002, and again on April 12, 2006, at a dinner to honor Arizona native Supreme Court Justice Sandra Day O'Connor.

September 18
Working Dinner with President Jacques Chirac of France
Pride Mountain Viognier 1999, California

Phelps Syrah 1997, California

Dolce 1993, California

September 19
Working Luncheon with President Megawati Suekarnoputri of Indonesia
Navarro Pinot Gris 2000, California

September 20
Working Dinner with Prime Minister Tony Blair of the United Kingdom
Gary Farrell Westside Chardonnay 1999, California

Iron Horse Thomas Road Pinot Noir 1998, California

Phelps Late Harvest Eisrebe 1996, California

September 24
Working Luncheon with Prime Minister Jean Chrétien of Canada
Ramey Chardonnay Carneros 1998, California

October 15
Working Luncheon with President Silvio Berlusconi of Italy
Paul Hobbs Chardonnay 1999, California

November 6
Working Luncheon with President Jacques Chirac of France
Paul Hobbs Chardonnay Carneros 1998, California

November 9
Working Luncheon with Prime Minister Atal Bihari Vajpayee of India
Archery Summitt Vireton 2000, Oregon

November 13
Working Luncheon with President Vladimir Putin of Russia
Paul Hobbs Chardonnay Carneros 1998, California

November 14
Dinner at Prairie Chapel Ranch with President Vladimir Putin of Russia
Becker Reserve Chardonnay 2000, California

Becker Reserve Cabernet Sauvignon 1999, California

November 28
Working Luncheon with President José María Aznar of Spain
Artesa Chardonnay Carneros 1999, California

December 3
Working Luncheon with Prime Minister Ariel Sharon of Israel
Hagafen Chardonnay Carneros 1999 (Kosher), California

2002

January 31
Working Dinner with Chancellor Gerhard Schroeder of Germany
Navarro Pinot Gris 2000, California

Shafer Hillside Select Cabernet 1994, California

February 24
Dinner in honor of Governors
Dos Cabezas Pinot Gris 2000, Arizona

Ste. Michelle Col Solare 1998, Washington

Chateau Biltmore Blanc de Blancs 1998, North Carolina

February 25
Luncheon in honor of the Spouses of Governors
MacRostie Chardonnay 1999, California

March 14
Private Dinner with Prime Minister Jean Chrétien of Canada
Etude Pinot Gris 2000, California

Phelps Insignia 1994, California

April 6
Dinner at Prairie Chapel Ranch with Prime Minister Tony Blair of the United Kingdom
Gary Farrell Westside Chardonnay 1999, California

Duckhorn Estate Merlot 1997, California

April 9
Dinner in honor of Secretary General Robertson of NATO
Ramey Chardonnay Hyde 1998, California

Paul Hobbs Pinot Noir Hyde 1999, California

May 3
Working Dinner at Camp David with President José María Aznar of Spain
Gloria Ferrer Carneros Chardonnay 2000, California

Artesa Reserve Cabernet Sauvignon 1997, California

Bonny Doon Muscat Ice Wine 1999, California

June 10
Working Luncheon with Prime Minister Ariel Sharon of Israel
Hagafen Chardonnay 1999 (Kosher), California

June 10
Dinner in honor of the Leaders of the International Democrat Union
Kistler Chardonnay Durrell 1999, California

Rochioli Pinot Noir Little Hill 1997, California

July 17
State Dinner in honor of President Kwaśniewska of Poland
Robert Pecota Sauvignon Blanc 2000, California

Stag's Leap Wine Cellars Fay Vineyard Cabernet 1998, California

Bonny Doon Muscat Vin Glaciere 2000, California

September 14
Luncheon at Camp David with Prime Minister Silvio Berlusconi of Italy
Ponzi Reserve Chardonnay 1999, Oregon

September 18
Dinner in honor of President Václav Havel of the Czech Republic
Ponzi Reserve Chardonnay 1999, Oregon

Paul Hobbs Pinot Noir Hyde 1999, California

Soter Brut Rosé 1997, Oregon

September 25
Working Luncheon with President Álvaro Uribe Vélez of Colombia
J Pinot Gris 2000, California

November 5
Dinner with Speaker of the House Dennis Hastert and Senate Majority Leader Trent Lott
Sonoma-Loeb Chardonnay Sonoma 2001, California

Storybook Zinfandel Eastern Exposure 1999, California

November 17
Working Dinner with Prime Minister Rafiq al-Hariri of Lebanon
Rochioli Chardonnay Estate 2000, California

Rancho Zabacho Zinfandel Dancing Bull 2000, California

Rochioli Pinot Noir Little Hill 1997

The Rochioli family operation began in the 1940s with farming in the Russian River Valley of California, but grape growing soon became its focus. Rochioli Pinot Noirs and Chardonnays were served at four events during the George W. Bush presidency. Its 1997 Little Hill Pinot Noir was featured at the president's dinner in honor of leaders of the International Democrat Union on June 10, 2002.

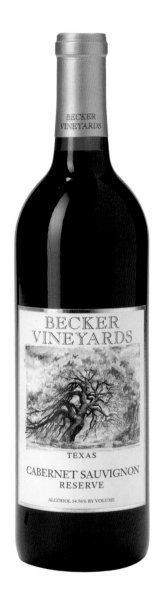

Becker Vineyards Cabernet Sauvignon

Located in Texas Hill Country, Becker Vineyards' wines have been served at the White House on several occasions and at President George W. Bush's Prairie Chapel Ranch. Its 2001 Cabernet Sauvignon was served at the Governors' Dinner at the White House, February 23, 2003.

November 25
Dinner in honor of Recipients of the Presidential Awards for Management Excellence
Sonoma-Loeb Chardonnay 2001, California

Baystone Shiraz Dry Creek Valley 2000, California

December 6
Christmas Dinner
Ponzi Reserve Chardonnay 1999, Oregon

Pride Mountain Cabernet 1999, California

December 18
Working Luncheon with President José María Aznar of Spain
Ponzi Reserve Chardonnay 1999, Oregon

Selby Syrah 1999, California

2003

January 22
Dinner in honor of Kofi Atta Annan, Secretary General of the United Nations
MacRostie Chardonnay Carneros 2000, California

Storybook Mountain Zinfandel Eastern Exposure 1999, California

January 28
Luncheon for Television Correspondents
Sonoma-Loeb Chardonnay 2001, California

January 30
Private Luncheon with President Silvio Berlusconi of Italy
Ponzi Reserve Chardonnay 1999, Oregon

January 31
Working Dinner with Prime Minister John Howard of Australia
Baystone Chardonnay Russian River 1999, California

Geyser Peak Reserve Shiraz 1998, California

February 23
Dinner in honor of Governors
Wolffler Estate Chardonnay Reserve 2000, New York

Becker Cabernet Reserve 2001, Texas

Domaine Merriwether Discovery Cuvée, Oregon

March 6
Dinner for Recipients of the National Medal of Arts
Etude Pinot Gris Carneros 2001, California

Paloma Merlot Napa 2000, California

Three Rivers Late Harvest Gewurtztraminer 2001, Washington

May 7
Working Dinner with President José María Aznar of Spain
Gloria Ferrer Chardonnay 2000, California

Artesa Cabernet Napa 1999, California

May 14
Working Dinner with President Roh Moo-hyun of South Korea
J Chardonnay Russian River 1999, California

Rochioli Pinot Noir Three Corners 1999, California

May 19
State Dinner in honor of President Mwai Kibaki of Kenya
Shafer Chardonnay Red Shoulder 2001, California

Soter Pinot Noir Beacon Hill 1999, Oregon

Honig Sauvignon Blanc Late Harvest 2002, California

November 20
*Dinner at Winfield House, London,
in honor of Queen Elizabeth II*

Newton Chardonnay 2000,
California

Peter Michael Les Pavots
1997, California

Schramsberg Crémant
1999, California

2004

January 14
*Working Dinner with
President Aznar of Spain*

Ortman Family Chardonnay
2001, California

DuMol Syrah Eddie's Patch
2000, California

February 13
*Luncheon in Recognition of the
National Park Foundation*

Navarro Rosé Old Vine
Cuvée 2002, California

March 31
*Luncheon in honor of the
Members of the National
Baseball Hall of Fame*

Ferrari-Carano Chardonnay
Reserve 2001, California

April 16
*Working Luncheon with
Prime Minster Tony Blair
of the United Kingdom*

Rochioli Chardonnay South
River 2001, California

June 21
*Luncheon in honor of the
Spouses of the Senate*

MacRostie Chardonnay
Reserve 2000, California

July 19
*Working Luncheon with President
Ricardo Lagos of Chile*

Neyers Chardonnay Carneros
2002, California

November 11
*Working Dinner with
Prime Minister Tony Blair
of the United Kingdom*

DuMol Chardonnay Chloe
2001, California

November 24
*Luncheon at Prairie Chapel Ranch
with King Juan Carlos of Spain*

Patz and Hall Hyde Chardonnay
2002, California

December 3
Holiday Dinner

Patz and Hall Hyde Chardonnay
2002, California

Paloma Merlot Napa 2001, California

Mumm Napa Cuvée Blanc
de Noirs, California

December 14
Holiday Dinner

Crocker Starr Napa Sauvignon
Blanc 2003, California

Penner-Ash Pinot Noir
Willamette 2002, Oregon

Iron Horse Classic Vintage
Brut 1999, California

December 15
*Working Luncheon with Prime
Minister Silvio Berlusconi of Italy*

Ponzi Reserve Chardonnay
2002, Oregon

Penner-Ash Pinot Noir 2002

Founded in 1998 by Lynn Penner-Ash, who
made history earlier as the first woman
winemaker hired in Oregon, Penner-Ash is
a sustainable, gravity-flow winery. Its 2002
Pinot Noir Willamette was paired with the
main course for George W. Bush's holiday
dinner on December 14, 2004.

RdV Rendezvous 2010

RdV Vineyard's Rendezvous was served by President and Mrs. Obama at a State Dinner in honor of Nordic Leaders on May 13, 2016

2005

July 18
Official Dinner in honor of Prime Minister Manmohan Singh of India

Chappellet Chardonnay Napa Valley 2003, California

Hartford Court Pinot Noir Arrendell 2002, California

Mer Soleil Late 2001, California

November 2
Luncheon in honor of Prince Charles and the Duchess of Cornwall

Peter Michael L'Aprs Midi 2004, California

November 2
Dinner in honor of Prince Charles and the Duchess of Cornwall

Newton Chardonnay Unfiltered 2002, California

Peter Michael Pinot Noir Le Moulin Rouge 2002, California

Iron Horse Wedding Cuvée 2002, California

December 9
Holiday Dinner

Hartford Court Chardonnay Seascape 2002, California

Archery Summit Pinot Noir Estate 2002, Oregon

Argyle Brut Rosé 2003, Oregon

December 11
Holiday Dinner

Pine Ridge Chardonnay Dijon Clones 2003, California

W. H. Smith Pinot Noir Hellenthal 2003, California

Ste. Michelle Ice Wie 2003, Washington

2006

February 6
Dinner in honor of Arthur Mitchell and the Dance Theatre of Harlem

Truchard Chardonnay Carneros 2004, California

Pride Mountain Merlot 2003, California

Adelsheim Pinot Noir Deglace 2004, Oregon

February 26
Dinner in honor of Governors

Becker Chardonnay Reserve 2004, Texas

Cardinale 2001, California

Sheldrake Point Riesling Ice Wine 2004, New York

April 12
Dinner in honor of Supreme Court Justice Sandra Day O'Connor

Dos Cabezas Pinot Gris 2004, Arizona

Callaghan Claire's Cuvee 2004, Arizona

May 16
Official Dinner in honor of Prime Minister John Howard of Australia

Greg Norman Chardonnay Santa Barbara 2004, California

Argyle Pinot Noir Reserve 2004, Oregon

Beringer Nightingale 2002, California

June 29
Official Dinner in honor of Prime Minister Junichiro Koizumi of Japan

Clos Pegase Chardonnay Mitsuko 2004, California

Ridge Zinfandel Lytoon Springs 2004, California

Iron Horse Classic Vintage Brut 2000, California

July 10
Dinner in honor of the Special Olympics
Hartford Court Chardonnay Seascape 2003, California

Duckhorn Cabernet Napa 2002, California

Argyle Brut Rosé 2003, Oregon

2007

January 4
Working Dinner with Chancellor Angela Merkel of Germany
Peter Michael Chardonnay Point Rouge 2002, California

Duckhorn Paraduxx 2001, California

February 11
Dinner in honor of Abraham Lincoln's Birthday
MacRostie Chardonnay Carneros 2005, California

Caymus Cabernet Napa 2004, California

Schramsberg Crémant 2003, California

February 25
Dinner in honor of Governors
Martinelli Chardonnay Martinelli Road 2004, California

Vine Cliff Cabernet Oakville 2004, California

Joseph Phelps Eiserebe 2005, California

May 7
State Dinner in honor of Queen Elizabeth II of the United Kingdom
Newton Chardonnay Unfiltered 2004, California

Peter Michael Les Pavots 2003, California

Schramsberg Brut Rosé 2004, California

November 6
State Dinner in honor of President Nicolas Sarkozy of France
HdV Chardonnay Carneros 2004, California

Dominus Napa Valley 2004, California

La Fayette's Legacy Chandon Rosé, California

November 9
Working Dinner at Prairie Chapel Ranch with Chancellor Angela Merkel of Germany
Kistler Chardonnay Carneros 2005, California

Caymus Cabernet Napa 2004, California

December 15
Senior Staff Holiday Dinner
Peter Michael Chardonnay Ma Belle Fille 2004, California

Shafer Hillside Select Cabernet Sauvignon 2003, California

Schramsberg J Schram 1999, California

2008

January 20
Dinner to Recognize Staff Service
Newton Chardonnay Unfiltered 2004, California

Pride Mountain Cabernet Napa 2002, California

Graff Family July Muscat 2005, California

February 24
Dinner in honor of Governors
Beringer Chardonnay Reserve 2005, California

Sebastiani Cabernet Secolo 2005, California

Stone Hill Late Harvest Vignoles 2005, Missouri

Shafer Chardonnay Red Shoulder 2006

Shafer's Hillside Select Cabernet Sauvignon and Red Shoulder Chardonnay were served more than six times during the Bush presidency. Shafer Chardonnay Red Shoulder 2006 was served at the State Dinner in honor of President Agyekum Kufuor of Ghana on September 15, 2008.

Thibaut-Janisson Brut

A joint venture between Claude Thibaut and Manuel Janisson, both of whom come from French champagne-making families, Thibaut-Janisson is set in Charlottesville, Virginia. Its sparkling wine was selected by the Obamas for three State Dinners, including their first, on November 24, 2009, in honor of Prime Minister Manmohan Singh of India.

March 17
Dinner celebrating St. Patrick's Day and the 250th Birthday of James Hoban, the Architect of the White House
Lynmar Chardonnay Russian River 2005, California

Spring Valley Merlot Uriah 2005, Washington

Chandon Etoile Rosé, California

May 5
Dinner in Celebration of Cinco de Mayo
Robledo Chardonnay Los Carneros 2006, California

Mi Sueño Pinot Noir Russian River 2006, California

Alex Sotelo Muscato Seven Stars 2005, California

July 21
Dinner in honor of American Olympians
Etude Pinot Gris Carneros 2006, California

DuMol Chardonnay Chloe 2005, California

Chandon Blanc de Noirs, California

September 15
State Dinner in honor of President John Agyekum Kufuor of Ghana
Shafer Chardonnay Red Shoulder 2006, California

Pride Mountain Merlot Vintner Select 2005, California

Schramsberg Crémant 2004, California

October 13
Official Dinner in honor of Prime Minister Silvio Berlusconi of Italy
Ponzi Reserve Chardonnay 2005, Oregon

Robert Mondavi Reserve Cabernet Sauvignon 2005, California

Iron Horse Russian River Cuvée 2003, California

October 22
Dinner in honor of the Chief Justice and Associate Justices of the Supreme Court
Sebastiani Chardonnay Dutton Ranch 2005, California

Vision Cellars Pinot Noir Las Alturas 2006, California

Chandon Blanc de Noirs, California

November 14
Dinner in honor of the G-20 Economic Summit Meeting
Landmark Chardonnay Damaris Reserve 2006, California

Shafer Hillside Select Cabernet Sauvignon 2003, California

Chandon Etoile Rosé, California

November 24
Working Dinner with Prime Minister Ehud Olmert of Israel
Baron Herzog Chardonnay Central Coast 2006 (Kosher), California

2009

January 16
The President and First Lady's Farewell Luncheon
DuMol Chardonnay Chloe 2005, California

Barack Obama Presidency
2009–2017

2009

November 24
State Dinner in honor of Prime Minister Manmohan Singh of India

Modus Operandi Sauvignon Blanc 2008, California

Brooks Ara Riesling 2006, Oregon

Beckman Granache 2007, California

Thibaut-Janisson Brut, Virginia

2010

May 19
State Dinner in honor of President Felipe Calderón of Mexico

Valdez Silver Eagle Chardonnay 2008, California

Mi Sueno Herrera Cabernet Sauvignon 2006, California

Mumm Napa Carlos Santana Brut, California

2011

January 19
State Dinner in honor of President Hu Jintao of China

DuMol Chardonnay Russian River 2008, California

Quilceda Creek Cabernet Columbia Valley 2005, Washington

Long Shadows Poet's Leap Riesling Botrytis 2008, Washington

June 7
State Dinner in honor of Chancellor Angela Merkel of Germany

Woodward Canyon Chardonnay Washington 2009, Washington

Kosta Browne Pinot Noir Koplen Vineyard 2008, California

Schramsberg Crémant 2006, California

2012

March 14
State Dinner with Prime Minister David Cameron of the United Kingdom

Thibaut-Janisson Brut, Virginia

Peter Michael Chardonnay 2009, California

Leonetti Cellar Cabernet Sauvignon 2008, Washington

Iron Horse Russian Cuvée 2007, California

2014

February 11
State Dinner in honor of President François Hollande of France

Morlet La Proportion Dorée, California

Long Shadows Chester Kidder Red Blend 2009, Washington

Thibaut-Janisson Blanc de Chardonnay, Virginia

2015

April 28
State Dinner in honor of Prime Minister Shinzō Abe of Japan

Freeman Ryo-fu Chardonnay 2013, California

Morlet Joli Coeur Pinot Noir 2010, California

Iron Horse Russian River Cuvée 2007, California

September 25
State Dinner in honor of President Xi Jinping of China

Shaoxing, China

Penner-Ash Viognier 2014, Oregon

Pride Mountain Merlot Vintner Select 2012, California

Schramsberg Crémant Demi-Sec 2011, California

Villa Ragazzi Sangiovese 2012

Owned by the Rodenos, a family with Italian roots, Villa Ragazzi released Napa Valley's first Sangiovese wine in 2011. Its 2012 Napa Sangiovese was featured by the Obamas at a State Dinner in honor of Italian Prime Minister Matteo Renzi on October 18, 2016.

**Domaine Drouhin Laurène
Pinot Noir 2014**

Domaine Drouhin's Oregon vineyard carries on a family legacy with roots in the winemaking traditions of Burgundy, France. Its French-style 2014 Pinot Noir Laurène was served by President and Mrs. Trump at the State Dinner in honor of President Emmanuel Macron of France on April 24, 2018.

2016

March 10
State Dinner in honor of Prime Minister Justin Trudeau of Canada

Pence Chardonnay Sebastiano 2013, California

Cliff Lede High Fidelity 2012, California

Chateau Chantal 2013 Ice Wine, Michigan

May 13
State Dinner in honor of Nordic Leaders

Grgich Hills Fumé Blanc Estate 2013, California

Trisaetum Dry Riesling Estates 2014, Oregon

RdV Rendezvous 2010, Virginia

August 2
State Dinner in honor of Prime Minister Lee Hsien Loong of Singapore

Margerum Sauvignon Blanc Sybarite 2014, California

Pence Chardonnay Sebastiano 2013, California

Waits-Mast Pinot Noir Deer Meadows 2012, California

Wolffer Estate Noblesse Oblige Sparkling Rosé 2012, New York

October 18
State Dinner in honor of Prime Minister Matteo Renzi of Italy

Palmina Vermentino Santa Ynez 2015, California

Villa Ragazzi Sangiovese Napa 2012, California

Ridge Vineyards Zinfandel East Bench 2014, California

Donald J. Trump Presidency
2017–

2017

January 20
Inaugural Luncheon at the Capitol

J. Lohr Arroyo Vista Chardonnay 2013, California

Black Stallion Estate Cabernet Sauvignon 2012, California

Korbel Special Inaugural Cuvée, California

April 6
Dinner at Mar-a-Lago for President Xi Jinping of China

Chalk Hill Chardonnay 2014, California

Girard Cabernet Sauvignon 2014, California

2018

April 24
State Dinner in honor of President Emmanuel Macron of France

Domaine Serene Chardonnay Evenstad Reserve 2015, Oregon

Domaine Drouhin Pinot Noir Laurène 2014, Oregon

Schramsberg Crémant Demi-Sec 2014, California

2019

May 15
Dinner in honor of the White House Historical Association

Stag's Leap Chardonnay Karia 2015, California

Hartford Zinfandel Fanucchi Wood Road 2014, California

Schramsberg Crémant Demi-Sec 2014, California

June 4
*Dinner at Winfield House,
London, for Charles, Prince of
Wales, and Camilla, Duchess of
Cornwall, of the United Kingdom*

Iron Horse Heart of the Vineyard
Chardonnay 2016, California

Iron Horse North Block Pinot
Noir 2016, California

Iron Horse Joy Brut 2005, California

September 20
*State Dinner in honor
of Prime Minister Scott
Morrison of Australia*

Spring Mountain Sauvignon
Blanc Napa 2017, California

Argyle Pinot Noir Reserve
2016, Oregon

J Vineyards Demi-Sec, California

Argyle Pinot Noir Reserve 2016

Argyle's Pinot Noir Reserve from Oregon
was served by President and Mrs. Trump at
the State Dinner in honor of Prime Minister
Scott Morrison of Australia on September
20, 2019.

ACKNOWLEDGMENTS

THIS BOOK WOULD NOT HAVE BEEN POSSIBLE without the commitment of the very talented team at the White House Historical Association. Nearly sixty years ago, First Lady Jacqueline Kennedy helped establish the Association to educate the public about the unique history of the White House and to assist with the acquisition and preservation of art for the Executive Residence. Today, through his support of this book, his dedicated stewardship of White House history, and his innovative leadership of all the Association's endeavors, President Stewart McLaurin continues this important mission.

Marcia Anderson, an accomplished editor, skillfully leads the Association's publishing team, ably supported by Lauren McGwin, Kristen Hunter Mason, and Rebecca Durgin. Elizabeth Routhier and Ann Grogg contributed indispensable research and editorial guidance, and I am grateful for their thoroughness and creativity. I am also grateful to the Association's Gina Sherman, who has worked tirelessly to help ensure this book finds enthusiastic readers.

I am thankful to my *Washington Post* colleagues Meghan Kruger and Paul Van Deventer for their help. Meghan, a White House veteran herself, found additional hours in already full days to polish my early drafts, becoming perhaps the world's most knowledgeable nondrinker in the process. Paul drew on his exceptional research capabilities to track down hard-to-find primary sources.

Stefanie Prelesnik, my executive assistant and friend for many years, has my deep and ongoing appreciation. Her skilled management abilities kept sources and drafts organized and the researching, writing, and editing processes advancing smoothly. Although she, too, is a nondrinker, she has been an incredible resource for everything wine-related, including this book.

Many documents in this book were obtained through the courtesy of the National Archives and the Library of Congress. My particular thanks go to Joanne Drake, chief administrative officer of the Reagan Presidential Foundation, and Jennifer Mandel, archivist at the Reagan Presidential Library, for digging deep into the records and providing valuable material for this book. Archivists, librarians, and curators from more than a dozen other presidential sites around the country kindly shared their knowledge while providing valuable assistance with image research and fact checking.

The history of wine in the White House could not be told without the careful recollections of the men and women who lived and worked there. Two recent occupants, First

Lady Melania Trump and former First Lady Michelle Obama, generously contributed their reflections for inclusion in these pages. Seven former social secretaries from four administrations also shared their memories, which demonstrate the care with which White House wine service is planned.

Daniel Shanks made White House wine history when he became the first person to ever serve in the Executive Mansion as food and beverage usher. His deep knowledge of wine and his exquisite taste have shaped many memorable White House events, and his experience has provided unique insights into social life in the White House. He generously agreed to take readers behind the scenes by sharing his reflections in this book, and I am grateful for his contributions.

New photography of the White House collection of historic glassware and serving pieces was made possible by the White House Office of the Curator and Usher's Office and reflects the talent of photographer Bruce M. White. Jane Shadel Spillman, former curator at the Corning Museum of Glass, did the original research on White House glassware. Her book on the subject, first published by the Association in 1989, was instrumental for the text.

Six presidents of the United States have belonged to the Metropolitan Club of Washington, D.C., which, appropriately for this book, also has a Wine Committee. I've been fortunate to vastly expand my wine knowledge and build some wonderful friendships through the committee; each member has special expertise in at least one of the world's wine regions, and they generously share their knowledge—and contacts in the field of winemaking and collecting—with other club members.

I am grateful to so many private collectors of rare wine books who made their libraries available to me as I researched this book. The libraries of Boodle's and Brooks's, two storied clubs in London, proved especially helpful.

Renowned wine expert Steven Spurrier forever changed the wine world—and elevated American wines to the global stage—when he organized the blind tasting that came to be known as the Judgment of Paris. He kindly shared his firsthand recollections of that historic event and provided original material for this book.

Christopher Forbes has been a longtime friend, but he went above and beyond the ordinary call of friendship by agreeing to relive the memories—not always happy ones—of purchasing the world's most expensive bottle of wine and then witnessing its untimely demise.

I have been fortunate to call Philippe Sereys de Rothschild a friend for many years. He is a superb winemaker who has expanded on the innovations of his grandfather, Baron Philippe, and his mother, Philippine, to carry on an extraordinary legacy. He has also generously opened his doors, cellars, and museum to me on several occasions, and I am always grateful for his hospitality.

Michael Mondavi has been a friend of mine for decades. In that time, he has enriched my life in many ways, not least by sharing his vast knowledge of the wine industry. For this book, he also recounted incredible personal stories and anecdotes from his family's rise to prominence in the world of winemaking.

So much of what I have learned about wine has come from enjoying it in good company. In that respect, I owe a great debt to John Rogers, Michael Castine, Ray Pierce, and John Walsh for sharing their knowledge, their contacts in the wine world, their bottles, and, most of all, their friendship.

Finally, I'd like to thank my many friends in the wine industry. Several have kindly contributed insights that appear in this book. These men and women are reminders of the devotion, experience, and, sometimes, luck required to make the outstanding wines enjoyed at tables across the United States—including in the White House.

SOURCES

Two online sources for primary documents have been used extensively. They are the National Archives website, *Founders Online*, https://founders.archives.gov, and the University of California, Santa Barbara's *American Presidency Project*, directed by John Woolley and Gerhard Peters, www.presidency.ucsb.edu. These sources are cited in brief form below.

Conversions to 2020 dollars throughout the book are from "Inflation Calculator," U.S. Official Inflation Data, Alioth Finance, https://www.officialdata.org. Inflation rates are subject to change.

CHAPTER ONE

INTRODUCTION

a man of the soil: Genesis 9:20.

winemaking in Areni: Marc Kaufman, "Ancient Winemaking Operation Unearthed in Armenian Cave," *Washington Post*, January 6, 2011.

King Tut, twenty-six vessels of wine: Patrick E. McGovern, "Ancient Wine," Biomolecular Archaeology Project, University of Pennsylvania Museum of Archaeology and Anthropology website, www.penn.museum.

in vino veritas: Pliny, *Naturalis historia* (77 CE).

GEORGE WASHINGTON

three or four glasses of Madeira: Nelly Custis Lewis to Elizabeth Bordley Gibson, February 23, 1823, quoted in Mary V. Thompson, "Madeira," George Washington's Mount Vernon website, www.mountvernon.org. Washington's step-granddaughter wrote that "after dinner" Washington "drank 3 glasses of Madeira." A fuller description of George Washington's eating and drinking habits can be found in Ron Chernow, *Washington: A Life* (New York: Penguin Press, 2010), 120.

More than one thousand bottles: John Hailman, *Thomas Jefferson on Wine* (Jackson: University Press of Mississippi, 2009), 75.

"4 Neat and fashionable": Quoted in ibid., 19.

"You have taken a most effectual method": George Washington to François-Jean de Beauvoir, Marquis de Chastellux, July 19, 1781, *Founders Online*.

JOHN ADAMS

"I shall be killed with kindness": John Adams to Abigail Adams, Philadelphia, September 29, 1774, in *Familiar Letters of John Adams and His Wife Abigail Adams during the Revolution with a Memoir of Mrs. Adams*, ed. Charles Francis Adams (New York: Hurd and Houghton, 1876), 43.

"We had every Luxury": John Adams, diary, December 19, 1779, *Founders Online*.

"I beg you to take": quoted in James M. Gabler, *Passions: The Wines and Travels of Thomas Jefferson* (Palm Beach, Fla.: Bacchus Press, 1995), 27.

THOMAS JEFFERSON

French cuisine and the stately setting: Hailman, *Jefferson on Wine*, 256.

$3,200 annually: ibid.

"You drink as you please": quoted in Gabler, *Passions*, 197.

"Wine provided at Washington": Thomas Jefferson, Memorandum Books, 1803, *Founders Online*.

pipe containing 110 gallons on average: Hailman, *Jefferson on Wine*, 260.

Jefferson's wine orders by country: ibid., 266.

20,000 bottles of wine: Gabler, *Passions*, 200.

"I rejoice, as a Moralist": Thomas Jefferson to Jean-Guillaume, Baron Hyde de Neuville, December 13, 1818, *The Writings of Thomas Jefferson*, ed. Albert Ellery Bergh (Washington, D.C.: Thomas Jefferson Memorial Association, 1907), 3:177–79.

"We could in the United States": Thomas Jefferson to C. P. de Lasteyrie, July 15, 1808, *Founders Online*.

In 1807 he began cultivating grapes: "The Vineyards," Thomas Jefferson's Monticello website, www.monticello.org.

JAMES MADISON

"There were many French dishes": William Winston Seaton, diary, November 12, 1812, in A *Biographical Sketch, With Passing Notices of His Associates and Friends* (Boston: James R. Osgood, 1871), 85.

"the wine, of which": Margaret Bayard Smith, *The First Forty Years of Washington Society*, ed. Gaillard Hunt (New York: Charles Scribner's Sons, 1906), 110.

JAMES MONROE

"with a view to making wine": quoted in Gabler, *Passions*, 219–20. See also Scott H. Harris and Jarod Kearney, "Articles of the Best Kind': James Monroe Furnishes the Rebuilt White House," *White House History*, no. 35 (Summer 2014): 28–45.

1,200 bottles of champagne and Burgundy wine: Esther Singleton, *The Story of the White House* (New York: McClure, 1907), 1:110, citing John LaFarge to James Monroe, September 15, 1817, Record Group 233, Records of the House of Representatives, 18th Cong., 1st sess., C20.4. On Monroe's purchases for the White House, see Harris and Kearney, "Articles of the Best Kind." Harris and the editor of the Papers of James Monroe refute the implication in Lucius Wilmerding, *James Monroe, Public Claimant* (New Brunswick, N.J.: Rutgers University Press, 1960) that Monroe used public funds for his private wine purchases.

"uncommonly social and pleasant": Louisa Catherine Johnson Adams to John Adams, January 8, 1819, *Founders Online*.

JOHN QUINCY ADAMS AND ANDREW JACKSON

"They sit after dinner": John Quincy Adams, *Memoirs of John Quincy Adams Comprising Portions of His Diary from 1795 to 1848*, ed. Charles Frances Adams (Philadelphia: J. B. Lippincott, 1874), 2:656.

"I do not believe": quoted in Benjamin Perley Poore, *Perley's Reminiscences of Sixty Years in the National Metropolis* (Philadelphia: Hubbard Brothers, 1886), 1:70–71.

Jackson Inauguration scene: William Seale, *The President's House: A History*, 2nd ed. (Washington, D.C.: White House Historical Association, 2008), 1:174–77.

"I suppose all the wines": Andrew Jackson to Andrew Jackson Jr., October 23, 1834, quoted in Pauline Wilcox Burke, *Emily Donelson of Tennessee* (Richmond, Va.: Garrett and Massie, 1941), 2:70. See also Jon Meacham, *American Lion: Andrew Jackson in the White House* (New York: Random House, 2009), 292.

"sherry, madeira, and champagne," "a significant nod": Robert C. Caldwell to Samuel Caldwell, December 29, 1834, reprinted in "Washington in 1834," *American Historical Review* 27 (October 1921): 273.

"The wines on the table": John R. Montgomery to his daughter, quoted in John Whitcomb and Claire Whitcomb, *Real Life at the White House: 200 Years of Daily Life at America's Most Famous Residence* (New York: Routledge, 2002), 64.

MARTIN VAN BUREN

"about fifteen or twenty gallons of table wine": Martin Van Buren to Jesse Hoyt, November 17, 1819, in William L. Mackenzie, *The Life and Times of Martin Van Buren: The Correspondence of His Friends, Family and Pupils* (Boston: Cooke, 1846), 183–84.

fondness for Italy's powerful red wine: Hailman, *Jefferson on Wine*, 303–05.

favorite French vintages: wine purchases are mentioned in two letters from William Cabell Rives to Martin Van Buren, November 12, 1831, and February 20, 1832. Elizabeth Howard West, *Calendar of the Papers of Martin Van Buren, Prepared from the Original Manuscripts in the Library of Congress* (Washington, D.C.: Government Printing Office, 1910), 166,177. Their correspondence also discussed tariffs on French wine.

stylish entertainments, European courts: Seale, *President's House*, 1:209–11.

Charles Ogle, "The Regal Splendor of the Presidential Palace," speech in the House of Representatives, April 14, 1840, reprinted in full in *White House History*, no. 10 (Winter 2002): 35–52, quotations on 72, 54.

WILLIAM HENRY HARRISON AND JOHN TYLER

whiskey distillery: William Osborn Stoddard, *William Henry Harrison, John Tyler and James Knox Polk* (New York: Frederick A. Stokes & Brother, 1888), 110–11.

"During the meal": John Sergeant Wise, *Recollections of Thirteen Presidents*

(New York: Double, Page, 1906), 26–27.

JAMES K. POLK

"The table & dinner": Elizabeth L.C. Dixon, diary, December 19, 1845, "Journal Written During a Residence in Washington During the 29th Congress, Commencing with the first of December 1845," Connecticut Historical Society, transcription in *White House History*, no. 33 (Summer 2013): 48.

relying heavily on wine, biggest expenses: Seale, *President's House*, 1:255–56.

ZACHARY TAYLOR, MILLARD FILLMORE, AND FRANKLIN PIERCE

"I am chiefly a water drinker": Millard Fillmore to Salmon P. Chase, July 23, 1850, in *Millard Fillmore Papers*, ed. Frank H. Severance, *Publications of the Buffalo Historical Society* 11 (Buffalo: Buffalo Historical Society, 1907), 2:296–95.

"There's nothing left to do": quoted in Sidney Blumenthal, *All the Powers of Earth: The Political Life of Abraham Lincoln*, vol. 3, 1856–60 (New York: Simon & Schuster, 2019), 8.

JAMES BUCHANAN

feast at Carusi's Saloon: Robert Strauss, *Worst. President. Ever.: James Buchanan, the POTUS Rating Game, and the Legacy of the Least of the Lesser Presidents* (Guilford, Conn.: Lyons Press, 2017), 106–07.

Inaugural Ball: Singleton, *Story of the White House*, 2:42.

"The Madeira and sherry": quoted in Stephanie Townrow, "'Finer Than the Best Monongahela': President Buchanan's Drinking Habits," posted September 22, 2017, Lancaster History website, www.lancasterhistory.org.

Buchanan was renowned: ibid.

"I was never in better health": quoted in Blumenthal, *All the Powers of Earth*, 3:453.

"awkward," "not being able": James Buchanan to Harriet Lane Johnston, Cape Island, New Jersey, August 14, 1867, in George Ticknor Curtis, *Life of James Buchanan Fifteenth President of the United States* (New York: Harper & Brothers, 1883), 2:656.

ABRAHAM LINCOLN

Berry and Lincoln grocery store: see the account in Benjamin P. Thomas, *Abraham Lincoln: A Biography* (Carbondale: Southern Illinois University Press, 2008), 36–37.

"barely touch his lips" and "perceptible diminution": William Osborn Stoddard, *Inside the White House in War Times: Memoirs and Reports of Lincoln's Secretary*, ed. Michael Burlingame (Lincoln: University of Nebraska Press, 2000), 200.

1859 vintage California wine: Perkins Stern & Co. to Abraham Lincoln, December 16, 1864, Abraham Lincoln Papers, ser. 1, General Correspondence, 1833 to 1916, Library of Congress,

Washington, D.C., online at www.loc.gov.

six different wines, liqueurs in the Red Room: Seale, *President's House*, 1:473.

"a coup d'oeil of dazzling splendor": *New York Herald*, February 6, 1862, 5.

ANDREW JOHNSON AND ULYSSES S. GRANT

"It was lucky": Rutherford B. Hayes to Mrs. Hayes, March 12, 1865, *Diary and Letters of Rutherford Birchard Hayes*, vol. 2, *1861–1865*, ed. Charles Richard Williams (Columbus: Ohio State Archaeological and Historical Society, 1922), 566.

"I never drink wine," "I refused wine": quoted George S. Hilton, *The Funny Side of Politics* (New York: G. W. Dillingham, 1899), 240. The anecdote is repeated in Feather Schwartz Foster, "Andrew Johnson and Strong Drink," posted November 12, 2018, *Presidential History Blog*, featherfoster.wordpress.com.

William Seward bet a case of champagne: Glyndon Van Deusen, *William Henry Seward* (New York: Oxford University Press, 1967), 481; Walter Stahr, *Seward: Lincoln's Indispensable Man* (New York: Simon & Schuster, 2012), 513.

"chose the wines himself": William H. Crook, *Through Five Administrations: Reminiscences of Colonel William H. Crook, Body-Guard to President Lincoln*, comp. and ed. Margarita Spalding Gerry (New York: Harper and Brothers, 1910), 188.

wine bill nearly $1,500: Mary Clemmer Ames, *Ten Years in Washington* (Hartford: A. D. Worthington, 1874), 250.

description of the dinner: Edward Winslow Martin, *Behind the Scenes in Washington* (New York: Continental Publishing Co., 1873), 380–82.

fruit punches: Seale, *President's House*, 1:473.

RUTHERFORD B. HAYES

Grand Duke Alexis dinner: "State Dinner at the White House," *New York Times*, April 20, 1877, 5.

"The water flowed": quoted in Paul Leland Haworth, *Reconstruction and Union, 1865–1912* (New York: Henry Holt and Company, 1912), 87.

temperance fountain: James M. Goode, *The Outdoor Sculpture of Washington, D.C.: A Comprehensive Historical Guide* (Washington, D.C.: Smithsonian Institution Press, 1974), 358–59.

JAMES A. GARFIELD

"to reject the reform," "You . . . will be regarded": Rutherford B. Hayes, "Memorandum for Garfield," January 17, 1881, *Diary and Letters of Hayes*, vol. 3, *1865–1881*, ed. Williams, 639.

"Shall wine be banished": "Wine at the White House," *Washington Post*, February 3, 1881, 4.

"It is expected": "Wine at the White House," *Boston Independent*, February 17, 1881, 16.

"My Darling," "For two nights": Lucretia Garfield to James R. Garfield, June 30, 1881, *Personal Letters of Lucretia and James Garfield*, ed. John Shaw (East Lansing: Michigan State University Press, 1994), 389.

CHESTER A. ARTHUR

Tiffany & Co. renovation: Seale, *President's House*, 1:517–23.

fourteen or more courses, eight different wines: Poore, *Perley's Reminiscences*, 2:462.

"Arthur would drink wine": James R. Bumgarner, *The Health of the Presidents: The 41 United States Presidents Through a Physician's Point of View* (Jefferson, N.C.: McFarland, 2004).

"far surpassed all," menu for Diplomatic Corps dinner: "The President's Table," *New York Times*, July 21, 1884, 5.

refuses to hang Lucy Webb Hayes's portrait in East Room: Gregory J. Dehler, *Chester Alan Arthur: The Life of a Gilded Age Politician and President* (New York: Nova History Publications, 2007), 79. Before the 1882 elections, Arthur hung the portrait in the Green Room. William Kloss, *Art in the White House: A Nation's Pride*, 2nd ed. (Washington, D.C.: White House Historical Association, 2008), 32, says the portrait, which was funded by the National Woman's Christian Temperance Union, was hung "just as the Hayes Administration ended."

"Madam, I may be": quoted in Dehler, *Chester Alan Arthur*, 78–79.

GROVER CLEVELAND AND BENJAMIN HARRISON

"when wine flowed freely," "At the large dinners": Irwin Hood Hoover, *Forty-Two Years in the White House* (Boston: Houghton Mifflin, 1934), 288.

"an epicure and connoisseur of wines": ibid., 14.

Cleveland's cabinet dinners: Singleton, *Story of the White House*, 208, 240.

"a pleasant, cheerful dinner": Benjamin Harrison to his wife, November 27, 1863, quoted in Harry J. Sievers, S.J., *Benjamin Harrison, Hoosier Warrior: Through the Civil War Years, 1833–1865*, 2nd ed. (New York: University Publishers, 1960), 230.

centennial of George Washington's Inauguration: "Centennial Celebration of Washington's Inauguration," George Washington's Mount Vernon website, mountvernon.org.

The Harrisons also opened: "Leland Stanford Winery," California Office of Historic Preservation website, ohp.parks.ca.gov; Ernest P. Peninou, comp., *Leland Stanford's Great Vina Ranch, 1881–1919: A Research Paper; The History of Senator Leland Stanford's Vina Vineyard and the World's Largest Winery* (San Francisco: Yolo Hills Viticultural Society, 1991).

Schramsberg Vineyards: "History," Schramsberg Vineyards website, schramsberg.com.

WILLIAM MCKINLEY

McKinley wrongly associated with a drunkard: William H. Armstrong, *Major McKinley: William McKinley and the Civil War* (Kent, Ohio: Kent State University Press, 2000), 111.

THEODORE ROOSEVELT

champagne at official dinners: "Never Drunk, Says Roosevelt," *Washington Post*, May 28, 1913, 1.

avoided hard liquor, buying his own wine: Archibald Butt, *The Letters of Archie Butt*, ed. Lawrence F. Abbott (Garden City: Doubleday, Page, 1924), 19, 246.

dinner menus: Menu, December 17, 1903, Records of Official Functions with the Official Diary of the President, 1901–16, Record Group 42.159, National Archives, Washington, D.C. This record group contains menus, invitations, seating charts, and other various correspondence related to White House social events from 1901 to 1916.

"You are further informed": Colonel Bromwell to Charles Rauscher, November 18, 1907, Letters Sent Relating to Executive Mansion Social Official Functions, 1898–1917, Record Group 42.155, National Archives.

visit of Prince Henry of Prussia: Henry Voigt, "Compliments of George Kessler," posted April 14, 2012, *The American Menu* website, theamericanmenu.com. See also Karen Sieber, "State Dinner for the Prince," posted February 22, 2019, Theodore Roosevelt Center at Dickinson State University website, theodorooseveltcenter.org; "Note Regarding the Champagne Controversy," Library of Congress, also posted on the same website.

Ethel Roosevelt's debut: Seale, *President's House*, 1:700–702.

"I did not see a single youth": quoted in ibid., 1:701.

"gets drunk": quoted in *Roosevelt vs. Newett: A Transcription of the Testimony Taken and Depositions Read at Marquette, Mich.* (Privately printed by W. Emlen Roosevelt, 1914), 12.

"I do not drink either whiskey or brandy": quoted in ibid., 13–14. For more information on the trial, see "The Roosevelt-Newett Libel Trial," *Michigan Legal Milestones*, State Bar of Michigan website, www.michbar.org.

WILLIAM HOWARD TAFT AND WOODROW WILSON

"We had in the wine closet": Archibald Willingham Butt, *Taft and Roosevelt: The Intimate Letters of Archie Butt, Military Aide* (Garden City, N.Y.: Doubleday, Doran & Company, 1930), 1:171.

Wilson's New Year's Eve party: Arthur Walworth, *Wilson: American Prophet* (New York: Longman's Green, 1958), 78. These memories are from Wilson's cousin Helen Woodrow Bones and also from Margaret Randolph Axson Elliott, Wilson's sister-in-law, *My Aunt Louisa and Woodrow Wilson* (Chapel Hill: University of North Carolina Press, 1944), 247.

"had wine brought in": Cary Grayson, diary, June 28, 1919, Cary T. Grayson Papers, WWP17210, Woodrow Wilson Presidential Library and Museum, Staunton, Va.

moving Wilson's wine collection: "A News Item: Wilson's Stock of Liquor Is Moved," *New York Times*, March 5, 1921.

WARREN G. HARDING, CALVIN COOLIDGE, AND HERBERT HOOVER

"trays with bottles": quoted in Robert H. Ferrell, *Presidential Leadership: From Woodrow Wilson to Harry S. Truman*

(Columbia: University of Missouri Press, 2006), 42.

Harding enjoyed drinking, golfing: Lawrence L. Knutson, *Away from the White House: Presidential Escapes, Retreats, and Vacations* (Washington, D.C.: White House Historical Association, 2014), 196; Edward Starling, *Starling of the White House: The Story of the Man Whose Secret Service Detail Guarded Five Presidents* (New York: Simon & Schuster, 1946), 169.

Harding's sources for his liquor supplies: Seale, *President's House*, 2:99.

Justice Department employee, party scene: Carl Sferrazza Anthony, "A President of the Peephole," *Washington Post*, June 7, 1998, an excerpt from Anthony's *Florence Harding: The First Lady, the Jazz Age, and the Death of America's Most Scandalous President* (New York: Morrow, 1998).

Coolidge and Tokay wine: Donald R. McCoy, *Calvin Coolidge: The Quiet President* (New York: Macmillan, 1967), 397.

Hoover World Series, "We Want Beer!": Joel D. Treese, "President Herbert Hoover and Baseball," White House Historical Association website, www.whitehousehistory.org.

FRANKLIN D. ROOSEVELT

"stupendous blunder": Franklin D. Roosevelt, "Speech of Governor Franklin D. Roosevelt: Prohibition," August 27, 1932, 7, Master Speech File, 1898–1945, Franklin D. Roosevelt Presidential Library and Museum, Hyde Park, N.Y.

"I believe this would": quoted in Jean Edward Smith, *FDR* (New York: Random House, 2007), 316; see also fdrlibrary.tumblr.com. Roosevelt made this statement on March 12, 1933, and he signed the legislation to amend the Volstead Act on March 22, 1933.

"Wines will be served," "light wines," "With us": quoted in "Wine Returns to White House Functions," *New York Times*, November 9, 1934, 1.

California Wine Institute: "Wine Men Thank Mrs. Roosevelt," *Los Angeles Times*, November 13, 1934, 3.

"Wine was served for the first time": Harold L. Ickes, *The Secret Diary of Harold L. Ickes: The First Thousand Days, 1933–1936* (New York: Simon and Schuster, 1953), 248–49.

"so rare as to be almost curios," wines presented by Simon: "British Epicurean to Teach Us to Eat," *New York Times*, May 2, 1935, 13.

"President Roosevelt refused": "Kinds of Wine for King Here Kept Secret," *Washington Post*, June 7, 1939, 5.

"On his breakfast tray," "At lunch": Alonzo Fields, *My 21 Years in the White House* (New York: Coward-McCann, 1961), 80–81.

HARRY S. TRUMAN

wartime service of wine: Seale, *President's House*, 2:182.

bourbon and branch water: Knutson, *Away from the White House*, 254; Philip

Kaiser, oral history by Niel M. Johnson, June 8, 1987, 34, and Edward D. McKim, oral history by James F. Fuchs, 111, Harry S. Truman Presidential Library and Museum.

DWIGHT D. EISENHOWER

Eisenhower menus: Eisenhower administration menus are in White House Office, Social Office (A. B. Tolley) records, 1952–61, Dwight D. Eisenhower Presidential Library and Museum.

gift of state: Cyril Ray, *Ray on Wine* (London: J. M. Dent, 1979), 65.

For luncheons and less formal dinners: Dorothy McCardle, "President Treats VIP Guests to Wealth of U.S. Wines," *Washington Post* and *Times Herald*, February 14, 1958, C1.

wine cellar upgraded: ibid.

JOHN F. KENNEDY

Kennedy menus: Kennedy administration menus are in following collections at the John F. Kennedy Presidential Library and Museum: Papers of John F. Kennedy. Presidential Papers. White House Staff Files of Sanford L. Fox, and Jacqueline Bouvier Kennedy Onassis Personal Papers.

Known for their stylish entertaining: Barbara Gamarekian, "The White House: All the President's Wines," *New York Times*, January 15, 1986, B10.

Veuve Cliquot: Mark Will-Weber, *Drinking with the Democrats: The Party Animal's History of Liberal Libations* (Washington, D.C.: Regnery History, 2016), 157.

"The champagne was flowing": Ben Bradlee, *Conversations with Kennedy* (New York: W. W. Norton, 1975), 52.

September 19, 1961, dinner: C. K. Hickey, "All the Presidents' Meals," posted February 16, 2019, *Foreign Policy: The Global Magazine of News and Ideas*, https://foreignpolicy.com.

Khrushchev and wine: Ray, *Ray on Wine*, 101–02.

"a most lovely wine": Michael Broadbent, *Vintage Wine: Fifty Years of Tasting Three Centuries of Wine* (New York: Harcourt, 2002), 55.

gift of five crates of Georgian wine: "Top Red Sends Kennedy Wine," *The Baltimore Sun*, September 11, 1962, 1. See also "Memorandum of Conversation," September 13, 1962, *Foreign Relations of the United States, 1961–1963*, vol. 5, *Soviet Union*, Department of State website, www.history.state.gov.

Kennedy sees James Bond movies: Kenneth T. Walsh, *Celebrity in Chief: A History of the Presidents and the Culture of Stardom* (Boulder, Colo.: Paradigm, 2015), 140.

James Bond movie references: "Dom Pérignon Champagne" and "Château Mouton-Rothschild," *James Bond Lifestyle* website, jamesbondlifestyle.com.

LYNDON B. JOHNSON

Johnson menus: Johnson administration menus are in the Henry Haller Collection, White House Historical Association.

American wines at the Waldorf Astoria Hotel: Eric Pace, "Domestic Wines Served at Dinner at Johnson's Wish," *New York Times*, May 23, 1965, 1.

"No President has done more": quoted in Marie Smith, "Imported Wines—by Choice," *Washington Post*, February 7, 1969, B2.

fifty-three State Dinners: Stewart D. McLaurin, *White House Miscellany* (Washington, D.C.: Thornwillow Books, White House Historical Association, 2016), 52.

Mondavi family feud: account based on the author's conversations with Michael Mondavi. For published versions, see Michelle Locke, "The Family Feud That Juiced the Rise of the Napa Valley," posted April 9, 2016, *Vivino*, vivino.com; "The Mondavi Family," *Wine Spectator's 40th Anniversary*, winespectator.com; John Mariani, "Mondavi Family Winery Shows Multiple Personalities," posted April 3, 2015, updated December 6, 2017, *Huffington Post*, huffpostcom.

RICHARD M. NIXON

Nixon menus: Nixon administration menus are in the Henry Haller Collection, White House Historical Association.

Nixon visit to China: Robert Lawrence Balzer, "Schramsberg's 25th," *Los Angeles Times*, January 14, 1990.

Wine Institute delivers wine: "Coast Vintners Stock White House Cellars," *New York Times*, April 8, 1970, 40.

"Nixon was particular about wine": Seale, *President's House*, 2:413.

oft-repeated story: Joseph Temple, "10 Interesting Facts about RN and Wine," posted June 17, 2018, International Wine and Food Society blog, blog.iwfs.org. "Pulling a Nixon" seems to have a variety of meanings.

Nixon wine on presidential yacht: Bob Woodward and Carl Bernstein, *The Final Days* (New York: Simon and Schuster, 1976), 238.

GERALD R. FORD

Ford menus: Ford administration menus are in the Gerald R. Ford Presidential Library and Museum.

"representing everything American": Maria Downs, "My Very Special Lady—Betty Ford," 7, typescript, Maria Downs Papers, box 1, Gerald R. Ford Presidential Library and Museum, online at fordlibrarymuseum.gov. A more general article is Gamarekian, "All the President's Wines."

State Dinner for Austria: "White House Cellar Adds Michigan Wine," *Los Angeles Times*, November 12, 1974, A17.

"I'd give myself four stars": quoted in Lisa McCubbin, *Betty Ford: First Lady, Women's Advocate, Survivor, Trailblazer* (New York: Gallery Books, 2018), 224.

"On Ford's last night": Ron Nessen, *Making the News, Taking the News: From NBC to the Ford White House* (Middletown, Conn.: Wesleyan University Press, 2011), 238.

JIMMY CARTER

Carter menus: Carter administration

menus are in the Jimmy Carter Presidential Library and Museum.

"We served wine, punch, and cordials": quoted in Bob Colacello, "The White House's Dinner Theater," *Vanity Fair*, June 2010, 176.

Jimmy Carter winemaking postpresidency: Ryan Isaac, "Wine Talk: Jimmy Carter the Former President of the United States Is Now an Amateur Winemaker," posted February 7, 2005, *Wine Spectator*, winespectator.com.

RONALD REAGAN

Reagan menus: Reagan administration menus are in the Ronald Reagan Presidential Library and Museum.

Reagan's interest in California wine: Robert Lewis Thompson, "Presidential Wine Policy: The Californians Have Arrived," *Washington Post*, December 3, 1981.

Trudeau buying a case of 1976 Jordan Cabernet Sauvignon: Ben O'Donnell, "Red Wine, White House," posted February 17, 2012, *Wine Spectator*, winespectator.com.

California Zinfandel and Merlot first served at the White House: Hickey, "All the Presidents' Meals."

"the best-informed administration": quoted in Thompson, "Presidential Wine Policy."

luncheon for media editors and reporters: Josh Getlin, "French Wine at White House Luncheon Riles California Vintners: Reagan Stirs Tempest in a Bottle," *Los Angeles Times*, September 20, 1985, D2.

"At dinner we opened": Ronald Reagan, *An American Life: The Autobiography of Ronald Reagan* (New York: Simon & Schuster, 1990), 610.

Reagan's private visit to London: Sheila Rule, "Reagan Gets a Red Carpet from British," *New York Times*, June 14, 1989, 6.

"without firing a shot": Margaret Thatcher, Eulogy for President Reagan, Washington National Cathedral, June 11, 2004, Margaret Thatcher Foundation website, www.margaretthatcher.org.

wines served by Margaret Thatcher: Bruce Anderson, "A Vintage Tale of Thatcher, Reagan, and Some Truly Great Wines," *Wine Spectator*, October 12, 2019, spectator.co.uk.

GEORGE H. W. BUSH

Bush menus: George W. H. Bush administration menus are in the George H. W. Bush Presidential Library and Museum.

WILLIAM J. CLINTON

Clinton menus: Clinton administration menus are in the William J. Clinton Presidential Library and Museum.

State Dinner for China: "The President and Mrs. Clinton Host His Excellency Jiang Zemin President of China and Madame Wang Yeping at a White House State Dinner," Clinton White House website, clintonwhitehouse3.archives.gov.

GEORGE W. BUSH

Bush menus: George W. Bush administration menus are in the George W. Bush Presidential Library and Museum.

first female White House executive chef: Hickey, "All the Presidents' Meals."

BARACK OBAMA

Michelle Obama's appreciation for wine: Cailey Rizzo, "Michelle Obama Is Better at Wine Than Her Husband," posted May 25, 2017, *Travel and Leisure*, travelandleisure.com.

Barack Obama and beer: Scott Horsley, "Obama Polishes His 'Regular Guy' Image with Beer," *All Things Considered*, September 15, 2012, National Public Radio, npr.org.

"It will be out soon!": quoted in Byron Tau, "Obama: Beer Recipe Will Be Released," posted August 29, 2012, *Politico44 Blog*, politico.com.

White House ale and porter recipes: J.L., "Release the Recipe for the Honey Ale Home Brewed at the White House," posted August 18, 2012, *We the People*, petitions.obamawhitehouse.archives.gov; Sam Kass, "Ale to the Chief: White House Beer Recipe," posted September 1, 2012, Obama White House, obamawhitehouse.archives.gov/blog.

Obama final State Dinner: menu and comments, obamawhitehouse.archives.gov.

DONALD J. TRUMP

Kluge Estate Winery: Annie Gowen, "Trump Buys Former Kluge-Owned Winery," *Washington Post*, April 7, 2011.

State Dinner for Australia: "First Lady Melania Trump Releases Details for the Trump Administration's Official Visit and State Dinner with Australia," September 19, 2019, Trump White House, whitehouse.gov.

State Dinner for France: Emily Heil, "Here's What Guests Will See at the White House State Dinner for France," posted April 24, 2018, washingtonpost.com.

SIDEBAR, JEFFERSON'S COLLECTION: WINE PROVIDED AT WASHINGTON

"Wine provided at Washington": Thomas Jefferson, Memorandum Books, 1803, *Founders Online*.

SIDEBAR, THOMAS JEFFERSON'S 1787 CHÂTEAU LAFITE

Good summaries are in Patrick Radden Keefe, "The Jefferson Bottles," *New Yorker*, September 3, 2007; John Hailman, *Thomas Jefferson on Wine* (Jackson: University Press of Mississippi, 2006), 397–404. This account is also based on the author's conversations with Christopher Forbes.

"We don't believe": quoted in Keefe, "Jefferson Bottles."

"I used to brag": quoted in ibid.

"I wish Jefferson had drunk": quoted in Hailman, *Jefferson on Wine*, 398.

CHAPTER TWO

ten thousand wineries: "General Industry Stats 2019," *WineAmerica*, National Association of American Wineries website, wineamerica.org.

"Being just now informed": Thomas Jefferson to William Short, August 12, 1790, *Founders Online*.

Jefferson letter, "M. la comte de Lur-Saluce," "Be so good": Thomas Jefferson to Joseph Fenwick, September 6, 1790, *Founders Online*.

Jefferson's stylized initials: Lucia Goodwin [Stanton], "Research Report: Chateau Lafite 1787, with initials 'Th. J.,'" posted December 12, 1985, Thomas Jefferson's Monticello website, www.monticello.org.

The vineyard owners responded: Madame de Lur-Saluces to Thomas Jefferson, February 25, 1791; Miroménil to Thomas Jefferson, January 18, 1791; Madame de Rausan to Thomas Jefferson, [January] 30, 1791; Lambert to Thomas Jefferson, February 10, 1791; all *Founders Online*.

"I shall not waste your time": Thomas Jefferson to James Monroe, April 8, 1817, *Founders Online*.

wines for March 1983 dinner for Queen Elizabeth II: David Berkley to Michael K. Deaver, February 9, 1983, Michael K. Deaver Papers, David Berkley Correspondence 2 box 62, Ronald Reagan Presidential Library and Museum.

"ice house": Seale, *President's House*, 1:101; Travis McDonald, "The East and West Wings of the White House: History in Architecture and Building," *White House History*, no. 29 (Summer 2011): 57, 60.

"President Jefferson, after experiencing": Sir Augustus John Foster, *Jeffersonian America: Notes on the United States of America Collected in the Years 1805–1806–1807 and 1811–1812*, ed. Richard Beale Davis (San Marino, Calif.: Huntington Library, 1954), 12.

Floored with brick: Seale, *President's House*, 1:193.

Wise, *Recollections of Thirteen Presidents*, 26–27.

SIDEBAR, JEFFERSON'S ADVICE

Thomas Jefferson, memorandum to Henry Sheaff, [after February 20, 1793], *Founders Online*.

SIDEBAR, WELCOMING WHITE HOUSE GUESTS WITH WINE

contributions by First Lady Melania Trump and former First Lady Michelle Obama and from White House social secretaries written for this book.

SIDEBAR, WHITE HOUSE WINE SERVICE: A CHOREOGRAPHED BALLET

contribution by Daniel Shanks written for this book.

CHAPTER THREE

contributions by vintners and owners written for this book.

INTRODUCTION

"We could, in the United States": Thomas Jefferson to C. P. de Lasteyrie, July 15, 1808, *Founders Online*.

"Wine being among": Thomas Jefferson to John Dortic, October 1, 1811, *Founders Online*.

FRENCH BEGINNINGS

"The best red wines": Thomas Jefferson, memorandum on wine [after April 23, 1788], *Founders Online*.

"I hope you all enjoy": President Ronald Reagan, "Toasts at the State Dinner for Prime Minister Jacques Chirac of France," March 31, 1987, *American Presidency Project*.

THE ITALIAN INFLUENCE

"a necessary of life": Thomas Jefferson to Thomas Appleton, January 14, 1816, *Founders Online*.

"truly the best": Thomas Jefferson to Thomas Appleton, April 29, 1806, *Founders Online*.

THE FORTIFIED WINES OF PORTUGAL

a pint a day: Sarah Ramsey, "Drink Like the Founding Fathers (and Mothers) with This Wine," posted June 29, 2018, *Wide Open Eats*, wideopeneats.com.

ordered two pipes: Mary V. Thompson, "Madeira," George Washington's Mount Vernon website, www.mountvernon.org.

water was unhealthy: Tom Jewett, "Spirits of Our Forefathers: Alcohol in the American Colonies," *Archiving Early America* website, www.varsitytutors.com.

John Hancock: Brittany Dust, "How Madeira Fueled the American Revolution," posted July 2, 2015, *Wine Notes*, blog.wine.com.

Signers drank: Ramsey, "Drink Like the Founding Fathers."

distributed at the polls: Dust, "How Madeira Fueled the American Revolution."

about one-quarter: "Ramsey, "Drink Like the Founding Fathers."

white wine for export: "The History of Madeira Wine in America," *Discovering Madeira* website, discoveringmadeira.com; Daniel Crown, "How a Thirst for Portuguese Wine Fueled the American Revolution," posted December 13, 2017, *Atlas Obscura* website, www.atlasobscura.com.

Madeira actually improved: "History of Madeira Wine in America," Emily Arden Wells, "Madeira Is the Oldest Wine in the World That's Worth Drinking," posted August 9, 2016, *Town and Country*, www.townandcountrymag.com.

20 percent by volume: Karen MacNeil, *The Wine Bible* (New York: Workman Publishing, 2001), 500.

A 1703 trade agreement: Joshua Malin, "The British Paradox: How a Cold, Rainy Island Invented Modern Wine," *Vinepair* newsletter, https://vinepair.com.

three-quarters of the wine: "History of Madeira Wine in America." Between 1700 and 1775, 64 percent of the wine imports

were from Madeira. Fred M. Leventhal and Rowland Quinault, *Anglo-American Attitudes: From Revolution to Partnership* (Burlington, Vt.: Ashgate, 2000), tables 3.2, 3.3.

"The taste of this country": Thomas Jefferson to Stephen Cathalan, [before June 6, 1817], *Founders Online*.

Madeira gradually dropped, fruit and nut course: Thompson, "Madeira"; Poppy Cannon and Patricia Brooks, *The Presidents' Cookbook* (New York: Funk and Wagnalls, 1986), 6–11.

much reduced by disease: "Vintage Madeira," *Finest & Rarest* website, www.finestandrarest.com.

HUNGARIAN TOKAJI: "THE WINE OF KINGS, THE KING OF WINES"

Located near the Carpathian Mountains: "Grape Varieties of Tokaj," *Tokaji* website, www.tokaji.com.

"silky" character: Thomas Jefferson to Justus Erich Bollman, February 6, 1803, *Founders Online*.

It was the highest price: Thomas Jefferson, Memorandum Books, 1803, *Founders Online*; "Hungary," *Thomas Jefferson Encyclopedia*, Thomas Jefferson's Monticello website, www.monticello.org.

"Your specimen from an American grape": James Madison to John Adlum, April 12, 1822, *Letters and Other Writings of James Madison* (Philadelphia: J. B. Lippincott, 1867), 3:263.

The agricultural practices of Soviet Communism: William Echikson, "Tokay: King of Wines," *Wall Street Journal*, April 30, 2004.

$40,000 a bottle: Clay Dillow, "The World's Most Expensive Wine Is from Hungary," posted March 9, 2019, *Fortune*, fortune.com.

GERMANY'S RIESLING RETURNS

Jefferson had traveled: Thomas Jefferson, "Notes on a Tour Through Holland and the Rhine Valley, 3 March–23 April 1788," *Founders Online*.

since the fifteenth century: "1200 Years of Winegrowing History," Schloss Johannisberg website, www.schloss-johannisberg.

"the most noble and unique": MacNeil, *The Wine Bible*, 51.

as low as 8 percent: ibid.

term "hock": "Hock," *Oxford Companion to Wine*, Wine Pros Archive website, https://web.archive.org.

first 100 percent Riesling vineyard: "1200 Years of Winegrowing History."

"of the very first quality": Thomas Jefferson, "Notes on a Tour Through Holland and the Rhine Valley."

Riesling vineyards were devastated: "History: Riesling Origins—Germany," Pacific Rim Winery website, pacificrim-winery.com."

CALIFORNIA ARRIVES

first commercial winery in California: "Complete Napa Valley California Wine History from Early 1800's to Today," *Wine Cellar Insider*, thewinecellarinsider.com.

missions moved north: Tom Gregory, *History of Sonoma County, California* (Los Angeles: Historic Record Company, 1922), 104.

first winery in Napa: Nancy S. Brennan, "John Patchett: Introducing One of Napa's Pioneers," *Napa Valley Register*, November 21, 2010.

repeal in 1933: Axel Borg, "A Short History on Wine Making in California," July 5, 2016, UC Davis Library website, library.ucdavis.edu.

California's more 4,500 vineyards: *Wine America*, "United States Wine and Grape Industry FAQs," *WineAmerica*, National Association of American Wineries website, wineamerica.org.

President Benjamin Harrison: "A President's Visit to Sutro Heights," *San Francisco Morning Call*, April 28, 1891, 1.

1938 luncheon: Jack James and Earle Vonard, *Treasure Island, the "Magic City," 1939–1940: The Story of the Golden Gate International Exposition* (San Francisco: Pisani Printing and Publishing Company, 1941), 55.

VIRGINIA AND BEYOND

"Acte 12": Patricia Keppel, "The Birthplace of American Wine: The Untold Story Behind Virginia's Vines," posted March 31, 2017, *Virginia Travel Blog*, Official Tourism Travel Blog of the Commonwealth of Virginia, blog.virginia.org.

Virginia was the fifth largest: ibid.

Oregon is known for its Pinot Noir: "Pacific Northwest Wine Region," *Truly Fine Wine*, trulyfinewine.com.

SIDEBAR, THE 1855 BORDEAUX CLASSIFICATION

Chambre de Commerce de Bordeaux.

SIDEBAR, PHYLLOXERA: THE TINY PEST THAT DEVASTATED FRENCH VINEYARDS

reward of 300,000 francs: Laura Clark, "American Bugs Almost Wiped Out France's Wine Industry," posted March 19, 2015, *Smithsonian Magazine*, www.smithsonianmag.com.

70 percent of the vines in France: "There's Still No Cure for Grape Phylloxera," posted March 18, 2013, *Winefolly*, https://winefolly.com.

SIDEBAR, THE JUDGMENT OF PARIS

account based in part on the author's conversations with Steven Spurrier.

See also George Taber's account in *Time*, July 7, 1976, 58, and his book, *Judgment of Paris: California vs. France and the Historic 1976 Paris Tasting That Revolutionized Wine* (New York: Scribner, 2005).

CHAPTER FOUR

This chapter is derived from Jane Shadel Spillman, *White House Glassware: Two Centuries of Presidential Entertaining* (Washington, D.C.: White House Historical Association, 1989; reprinted 2007, 2013). It has been condensed for publication here, and updated by the Office of the Curator, The White House, to reflect more recent research. Some of the passages pertaining to White House entertaining have been incorporated into chapter 1. All photography is new. The White House Historical Association is grateful to Spillman for her original research and for the opportunity to bring it to the public in this new format.

INTRODUCTION

in keeping with the law: *United States Statutes at Large* (Boston: Charles C. Little and James Brown, 1846), 4:194, quoted in William C. Allman, *Official White House China, From the 18th to the 21st Centuries*, 3rd ed. (Washington, D.C.: White House Historical Association, 2016), 46.

FROM GEORGE WASHINGTON TO JOHN QUINCY ADAMS, 1789 TO 1829

"One idea": George Washington to Gouverneur Morris, October 13, 1789, *Founders Online*.

"Nothing has been said": List of Articles, Public and Private, February or March 1797, George Washington Papers, vol. 110, Library of Congress (hereafter LOC), Washington, D.C.

"glass tumblers": David Brooks to Maria Mallam Brooks, June 9, 1797, Office of the Curator, The White House (hereafter OCWH), Washington, D.C.

John Adams inventory, "a plentiful quantity," February 26, 1801: Joint Committee Appointed to Consider . . . Accommodations of the President of the United States, House of Representatives Report, 6th Cong., 2nd sess., February 27, 1801, 12.

"Never before had such dinners": Smith, *First Forty Years*, 391–92.

"One great reform": Mrs. Harrison Smith [Margaret Bayard Smith], "The President's House Forty Years Ago," *Godey's Lady's Book*, November 1843, 215.

Thomas Jefferson inventory, February 19, 1809: Thomas Jefferson Papers, vol. 186, LOC, copy in OCWH.

"Sir, convinced that you": Benjamin Bakewell to James Madison, February 19, 1816, James Madison Papers, LOC.

James Monroe glassware sold to the White House, March 15, 1817: Miscellaneous Treasury Accounts for the President's House, Record Group 217 (hereafter MTA), account 43.754, voucher 86, National Archives (hereafter NARA), Washington, D.C.

"a full set of Decanters": *Pittsburgh Gazette*, November 10, 1818, 3. Alexander Jardel was a French glass engraver who had recently moved to Pittsburgh.

"wine was handed about": quoted in Esther Singleton, *The Story of the White House* (New York: McClure, 1907), 1:148–49.

James Monroe inventory, March 24, 1825: "Inventory of Furniture in the President's House, taken the 24th day of March, 1825," House of Representatives, Report No. 2, 19th Cong., 1st sess., December 7, 1825, 131.

John Quincy Adams order, April 1825: MTA, account 51.873, voucher 10, NARA.

"very much crowded": quoted in Betty C. Monkman, *The Living White House*, 14th ed. (Washington, D.C.: White House Historical Association, 2017), 39.

"all furniture purchased": *United States Statutes at Large*, quoted in Allman, *Official White House China*, 46.

FROM ANDREW JACKSON TO JAMES BUCHANAN, 1829–1861

"Orange punch by barrels full": quoted in Edwin A. Miles, "The First People's Inaugural—1829," *Tennessee Historical Quarterly* 37 (Fall 1978): 305.

"a rabble": Smith, *First Forty Years*, 295.

Andrew Jackson order, "richest cut," 1829: MTA, account 61.369, voucher 54, NARA.

"pellucid as crystal": quoted in Hortense F. Sicard, "Glassmaker to Two Presidents," *Magazine Antiques* 25, no. 2 (February 1934): 56.

"charming little dinners": Jessie Benton Fremont, *Souvenirs of My Time* (Boston: D. Lothrop, 1887), 94.

"Gold Spoon Oration": Charles Ogle's speech is printed in full in *White House History*, no. 10 (Winter 2002): 35–52, together with essays that relate to it.

John Tyler orders, to May 28, 1842, June 1842–April 1845: MTA, account 87.086, and account 93.470, voucher 28, NARA.

James K. Polk orders, April, May 24, 1845: MTA, account 93.470, vouchers 2, 3, NARA.

Zachary Taylor orders, May 30, 1849, January 24. 29, 1850: MTA, account 101.316, and account 103.151, voucher 4, NARA.

Millard Fillmore orders, December 1850, 1851: MTA, account 107.778, vouchers 6, 10, 16, NARA.

Franklin Pierce receptions and formal dinners: Mrs. E. F. Ellett, *Court Circles of the Republic* (Philadelphia: Philadelphia Publishing Company, 1872), 460.

New York exhibition: *Official Catalogue of the New-York Exhibition of the Industry of All Nations* (New York, 1853), 80; see also Allman, *Official White House China*, 73–75.

Franklin Pierce glassware order, 1853: MTA, account 113.810, voucher 4, NARA.

"At the right hand": Miss [Eliza] Leslie, *The House-Book; or, A Manual of Domestic Economy* (Philadelphia: Henry Carey Baird, 1840), 258.

James Buchanan orders, December 16, 19, 1857, July 22, 1858, MTA, account 130.243, vouchers 9, 12, and account 134.023, voucher 31, NARA.

James Buchanan orders, November 18, December 2, 1858, Accounts Received, voucher 13, Office of Public Buildings and Grounds, Record Group 42 (hereafter OPBG), NARA.

James Buchanan order, July 1859: MTA, account 134.023, voucher 19, NARA.

FROM ABRAHAM LINCOLN TO GROVER CLEVELAND, 1861–1889

Abraham Lincoln reception and first State Dinner: Elizabeth Todd Grimsley, "Six Months in the White House," *Illinois State Historical Society Journal* 19, nos. 3–4 (October 1926–January 1927): 50.

Abraham Lincoln order, 1861: order missing from MTA, but invoice from Zimaudy is MTA, account 141.158, no voucher, NARA.

Abraham Lincoln order, 1865, "ruby": MTA, account 157.178, voucher 9, NARA.

"The rabble ranged": Ames, *Ten Years in Washington*, 240.

Andrew Johnson order (by Martha Patterson), January 1866: MTA, account 157.178, voucher 18, NARA.

Andrew Johnson order (by Martha Patterson), December 26, 1868, January 19, 1869, "Liqueurs,": MTA, account 173.118, voucher 7, NARA.

"filled with fadeless French flowers": Ames, *Ten Years*, 250.

Ulysses S. Grant order for Nellie Grant's wedding, 1874: MTA, account 192.686, voucher 90, NARA.

"seven dozen": *Oakland (Calif.) Daily Herald*, January 5, 1874.-

Ulysses S. Grant order for family use, 1874: MTA, Account 192.686, voucher 81, NARA.

Chester A. Arthur sale, April 1882: *Washington Post*, April 15, 1882; Allman, *Official White House China*, 123.

Chester A. Arthur inventory, May 13, 1882: "List of Articles, in serviceable condition, in the Executive Mansion," OCWH.

"Dinner was served": Poore, *Perley's Reminiscences*, 459, 462.

"The fifty dozen pieces": "Executive Cut Glass," *Crockery and Glass Journal* 22, no. 10 (September 3, 1885): 28.

Grover Cleveland order, July 29, 1885: Col. John M. Wilson to Thomas G. Hawkes, July 29, 1885, OPBG, NARA.

"At each plate": Poore, *Perley's Reminiscences*, 499. Despite the label "Bohemian," the glassware was in the Lincoln pattern.

Frances Folsom Cleveland's prediction: Seale, *President's House*, 1:549.

FROM BENJAMIN HARRISON TO WOODROW WILSON, 1889–1921

"the straight shape": Col. Oswald Ernst to M. W. Beveridge, June 17, 1891, OPBG, NARA.

Benjamin Harrison order, June 17, 1891: ibid.

"guests at the state dinners": unidentified newspaper clipping, June 1891, OCWH.

Grover Cleveland replacement order, June 26, 1896: MTA, accounts received, voucher 10, NARA.

William McKinley orders, July 22, 1898, April 18, 1900: Theodore A. Bingham to Estate of M. W. Beveridge, July 22, 1898; Theodore A. Bingham to Dulin & Martin, April 18, 1900, February 27, 1901, OPBG, NARA.

Theodore Roosevelt orders, 1901, 1902: Van Heusen Charles Co. to Miss T. S. Hagner, December 1, 1901, March 24, 1902, Letters Received, OPBG, NARA; Edwin A. Barber to W. F. Dorflinger, May 16, 1903, and Dorflinger to Barber, May 19, 1903, Philadelphia Museum of Art Archives.

"Joseph F. Haselbauer and son Frederick": *Corning (N. Y.) Daily Journal*, September 19, 1906.

"cheapens the White House," "In former years": Butt, *Letters of Archie Butt*, ed. Abbott, 237–38.

Woodrow Wilson order: Col. W. W. Harts to Dulin & Martin, July 12, 1917, Letters Sent, OPBG, NARA; General Accounting Office, no. 46383, voucher 100, and no. 51956, vouchers 121, 122, NARA.

FROM WARREN G. HARDING TO DONALD J. TRUMP, 1921 TO THE TWENTY-FIRST CENTURY

"etched and filled in with gold": *Crockery and Glass Journal*, May 26, 1921, 16.

Franklin D. Roosevelt order, 1933: Howard Ker to Mrs. William B. Umstead, June 15, 1939, OCWH.

T. G. Hawkes engravers, president sent them back, choices were limited: Henrietta Nesbitt, *White House Diary* (Garden City, N.Y.: Doubleday, 1948), 198–99.

Franklin D. Roosevelt order, 1939: correspondence from Hawkes, April 3, 1939, OCWH. Records of the orders are in OCWH.

"Embassy" glassware: OCWH records.

USS *Williamsburg* glassware: ibid.

John F. Kennedy order, 1961: Morgantown Glassware Guild invoice, May 31, 1961, OCWH.

"I really love": Mrs. John F. Kennedy to Mrs. Henry Parrish, July 16, 1962, OCWH.

SIDEBAR, 1901 GLASSWARE INVENTORY

"Inventory of Public Property in the Executive Mansion," June 30, 1901, Appendix A, *Annual Report of the Chief of Engineers for 1901*, Appendix DDD (Washington, D.C.: Government Printing Office, 1901), 3747–48.

CHAPTER FIVE

INTRODUCTION

In ancient Rome, banquet guests: Jeff Herman and Deborah Herman, *Toasts for All Occasions* (n.p.: Weiser, 2003), 40.

The Roman Senate even passed: Paul Dickson, comp., *Toasts: Over 1,500 of the Best Toasts, Sentiments, Blessings, and Graces* (New York: Crown Publishers, 1991), 6.

Attila the Hun reportedly: ibid.

drink from the skull: Richard Valpy French, *The History of Toasting, or, Drinking of Healths in England* (London: National Temperance Publication Depôt, 1881), 46–47.

"drinking on the sly.": Dickson, *Toasts*, 11.

Toasting became so prevalent: ibid., 14.

In 1634, Massachusetts officials: ibid., 17.

thirteen separate toasts: ibid., 23.

"sufficient powers to Congress": quoted in ibid.

"The dinners are neat and plentiful": quoted in Hailman, *Thomas Jefferson on Wine*, 298.

At a dinner in the unfinished Rotunda: ibid., 320–21.

What was perhaps America's "golden age" of toasting: Dickson, *Toasts*, 24.

"Here's to Prohibition": quoted in ibid., 29.

1975 State Visit of Zambian President Kenneth Kuanda: ibid., 3.

"a rambling forty-minute dissertation": Dickson, *Toasts*, 2009 ed., 3.

State Department recommendation: ibid.

"make sure that the toast is authenticated.": State Dinner for President José Lopéz Portillo of Mexico, September 28, 1979, *American Presidency Project*.

"When the toast comes first": quoted in Donnie Radcliffe and Joseph McLellan, "Toast with Oil at White House Dinner," *Washington Post*, September 29, 1979.

"great people and the government": quoted in Dickson, *Toasts*, 2009 ed., 3.

"people of Bolivia.": quoted in ibid.

"diplomacy by dinner toast.": quoted in ibid., 4.

TOASTS

Andrew Jackson, April 13, 1830, toast: Jackson's famous toast is oft reported.

Andrew Jackson, April 13, 1830, broadside: *Niles' Weekly Register*, Baltimore, April 24, 1830, 1.

All other presidential toasts are presented in full on the *American Presidency Project* website.

CHAPTER SIX

The menus reproduced here are primarily from the respective presidential libraries. A few are in the collection of the White House Historical Association or have been supplied by the Office of the Curator, The White House. News articles were also consulted.

February 25, 1902: for the events surrounding the visit Prince Henry of Prussia and the launching of the kaiser's yacht, see Henry Voigt, "Compliments of George Kessler," posted April 14, 2012, *The American Menu* website, theamerican-menu.com. See also Karen Sieber, "State Dinner for the Prince," posted February 22, 2019, Theodore Roosevelt Center at Dickinson State University website, theodorerooseveltcenter.org; "Note Regarding the Champagne Controversy," Library of Congress, also posted on the same website.

June 8–9, 1939: for Ambassador William C. Bullitt's letter detailing the preferences of King George VI and Queen Elizabeth, see Alan Capps, "A Royal Tour on the Eve of World War II: King George VI and Queen Elizabeth Visit the White House," *White House History*, no. 46 (Summer 2017): 60–61.

CHAPTER SEVEN

The list of wines served, chronologically by administration, has been compiled directly from the menus for State Dinners, State Visits, official dinners, working dinners, luncheons, and other official events. A complete list of "Visits by Foreign Leaders," with information about the status of the visit (State Visit, official working visit, working visit, private visit, and others) is available from the Department of State's Office of the Historian, https://history.state.gov. Information in the captions has drawn on the websites of the vintners.

Note that guests identified as from "Germany" are all from the Federal Republic of Germany until German unification in 1990.

QUOTATIONS IN MARGINS

There are lots of quotations about wine, attributed to famous people, circulating on the web. We did our best to verify them before using them in the margins of this book, and sources are listed below. A few that could not be verified were too good not to use, however, and those are identified as "attributed." Their appearance in this book does not confer legitimacy on them, but we hope they bring readers some cheer and ideas for toasts.

INTRODUCTION

Pliny the Elder: *Naturalis Historia* (77 BCE), bk. 14, chap. 28.

CHAPTER ONE

Wine to gladden: Psalm 104:15

Ovid: *Ars Amatoria* (2 CE), bk. 1.

Thomas Jefferson: letter to John F. Oliveira Fernandes, December 16, 1815, *Founders Online*.

James Madison: quoted in Ralph Ketcham, *James Madison: A Biography* (Charlottesville: University Press of Virginia, 1990), 606.

Benjamin Franklin: attributed.

John Quincy Adams: letter to his sister, Abigail Adams, May 18, 1786, *Founders Online*.

Homer: *The Odyssey* (eighth century BCE), bk. 14.

Madame de Pompadour: attributed.

Millard Fillmore: *Millard Fillmore Papers*, ed. Frank H. Severance (Buffalo, N.Y.: Buffalo Historical Society, 1907), 2:489.

Charles Dickens: *Barnaby Rudge: A Tale of the Riots of Eighty* (1841), chap. 32.

Oliver Wendell Holmes: "Ode for a Social Occasion, with Slight Alterations by a Teetotaler," *The Complete Poetical Works of Oliver Wendell Holmes* (Boston: Houghton, Mifflin, 1900), 176.

Victor Hugo: *Contemplations* (Paris: Librairie Hachette et Cie, 1884), 1:86.

Lord Byron: *Sardanapalus, King of Assyria* (1821), act 1, scene 1.

Grover Cleveland: quoted in Alexander Leitch, *A Princeton Companion* (Princeton: Princeton University Press, 1978), 103.

Horace: *Epistle 5, To Torquatus* (20 BCE), trans. in Craufurd Tait Ramage, *Beautiful Thoughts from Latin Authors* (Cambridge, Mass.: E. Howell, 1869), 198.

Mark Twain: letter to William Dean Howells, February 15, 1887, *Mark Twain's Letters, 1886–1900*, vol. 4, Project Gutenberg EBook, gutenberg.org.

W. C. Fields as Cuthbert J. Twillie: film *My Little Chickadee* (1940).

John Ciardi: epigraph on dedication page of Charles W. Bamforth and David J. Cook, *Food, Fermentation, and Micro-Organisms* (Hoboken, N.J.: John Wiley & Sons, 2019).

Winston Churchill: *Churchill by Himself: The Definitive Collection of Quotations*, ed. Richard M. Langworth (New York: PublicAffairs, 2008), 577.

Winston Churchill: attributed.

Alben Barkley: attributed.

Winston Churchill: *The Story of the Malakand Field Force: An Episode of Frontier War* (New York: Longmans, 1898), 13.

Rose Kennedy: quoted in "Hundreds Gather to Celebrate Rose Kennedy's 100th Birthday," *Santa Fe New Mexican*, July 16, 1990, 8.

Sean Connery as James Bond: film *Goldfinger* (1965).

William Shakespeare: *Othello* (1604), act 2, scene 3 (Iago).

Pope John XXIII: quoted in John Bingham, "Like Good Wine, We Get Better with Age," *London Telegraph*, March 15, 2013.

Ovid: *Ars Amatoria* (2 CE). bk. 1.

Louis Pasteur: quoted in René Vallery-Radot, *The Life of Pasteur*, trans. Mrs. R. L. Devonshire, (New York: Doubleday, Page, 1915), 23.

Robert Mondavi: *Harvests of Joy: How the Good Life Became Great Business* (New York: Harcourt, 1998), 208–09.

Louis Pasteur: epigraph on Université Nice Sophia Antipolis Science Faculty website, unice.fr.

Napoleon Bonaparte: attributed.

Bill Clinton: *My Life: The Early Years* (New York: Vintage Books, 2005), 180.

Benjamin Franklin: attributed.

Ralph Waldo Emerson: "Montaigne; or, The Skeptic," in *Representative Men* (1850).

Robert Louis Stevenson: *The Silverado Squatters* (London: Chatto & Windus, 1906), 34.

CHAPTER TWO

Julia Child: attributed.

Thomas Jefferson: letter to Jean Guillaume Hyde de Neuville, December 13, 1818. *Founders Online*.

Ernest Hemingway: *Death in the Afternoon* (1932), chap. 1.

Thomas Jefferson: letter to Thomas Munroe, May 28,1804, *Founders Online*.

Salvador Dalí: *The Wines of Gala* (1977).

CHAPTER THREE

Dom Pérignon: attributed.

Winston Churchill: *Churchill by Himself*, ed. Langworth, 537.

Ernest Hemingway: *A Moveable Feast* (1964), chap. 17.

Benjamin Franklin: quoted in Hailman, *Jefferson on Wine*, 76.

Plato: attributed.

Ralph Waldo Emerson: "Bacchus," *Early Poems of Ralph Waldo Emerson* (Boston: Thomas Y. Crowell, 1899), 168.

Robert Mondavi: *Harvests of Joy: My Passion for Excellence* (New York: Harcourt Brace, 1998), chap. 1.

Galileo: attributed.

Miljenko ("Mike") Grgich: Grgich website, Grgich.com.

Thomas Jefferson: letter to C. P. de Lasteyrie, July 15, 1808, *Founders Online*.

Ovid: *Ars Amatoria* (2 CE), bk. 1.

CHAPTER FOUR

Heraclitus: attributed.

Thomas Aquinas: *Summa Theologica* (1265), pt. 2, pt. 2, question 38, answers 1, 5.

No one who has been drinking old wine: Luke 5:39.

Charles Dickens, *The Old Curiosity Shop* (1841), chap. 7

Ralph Waldo Emerson: "From the Persian of Hafiz," *Early Poems of Ralph Waldo Emerson*, 187.

Alexander Fleming: attributed.

Oliver Wendell Holmes: "The Banker's Dinner," *Complete Poetical Works*, 114.

F. Scott Fitzgerald: *The Beautiful and Damned* (1922), bk. 2, chap. 3.

Bette Davis as Kit Marlowe: film *Old Acquaintance* (1943).

CHAPTER FIVE

Aristophanes: *The Knights* (424 BCE).

Sources for quotations from toasts given in Chapter 5 citations, above.

CHAPTER SEVEN

M. F. K. Fisher: introd. to Marylou Scavarda and Kate Sater, *Vin et Fromage: An Odyssey for Wine and Cheese Lovers* (Santa Rosa, Calif.: Sonoma County Citizen Advocacy, 1981).

ILLUSTRATION CREDITS

All images in this book are copyrighted by the White House Historical Association, unless otherwise noted below and may not be reproduced without permission of the copyright owner.

AP	Associated Press
LOC	Library of Congress
NARA	National Archives and Records Administration
WH	White House Photo
WHHA	White House Historical Association

153	Eric Risberg, AP
154	Nik Wheeler, Alamy
155	Top: Eric Risberg / AP; Bottom: Charles Wollertz / Alamy
156	AP
157	Alamy
159	Top: Alamy
160	Getty Images
162–63	Rebecca Hopkins for Michael Mondavi Family Estate
164	Alamy
165	Getty Images
166	Alamy
167	Norma Jean Gargasz / Alamy
168	Courtesy of Early Mountain
169	Courtesy of Jean Case
170	Ricky Carioti / The Washington Post / Getty Images
171	Courtesy of Rutger de Vink

All photographs in Chapter 4 (pages 172–232) by Bruce M. White unless listed below

210	Artokoloro, Alamy
233	Getty Images
234	Ronald Reagan Presidential Library
238	Harper's Archive
241	Alamy
242	LOC
243	Alamy
244–45	AP
246–48	Getty Images
249	Keystone-France / Gamma-Rapho / Getty Images
250	Getty Images
251	John F. Kennedy Presidential Library
252–53	Lyndon B. Johnson Presidential Library
255	Shutterstock
256	Getty Images
257	Alamy
258	The Asahi Shimbu / Getty Images
259	Getty Images
260–61	AP
262–64	Alamy
265	Ronald Reagan Presidential Library

266	Dirck Halstead / The LIFE Images Collection / Getty Images
267	Shutterstock
268–69	AP
270–71	Alamy
272–73	AP
274	Barack Obama Presidential Library
275	AP
276	Alamy
277	WH

All menus belong to the Henry C. Haller Collection, unless listed below:

278	George W. Bush Presidential Library
280–81	Barry Landau, *The President's Table*
282	NARA
283	Henrietta Nesbitt Collection / LOC
284	WHHA
285–88	Harry S. Truman Presidential Library
289–90	Dwight D. Eisenhower Presidential Library
291	White House Collection
292–98	John F. Kennedy Presidential Library
299	Lyndon B. Johnson Presidential Library
326	Gerald R. Ford Presidential Library
355	Ronald Reagan Presidential Library
356–59	George H. W. Bush Presidential Library
360	WHHA
361	William J. Clinton Presidential Library
362–63	WHHA
364–65	George W. Bush Presidential Library
366	WHHA
367	George W. Bush Presidential Library
368	WHHA
369–70	George W. Bush Presidential Library
371	WHHA
372–73	George W. Bush Presidential Library
374	Barack Obama White House Archives Online

375	AP
376	Barack Obama White House Archives Online
377	White House Collection
378	WHHA
379	White House Collection

All wine bottle images are courtesy of the respective winemakers with the exception of the following:

385, 392, 393, 395, 396, Labels: White House Historical Association; Bottles: Shutterstock

384, 412, 417, 424, 426, 431, Labels: Courtesy of winemakers; Bottles: Shutterstock

383, 390, Labels: Courtesy of winemakers; Bottles: Alamy

382	Renzo Grosso / Wikimedia Commons
387	Domaine Clarence Dillon
397	Label: Roger W, Flickr; Bottle: Shutterstock
399	Deepix
400	Julien Domec
403	Label: Roger W, Flickr; Bottle: WHHA
404	Bottle: Bruce M. White Photography
413	Bottle: Getty Images
436	Bokeh Lane Photography
437	Bryan Gray